5th Edition
MYOB® Software For Dummies®

CW00434807

Cruising the Command Centres

Press the Ctrl (Cmd on Macs) key and at the same time hit one of these numbers and you'll arrive straight at the command centre of your desire.

Ctrl+1	Accounts command centre
Ctrl+2	Banking command centre
Ctrl+3	Sales command centre
Ctrl+4	Time Billing command centre
Ctrl+5	Purchases command centre
Ctrl+6	Payroll command centre
Ctrl+7	Inventory command centre
Ctrl+8	Card File command centre

Fiddling with Text

You can copy and paste text in MYOB software as you would in any word processor. Here are the shortcuts (Cmd for Macs):

Ctrl+C	Copy text
Ctrl+X	Delete or cut text
Ctrl+V	Paste copied text
Ctrl+Z	Undo last command

An Altercation with the Alt Key

On a PC, every command in MYOB software includes an underlined letter. To execute this command, press the Alt key followed by the relevant letter. For example

- ✔ In the Banking command centre, Alt-A . . . becomes Reconcile Accounts

- ✔ In the Payroll command centre, Alt-N . . . becomes Pay Superannuation

Moving Around

Learn to fall in love with your Tab key, moving forwards and backwards through every window in MYOB software. It's so much easier and quicker than using your mouse.

Tab	Move forwards to the next field
Shift+Tab	Move backwards to the previous field
Enter	Move forwards to the next field
Ctrl+Enter	Record or accept a transaction
Alt+F4	Quit out of MYOB software (PC only)
Esc	Takes you out of wherever you are
Ctrl+Tab	Cycles through open windows

MYOB® Software For Dummies®

Cheat Sheet

Super Shortcuts

On Macs use Cmd instead of Ctrl

Ctrl+B	Takes you to Receive Payments
Ctrl+D	Takes you to Receive Money
Ctrl+E	Takes you to Enter Purchases
Ctrl+F	Displays all your cards
Ctrl+G	Takes you to Record Journal Entry
Ctrl+H	Takes you to Spend Money
Ctrl+I	Displays the Reports menu
Ctrl+J	Takes you to Enter Sales
Ctrl+K	Takes you to the Bank Register
Ctrl+M	Takes you to Pay Bills
Ctrl+P	Prints what's on screen
Ctrl+R	Tells you about debits and credits
Ctrl+T	Takes you to your To Do List
Ctrl+Y	Takes you to Find Transactions

Windows Tricks

Home	Takes you to the beginning of a line
End	Takes you to the end of a line
Ctrl+→	Moves one word at a time to the right
Ctrl+←	Moves one word at a time to the left
F1	Brings up help, from wherever you are
	Minimises a window
	Maximises a window

Account Numbers

Account Types	Description	First Number
ASSETS	Things you own	1
LIABILITIES	Things you owe	2
EQUITY	Your stake in the business	3
INCOME	Money in!	4
COST OF SALES	Direct cost of a sale	5
EXPENSES	Overheads, general expenses	6

For Dummies®: Bestselling Book Series for Beginners

5th Edition

MYOB® Software FOR DUMMIES®

By Veechi Curtis

WILEY

Wiley Publishing Australia Pty Ltd

MYOB® Software For Dummies®

5th edition published by
Wiley Publishing Australia Pty Ltd
42 McDougall Street
Milton, Qld 4064
www.dummies.com

Copyright © 2006 Wiley Publishing Australia Pty Ltd

The moral rights of the author have been asserted.

National Library of Australia
Cataloguing-in-Publication data

Curtis, Veechi.
    MYOB Software for dummies.

    5th ed.
    Includes index.
    ISBN   978 0 73140 541 1.

    1. M.Y.O.B. (Computer file). 2. Accounting —
    Computer programs. 3. Small business —
    Accounting — Computer programs. I. Title.

657.0285536

Printed in Australia by
McPherson's Printing Group

10 9 8 7 6 5 4 3

About the Author

Veechi is a person who loves to teach and communicate with others (just try to stop her talking!). She's passionate about small business and loves helping people realise their dreams and to succeed.

Born in Scotland, Veechi attended university in Bathurst, NSW, where she completed her degree in Accountancy and Business Management. She has been an MYOB Certified Consultant for more than ten years, training hundreds of businesses in how to make MYOB software work for them. As a journalist, she has written for many publications including *Australian PC World*, *Australian Personal Computer*, *Australian Reseller News* and *CCH Australia Limited*, and has also been a columnist for *The Sydney Morning Herald*.

Running a business in theory is very different from running a business in practice. In *MYOB Software For Dummies*, Veechi draws on her experience of running her own business over the past 13 years, as well as her experience as director of the Blue Mountains Food Co-op, which has grown to become one of the most successful food co-operatives in Australia.

Veechi's first book was the bestselling *Making the Most of MYOB Business Software*, which is now in its 7th edition. Veechi is also the author of two other Australian *For Dummies* books: *Small Business For Dummies*, (now in its 2nd edition), and co-author of *Business Plans For Dummies*.

Veechi has three children and lives with her husband in the beautiful Blue Mountains of NSW.

Dedication

To Mum, whose courageousness and generosity is an example to live by.

Author's Acknowledgments

As with most things in my life, this book was a team effort. Without my energetic and zany family to encourage me and keep me laughing, I'm sure the first few pages would still be languishing, alone, in my computer. Extra special thanks also go to my husband, John, for his daily jokes and cryptic silliness. (Transforming accounting into a light-hearted subject can be quite a challenge.)

I'd also like to say thanks to Lesley Beaumont and Maryanne Phillips at John Wiley for their valuable support and editorial guidance. Also thanks to everyone at MYOB software, particularly Andrew Stebbing and Mario Galevski.

Publisher's Acknowledgments

Screen captures in *MYOB Software For Dummies*, 5th Edition, reproduced with permission. Copyright 2006 MYOB Technology Pty Ltd.

We're proud of this book; please register your comments through our Online Registration Form located at www.dummies.com.

Some of the people who helped bring this book to market include the following:

Acquisitions Development and Editorial

Project Editor: Maryanne Phillips

Acquisitions Editor: Lesley Beaumont

Copy Editor: Maryanne Phillips

Managing Editor: Gabrielle Packman

Production

Layout and Graphics: Wiley Composition Services, Wiley Art Studio

Cartoons: Glenn Lumsden

Proofreader: Liz Goodman

Indexer: Veechi Curtis

Contents at a Glance

Table of Contents

Foreword

··

*W*hen Veechi Curtis asked me to write the foreword for her book, *MYOB Software For Dummies*, I was delighted. At MYOB, we've known Veechi for many years, both in her capacity as a journalist (specialising in putting our software through its paces!) and later as the bestselling author of *Making the Most of MYOB Business Software*.

As the Australian leader in business management solutions, MYOB seeks to produce the best possible products that combine ease of use, powerful business reporting, streamlined administration and the latest technologies. Being Australian-owned ourselves, we intimately understand your business and accounting environment, which is why we're able to respond so quickly on your behalf to changes in taxation and administration requirements. To grow as fast as MYOB has and maintain the quality of customer service we're famous for is a challenge we're proud to have met. We strive to be innovative and creative in the way we serve businesses like yours, always looking for new ways to provide support, information and other resources. At MYOB, it's not enough to simply produce excellent products and services; we're committed to being there to help business people in the long term.

That's why our company welcomes the contribution of authors like Veechi. *MYOB Software For Dummies* takes a refreshing and new approach to our product and service range. In an accessible and humorous style, this book communicates to people of all skill levels and offers a comfortable learning curve to mastering the key tasks. No matter how simple our products are, every business has different needs, different skills and different levels of understanding. In an increasingly competitive business world, it's vital to use technology to simplify key business processes, such as producing printed Business Activity Statements or paying suppliers using MYOB M-Powered services. Veechi communicates these new tools, as well as time-proven techniques, in a practical way anyone can understand and apply in their own business. She provides a guide that both inspires you to get started and gives you the confidence to see it through.

Our company is proud of our products and services, and we're constantly inspired by you, the business people who form the foundation of our Australian economy. The MYOB team is grateful for the faith you have put in us to help you manage your business more effectively and we're committed to delivering on that promise. I wish you luck on your own business journey, and personally recommend *MYOB Software For Dummies* as your key guide for the road ahead.

— Craig Winkler, Founder and CEO, MYOB

Introduction

Not many people will talk to you in the dead of night, listen without answering back, offer advice whenever asked, and won't take up more than their fair share of the bed. It's these qualities (and many more besides) that make MYOB software such a perfect companion.

I admit that reaching this comfortable state of cohabitation can take a while. Lots of people feel totally overwhelmed by MYOB software at first, but fortunately, the sensation is always temporary. You can do it! I've taught MYOB software to literally hundreds of people over the years and I've yet to meet someone who hasn't mastered the software in the end.

In fact, it's often the very people who are the most unsure in the beginning who end up the best users of MYOB software. That's because being cautious pays off in the long run — it's a quality that carries real worth in accounting. So, however anxious you feel, I'd like to assure you that you can now cast your cares to the wind. Be brave, be confident, and read on . . .

About This Book

Whether MYOB software is a complete stranger or an old and trusted friend, my aim in *MYOB Software For Dummies* is to show you how you can get the most out of this wonderful software. I include a mixture of advice, explanations, warnings (often because I've learnt the hard way!) and examples of real-life businesses.

MYOB software isn't only about producing a set of accounts for tax time. More importantly, it's about giving you the tools to help you understand your business better. This book does the same thing. Not only do I explain the mechanics of everyday transactions, I also describe how to set up your company file in the best possible way, so that you can see what's going on in your business.

Last, I understand that your time is precious and you'd much rather be out running your business than learning about software. For this reason, I stick to the practicalities and, wherever possible, steer clear of boring theories and explanations. (I've even decided to save my treatise on quantum physics for a future edition.)

How to Use This Book

MYOB Software For Dummies is not a gripping novel to be read from cover to cover. Even the most determined of readers will go numb after reading relatively few pages. Instead, this is a pick 'n' mix type of book. Read a bit here, browse another bit there, or head for the end without missing a beat. Or, pluck this book off the shelf only when something is causing you grief.

However, if you're setting up MYOB software for the first time, I suggest you read Chapter 1, 'Hitting the Road', and Chapter 2, 'Creating Accounts and Cards', before moving on to other areas. That's because a number of the decisions you make at the beginning affect everything else that follows. A clean start takes a bit of planning and, hopefully, these early chapters will help you do just that.

Conventions Used in This Book

On occasions, I supply you with step-by-step descriptions of tasks. For each task, I highlight the action itself in bold. If you understand this process, you don't need to read the blurb underneath, meaning you can whiz through instructions in a few minutes flat. For instance:

1. **Click the font tool on your forms toolbar.**

    The font tool is the third icon along from the right, the one with the two capital 'T's.

My point? If you know where the font tool on your forms toolbar is, you don't have to plough through the description telling you how to find it.

If a step-by-step instruction consists of menus within menus, then I simplify things further:

Choose Setup⇨Preferences

This command means you need to choose the Setup menu and then choose the Preferences command.

You may also come across keyboard combinations such as:

Ctrl-P or Cmd-P

This combination means you press and hold the Ctrl key, type the letter **P** and then release the Ctrl key. Or, if you're in Mac land, you hold down the Cmd key (the one with the squiggly sign that sits next to the apple key on the bottom row of your keyboard) and then type the letter **P** before releasing the Cmd key.

This combination means you press and hold the Ctrl key, type the letter **P** and then release the Ctrl key. Or, if you're in Mac land, you hold down the Cmd key (the one with the squiggly sign that sits next to the apple key on the bottom row of your keyboard) and then type the letter **P** before releasing the Cmd key.

Different Software Versions

Although a certain amount of hullabaloo reigns about the different MYOB software versions, you won't find that version differences affect this book unduly. I have written this book with MYOB BusinessBasics, MYOB FirstEdge, MYOB Accounting 16, MYOB Accounting Plus 16, MYOB Premier 10 and MYOB AccountEdge 6 in mind, but this book is still relevant to earlier versions.

As far as the different MYOB products are concerned, I explain tasks in a way relevant to the product you have, whether it be MYOB BusinessBasics, MYOB FirstEdge, MYOB Accounting, MYOB Accounting Plus, MYOB AccountEdge or MYOB Premier. On the whole, this is easy because the core accounting activities in each family member are identical. However, if you have MYOB BusinessBasics or MYOB FirstEdge, you may come across references to features that don't exist, such as inventory or payroll, and occasionally there are slightly different ways of doing things. I point out these differences wherever possible.

This book is suitable for PCs (Windows) and Macintosh computers. The beauty of a purple iMac may be hard to ignore, but MYOB software is not guilty of favouritism. Most of the features and procedures in MYOB software are identical, whichever camp you belong to, and in the few circumstances where they do differ, I point out the correct commands for each.

How GST Fits In

Although Chapter 12 is exclusively about GST and nothing else, the truth of the matter is that GST affects almost every transaction. Because of this, you'll find items relating to GST scattered throughout most chapters and, to make them easy to spot, they are flagged with a special GST icon.

This book doesn't attempt to provide an explanation of the intricacies of GST, or impart advice on the many different GST rulings. Instead, I focus on how to account for GST in everyday transactions and produce your Business Activity Statement with a minimum of fuss.

How This Book is Organised

MYOB Software For Dummies is divided into five parts:

Part I: The Building Blocks

The first part of this book is the stuff you need to know when you first set up MYOB software. I talk about the initial setup interview, what the Accounts List is all about, and explain how card files fit into the picture.

Part II: Everyday Activities

This part deals with everyday business transactions. Making sales and receiving money (the fun bit); making purchases and shelling out money (the not-so-fun bit); handling inventory; and paying employees.

Part III: Moving On

This part covers a range of topics including customising your own business forms, creating custom reports, backing up your files, coming to grips with GST and working with MYOB M-Powered services. I also dedicate a whole chapter to understanding financial statements and analysing where you make your money, and where you don't.

Part IV: The Part of Tens

This is the list (but not last) part of the book. You'll find a list of necessary chores, a list of petrifying pitfalls, a list of tips to help speed your work and a list of tips for running your business. I've even included a list that explains everything you need to know about starting a new year.

Part V: Appendixes

Appendix A tells you where to go when you need more help, Appendix B describes the different products in the MYOB software range and Appendix C provides a handy reference of the Web sites mentioned in the first four parts of this book, plus a few more besides.

Special Icons

Tips are the little ways to make life easier, including shortcuts and handy brainwaves.

Don't forget these little pearls of wisdom.
Remember, remember, remember . . .

Warning icons are serious stuff. If you want to keep your accounts clean and mean, read warnings carefully and take heed.

The Internet icon flags handy Web sites related either to MYOB software or small business.

You guessed it! This icon marks content relating to everyone's favourite topic — our beloved Goods and Services Tax.

This icon flags tricky procedures or in-depth detail. Depending on your level of skills, you may want to ask your accountant for further advice on topics marked with this icon.

If you want to streamline business processes and work online as much as possible, then subscribing to MYOB M-Powered services is the way to go. This icon flags all the snazzy things you can do when you sign up.

Part I
The Building Blocks

Glenn Lumsden

'I'll install this MYOB software the minute I find my computer.'

In this part . . .

Setting up MYOB software is like laying the foundations of a house — you need to plan carefully and make sure those first building blocks are perfectly in place.

This part of the book is about building solid foundations that are made to last. You need to set aside some quiet time and prepare yourself for a bit of brain-drain to get things right but, as with any grand castle or illustrious edifice, the results will be worth the trouble (I promise!).

Chapter 1

Hitting the Road

• •

In This Chapter

▶ Choosing the MYOB software that's right for you

▶ Getting started in a hurry

▶ Taking a bit more time with your setup

▶ Getting back in after you've quit

▶ Activating and re-activating your MYOB software

▶ Fixing date settings

• •

*W*elcome to the splendiferous world of MYOB software. Some may call it a daunting journey, but it's one that's well worth the experience. MYOB software can transform the way you do business, save you untold hours of tedious bookkeeping and even provide some fun along the way.

I run my own small business, so I understand how busy you are. That's why to show you how to get started with MYOB software this chapter includes a 'quick and dirty method' as well as a 'getting it perfect method'. But please, don't leap automatically to the quick and dirty section. You're about to make decisions for your business that you'll be stuck with for months, if not years. If you can possibly afford to, take some time out to read this entire chapter carefully. Send everyone away for the weekend, buy in a bulk load of coffee, cut the cord on the television — do whatever you have to do to get some peace and quiet.

The good news is that the Easy Setup Assistant makes getting started pretty simple. It asks lots of questions during the setup process — rather like an interrogation only without the bright white lights and barbed wire. All you need is a bit of time, some patience and a willingness to see the big picture.

The MYOB Software Family

When it comes to accounting, you need to use the right tool for the job. Just as there's no point in trying to fell a tree with a Swiss army knife, there's little to be gained from trying to run the accounts of your multinational corporation using MYOB software. But, if you have a small or medium-sized business and want to smarten up your accounts and business management, MYOB software is just the ticket.

MYOB software is available in seven different versions, ranging from MYOB BusinessBasics to MYOB Premier Enterprise for the PC, and from FirstEdge to AccountEdge for the Macintosh. Which one is best for you depends on the size and nature of your business. Here's the low-down:

- ✔ If you're a small service business running from home, either MYOB BusinessBasics (for Windows) or MYOB FirstEdge (for Macs) is your best bet.

- ✔ When you're more established or need to use inventory features, then MYOB Accounting is the go.

- ✔ If you have four employees or more, MYOB Accounting Plus (for Windows) or MYOB AccountEdge (for Macs) includes everything you find in MYOB Accounting, but throws in payroll and time billing as well.

- ✔ At the top of the range, MYOB Premier (for Windows) and MYOB Premier Enterprise (also for Windows) provide both enhanced inventory and multi-currency features, as well as multi-user accounting, which is essential if your computers are networked and more than one employee needs to work on your accounts at any one time. (MYOB AccountEdge, the highest-level product available for Macintosh, also provides enhanced inventory and multi-user accounting, but with some restrictions.)

Whichever member of the MYOB software family you choose, you can adapt it to lots of different situations. I've set up MYOB software in childcare centres, vet surgeries, even butchers' shops and wineries. The secret to success lies in the skill of the setup, and that's what this chapter is all about.

What You Need to Do First

You wouldn't set off across the Nullarbor Plain without water or fuel, would you? Nor should you attempt to set up MYOB software without a couple of essentials close to hand. Here's what you need:

- A computer, your MYOB software, this book, and maybe some chocolate cake. Yes, I know I'm stating the obvious. But the chocolate cake will help heaps.

- Tax returns/final accounts for the most recent financial year. Even if these reports aren't completely up-to-date, they come in handy, helping you to work out which categories to include in your Accounts List.

- Cheque books, deposit books, bank statements and credit card statements. These documents are your basic supplies for the trip ahead. Without these, you won't be able to get started, enter transactions or balance your bank account the first time.

- A list of who owes you money. It's always cheering when you realise that if everyone coughed up tomorrow, you'd actually be quite rich. This list should include everyone who owed you money on the day that you started recording transactions, along with the date of the original invoice and the invoice number.

- A list of everyone you owe money to. This is the serious (and sometimes scary) bit. If you intend to record supplier invoices (I talk lots more about them in Chapter 6), make a list of everyone you owe money to. Include dates, amounts and invoice numbers on the list.

Deciding when to begin

Here's a tip I learnt the hard way. The very best time of year to start off your accounts is the beginning of the financial year (1 July for 99 percent of businesses). It doesn't matter if it's September, December or even February and you're sitting there, ready to roll. It's still probably best to go back and enter accounts from the beginning of your financial year.

Why? If you start on the first day of a new financial year, the transition from your old accounting system to your new one is a cinch. That's because accounts are always finalised at the end of each financial year. These final accounts provide the opening balances for the following year and save you paying your accountant to draw up the interim accounts.

That's not to say that you can't start at any time of year. You may prefer to start in May and June, have a trial run and make all your mistakes when it doesn't count. Then by the time 1 July comes around, you know how to use the software, have things under control and you're ready for a flying start. However, even if you do it this way around, you're still not starting for real until that July.

With suitably religious overtones, the date from which you start recording transactions is called your *conversion date*. So if you're entering information from July onwards, then your conversion date is July. (Or if you're entering information from January onwards, your conversion date is January.)

Don't be tricked into thinking that this conversion date is the current month. Even if it's February when you install MYOB software, if you want to go back later and enter transactions from July in the previous year, your conversion date should be July.

Your First Company File

Okay, you've just installed MYOB software on your computer. Now you're ready to divulge everything about yourself (well, maybe not absolutely everything) in a special question and answer session.

1. **Fire up your MYOB software and click Create to start a new company file.**

   If you're using a PC, double-click the MYOB software icon on your desktop. If you're using a Macintosh computer, open up your Finder and double-click the MYOB software icon. When the Welcome window appears, as shown in Figure 1-1, click Create.

Figure 1-1:
The MYOB
software
Welcome
window.

2. **Add some details about yourself — your business name and address and so on.**

   This is the easy bit. Hopefully you know your name and address by now.

3. **Set the Current Financial Year and confirm when this year ends.**

   To answer this question, ask yourself what year it will be when the current financial year ends. If it's July 2006 now, it will be June 2007 by the time you're next due to complete a tax return. Therefore, type **2007** as your Current Financial Year.

   Be careful to answer this question correctly, because once you've selected a year, you can't change it!

4. Specify your conversion date and choose whether you want to run with 12 or 13 periods a year.

For more information about conversion dates, check out the sidebar, 'Deciding when to begin' earlier in this chapter. However, if you're still not sure, pick July. Whether you want 12 or 13 periods is kind of up to your accountant and the way they work. But again, if you're not sure, choose 13. There's nothing to be lost by doing this.

5. Build your Accounts List.

You have a choice to start with a ready-made list, import a list from another file or build your own list from scratch. Unless you have an accounting background, you're best to start with one of the standard lists. Select your Industry Classification and Type of Business, as shown in Figure 1-2, picking the business type most similar to yours. Whatever you choose, don't worry if the suggested Accounts List isn't perfect; you can always adapt it later (see Chapter 2 for more details).

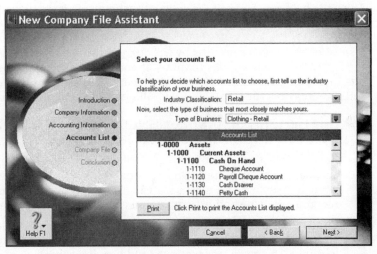

Figure 1-2:
Select the business type closest to yours to create your Accounts List.

6. Name your company file.

You can click Next to accept the suggested name or select Change to create your own.

You did it! Now click Setup to continue, or Cancel if it's time to walk the dog.

The Easy Setup Assistant

So, you've created your company file. Now you need to customise it to fit your particular business (choosing account names, listing who owes you money and so on). This process is made as easy as possible with the Easy Setup Assistant.

- ✔ If you just created your first company file, clicking Setup automatically takes you to the Easy Setup Assistant.

- ✔ Did it last week? Fire up your MYOB software, open your company file and click Setup⇨Easy Setup Assistant.

Customising your company file

Your first stop on the Easy Setup Assistant menu is the Customise button. This little baby lets you call the shots; it's where you design your accounts so that they work the way you want them to.

Instead of boring you senseless by walking you through every single question the Easy Setup Assistant has to throw at you, I only expand on the important bits that need your attention — or extra care. And as far as the remaining settings are concerned, I suggest you blithely accept all that's on offer.

- ✔ **Data Entry.** Tick the Use Expandable Data Entry Fields in Windows box if you want to record long descriptions on invoices.

- ✔ **Record Selection.** If you're no good at remembering numbers and account codes, tick the option Select and Display Account Name, Not Account Number. This means instead of entering account numbers when recording income and expenses, you can just type the account name.

- ✔ **Contact Logs.** Don't tick any of the contact log boxes — unless you've already thought of a good reason why you would want to run contact logs on all financial transactions (and I can't easily think of one!). All they do is make your file run slower and take up space on your hard disk. You can switch contact logs back on later if you come across some special situation where you need them.

- ✔ **Ageing Options.** Most businesses in Australia use monthly ageing periods.

- ✔ **View Options.** If you're usually hooked up to the Internet when you're working on your accounts, choose to search MYOB's Web site for help, rather than use the help files that come with the software. (However, if the Internet proves too slow, toss this suggestion out the window.)

Setting up your accounts

When you've completed the Customise section, saddle up for the Accounts section of the Easy Setup Interview. Again, follow your nose and accept all suggestions, but keep in mind these extra tips.

The Accounts List

The Accounts List is simply a list of asset, liability, equity income and expense categories that apply to your business. Your starting point is a standard list of categories, depending on the business type you chose in the Setup Interview.

If you're in a hurry to get up and running, you don't have to add or change any categories in your Accounts List right now. However, if you have the time, you're best to start by customising your Accounts List properly, so that it has all the categories you need for your business. Go to Chapter 2 to find out how.

I find the Accounts List in the Easy Setup Assistant rather squishy and difficult to work with. It's much clearer if you go to the Command Centres menu at the top, and choose Accounts⇨Accounts List.

Opening balances

The next step in the Easy Setup Assistant (still in the Accounts menu) asks you to set up your opening balances. If you're in a hurry, you don't need to enter all of your account opening balances at this point. You can get away with just entering the opening balance of your bank account and, if you intend to use the Sales command centre, the balance of your trade debtors. You may also need to ask your accountant about opening balances for GST.

On the other hand, if you want to get things as accurate as you possibly can, you can do one of two things — depending on whether or not your accountant has finished your accounts for the year just gone.

✔ If your accountant has finalised last year's accounts, fish out the balance sheet and enter opening balances one by one, copying the figures one at a time until the amount left to be allocated is zero.

✔ If your accountant hasn't finished last year's accounts yet, start by entering the opening balances that you do know for the time being, then return later to the Easy Setup Assistant and complete the process. Important balances include your bank account balance, the balance of trade debtors if you intend to use the Sales command centre, and the amount you owed in GST as at 30 June.

Account Opening Balances

Enter the balance of your accounts as of 1/07/2005 (Balance Sheet Only).

(Remember, enter all balances as positive numbers, unless the balance really was negative.)

Acct #	Name	Opening Balance
Asset		
1-1110	Cheque Account	$1,023.50
1-1120	Payroll Cheque Account	$0.00
1-1130	Cash Drawer	$226.35
1-1140	Petty Cash	$100.00
1-1150	Provision Account	$0.00
1-1160	Investment Account	$25,060.00
1-1180	Undeposited Funds	$0.00
1-1190	Electronic Clearing Account	$0.00

Amount left to be allocated: $0.00

This will be the Opening Balance of the Historical Balancing Account.

Help F1

OK

Figure 1-3: Getting the Amount Left To Be Allocated down to zero.

Regardless of your approach, you have to complete your account opening balances sooner or later. At this point, the aim of the game is to get the Amount Left To Be Allocated down to zero (this amount appears at the bottom of the Account Opening Balances window as shown in Figure 1-3). If you can't, it means you've made a mistake. Read on for some tips to help you get to the bottom of the mystery.

By the way, are you feeling muddled about the difference between trade debtors and creditors? I always used to be too. *Trade debtors* (also sometimes described as Accounts Receivable) are the ones who owe you money. *Trade creditors* (also sometimes described as Accounts Payable) are the ones you owe money to.

When opening balances don't balance . . .

Congratulations, you're human. The following mistakes are common:

- ✔ **Have you made minus figures positive?** Anything appearing in brackets on your balance sheet should be in brackets on your Opening Balances list. (Enter figures that are in brackets by typing a minus first.) Accumulated depreciation accounts are always minus figures.

- ✔ **Are you missing any accounts?** Count the number of accounts on your accountant's balance sheet and then count the accounts listed in your Opening Balances list.

   ✔ **Have you entered an incorrect amount somewhere?** Spot this at a glance by going to the Reports menu on the top menu bar, clicking Index to Reports and then the Accounts tab. Highlight the Standard Balance Sheet report, click Customise and enter your starting date. Print the report and compare it with your accountant's balance sheet and then play Spot the Difference.

   ✔ **Is your Out of Balance Amount a multiple of nine?** If so, you have probably reversed a figure — for example, typing $63 instead of $36.

If your opening balances still don't balance (that is, if the Amount Left To Be Allocated displayed at the bottom of your list of opening balances isn't zero), then this out of balance amount ends up in a special account called Historical Balancing — the accounting version of a too-hard basket.

Even if you end up with an amount in Historical Balancing, you can still continue with the rest of the Easy Setup Interview. Just bear in mind that, sooner or later, you (or some other lucky soul) has to get to the bottom of why it doesn't balance, and postponing the pain won't make it hurt any less.

Setting up customers and sales

You only need to set up customers and sales in the Easy Setup Assistant if you plan to use MYOB software to create invoices for your customers. Again, I don't need to bore you by explaining every little itsy bit. I just clarify the stuff most likely to cause you strife. To get to all of the menus mentioned below, you click the Sales button in the Easy Setup Assistant.

Choose your invoice layout

Decide on an invoice layout that best suits your business: Service, Item, Professional, Time Billing or Miscellaneous. (The Time Billing layout is only an option in MYOB Accounting Plus, MYOB Premier and MYOB AccountEdge.) If you're not sure which layout to pick, select No Default (it's easy to change your invoice layout later). I talk lots more about invoice layouts in Chapter 3.

Record selling details and tax codes

When you click the Selling Details button, you need to select the Income Account that you plan to use for most of your sales. Don't worry if this income account won't apply to all customers; simply choose the account you know you'll use most frequently.

Under the Tax Codes button, choose the Tax Code you use most often for sales (this code is usually GST, unless you're in the business of selling GST-free food, childcare or medical services). However, if you're not registered for GST (maybe you're turning over less than $50,000 a year), then select N-T (standing for Not Reportable) as your Tax Code.

Set up your payment information

It doesn't matter if you offer different credit terms to different customers. In this window, simply specify the credit terms you offer most often (you can adjust individual customer credit terms later). Also, select the Payment Method that the majority of your customers use, such as Cheque, Cash or Eftpos.

Check your linked accounts

Linked accounts (see Figure 1-4) are a clever way of figuring out the debits and credits of each transaction so that ordinary mortals such as you and I never have to think about such accounting complexities. However, because they are so clever, they're also crucial to the accuracy of your accounts.

You can really stuff things up by fiddling with the account numbers for linked accounts. I recommend you look at your Linked Accounts window, say to yourself, 'How wonderful!' then click Next.

Figure 1-4:
Don't fiddle with linked accounts unless you're sure you know what you're doing.

Create your customer's cards

Before entering sales, you need to set up your customer list in the Customer Cards menu. If you're in a hurry, it's okay at this stage to enter customer names only — you can return later to fix up the address and phone details. If you're in a *real* hurry, you can get away with only entering names for those customers who owe you money at the moment, and then add remaining names and details later when you have more time.

Enter historical sales

At last! You can finally tell the Sales Easy Setup Assistant how much money you are owed.

Start by getting together a list of all customers who owed you money as at your start date. Make sure this list includes invoice numbers, invoice amounts and total GST for each invoice. Then, with this list in your sticky hand, hit the Historical Sales button — a list of all your customers appears.

Click Add Sale to record the details of the first invoice in your list. Date each entry with the original date of the sale, stick the invoice number in the Invoice # field and write a comment such as 'Brought forward sale' as the Memo. Repeat this over and over again until all outstanding amounts are recorded.

If any historical sales include GST, enter GST as your Tax Code and check that the right amount of GST comes up in the Tax box. (If the sale was only partly taxable, you need to enter two historical sales, the first sale with the taxable amount and GST as the Tax Code, the second sale with the GST-free amount of the sale and FRE as the Tax Code.) Getting the amount of GST right is important, especially if you report for GST on a cash basis.

After you enter all outstanding sales from your list, you should find that Total Sales in the Historical Sales window equals the amount you entered for trade debtors in your account opening balances. In the perfect world, the Out of Balance Amount should be zero, as shown in Figure 1-5.

If it's not, stay cool. Look for your mistake by hopping up to Reports on the top menu bar. Click Index to Reports, followed by the Sales tab, then select the Receivables Ageing Detail report. Print this report and compare it with your original list of outstanding invoices. Try to spot the difference, keeping a keen eye out for credit notes. (It's easy to forget to stick a minus sign in front of credit notes when you enter them as historical sales.)

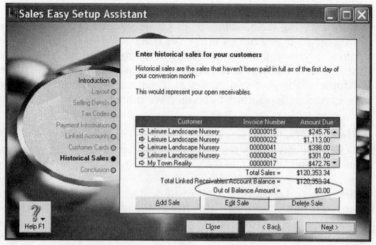

Figure 1-5:
The Out of
Balance
Amount for
your
receivables
should be
zero.

Setting up suppliers and purchases

You only need to complete this section if you plan to use MYOB software to create purchase orders or record supplier invoices. This part of the Easy Setup Assistant has eight steps, but here I only talk about the bits that could trip you up.

Choose your purchase order layout

You get five choices: No Default, Service, Professional, Item or Miscellaneous. The Service layout is usually the best option, unless you're buying inventory, in which case you need to opt for the Item layout. (It's unlikely you're ever going to need Professional or Miscellaneous layouts, so ignore these two.)

Of course, you can use more than one purchase order layout for your business, but at this stage just select the layout you think you may use most.

Select buying details and tax codes

Click the Buying Details button to select the Expense Account that applies to most of your purchases. Don't worry if this expense account won't apply to all suppliers; simply choose the account you know you may use most often.

Under the Tax Codes button, choose the Tax Code that you use most often for purchases (this code is usually GST, unless you're in the business of buying GST-free food, goods from overseas or medical equipment). However, if you're not registered for GST (maybe you're turning over less than $50,000 a year), then select N-T (standing for Not Reportable) as your Tax Code.

Select your payment information

Start by selecting the Payment Method you want to use to pay the majority of your suppliers, such as Credit Card, Cheque or Direct Credit.

The credit terms offered by your suppliers almost certainly vary, but don't worry about this right now. For this section, select the credit terms that suppliers offer you most often (you can adjust individual supplier credit terms later).

Set up linked accounts

The Account for Paying Bills should default to your general cheque account. This setting is fine; click Next to continue.

Record supplier details

Click the Supplier Cards button to see a list of names for all your suppliers (this list is empty if you haven't entered any yet). If you're in a hurry, it's fine at this stage to enter supplier names only, returning later to fix up the addresses and phone details. If you're in a real hurry, you can get away with only entering names for those suppliers who owe you money at the moment, and then add remaining suppliers and details later when you have more time.

Add historical purchases

Now for the not-so-fun bit, where you face up to the grim truth about how much money you owe.

Start by getting together a list of all the suppliers to whom you owed money as at your start date. Make sure this list includes invoice numbers, invoice amounts and the total GST on each invoice. Then, with this list in your now hot and sticky hand, hit the Historical Purchases button. The list of all your suppliers you added in the previous step appears.

Click Add Purchase to record the details of the first invoice on your list. Date each entry with the original date of the purchase, stick the invoice number in the Supplier Inv # field and write a comment such as 'Brought forward purchase' as the Memo. Repeat this over and over again until you've recorded all outstanding amounts.

If any historical purchases include GST, enter GST as your Tax Code and check that the amount of GST comes up correctly. (If the purchase was only partly taxable, you need to enter two historical purchases — the first purchase with the taxable amount and GST as the Tax Code, and the second purchase with the GST-free amount of the purchase and FRE as the Tax Code.) Getting the amount of GST right is important, especially if you report for GST on a cash basis.

After entering all outstanding invoices from your list, you should find that Total Purchases in the Historical Purchases window equals the amount you entered for trade creditors in your account opening balances. The Out of Balance Amount should be zero.

If your Out of Balance Amount doesn't equal zero, don't worry. Look for your mistake by going to Reports on the top menu bar, clicking Index to Reports, followed by the Purchases tab, then select the Payables Ageing Detail report. Print this report and compare it with your original list of outstanding supplier invoices. Try to spot the difference, keeping a special eye out for credit notes. (Remember: It's easy to forget to stick a minus sign in front of credit notes when you enter them as historical purchases.)

Payroll

If you're using MYOB Accounting Plus, MYOB Premier or MYOB AccountEdge, then there's one last button lurking in your Easy Setup Assistant — the Payroll button. Payroll is the most complex part of any accounting software setup, especially if you have several employees with different rates of pay and so on.

Don't set up Payroll right away. Complete the Easy Setup Assistant, but ignore the Payroll button. Instead, familiarise yourself with the rest of MYOB software — tune up your Accounts List and have a go at entering a few transactions (sales, payments and so on). When you feel confident doing these basics — and only then — return to the Easy Setup Assistant (found on the Setup menu) and click the Payroll button. I cover setting up payroll in detail in Chapter 9.

Two Methods to Help You Get Started

I've done literally hundreds of accounting software setups over the years, taking anything from 15 minutes to several days to complete. How long the setup for your business takes depends on the complexity of your business, the amount of time you've got on your hands and, last but not least, the kind of person you are.

My mother always used to torment me with the line, 'The tortoise always wins the race'. If you set up your accounts in a hurry, disregarding opening balances, customer accounts and most other fine detail, everything may appear to run okay, but only temporarily. At some time in the future you'll have to face the music. Searching through old invoices, convoluted supplier accounts and dog-eared cheque stubs can be a tricky and time-consuming process if put aside for too long, and doing your accounts this way will probably take longer than if you'd done them properly in the first place.

However, I realise this isn't a perfect world. That's why I give you the choice of two approaches: the getting-it-perfect method and the quick-and-dirty method. Pick which one suits you best.

The getting-it-perfect method

Perfection has its place in the world of accounting. If you're the kind of person who likes to get things just right and sleep easy at night, this method is for you.

1. **Make sure your books are as up-to-date as possible.**

   The more up-to-date your books before you start recording transactions, the easier your setup will be. Make sure all invoices have been sent out to customers and that you know how much you owe to suppliers. Write up your payments and deposits and balance your bank account. Then hassle your accountant mercilessly to finalise these accounts as soon as possible.

2. **Install your MYOB software.**

   Instructions for installing MYOB software are in your MYOB software user guide.

3. **Follow the steps in this chapter to complete the Setup Interview and the Easy Setup Assistant.**

   Earlier in this chapter I explain both these processes, in the sections 'Your First Company File' and 'The Easy Setup Assistant'. Follow these sections faithfully, step by step.

4. **Customise the Accounts List.**

   Once you've completed the setup interviews, you're well on your way. Go to your Accounts List and customise it a bit more for your business, adding accounts, changing account names and deleting accounts. See Chapter 2 for more details.

5. **Make sure that your Historical Balancing account is zero.**

   I talk more about the Historical Balancing account earlier in this chapter, but I'm mentioning it again now because it's so important to get right, especially when perfection is your aim. So tarry not. Go to your Accounts List, click the Equity tab, and check out the balance of account 3-9999 — your Historical Balancing account. The balance should be zero! (However, if you're still waiting for your accountant to finalise your previous year's accounts, then you'll have to wait a while before you can get this balance right.)

6. **If you deal in items for resale, set up your inventory.**

It's strange, but inventory isn't mentioned anywhere in the Easy Setup Assistant. Fear not. Progress to Chapter 8, read it faithfully, then set up your inventory before going any further.

7. **If you have MYOB Accounting Plus, MYOB Premier or MYOB AccountEdge, set up payroll.**

If you're going to use payroll, you should do so from the very beginning of the payroll year (July). When you've completed the rest of your setup and you're finding your way around with some degree of confidence, hop to Chapter 9 — it covers payroll in depth.

8. **Decide on a backup system and set it in place.**

Backing up is important, so be sure to establish a backup system. See Chapter 14 to find out more.

The quick-and-dirty method

If you have a simple business with only a few account customers (or none at all for that matter), no stock and not many expenses, you can get away with using this setup method. Your setup won't be perfect and you'll need to return later to fix up a few things, but at least you'll be up and running.

Here's what to do:

1. **Install your MYOB software and create a new company file.**

Instructions pop up automatically to help you install the software. Then, follow your nose to create a new company file (if you need help, check out 'Your First Company File', earlier in this chapter) until you arrive at the Easy Setup Assistant.

2. **Enter the balance of your bank account, trade debtors and trade creditors.**

In the Easy Setup Assistant, click Accounts. Click the Opening Balances button to see a list of accounts. Leave all these account balances blank with the exception of your bank account, total trade debtors and total trade creditors. Work out the balance of these accounts as at your starting date and enter these in the Opening Balance column.

3. **Work out how much GST you owe.**

If you owe any GST as at this date, work out the exact balance and pop this amount in your GST Collected from Customers liability account.

4. Create new cards and enter historical sales for all customers who owe you money.

a. If you plan to use MYOB software for invoicing and you have customers that owe you money, click Sales in the Easy Setup Assistant. Then select the Customer Cards button, as shown in Figure 1-6.

b. Now click New to create cards for all customers who owe you money. Every customer needs to have their own card, where you record their name, address, phone number and so on (see Chapter 2 for more details). But for the moment, don't bother with address and phone details — just enter their names and nothing else.

c. Click Next again to progress to Historical Sales. Then click Add Sale and, in the Historical Sales window, enter the details of all outstanding invoices.

5. Create new cards and enter historical purchases for all suppliers you owe money to.

a. If you plan to keep track of how much you owe to suppliers, then click Purchases in the Easy Setup Assistant. Go straight to the Supplier Cards button.

b. Now click New to create cards for all suppliers to whom you owe money. Again, don't bother with addresses or phone details; just enter their names and nothing else.

c. Once that's done, click Next to progress to Historical Purchases. Click Add Purchase and, in the Historical Purchases window, enter the details of all outstanding accounts.

6. Click Close to conclude the interview.

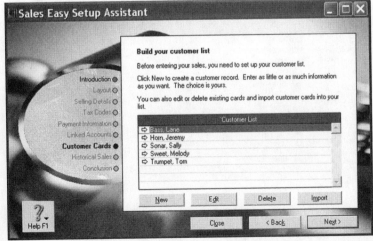

Figure 1-6: Setting up new cards for customers using the Easy Setup Assistant.

Getting In and Out

Agh! You're tired and want to go home — it's time to quit.

Go to File on the top menu bar, then select Exit (if you're using a PC) or Quit (if you're using a Macintosh).

When asked if you want to back up, click No if you don't, or Yes if you do (it's usually a good idea to click Yes). Depending on your settings in Preferences, a message may pop up asking you if you want to print a session report. Again, click No or Yes. (Actually, session reports are pretty useless, so I recommend you don't.)

'I want to do more, right now!'

Want to get back into your company file? Okay!

- ✔ **If you're using a PC:** Double-click the MYOB software icon on your desktop. When the Welcome window appears (refer to Figure 1-1), click the Open button, then select your company's file name from the list, similar to the one shown in Figure 1-7. Click Open once more and you're in.

- ✔ **If you're using a Mac:** Go to your Finder and look for your MYOB icon. Double-click it and the Welcome window appears. Click Open, select your company file from the list and click Open once more. You're there!

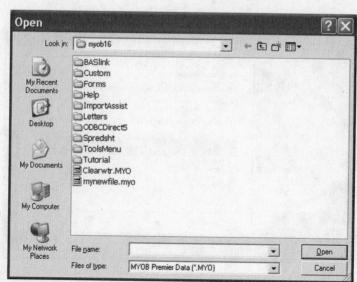

Figure 1-7:
Opening your
company file.

Activating your babe

So you thought piracy had faded out with Captain Jack Sparrow? Not so, for the business of piracy is alive and well in the pernicious practice of stealing software. In an attempt to prevent this, MYOB software requires that you activate your software within 30 days of creating your company file.

If you don't activate your software within the timeframe, your company file changes to read-only status on the 31st day, meaning you're still able to view your transactions, but you won't be able to change transactions or add new ones.

Doing it the first time

When you're first prompted to activate your software, you can choose between doing it online or by phone. Either method works fine; take your pick. This being the first time, you'll also have to register your software in the same hit. You're asked a few questions — your business name, contact details, industry type, grandmother's maiden name and so on — and as a reward, you receive a confirmation number. Type this number when prompted and you're away.

By the way, in order to get through the registration process, you need your serial number. You can find this little gem on the registration card that's in your MYOB software box. Or, it's on the back of your MYOB product CD sleeve.

Doing it again (and again and again)

Now for some bad news. After activating your software everything is hunky-dory. A few months pass by, then suddenly you get a message prompting you to confirm your file. What?

The idea is that by prompting you to confirm your software every few months, MYOB is protecting itself from people activating a legal version of the software, then passing their CD onto friends. The company says that by reducing piracy, its software will become cheaper for everyone who has legal versions (that's the party line, anyway).

Thankfully, re-configuring your company file is pretty straightforward.

✔ **Do it automatically, via the Internet:** Every few months, when the confirmation warning window pops up, simply click OK to send a response back to MYOB. Don't forget you need to be connected to the Internet before you click OK.

✔ **Use your phone:** If you don't have an Internet connection (or you're offline for some reason), you can confirm your file by phone using the telephone number that's shown on your screen. It's a 24-hour, 7-day-a-week service that only takes about 60 seconds to complete. You get a confirmation code over the phone to enter into your MYOB software. After your company file has been confirmed, you can chuck the code away.

If you open up an old file and receive a prompt to confirm this file, bear in mind that you can only activate up to five different company files at one time. To avoid reaching this limit, you're best to ignore the prompt to confirm old files — chances are you're only looking up historical information anyway, and it's of no consequence if this old file changes to read-only status.

Back-to-Front Dates

Back-to-front dates can be very confusing: You type in a date and it's rejected. You try and try again, then suddenly it dawns on you that your dates are back to front. That is, when you type 1/7/06, MYOB software thinks you're talking about the seventh day of the first month, 2006 — not the first day of the seventh month, 2006.

In fact, the problem isn't anything to do with MYOB software; it's the settings in your computer's Control Panel. Here's how to fix it:

For Windows:

Quit out of MYOB software and go to your Control Panel, then click on the Regional and Language Options icon. On the Regional Options tab, select English (Australia), as shown in Figure 1-8. Click Apply. Now, open up your company file again. Hey presto, problem fixed!

For Macintosh:

Go to System Preferences under the Apple menu. On the Personal tab, click International. Click Formats and select your region. Click Apply. (You may need to restart your Mac for your changes to take effect.)

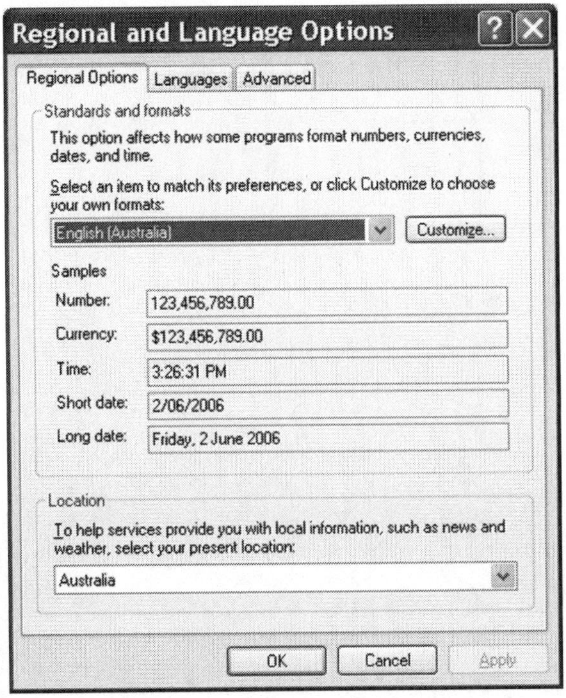

Figure 1-8: Fix up back-to-front dates in your Control Panel.

Chapter 2

Creating Accounts and Cards

In This Chapter

▶ Setting up your accounts

▶ Combining, creating and deleting accounts

▶ Creating cards for customers, suppliers and employees

▶ Organising customers into groups

▶ Importing customer or supplier details into your new company file

*W*hen I first started to teach people about MYOB software, I was overcome with the urge to explain every little detail to anyone who would listen, and full of enthusiasm to share the finest complexities. But, as the eyes of my students glazed over in mindless stupor, I discovered that words like debits and credits, general journals and reconciliation adjustments (I can hear you yawning already!) are best avoided. Easy explanations in plain English that demonstrate how to get the best job done in the shortest time are always preferable.

So in this chapter — which sometimes has to cover some pretty technical material — I explain the facts as simply as possible. You find out how to customise your Accounts Lists, organise accounts into groups, add new customers and suppliers, and much more. Best of all, you don't need a degree in accountancy before you start.

Understanding Your Accounts List

The first thing I do when I set up accounting software for a client is sit down with them and have a chat about organising their Accounts List. That's because your Accounts List affects everything else that happens, including how you record income and expenses, and the format of your Profit & Loss reports.

Put simply, your Accounts List is a list of categories describing what your business owns and what it owes, where money comes from and where money goes.

So, go to the Accounts command centre and click on Accounts List. Notice that your list shows lots of different accounts. It's a list that varies slightly from business to business, depending on the options you chose during the Setup Interview. If you have to, you can make do with this Accounts List just as it is, but it's more efficient to take the time to understand how it relates to your business, and how you can adapt it.

TIP

- ✔ Look at every account in your Accounts List and think about what it's doing there. If you don't need an account, you can get rid of it. If you need an extra account, you can add it in. You can even rename an account if you want. (I explain how to do all these things later in this chapter.)

- ✔ Dig out the most recent reports from your accountant and compare your accountant's categories with those in your Accounts List. If you need to add more accounts to make the two match, then do so.

- ✔ Go to the Income tab on your Accounts List and read what's there. If you have less than five income accounts, have a think about how you could describe your income in more detail. (The sidebar, 'Getting clever with accounts' explains how one newsagency breaks down its income into six different categories.)

If you can't decide how to describe your income accounts, take a coffee break — or drink a calming chamomile tea — away from your computer and think through all the different sources your earnings come from . . .

Maybe you're a builder who earns money from new houses, as well as renovations and extensions. Maybe you're like me, and earn money from a combination of journalism, consulting and teaching. Or maybe you've got a newsagency that doubles as a post office, and is also a drycleaning agency. No matter how you earn a crust, try to split your income into at least five different categories.

Picking your account classification

Whenever you do anything to your Accounts List — be it adding, deleting or changing an account — you have to decide which kind of account you're dealing with.

I explain each account classification in Table 2-1. Don't let your eyes glaze over as you meet this accounting jargon. If you can drive a car or operate a video player, then understanding the difference between account classifications such as assets and liabilities is a piece of cake.

Table 2-1	Account Classifications Used in the Accounts List
Account Classification	*When to Use It*
Assets	Assets are the good stuff — anything you own, such as computers, office equipment, motor vehicles and cash. **Asset account numbers start with 1.**
Liabilities	Liabilities are what keep you awake at night — that's everything you owe to other people. Liabilities include loans, GST, other taxes owing and outstanding supplier accounts. **Liability account numbers start with 2.**
Equity	Equity is a fancy term for your 'interest' in the business, the profit or loss that you have built up over time. Equity includes drawings, capital contributions, retained earnings and share capital. **Equity account numbers start with 3.**
Income	Income is all the money you earn and includes everything you invoice or sell to your customers, plus freight income and bank interest. **Income account numbers start with 4.**
Cost of Sales	Cost of Sales is the direct cost of selling goods or providing your service. It includes purchases, freight, commissions and subcontract labour. **Cost of Sales account numbers start with 5.**
Expenses	Overheads are the day-to-day running costs of your business and includes advertising, bank charges, rent, telephone and wages. **Expense account numbers start with 6.**
Other Income	Other Income is probably better described as Non Trading income. (This account classification isn't available in MYOB BusinessBasics or FirstEdge.) It includes income that's not really part of your everyday business, such as interest income, one-off capital gains, or gifts from mysterious benefactors (if only). **Other Income account numbers start with 8.**
Other Expenses	Again, think of Other Expenses as abnormal expenses that are not part of your everyday business, such as lawsuit expenses, capital losses or entertaining aliens from outer space. (This account classification isn't available in MYOB BusinessBasics or FirstEdge.) **Other Expenses account numbers start with 9.**

Getting clever with accounts

One of my clients is based in the bush and runs a newsagency that's a post office franchise as well. Everything goes through their Point of Sale system and then they journal daily income totals in their MYOB company file.

My client groups his income into six key categories: newspapers, magazines, stationery, post office, cards and all other items. His company file is set up in this way, with not only an income account for each of these categories, but a cost of sales account too. Every month he prints a Profit & Loss report that shows total income and purchases for each category.

My client loves this setup. It's simple, but powerful enough that he can see how his income patterns change from one year to the next, analyse where he makes most profit in his business, and even predict where his business is heading in the future.

Picking your Account Type

If you create a new account that's either an asset or a liability, you'll be prompted to select an Account Type. For those anxious to get everything picture perfect, read on to find out what type to choose.

When creating an asset account:

- ✔ Choose Bank as the Account Type if you're creating a new bank account (such as a cheque account, savings accounts or term deposit). Obvious really.

- ✔ Choose Accounts Receivable as the Account Type if you plan to use this account for tracking how much money customers owe you.

- ✔ Choose Other Current Asset as the Account Type for anything that isn't a bank account, but is a short-term asset. Examples include Prepaid Insurance, Employee Advances or Inventory.

- ✔ Choose Fixed Asset as the Account Type for anything material that you can touch, feel and see. Sounds kind of sensual but I'm talking about relatively mundane things such as Plant & Equipment, Land & Buildings and Fixtures & Fittings.

- ✔ Choose Other Asset as the Account Type for those odd things that accountants like to describe as 'intangibles'. Examples include Goodwill and Formation Expenses.

When creating a liability account:

- There's a bit of a trick here. Choose Credit Card as the Account Type not only for your credit cards, but also for any bank accounts that are always in the red, such as your Bank Overdraft.

- Choose Accounts Payable as the Account Type if you plan to use this account to track how much money you owe suppliers.

- Choose Other Current Liability as the Account Type for any money you owe that's relatively short term. Examples include Loans from Directors, Customer Deposits, PAYG Payable, GST Payable and Superannuation Payable.

- Choose Long Term Liability as the Account Type for Hire Purchase accounts, Bank Loans and long-term Loans from Directors.

- The last Account Type is described as Other Liability. Do send me an email if you figure out when you would use this Account Type (I'm blowed if I can find a good use for it) and I'll illuminate all readers in the next edition.

Adding a new account

So you want to create a new account. Here's what you do:

1. **Go to the Accounts command centre and click Accounts List.**

2. **Decide the classification of account you're creating, then click the appropriate tab.**

   Here's where you decide whether the account you want to create is an asset or a liability account, an income or an expense account, a Desiree potato or a rotting pumpkin. When you've made up your mind, click the right tab.

   (Refer to Table 2-1 if you're not sure.)

3. **Decide how to number your new account.**

   Look at the list of accounts already in the account group and decide where you'd like this new account to fit in. Then pick a number so that the new account falls in the right spot. Accounts are sorted in numeric order, not alphabetical order. So, if your Advertising Expense account is numbered 6-1000 and your Cleaning Expense account is numbered 6-3000, and you want to insert a new Bank Charge Expense account between these two, then you should choose a number between 6-1000 and 6-3000 — say 6-2000.

   Now, jot down the number on a scrap of paper.

4. Click New.

5. Choose whether the new account is a Header Account or a Detail Account.

If this new account is to be a heading that appears in bold with other accounts listed below it, select Header Account. If you want it to be an account that you add transactions to, select Detail Account.

(For more about header and detail accounts, see 'Becoming a groupie' in 'Getting your accounts to look just right' later in this chapter.)

6. Pick an Account Type (for asset and liability accounts only).

If this new account is an asset or liability, you need to pick the appropriate Account Type, such as Bank, Fixed Asset, Credit Card or Accounts Payable. If you're not sure what Account Type to select, refer to 'Picking your Account Type' earlier in this chapter. In particular, make sure you select Bank as the Account Type for cheque, savings or investment accounts, and Credit Card as the Account Type for credit cards or overdrafts.

7. Type in the Account Number and Account Name.

Now you can type in the account number you decided on at Step 3. Then, press the Tab or Enter key and type in the name of your new account. Your new account should now look similar to the one shown in Figure 2-1.

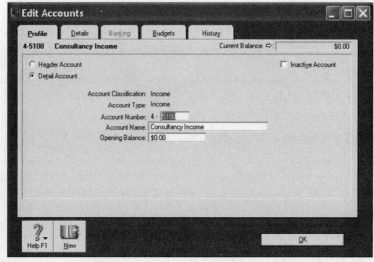

Figure 2-1:
Creating a new account.

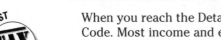

8. Click the Details tab then choose a Tax Code for the new account.

When you reach the Details tab, select the most appropriate default Tax Code. Most income and expense accounts should show GST as the Tax Code (unless you sell GST-free supplies), although some expenses, such as bank charges and donations, should have FRE as the Tax Code. Asset, liability and equity accounts almost always have N-T as the Tax Code, although fixed assets usually have CAP as the Tax Code. See Chapter 12 for more about GST, or talk to your accountant if you're not sure.

9. Click OK and you're done.

Fantastic! You just created your first new account.

Deleting unwanted and unloved accounts

Having accounts in your Accounts List that you don't use is like littering your lounge room with old socks. So, if there's an account that you don't need, get rid of it. You can always add it back later, if you change your mind.

To cull an account:

1. Go to your Accounts List and double-click on the name of the account you want to delete.

2. Click Edit (on the top menu bar) and select Delete Account.

3. *Poof!*

It's gone.

'I can't delete an account!'

What should you do if you try to delete an account but a warning message tells you that accounts with journal entries may not be deleted?

If an account has a current balance, (or a zero balance but there were transactions in the previous financial year), you won't be able to delete it — you have to wait until you start a new year, then try once more to delete it.

If you can't delete an account yet, but you don't want it cluttering up your reports or lists in the meantime, you can make it inactive.

Go to your Accounts List, double-click the offending account and then click the small box called Inactive Account.

Deleting pesky linked accounts

If you try to delete an account and receive a message saying that you can't because it's a linked account, you can still get rid of it.

Here goes:

1. **Go to your Accounts List and double-click on the account you want to delete.**

2. **Click the Details tab to reach the Edit Accounts window.**

3. **Zoom in on the white arrow next to the words Linked Account.**

   Figure 2-2 shows you where the arrow is located. When you click on it a list of linked accounts appears, including the one you're trying to delete.

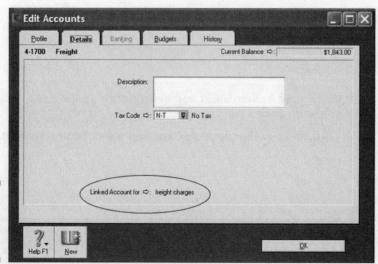

Figure 2-2: Deleting linked accounts.

4. **Remove the tick against the account you want to delete.**

   For example, if you're trying to delete your Freight Income account, then remove the tick from the option that lists its account number and is labelled 'I charge freight on invoices'.

   Don't be tempted to fiddle with linked accounts for Trade Debtors or Trade Creditors. These accounts are particularly important and should stay just as they are.

5. **Click OK.**

You're returned to the Edit Accounts window. You can now try once more to delete the account . . .

6. On the top menu bar, choose Edit⇨Delete Account.

Getting your accounts to look just right

After you delete any accounts you don't want, and add any new ones to suit your business, it's time for a little cosmetic surgery on your Accounts List, such as putting your accounts in the right order and sorting them into groups.

Good surgeons take their time so don't rush these tasks. Having a tidy Accounts List makes it easy to find any account no matter what you're doing, and it makes your reports look sensational!

Learn your A to Z

I'm a bit of a nutter about making sure my income and expense accounts are listed in the Profit & Loss reports in alphabetical order — it's a much easier way to work.

However, in your Accounts List, accounts are sorted in numeric order, not alphabetical order. This means that if you're not careful with numbering when you're creating new accounts, your Accounts List can soon get out of alphabetical order. To reorganise your accounts, you simply need to change some of your account numbers.

For example, Figure 2-3 shows that Cleaning (account 6-1105) is out of alphabetical order: It appears before Advertising and Bank Charges

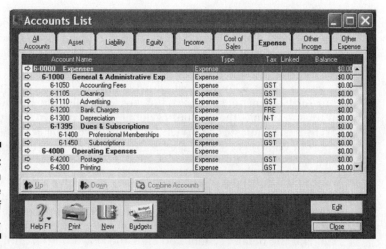

Figure 2-3:
You can change the order of accounts.

(accounts 6-1110 and 6-1200) in the Accounts List. To make it appear in the correct position, I change its number; for example, changing the number of Cleaning from 6-1105 to 6-1225.

Now it's your turn:

1. **Go to your Accounts command centre, click on Accounts List, then double-click on the account that's out of order.**

2. **Edit the account's number.**

3. **Click OK.**

Become a groupie

If you have many accounts that belong together, you can further categorise them into groups in your Accounts List using header and detail accounts. For example, you can create a group for your wages accounts, your motor vehicle expense accounts or your different kinds of marketing expense accounts.

Header accounts are the headings (surprisingly enough) and appear in bold in the list. Detail accounts are the accounts that belong under each header. For example, if you create a header account and name it Motor Vehicle Expenses, you can then add lots of detail accounts to sub-categorise your motor vehicle expenses, such as Fuel, Rego, Insurance and Repairs.

You can create groups of accounts within groups if you're really enthusiastic. For example, refer to Figure 2-3, which shows a header account called General & Administrative Expenses, along with several detail accounts. Another header account called Dues & Subscriptions follows, which then includes detail accounts to separate Professional Memberships from Subscriptions.

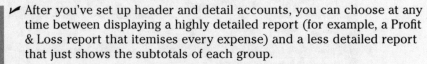

✔ After you've set up header and detail accounts, you can choose at any time between displaying a highly detailed report (for example, a Profit & Loss report that itemises every expense) and a less detailed report that just shows the subtotals of each group.

✔ To view a Profit & Loss report showing different levels of detail, go to your Analysis menu, select Profit & Loss and click the Up and Down buttons to change the amount of detail it displays. Or, if you're using MYOB BusinessBasics or MYOB FirstEdge, find your Profit & Loss report in your reports menu, click Customise and select your Report Level — 1, 2, 3 or 4.

✔ You can tell when detail accounts belong to header accounts because they're indented and sit in a bunch below the header account. However, sometimes things get muddled and detail accounts appear immediately below their header account without any indentation. This is easy to fix: Highlight the detail account and click the Down button until it sits in the right spot.

Paint by numbers

Alright, I'm being pedantic, but I think it's important to be clever when you choose account numbers in your Accounts List.

If you have an account you use again and again, make it a round number to the nearest thousand, such as 6-1000 or 6-2000. Then change all other account numbers so that this account is the only one in this thousand range. For example, Figure 2-4 shows four sales accounts, each with a round thousand number.

What's the big deal about rounding your account numbers? It means that if you have an account that is the only one in a thousand-number range, whenever you select the account, you only have to type the first two digits.

For example, to select account 4-1000, you only need to type '41' and the rest pops up automatically.

If you don't have too many accounts, making all your account numbers easy to remember and type is a good idea. It's easier to work with account numbers such as 6-1200, 6-1300 and 6-1400, rather than 6-1267, 6-1271 or 6-1292. Sure, you may save only a few seconds each time, but multiply those seconds by the hundreds and hundreds of entries that you're going to type, and you'll earn yourself hours of credit before you know it. And that's all the more time to spend at the beach.

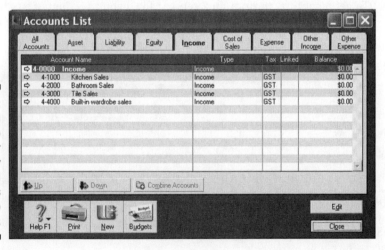

Figure 2-4:
Use round numbers to make your frequently used accounts easy to remember.

Merge into one

After you've been using MYOB software for a while, chances are you'll want to do a bit of housekeeping on your Accounts List. Maybe you realise that you accidentally created two separate accounts called Advertising Expense; maybe you realise that you've got too many accounts and you want to have a slightly less detailed Accounts List. Never fear, with the latest versions of MYOB software, you can now merge accounts.

For example, imagine you have two separate accounts, both of which are called Advertising Expense. You only want one account by this name, but both accounts already have transactions recorded in them. To merge these two accounts, go to your Accounts List, select the account you want to keep, and click Combine Accounts. In the Combine Accounts window that appears, select the account you want to merge, then click the Combine Accounts button. A warning message then pops up, as shown in Figure 2-5 (in this case, to show that my Bank Charges Other account is about to be merged into my regular Bank Charges account). Click Combine Accounts once more and in a blink of an eye, the two accounts are merged.

Get totalled

When you tweak your Accounts List, think about whether you want to print subtotals for every header account, or not. To me, subtotals look pretty good on a Profit & Loss report, but they can look awfully messy on a Balance Sheet, especially if you've got plenty of them.

To get a subtotal to print on a report, go to your Accounts List and double-click the header account to which the subtotal belongs. Click the Details tab and tick When Reporting, Generate a Subtotal for This Section.

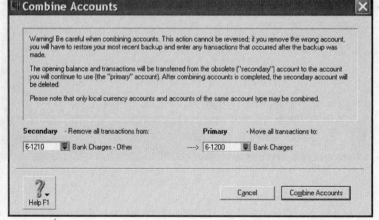

Figure 2-5:
Tidy up your Accounts List by merging duplicate or unwanted accounts.

Have a think about where jobs fit in

Some businesses are actually several businesses bundled under the one name — like the newsagent that doubles as a post office and drycleaning agency, or the handyman who fixes your cupboard doors and also mows the lawn. To use accounting jargon, some businesses have multiple *cost centres*.

Does this apply to you? If so, don't be tempted to create a swag of new accounts with a separate set for each cost centre. Instead, have a single set of accounts, but set up either job or category tracking to look after your cost centre reporting. Make your way to Chapter 15 to find out more.

Creating a New Card

In the old days, way back in the second millennium, people kept little handwritten A5 cards in neat boxes on top of their desks. Each card had the name and contact details of customers, suppliers or employees at the top so it was easy to flip through, in alphabetical order, and find the person they needed.

Cards in MYOB software are a computerised version of these A5 box sets. And like the cards of old, these cards list names, addresses, phone numbers and other details, such as banking information, employee start dates, customer payment terms and much more.

Creating the perfect card does involve quite a few steps. But don't fall into a heap of exhaustion at the thought of having to go through this level of detail every time you want to create a new card! When you're in a hurry, you can create a card that includes nothing more than a name. Then you can fill in the other details later.

Here's the full guide to creating a new card:

1. **From the main menu, choose Lists⇨Cards.**

   The Cards List window appears (which is probably empty if you haven't created a card before now).

2. **Select the card type and then click New.**

   Along the top are tabs labelled All Cards, Customer, Supplier, Employee and Personal. Pick the type of card you want and then click the New button.

3. **Indicate whether the card is a Company or an Individual and fill in the name.**

Click Individual if this is a person with a first name and a last name. Why? If you enter a name, such as Kathy Smith, and select Company, her name always appears under K, not under S, and she'll be forever hard to find.

4. **If you want, fill in a Card ID.**

MYOB software sorts cards by referring to names, not numbers. However, if you prefer to allocate numbers to cards (to issue customer numbers or membership numbers), then use the Card ID field.

5. **Press the Tab key, then fill in the Address, City, State and Postcode.**

When you press the Tab key lots of other white boxes pop up, ready for you to start filling in details. Begin by recording address information.

On the whole, the best way of moving around is to fall head over heels in love with your Tab key (that's the dinky little key with the arrows pointing in either direction, usually found next to the letter Q). However, if an address has more than one line to it (such as the one shown in Figure 2-6), you need to press the Enter key to move to the next line of the address. Then you can press the Tab key to progress to the next field.

6. **Complete additional addresses, if necessary.**

If a customer or supplier has an alternative location or shipping address that's different to the mailing address, select Address 2 from the Location field and record these details.

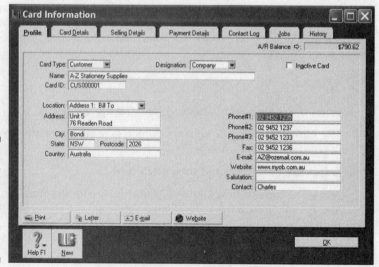

Figure 2-6:
The Enter key moves you from one line of an address to the next.

7. **Fill in phone numbers, fax number, email and so on.**

You have three fields for phone numbers, one for a fax, one for email and one for a Web site address. Fill in whatever info you have handy (you can always return and complete the rest of the details later).

8. **If you like, enter a Salutation and Contact Name.**

A salutation is the name that MYOB software uses as the addressee if it ever creates a mail merge file. If you don't intend to use mail merge, then ignore this field. But if you think you may use mail merge in the future, stick your contact's first name as the Salutation and their full name as the Contact Name.

9. **Click OK.**

The card details are now complete.

Thinking Smart about Your Card File

You can work your card file a little harder if you want, organising cards into groups, storing notes about customers or suppliers and setting up tax codes and invoice layouts.

Can MYOB software be your database?

The card file in MYOB software is wonderfully versatile and, in most cases, the best possible place for you to store information about customers. You won't need a separate database or a separate software program.

However, sometimes I come across a business that needs to maintain loads of very specific information about its customers. The business may be a club that wants to keep a record of golf scores for each member, a vet who wants to record every animal's vaccination history or an acupuncturist updating a client's treatment records. In these situations, you're probably best to maintain an independent database in addition to the cards in MYOB software.

If you do decide to maintain a separate database, make sure you're not duplicating information by typing customer details first into a database and again into your MYOB company file. Lots of third-party developers can help you integrate your database with MYOB software so that information flows automatically between the two applications. See Appendix C for more details.

Setting up customer selling details

In the section, 'Creating a New Card' earlier in this chapter, I explain how to set up basic card details — such as names, addresses and phone numbers. However, after you create your first customer card, additional tabs appear on the card along the top, including Card Details, Selling Details and Payment Details tabs (as shown in Figure 2-7). Of these, the Selling Details tab is the most important.

Don't worry if you're not sure what information to fill in — here's the low-down on what's hot (and what's not):

- **Select repeating invoice information:** If you intend to invoice a customer regularly, you can fill in the information that stays the same every time — such as the Sale Layout, the Shipping Method, Salesperson or Customer Billing Rate. If this information changes from invoice to invoice, simply leave these fields blank.

- **Check customer credit terms:** Credit details for customers default to whatever terms you set up in your Preferences (see 'The credit game' later in this chapter). If a customer has different credit terms from your default, record the changes in the Customer Terms Information fields.

- **Get the GST right:** Usually you can ignore the Tax Code and Freight Tax Code fields, because when you're creating a sale, GST information comes either from your Accounts List or from your Items List. However, if a customer is an overseas customer and you don't charge GST, then change the Tax Code fields to EXP and click the box Use Customer's Tax Code.

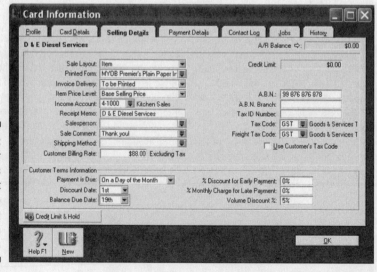

Figure 2-7: For customers with repeat sales, set up Selling Details in their card.

Setting up supplier buying details

To view supplier buying details, open a supplier's card and click the Buying Details tab. Here's what to do next:

- ✔ **Pick the Purchase Layout:** You only have to worry about this field if you print Purchase Orders, in which case, select your Purchase Order layout here.

- ✔ **Select the Expense Account:** Choose the expense account that normally applies to the supplier. For example, if this supplier is your landlord, select Rent Expense. Or, if the supplier sells you raw materials, select Purchases as your expense.

- ✔ **Check supplier credit terms:** Credit terms appear as whatever default terms you set up in Preferences (see 'The credit game' later in this chapter). If a supplier offers different terms, change these now.

- ✔ **Think about tax:** Despite rampant rumour-mongering, you're not obliged to complete suppliers' ABN information for tax or record-keeping purposes, so you can ignore these fields if you like. However, if a supplier's GST status differs from the norm (maybe they have an ABN but they're not registered for GST), you can complete the Tax Code fields and click the box Use Supplier's Tax Code.

Changing and deleting cards

If you make a mistake when you create a card, or if someone's details change, it's easy enough to fix. From the Lists menu, choose Cards and highlight the card in question. Click Edit, change any details that you need to, then click OK. You're done.

To delete a card, select the card in question and click Edit. Then, from the main menu, choose Edit⇨Delete Card. Zap, the card is gone.

If you get a warning that says, 'A card with journal entries may not be deleted', it means the card has transactions on it that belong to the current financial year, so you have to wait till the year rolls over before you can delete it. That's okay! If it really bugs you to see this card appearing in your drop-down lists all the time, double-click the card and tick the box Inactive Card. Now the card's details won't show up when you're selecting names from lists in MYOB software, although the card still appears in your Cards List, marked inactive.

By the way, if you end up with duplicate cards (maybe you have one card called 'St Mary's College' and another called 'Saint Mary's College'), you can merge the two cards together in the same way as you merge accounts. Refer to 'Merge into one' earlier in this chapter to find out more.

Finding cards when you need 'em

When you're chasing information, it's easy to get confused about the difference between card details (such as the address, phone and so on) and transactions that belong to a card.

✔ If you want to see card details — maybe to look up a phone number or check a contact name — go to your Cards List, highlight the card in question, then click Edit.

✔ If you want to look up financial transactions belonging to a card, select Find Transactions and then click the Card tab. Enter the card name, then select a date range in the Dated From and To boxes. Now you should see a list of all transactions for the card, as shown in Figure 2-8.

✔ You can also choose Reports and click the Card tab to see a whole range of other card-based reports.

✔ If you like, use the keyboard shortcut Ctrl+F (or Cmd+F on Macs) to hop directly to your Cards List from anywhere in the program.

Figure 2-8:
Go to your Find Transactions menu to see all the transactions belonging to a card.

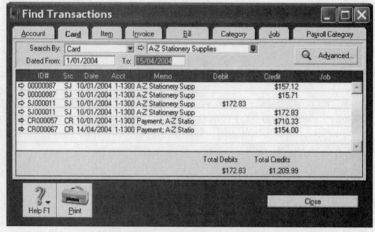

Separating customers into groups

I can think of a zillion reasons why it's a good idea to split your customers into groups. You can track how customers find out about you (for example, from radio, newspapers or word of mouth) or look at customer demographics (for example, male versus female, age groups and socioeconomic backgrounds). Or you can group customers in ways that are specific to your business, like a gym that groups its members according to the classes they attend.

So today, while you're multi-tasking away, making phone calls, paying bills and sweet-talking suppliers, why not organise your customers as well . . .

✔ **Decide how to group your customers or clients.** Without knowing your business, I can't tell you how do this. But to give you an idea, I know a recording studio that groups its clients according to business type, location and musical genre.

✔ **Set up labels for each customer group.** Head for the Lists menu and select Custom List & Field Names. Select Customers. Change the titles of Custom List #1, List #2 and List #3 so that they become the labels for each customer group. For example, the title for Custom List #1 may be Business Type and the title for Custom List #2 may be Location.

✔ **Set up lists for each customer group.** From the main menu, choose Lists⇨Custom Lists⇨Customers. Now decide what you want to appear under each custom list. For example, the recording studio sets up classical, country, folk, hip-hop, jazz and rock under Genre, as Figure 2-9 shows.

Figure 2-9: Organising customers into groups.

The credit game

Before you create too many new cards, it's a good idea to set up default credit terms for your customers and suppliers. Default credit terms are the terms you offer to the majority of your customers, or the terms you negotiate with the majority of your suppliers.

The default credit terms you set up for customers and suppliers appear every time you create a new card. However, if you create a new customer or supplier who has credit terms different to the default, that's fine too. Simply go to either the Selling Details or Buying Details tab of that particular customer or supplier and override the default settings.

Here's how to set up your default credit terms:

1. **From the main menu, choose Setup⇨Preferences and then click the Sales tab.**

2. **Click the Terms button in the bottom left corner.**

   Your current default customer terms appear.

3. **From the Payment is Due drop-down box, choose when you want your customers to pay, using Table 2-2 as a guide.**

4. **Repeat this process for your suppliers.**

   When you've completed setting up your customer credit terms, click OK to return to the Preferences menu, then click the Purchases tab. Click Terms once more to set up your default supplier terms.

Of course, you need to take extra special care when setting up customer credit terms. Here are a few tips to help you on your way:

✔ Don't forget to pick the Tax Code that applies to most of your customers. If you charge GST on most sales, pick GST as the Tax Code when setting up default customer terms. Otherwise, pick FRE (if the majority of your sales are GST-free) or N-T (if you're not registered for GST at all).

✔ If you're using MYOB Premier or AccountEdge, select the Price Level that applies to most of your customers when setting up default customer terms.

✔ If you would rather age your receivables based on something other than 30, 60 or 90 days, here's what to do: Stay in the Preferences menu, but this time click the Reports & Forms tab. Now you can choose between Daily Ageing Periods and Monthly Ageing Periods. (Most businesses in Australia and New Zealand work on a monthly ageing basis.)

✔ If you want to set credit limits for customers, you can. You can set an overall credit limit for all customers in your default credit terms, or individual limits by zooming into the credit terms on individual customer cards. You'll also need to visit the Sales tab on your Preferences menu and select how you want the warnings to work if a customer does exceed their limit.

Table 2-2	Customer Payment Options
Payment Method	*Payment Terms*
C.O.D.	Cash must be paid at the time of delivery.
Prepaid	All orders should be prepaid in advance.
In a Given # of Days	The given number (#) of days is the time you allow the customer to pay you after the invoice date. Use the Balance Due field to fill in the number of days.
On a Day of the Month	The due date is calculated by combining this day with the month on the invoice.
# of Days after EOM	The customer has to the end of the month (EOM) and then the number of days you nominate.
Day of Month after EOM	The due date is a certain number of days following the end of the month. Use this option if the due date is always the last day of the following month.

Importing Info from Other Programs

I often meet new clients who already have a customer or supplier listing set up on their computer, before they install MYOB software. They don't want to type in the information all over again, but don't know how to get the information into their MYOB company file. (This is important, which is the reason I deal with something so technical so early in the book.)

If you have better things to do than labour over a hot keyboard hour after hour, read on. Believe me, to get information out of a word processor, spreadsheet or database and into MYOB software isn't too difficult.

Translating from Swahili into pig Latin (or MYOB-speak)

Your first step is to get your customer or supplier details into a format that MYOB software can understand. I find that a spreadsheet program is the easiest. Microsoft Excel, Lotus 1-2-3 and Microsoft Works are examples of spreadsheets that you may have on your computer.

1. **If your customer or supplier details are currently in a word processor or database, try to get them into a spreadsheet before you send the information to your MYOB company file.**

   I can't be too specific here because I don't know exactly what software you're using, but try to open your word processing document directly from your spreadsheet program (sometimes it works and sometimes it doesn't). Or, see if you can save the data in your database as a file in a format that can be opened up as a spreadsheet.

2. **Arrange the information neatly in columns.**

   Tidy things up so that all names are listed one after the other, all addresses are listed one after the other and so on. (With addresses, separate the street, city, state and postcode into four separate columns.)

3. **Insert a row at the very top of your list (if you haven't got one already) that labels the columns.**

   For example, Name, Phone 1, Phone 2, Contact and so on. This row is called your Header row.

4. **From the main menu, choose File⇨Save As and then select Tab-Delimited as the File Type.**

   The Tab-Delimited file format makes it easy for MYOB software to read.

Translating from pig Latin

Now you're ready to import your Tab-Delimited file into your MYOB company file. Hold tight, here goes:

1. **Fire up MYOB software and make a backup of your file.**

   Guess why I start with this step? If you really mess up your import (which sometimes happens the first time around), you can restore your backup and start again. Trust me, I know about first-time attempts!

2. **Choose File⇨Import Data. Then choose Cards and pick the type of card you want to import.**

   The Import File dialogue box appears.

3. **Fiddle with the settings and click Continue.**

   It's getting pretty damned technical at this point. But never fear! Select Tab-Delimited as your Import File Format, and click the option to include your Header Record. As for Duplicate Records, choose to Add Them. (This means that if you have two customers called John Stuart, both are added.)

4. Locate the file you're importing, then click OK.

Find the spreadsheet file that has your customer or supplier list. If it's not stored in your MYOB program folder, you may have to change folders to look for it. When you find it, highlight it and click OK to progress to the Import Data window.

5. Match your import fields and click Import.

Aha! This is the good bit. The idea is that you grab your trusty mouse and highlight the first field on the left-hand side. Then click in the Matching Import Field on the right-hand side. Do this one by one until every field on the left-hand side is matched with a field on the right-hand side.

6. Watch and marvel as the fun begins.

Sometimes importing takes a painfully long time, sometimes only a few seconds. However, the import is complete when a delightful message pops up to inform you of your success (or failure). If your import failed, read the message carefully!

Get that shag off the rock

Once you're up and running with MYOB software, you're literally sitting on a goldmine of information. All those supplier and customer details, account balances, email addresses and so on could be used in many other areas of your business, right? Well, such information isn't so handy if MYOB software runs in isolation, not talking to the rest of your business software.

If you have ACT! contact management software, you can purchase a nifty little utility that sucks customer or supplier contact details straight from your MYOB company file so that they appear in ACT!, without you having to type a single keystroke. (For more info, visit www.acttoday.com.au and search for 'ACT! Link for MYOB'.) Similarly, if you use Microsoft Outlook to manage your contacts and diary, go to www.datapel.com, and for a modest fee, download the utility that automatically synchronises contact names and email addresses between your MYOB software and your Outlook address book.

Smart Tags is another way of exchanging information between MYOB software and Microsoft Office XP products (Word, Excel, Outlook and so on). For example, if you're working in Microsoft Word and you type the name of a customer that exists in your MYOB company file, a Smart Tag icon appears above the customer's name. You can then right-click with your mouse to reveal a list of options, such as inserting the customer's address, their unpaid invoice details or their credit limit. To delve into the fine detail of this topic, check out the Smart Tags help document at www.myob.com.au/support.

Understanding what went wrong

Importing card details into your MYOB company file should be easy, but plenty of gremlins can throw an error message your way.

- ✔ If a record is skipped, it means that something was so bad that it was ignored completely.
- ✔ If a record is imported with a warning, it means there was a minor problem causing a part of the record to be rejected.

The good news is that MYOB software is pretty helpful when it comes to pinpointing import errors, documenting all problems in a special file called 'myoblog.txt', which notes exactly which records — or parts of records — are rejected, and why. This file is saved in the same folder as your MYOB company file (usually your MYOB program folder).

If you get an error message, go to your word processor and open up myoblog.txt to view the error log. It shows a list of every record that has a problem, with an error code showing at the beginning of each one. At first, these error codes look like unintelligible jargon (Error -7 doesn't mean much to the uninitiated). Now go to the bottom of the document to see a list of what each error message means.

After you identify which records didn't import properly and why, you can make one of two moves. If only a few cards are affected, open up your company file and fix up these cards one by one. If most of the import was a disaster, your best bet is to restore your backup, fix up the import file and try again.

Part II
Everyday Activities

Glenn Lumsden

'This is one of my favourites . . . notice how
the purchases perfectly counter-balance
supplier payments, while the profits seem
to follow you around the room.'

In this part . . .

*E*veryday business transactions are the heart and soul of any enterprise. In this part, I cover making sales and receiving money (the fun bit), making purchases and shelling out money (the not-so-fun bit), and handling stock and paying employees.

Once you're in the swing of things, MYOB software makes these everyday activities feel like second nature, just like brushing your teeth, having a shower or making breakfast.

Chapter 3

Making a Sale

. . . .

In This Chapter

▶ Choosing your invoice layout

▶ Creating your first sale

▶ Calculating GST

▶ Finding invoices and fixing your mistakes

▶ Invoicing tips and shortcuts

▶ Getting a hard copy

▶ Saving paper with emails and faxes

. . . .

The sales end of town forms the guts of your accounting software. This is where you want MYOB to bend to your every whim and deliver a smart and spectacular solution.

With this in mind, in this chapter I talk about everything you need to know in order to produce your first invoice: what kind of layout to choose, how to calculate GST, how to bill for time, what to do if you make a mistake and much more. I also explain how to set up recurring sales templates, ideal if you need to generate the same invoice again and again.

This chapter then delves into ancient history, explaining how it's possible to print invoices, fold them into a special piece of packaging called an envelope and employ the Australian postal service to take this envelope from one destination to another. To be even-handed in my historical approach, I then move to more recent times and explain more modern methods of delivery — how to dispatch customer invoices by email, sending them on a virtual journey that takes but a few fleeting seconds.

Deciding Which Invoice Layout Fits Best

Producing your very first invoice can be a pretty amazing experience: Type in your customer's details, describe what you're selling and press Print. There, in your hot little hand, is a stylish invoice ready to go.

To make it easy, you choose from one of four standard invoice layouts: Service, Item, Professional and Time Billing. Actually, MYOB also has a fifth invoice layout called Miscellaneous, but this type is only useful if you want to make adjustments to a customer's account (see Chapter 4 for details). Also, note that the Time Billing layout is only available in MYOB Accounting Plus, MYOB Premier and MYOB AccountEdge.

The different invoice layouts let you best describe the contents that appear on your invoices. All you have to do is decide which type best suits your business . . .

Service and Professional invoices

Service and Professional invoices suit the majority of businesses.

Service invoices give you plenty of room to include a detailed description (in the body of the invoice) of the excellent goods or services you have just provided for your customer. Probably most businesses that use MYOB Software use the Service invoice template. (*Tip:* To see what a Service invoice looks out, check out Figure 3-3 in this chapter.)

Professional invoices are almost the same as Service invoices, but not quite. Professional invoices have an additional column on the left-hand side for listing dates, which comes in really handy if you charge by the hour and take several days — or even weeks — to do a job. You can show the client precisely how much time was required to complete the work.

The only fields excluded on Professional invoices, compared to Service invoices, is the Ship Via field.

The kinds of people who use Professional invoices include accountants, barristers, consultants and so on. For example, Figure 3-1 shows a consultant's Professional invoice, billing for on-site training, meetings and parking.

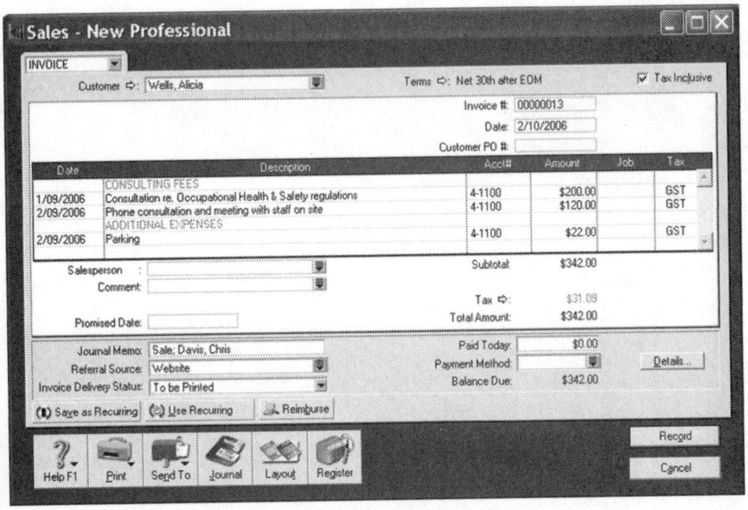

Figure 3-1:
A typical
Professional
invoice.

Item invoices

Item invoices are designed for businesses that sell products — be they computers, fine porcelain, teddy bears or water filters. The Item invoice layout includes columns for quantity, back orders, description, pricing and discounts.

Item invoices are also useful for businesses that include units of time spent on a job. I talk more about this in Chapter 8, but you can get an idea of how this works by checking out Figure 3-2. This typical Item invoice combines products (coffee powder and pottery) and time (labour) as items. You can see products on the first two lines. Labour comes up on the third line, showing four hours at $65 an hour.

If you're going to use Item invoices, you first need to venture into the Inventory command centre and set up descriptions for the items that you sell. Sure, labour isn't something that you can physically count, but you set up hourly rates as inventory items that you sell only (you don't select to buy or inventory these items). I talk more about items and inventory in Chapter 8.

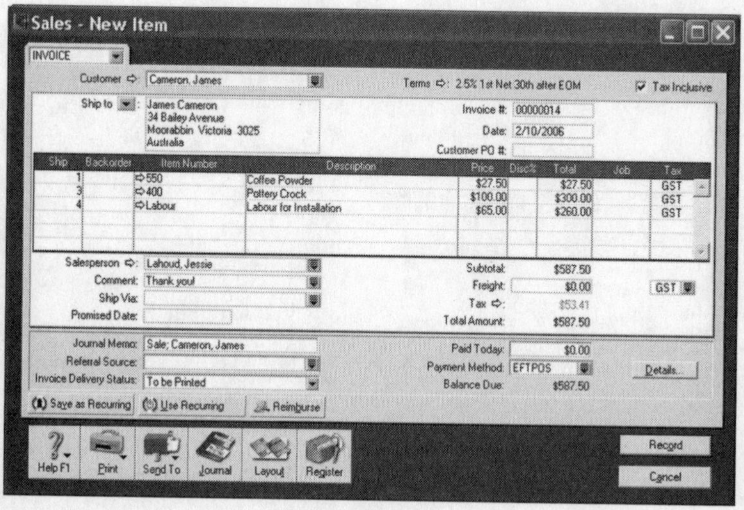

Figure 3-2:
A typical
Item invoice.

Time Billing invoices

The most exclusive invoice template, Time Billing, exists in MYOB Accounting Plus, MYOB Premier and MYOB AccountEdge — but not in MYOB BusinessBasics, FirstEdge or MYOB Accounting.

Time Billing has a financially successful ring to it, don't you think? It conjures up images of professional types who charge $200 just for shaking your hand and saying hello, and thousands more just to give you advice. Yes, indeed.

- Time Billing is designed for those who like to bill in detail for their working hours. You can itemise each date, activity, the number of hours and minutes spent on that activity, and add notes about the particular skills required and the rates charged for them.

- Time Billing invoices are a little different from other invoice layouts in that you generate these invoices automatically. The idea is that you log all the minutiae of your day in the Activity Slips area of the Time Billing command centre. That's everything from a phone call to a photocopy, or a trip to the back door to collect a courier parcel. Time is money!

- When it comes time to bill a client, all you do is click the Prepare Time Billing Invoice button to view all unbilled activity slips relating to any particular client. You then add descriptions, write down unbillable time (or even add some extra time!), consolidate activities so they appear as a single line on the sale and much more. Click Prepare Invoice and there you have it, living proof of your own inestimable worth, charged minute by minute.

Knocking Up Your First Invoice

Finding your way through your first invoice is like finding your way through a foreign city for the first time. Although it's possible to reach your destination by sheer animal instinct, it's much easier if you have a map with detailed street directions. So, with the aim of finishing your first invoice by the shortest possible route, I suggest you provide the animal instinct and let me provide the street directions.

Creating a Service invoice

If your business provides some sort of service and it's successful, you're gonna do this a lot. So, fasten your seatbelt . . .

1. **From the Sales command centre, click Enter Sales (or, if you're using MYOB BusinessBasics or MYOB FirstEdge, go to the Sales Register and click New Sale).**

2. **Click the Layout button and choose Service as your invoice type.**

   Or, if you change your mind at this point, you can choose a different layout.

3. **Fill in the customer's name.**

   If the customer already exists in your list, all their details come up automatically. If not, when you type the customer's name and press Enter, you see a list of all the customer names you've used so far. If the list doesn't include the name you want, you need to create a new card for the customer. You can either click New to enter the customer's name, address and a thousand other details, or you can click Easy-Add to create a new card that contains the customer's name and nothing else.

4. **Accept the invoice number and check the date.**

   Most of the time, you're fine to accept whatever invoice number suggests. (The invoice number automatically goes up one with every new invoice.) However, if you want to change the invoice number, you can do so.

5. **If you have a customer purchase order number, type the number in the Customer PO# field.**

6. **Type a description in the Description column.**

   This bit is pretty easy. Just type a description, then press Enter if you want to continue to a new line of description. If you don't want to continue, press the Tab key.

7. Choose the income account best suited for this invoice.

Next to the Description column is a narrow column headed Acct #.
Select the type of income this sale is generating and click Use Account
to return to the invoice.

8. Enter the amount of the sale in the Amount column.

Real easy. If you enter an amount that's in round dollars, say $50 or $100,
you can get away with entering the dollars only — you don't need to
bother with the decimal point or the cents.

9. If you're using jobs, enter a Job number now.

If you want to track job income and expenses, enter the job number
now. (For more about jobs see Chapter 15, where I show you how to
track the profit from any job, project, venture or cost centre.)

10. Check the tax code in the Tax column.

If you're registered for GST, then you need to check that you have the
right tax code for these goods or services in the Tax column. I talk about
which tax code to pick later in this chapter.

**11. If there's lots of information on this invoice and you can think of a
way to organise this info into groups (maybe by service type, location
or consultant name), insert headers for each group.**

Figure 3-3 shows how you can organise any invoice by inserting headers
to group information. To insert a header, click on the spot in the
Description area where you want to insert the header, go up to the Edit
menu and select Insert Header. Type your heading and then press the
Tab key to accept this change.

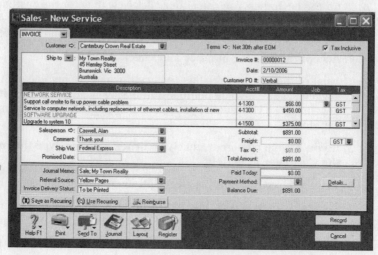

Figure 3-3:
A typical
Service
invoice.

By the way, you can't select different fonts or colours for invoice headers — the header is going to print out using the same font as the rest of your invoice description. For this reason, you're best to type headers using capital letters.

12. Fill in any other information, if it takes your fancy.

The other fields in a Service invoice are optional, and pretty self-explanatory. You can enter the name of a salesperson, add comments or shipping details or even slot in a promised date for delivery. I like to include comments to make my invoices more personal, anything from 'Happy Christmas' to 'Thanks for the lunch'.

13. Leave the Journal Memo as is.

You can use this box for additional notes if you're really stuck, but the Comments field is a better spot.

14. If this is one of those rare (these days) cash sales, record the payment in Paid Today.

The Paid Today field is really handy if the customer wants to pay on the spot, or you've just been paid for this sale. All you have to do is feed the amount into the Paid Today field and record the Payment Method details.

15. Click Print when you're done.

You have to select what form you want to use for printing this invoice. If you're not sure, just select the default form that comes up (for more about printing invoices, see 'Printing Invoices and Credit Notes' later in this chapter). You'll also get a warning that this sale will be recorded before it's printed. That's cool, so click OK when prompted. The printer crunches away and your invoice appears in all its glory.

Creating a Professional invoice

Creating a Professional invoice is almost exactly the same as creating a Service invoice. The only difference is that at Step 2 (described in 'Creating a Service invoice' in the preceding section), you select Professional as your layout type, instead of Service. Professional invoices include an additional date column and are missing the Ship Via field.

When typing dates in Professional invoices — actually, this tip applies to dates anywhere in the program — only type in the numbers that require changing. For example, if the date reads 07/09/06 and you need to change it to 08/09/06, all you have to do is type the number '8', press the Tab key and the rest of the date fills in automatically. Try it and see!

Taking the expressway

Why go on the back roads when you can take the expressway? Hop straight to Sales from anywhere in the program by holding down the Ctrl key (if you're using a PC) or the Command key (if you're using a Mac) and at the same time pressing the letter J.

Creating an Item invoice

Creating an Item invoice is almost exactly the same as creating a Service invoice. So, again, instead of repeating all the instructions listed in 'Creating a Service invoice' earlier in this chapter, I only point out the stuff that's different.

- Select Item as your invoice layout, not Service.
- Enter the quantity of the item you're shipping in the Ship column. (Sorry if I'm spelling out the obvious.)
- If you can't yet supply the full amount that your customer ordered, enter the quantity that you can't supply in the Backorder column.
- Type the item code in the Item Number column. I explain how to set up item numbers and names in Chapter 8.
- The Item Description and Price pop up automatically, based on whatever details you keyed into your Items List when you created this item. However, it's fine to change the standard description or the price if you need to.

If you wish to enter item prices including GST, you can. Simply click the Tax Inclusive box at the top right of the invoice.

Creating a Time Billing invoice

Time Billing invoices are different from other invoices. For a start, these invoices are easiest to create from the Time Billing command centre, rather than the Sales command centre (by the way, Time Billing features only exist in MYOB Accounting Plus and MYOB Premier).

With Time Billing, you make a list of all the different activities you do in the Activity List, and then record how long you spend doing these activities in the Enter Activity Slips. (If you're not sure about how to create Activity Slips, see your MYOB software user guide for more details.)

After you accumulate a few activity slips and it's time to bill the client, here's what to do:

1. **From the Time Billing command centre, click Prepare Time Billing Invoice.**

2. **Select your customer's name from the Work in Progress window.**

   The Work in Progress window shows the list of customers for whom you've already recorded activity slips. Choose the one you want to invoice, then click OK.

3. **Enter the amount of the invoice in the Bill column. You can enter an adjustment, if you like.**

   The first column shows the amount you're billing the customer if you're charging for all the hours logged at your normal rate. You can leave the Bill column as is if you're satisfied with this amount, or you can alter the amount to deduct a discount or add extra costs.

   If you want to write off some of the bill, enter the amount you want to write off as a minus figure in the Adjustment column. If you want to increase the bill (and the temptation to make a lawyer joke at this point almost overwhelms me), then enter the adjusting amount as a positive figure. Figure 3-4 shows an invoice that has been adjusted downwards by $40.

4. **Click Prepare Invoice.**

   A customer invoice comes up automatically, showing all the time that you've logged, with any adjustments that you've made. If you like, you can change the invoice further at this point, adding descriptions, comments or additional items.

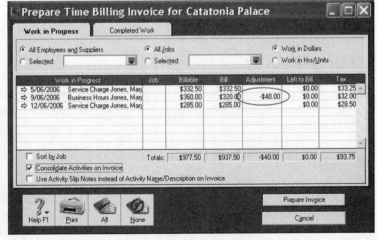

Figure 3-4: You can adjust Time Billing invoices upwards or downwards.

Falling in love with your Tab key

Don't rely on your mouse too much. It's fiddly and, unlike the real guys, it's slow. It also tends to make your forearm ache.

Instead, learn to move around invoices (and indeed, most areas of the program) using the Tab key. (That's the very versatile key with the arrows pointing in either direction, positioned next to the letter Q.) The Tab key, used on its own, moves you forwards. The Shift key and the Tab key,

used together, move you backwards — kind of like first gear and reverse gear, except driving MYOB software is safer than driving your car.

Also, when you finish a transaction, you don't have to click Record with your mouse. Instead, you can press the Ctrl key and the Enter key at the same time, or if you're using a Mac, simply press the Enter key.

---

5. If you're using jobs, check the info in the Job column now.

If you want to include job information, check that it comes up correctly at this point. See Chapter 15 for details on jobs.

6. Check the tax code in the Tax column.

Make sure that the Tax column displays the right tax code for the goods or services you've supplied. And the rule again: The code is almost always going to be GST, but if the goods or services you're providing are GST-free, then the code should be FRE.

7. Leave the Journal Memo as is.

8. Click Record when you're done.

Click Record to record and save your invoice. Or you can click Print to record your invoice and print it too. What more could you ask for!

Invoicing and GST

Although MYOB software handles GST perfectly, it can't guarantee that you produce legit and perfect tax invoices every time. You have to complete your part of the deal as well.

For example, MYOB software always prints Tax Invoice at the top of the first page, but if you don't type the description of what you're supplying in the body of the invoice, the invoice won't meet the requirements for a tax invoice. Similarly, if you sell goods that cost more than $1,000 but forget to type in the customer's address or ABN, the invoice won't meet requirements either.

I explain all you need to do in the next couple of sections.

Keeping within the law

If you're registered for GST and you send a client an invoice that's $50 or more (before GST), you have to issue a tax invoice. The invoice needs to include the following:

- ✔ Your Australian Business Number (ABN). This is the number that the Australian Taxation Office gives you when you register your business, or when you register for GST. (If you haven't done so already, go to Setup and fill in your ABN details in the Company Information window.)

- ✔ The words Tax Invoice written clearly in nice big letters on the first page of the invoice.

- ✔ Your business name or trading name.

- ✔ The date.

- ✔ A brief description of whatever it is that you're supplying.

- ✔ Either the amount of GST charged or a statement saying that the total price includes GST.

If you give a client an invoice that comes to more than $1,000 (including GST), you need to show all the information listed above. As well as this requirement, you need to include:

- ✔ Either your customer's name and address or your customer's name and ABN.

- ✔ The quantity or volume of whatever it is that you're supplying. For example, the number of hours charged, or the number of units supplied.

Showing your prices

One of the neat things about MYOB software is that it can produce tax-inclusive or tax-exclusive invoices.

- ✔ Tax-exclusive invoices exclude GST in the price, so that GST is shown separately at the bottom of the invoice.

- ✔ Tax-inclusive invoices include GST in the price, so GST isn't shown separately, making for a simpler-looking invoice. Figure 3-5 shows a GST-inclusive invoice, which has been prettied up using the Customise Forms feature (I show you how to customise forms in Chapter 10). Although the invoice total shows the amount including GST, the invoice has been customised to include a comment that tells the customer how much GST was actually charged.

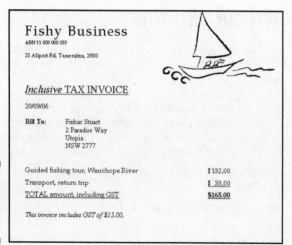

Figure 3-5:
A GST-
inclusive
invoice.

When you go to customise your form, you choose one of the standard templates as your starting point. The template called simply 'MYOB Accounting Plain Paper Invoice' is tax-exclusive. The template called 'Tax Inclusive Plain Paper Invoice' is — you guessed it! — tax-inclusive. Choosing the closest standard template as your starting point makes life a whole lot easier.

Choosing your tax codes

Short of closing your eyes, wiggling your mouse at random and accepting whatever Tax code first appears, you're going to have to get a grip on which code to pick. Doing so may scramble your brain at first, so here are some pointers:

- If you're registered for GST, and charge GST on your sales, select GST as your tax code.

- If your business sells GST-free goods such as child-care or medical services, choose FRE as your tax code.

- If your business sells a mixture of goods, some attracting GST and some GST-free, choose the appropriate code (either GST or FRE) as your tax code.

- If your turnover is less than $50,000 annually, and you have chosen not to register for GST, select N-T (stands for Not Reportable) as your code.

- If this is a sale to an overseas customer, select EXP as your tax code.

Calculating GST backwards

I hope you realise that the introduction of GST heralded a major shift in our education system. Forget multiplying by two, dividing by five or understanding fractions. Cast algebra to the wind, and speak not of spelling or grammar. To get by in the world of GST, our children need to be wizards at multiplying by ten and dividing by eleven.

Fortunately, MYOB software can divide by eleven sooner than you can say the words. You can enter sales prices including GST, and then click the Tax Inclusive button to calculate the GST component. All you have to do is click the Tax Inclusive box, found at the top right of your sales invoice.

Figure 3-6 shows how this works. When the Tax Inclusive box is ticked, the Amount is $110 but Tax comes up at $10. If the Tax Inclusive box is unticked, the Amount changes to become $100.

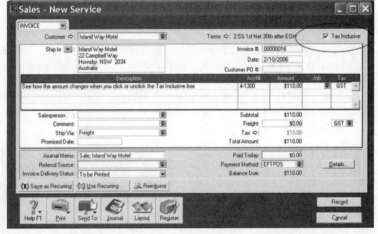

Figure 3-6:
You can mark sales invoices as Tax Inclusive or Tax Exclusive.

When Things Go Wrong

Admit it! You rarely spend a day at work when something doesn't go amiss. It happens to all of us. But if you're the kind who can treat problems as challenges, the following workarounds can help.

Finding an invoice

Assuming you know the invoice number, the very quickest and easiest way to find an invoice is to go to your Find Transactions menu and click the Invoice tab. Enter the invoice number and the invoice details pop up in a flash. From here, you can zoom in on the white arrow next to the invoice number to view the invoice in detail.

If you'd rather look up all invoices belonging to a particular customer, go to your Sales Register, click the All Sales tab and select the customer's name from the Search By field. If you need to, change the dates that come up in the Dated From and To boxes. A window then appears, like the one shown in Figure 3-7, listing a summary of every invoice for that customer. You can find more details for any of these invoices by clicking the zoom arrow on the left-hand side.

By the way, in the Sales Register you can see the Status listed for every invoice. For the uninitiated, 'Open' means unpaid and 'Closed' means paid. (Yes, I agree, software programmers speak a different kind of English to the rest of us.)

Whenever you see Dated From and To fields in any transaction journals or registers, don't forget to press the Tab or Enter key after you've entered the To date. If you do forget, nothing at all happens — at which point, you're left with that hysterical feeling that maybe all your transactions have disappeared, never to be seen again!

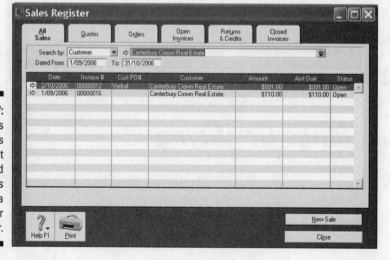

Figure 3-7:
The Sales Register is the quickest way to find all invoices for a particular customer.

Fixing up mistakes and GST

Life's a bit more serious these days, thanks to GST. Before you change or delete an invoice, always ask yourself, 'Does this invoice belong to a prior GST period?' Because if it does, you shouldn't change or delete the invoice. Instead, you should fix your mistake by either creating a credit note or recording a reversal.

Here's an example: Jim, a mechanic, uses MYOB software for all his invoicing and submits his Business Activity Statement every quarter. One day in November, he looks up the list of how much he's owed from outstanding invoices and finds, to his surprise, that the usually reliable Katy still owes him for work he did on her car in September. Strange, he thinks to himself. He investigates further and discovers that the reason his receivables report says that Katy still owes him money is that in September he accidentally created two identical invoices for Katy.

In the days before GST, Jim would simply have displayed the unpaid invoice and deleted it. But if he did this now, Jim's income figures for the first quarter of the year would change — figures that he has already submitted in his last Business Activity Statement. Instead, Jim's best course of action is to reverse the invoice (kind of like creating a credit note) but date this reversal with the current date. (For more about reversing transactions, see 'Reversing invoices' later in this chapter.)

So, what's the moral of this tale? The moral is that sure, it's possible to change or delete invoices when you make mistakes, but doing so should be done only if the invoice belongs to the current GST period.

Fixing and deleting an invoice

So you've recorded your invoice, maybe you've even printed it out, then you realise that you've messed up. You have to move quickly if you're going to stop Madame Gautier in Paris receiving the assignment of haggis intended for Mrs MacDonald's store in Edinburgh.

If you can solve the problem by altering the invoices, all you need to do is find each invoice and display it. (I explain how to find missing invoices in the preceding section, 'Finding an invoice'.) You can change dates, prices, invoice numbers, descriptions — pretty much anything you like. Click Record once you're done.

If you've really messed up and the invoice hasn't been sent yet, you can always choose to delete it. To do this, first find the invoice and zoom in on it (your Sales Register is the easiest place to find sales transactions). Then go to Edit (in the top menu bar) and select Delete Invoice. Close your eyes and . . . whoosh, the invoice is gone forever.

Of course, if you've already sent this invoice to your customer, you shouldn't make any changes at all, no matter how bad your mistakes. Instead, a better approach is to create a credit note if your customer has been overcharged (see 'Raising credit notes' later in this chapter), or create an additional invoice if your customer has been undercharged.

If you find that you can't delete an invoice — maybe the sale belongs to a previous financial year or you've already applied a payment to this sale — then you will have to reverse it instead. Read on to find out more . . .

Reversing invoices

To reverse an invoice, first check your preferences. Go to Setup⇨Preferences and click the Security tab. Make sure this option is ticked: Transactions CAN'T be Changed; They Must be Reversed.

Now, to reverse a sale, zoom in on the invoice, head up to the Edit menu and select Reverse Sale. A transaction pops up that is the reverse of your original sale, with the only difference being that the amount is negative. All you have to do is change the date (usually the current date makes most sense) and click Record.

Oh, and one thing. When you've finished recording this reversal, don't forget to return to your preferences and remove the tick from the option Transactions CAN'T be Changed; They Must be Reversed.

Raising credit notes

In principle, creating a credit note is just the same as creating an invoice; the only difference is you use negative quantities in the Ship column (if it's an Item invoice) or negative amounts in the Amount column (if it's any other kind of invoice).

Here's what you have to do:

1. **Click Enter Sales to create a new sale for this customer (or, for MYOB BusinessBasics and MYOB FirstEdge, click New Sale from your Sales Register).**

2. **Enter the customer's name, then press the Tab key.**

   Before you press the Tab key, make sure the customer's address details are complete if the credit is for more than $1,000.

3. Enter the details of this credit.

If this is an Item invoice, use negative figures in the Ship column, followed by the items you're crediting in the Item Number column. If this is a Service or Professional invoice, stick negative figures in the Amount column. For the credit note's tax code, use whatever tax code you had on the original invoice.

4. Enter a brief explanation for this credit in the Description field.

Your credit note should look something like the one shown in Figure 3-8.

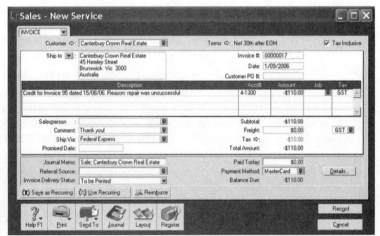

Figure 3-8: Creating a credit note.

5. Click Print.

This records (saves) the credit note and prints a copy. You'll find that because the total is a negative amount, MYOB software automatically knows to print Adjustment Note at the top rather than Tax Invoice.

6. Go to Returns & Credits and apply the credit to the original invoice.

Go to your Sales Register and click the Returns & Credits tab. Find your credit in the list and click Apply to Sale. Apply the negative balance of this credit invoice against the original invoice.

Invoicing Tips

Invoicing customers is almost the most pleasurable part of running your own business. (The most pleasurable part is when the invoice results in a quick payment.) So, to help you add even more joy to the times you sit down to run off a ream of invoices, here are some very handy hints.

Getting invoices where you want them

Go ahead, tweak your invoices so they work well and look good.

✔ Does that big description box that appears in every sale drive you bananas? Me too. Whenever you work in the Description field, a large empty box pops up, taking up the line you're on, plus a few lines below. This box is called an expandable data entry field. To switch expandable fields off, go to Setup, click Preferences, then find the Windows tab. Remove the tick from Use Expandable Data Entry Fields in Windows.

✔ If you make a one-off sale to someone you think you'll never see again, you don't have to create a new card just for them. Simply create a new card called 'Cash Customer', then fill in the name and address details in the Ship To field if necessary.

✔ To insert a blank line in an invoice, choose Edit⇨Insert Line.

✔ To insert a header or subtotal in an invoice, choose Edit⇨Insert Header or Edit⇨Insert Subtotal. If you want to attract more attention to your header (there's no way to make invoice header fonts different from invoice description fonts), type your header in capital letters.

✔ If you want to track where your sales come from, as well as the effectiveness of different advertising campaigns, then use the Referral Source field that appears at the bottom of every sale. So if a sale came via your Web site, enter 'Web site' as the Referral Source. Or if a sale came via word of mouth, enter 'Word of Mouth' as the Referral Source.

✔ For more details about changing fonts, shifting stuff around and getting your final invoice to look generally fab, flip over to Chapter 10.

Setting up recurring invoices

Do you send some customers the same invoice month after month, or year after year? Maybe you're a music teacher and you send out tuition fees term after term, or a security firm with a set monthly fee, or an air-conditioning technician with a standard monthly service retainer.

The good news is you can set things up so that you don't have to wear out your fingers typing the same invoice every month. Instead, you can create this invoice automatically.

The first step is to create a *recurring invoice*, just like a template that you use to produce identical products again and again.

1. **Create your customer's invoice, but instead of clicking Record, click Save as Recurring.**

   Go to the Sales command centre, click Enter Sales and create your customer's invoice as explained earlier in this chapter. Then, just before you click Record, say to yourself, 'No, no, no — don't!' and find the Save as Recurring button (one of those buttons in a row at the bottom of the invoice) then hit it with abandon.

2. **Give your recurring sale a name.**

   Type a name for your recurring sale into the dialogue box that appears. Call it whatever you like, as long as it's something you can recognise (the customer's name usually works pretty well).

3. **Select how often the sale happens and on what day of the month.**

   In the Schedule window that pops up (see Figure 3-9 for a preview of what you're up for), indicate whether you make this sale every week, every month, every quarter, or whenever. Specify when you next want this sale to occur (this date has to be at some point in the future; you can't travel back in time). You can even say how many times you want this sale to be recorded.

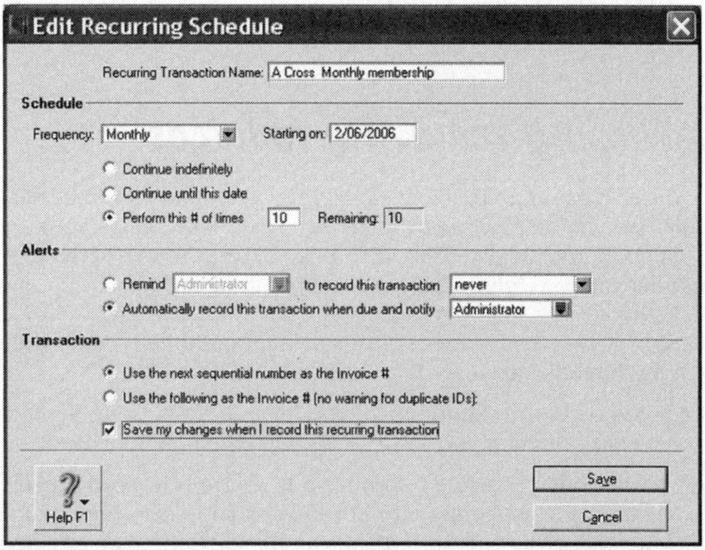

Figure 3-9:
Setting up
the
frequency,
automation
and
individual
settings of
recurring
sales.

4. **Decide whether you want MYOB software to record this transaction automatically, or whether you'd prefer to receive reminders.**

In the Alerts section, you can ask to be reminded when this transaction falls due (it will pop up a reminder whenever you open up your company file). Reminders are your best bet if this transaction changes or needs regular review. Alternatively, you can choose to have MYOB software record this transaction automatically. The automatic method works well for sales that proceed like clockwork, such as monthly subscriptions.

5. **Decide whether you want your changes to be saved every time you record this transaction.**

Ah, this is such an innocent looking question. However, it's crucial to get this one right. Imagine you bill a customer a set fee every month but, from time to time, you increase your rate. If you select the box Save My Changes When I Record This Recurring Transaction, then MYOB software knows to update the template if you ever edit the value of the sale, so that future invoices automatically come up at your new rate.

6. **Click Save.**

When you click Save, you're flicked back to your original invoice. Don't get confused and think that nothing has happened. It has. All you have to do now is click Record one last time to record the sale and save this template for the next time you want to bill this customer.

Recording recurring invoices

So you've created an invoice, saved it as a template so that you can use it again, and you've recorded the invoice itself. Now, close your eyes and imagine time ticking by. Tick, tick, tick . . . Aha! You've arrived at the future, and now you're ready to bill your customer again.

✔ If MYOB software records this sale automatically, then there's not a lot you have to do. Just sit back and relax.

✔ If you receive a reminder, all you have to do is zoom in on the reminder, change anything you want to change, then click Record.

✔ If you don't receive a reminder but you're now ready to record that recurring sale again, go to Enter Sales and click Use Recurring. Find your recurring sale in the list, double-click it, make any necessary changes and click Record.

Copying and changing recurring invoices

From time to time you'll want to edit your sales template, maybe fixing up schedules, changing billing amounts or deleting old templates. To do any of these things, make your way to the Lists menu and select Recurring Transactions.

✔ To change the name, frequency or dates of a recurring transaction, highlight the transaction and click the Edit Schedule button in the bottom left.

✔ To change the details within a recurring transaction, such as the billing amount or the items billed, click the Edit button in the bottom right, as shown in Figure 3-10. (If you double-click on the sale itself, you won't change the details; you just end up recording a new sale.)

✔ To copy a template from one customer to another (or to a whole batch of customers), click Create Copy and then choose the customers from the list. For example, a membership organisation would create one recurring sale for membership dues and then copy this template across to all customers.

✔ To delete a template, highlight the template and click Delete. This only deletes the template, and doesn't delete any transactions you recorded in the past using that template.

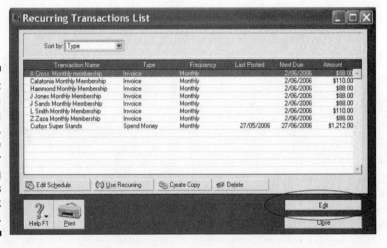

Figure 3-10: To change a recurring sale, highlight the sale in your Recurring Transactions List and click Edit.

Creating quotations and sales orders

The good news is, if you know how to create a sale, you already know how to create a quote or a sales order. Simply go to the Sales command centre and choose Enter Sales. Now, can you see the drop-down box in the top-left corner? Click here to toggle between Quote, Order and Invoice.

Working with quotes and sales orders

Sometimes novices get a little bamboozled by quotes and sales orders, so here are a few pointers to give you an extra hand:

✔ To see a list of all outstanding quotes or sales orders, go to the Sales command centre and click the Sales Register button (as shown in Figure 3-11).

✔ If a customer accepts your quote and you want to change it into an invoice when the job is complete, go to your Sales Register and click the Quotes tab. Highlight the quote and then click Change to Invoice. The quote comes up, ready for you to update as necessary and record as a final invoice.

✔ For a quick snapshot of all outstanding quotations or sales orders for a particular customer, go to Enter Sales in the Sales command centre, type in the customer's name and press Tab. A list of all outstanding quotes and sales orders for this customer pops up.

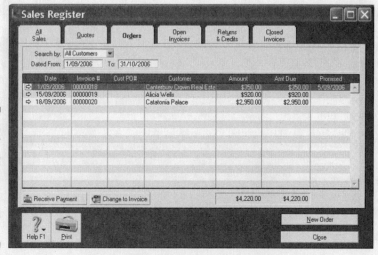

Figure 3-11:
Go to your Sales Register to view all outstanding quotes and sales orders.

✔ To print quotes or orders from the Print/Email Invoices menu, click Advanced Filters and change the Sales Status (which normally defaults to Open) to Quotes or Orders.

✔ You can create a special invoice layout for quotations, basing it on your normal invoice but adding comments at the bottom about the conditions that apply (for example, 'This quote is only valid for 30 days'). See Chapter 10 for lots more on creating customised forms.

Printing Invoices and Credit Notes

You have three ways to print your invoices: the simple way, the very simple way and the not-so-simple (but quite efficient) way. This section explains all three.

The simple way

You can print an invoice simply by clicking the Print button (you find this button at the bottom of the invoice) just before you record it. From here, you can choose between the default form or you can choose Select Another Form.

Using the Print button to print an invoice works best if you only create one or two invoices at a time and your desk is close to the printer.

The very simple way

If you want to print invoices with no brain-drain whatsoever, then set up your preferences to print invoices automatically every time you record them. Here's what to do:

1. **Go to the Setup menu and select Preferences.**

2. **Click on the Sales tab.**

3. **Select the option Automatically Print Sales When They Are Recorded.**

4. **Click OK.**

Now your invoices print automatically every time you choose Record. (All you have to do is make sure your printer is actually switched on.)

Automatically printing your invoices works best if you only create one or two invoices at a time and you always want to print invoices as soon as you create them.

The not so simple (but quite efficient) way

If you prefer to print invoices in batches, then the Print/Email Invoices command is the way to go. This feature is pretty efficient because you can walk away and leave your invoices printing, one after the other, while you have a snooze, talk to your loved ones or nibble on some caramel fudge.

After creating a batch of invoices, go to the Sales command centre and click Print/Email Invoices. A list of unprinted invoices appears before your eyes. Select those you want and click Print.

Sounds simple enough, but you may have a hiccup if you've already printed an invoice and you want to print it again. If this happens, head to Print/Email Invoices as normal but click the Advanced Filters button that appears on the right-hand side. Unclick the button that says Unprinted or Unsent Sales Only, select a date range or invoice number range, and click OK. All you have to do now is send them off then wait for the money to roll in.

When printing blues call

Still having a problem printing your invoices? Stay cool; here are some problems, along with solutions to fix 'em:

- ✔ **The invoice layout always defaults to the wrong form when you try to print it direct from the invoice.** Go to Print/Email Invoices and click Advanced Filters (the window shown in Figure 3-12 appears on your screen). Choose your preferred form from the Selected Form for Sale and click OK.

- ✔ **All the invoices that have changes didn't print.** If you already printed a batch of invoices, then made some changes to them and now you want to print them again, these invoices won't appear in the Print/Email Invoices window. The solution is to click Advanced Filters. Remove the tick from Unprinted or Unsent Sales Only, specify a date range or invoice number range, and the invoices that you want to reprint should show up in the list.

- ✔ **Credit notes didn't print.** When printing credit notes, you need to go to Print/Email Invoices, click Advanced Filters and change the Sales Status to All or Credit. (The safest way to guarantee all invoices are printed is to select All as your Sales Status.)

- ✔ **None of the invoices that are fully paid print.** Again, go to Print/Email Invoices, click Advanced Filters and change the Sales Status to All or Closed.

✔ **All invoices that are a different layout from usual didn't print.**
You need to print a separate batch for each Sales Type (you select the
Sales Type at the top of the Print/Email Invoices window). For example,
you need to print one batch for Item invoices and another batch for
Service invoices.

✔ **The invoice looks like something the cat dragged in.** The fact that it's
first thing in the morning after a big weekend is no excuse. You may
need to customise your invoice layout to smarten it up. Flip over to
Chapter 10 to find out about customising forms.

✔ **The invoice prints out using the wrong form and you can't see where
to select a different form.** Again, go to Print/Email Invoices and click
Advanced Filters. Choose the form that you need from the Selected
Form for Sale and click OK.

Chapter 10 explains more about how you can create multiple forms,
designing different invoice layouts for different customers. If you have more
than one sales form, it makes sense to go to the Selling Details tab of every
customer card and select the correct layout for this customer in the Printed
Form field. That way, you can rest assured that the correct layout will print
out every time.

Figure 3-12:
Advanced
Filters (found
within the
Print/Email
Invoices
window)
provide the
salvation to
most printing
blues.

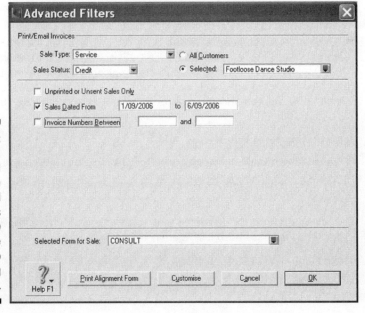

Emailing and Faxing Sales

Did you know that you can email or fax invoices direct from MYOB software to your customers? No longer do you need to sacrifice forests in the name of the printed word, suffer the pace of snail mail or be revolted by the taste of envelope glue. Instead, a couple of clicks of a button and your customer invoices travel meekly through cyberspace until they reach their final destination.

Evolving from snail mail to email

To email a customer invoice, do the following:

1. **For each customer, zoom in on their card and make sure you've entered an Email address for them.**

   Sometimes a customer has more than one email address (maybe an email for their accounts department, but another for management). Under the Location, you can select up to five different locations and MYOB software lets you enter a different email address for each one.

2. **When you're creating new sales for customers, select To be Emailed as the Invoice Delivery Status in the bottom-left corner.**

   Or, if you want to keep a foot in both camps, you can select To be Printed and Emailed as the Invoice Delivery Status. By the way, if you don't want have to fiddle around changing this status every time you invoice this customer, just zoom in on the customer's card, click the Selling Details tab and change the Invoice Delivery field so that it reads To Be Emailed.

3. **Click Record to finalise the sale.**

4. **Go to Print/Email Invoices and click the To Be Emailed tab.**

   You'll see a list of all invoices where you selected To Be Emailed as the status.

5. **Click against all the invoices you want to email, checking that each one has an email address against it.**

   See Figure 3-13 for an example. Note that if someone on your list is missing an email address, just highlight the customer name and enter their details using the Email Address field.

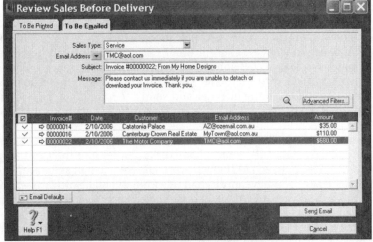

Figure 3-13:
It's easy to
email
invoices to
your
customers,
all in one
batch.

6. **Review the default message or, if you want to send a particular message to just one customer, highlight that customer's name and change the Message that appears at the top.**

   Click the Email Defaults button to change the default message that will go out on every customer email. I like to include my 'signature' in this default message also — the bit that says my name, my phone number and other deeply personal stuff. Speaking of deeply personal stuff, if you want to send one customer a different message from the rest, don't change the default message. Instead, just click on that customer's invoice and then edit that invoice's Message field.

7. **Click Send Email.**

   Things go quiet for a few seconds as MYOB software sends you a 'please-don't-hassle-me-I'm-working-really-hard' kind of message. Then you arrive back at the Sales command centre, ready to continue your day. (Oh yes, and your emails will be sitting in your Outbox, ready to go.)

By the way, if you only want to send one invoice, rather than a whole batch, there's an easier way. When you've finished entering the detail of a sale, don't click Record, but instead click the Send To button (found at the bottom next to the Print button) before recording the sale. Choose Email and then click Send.

Getting MYOB software to talk

When you emailed your customer invoice directly from MYOB software, did you pause to wonder where it was heading? That's a fair question. What happens is that MYOB software creates an email for each customer, with an invoice attached to each one. These emails sit in your Outbox until you're ready to log on to the Internet and send them or, if you're always connected to the Internet, your mail program sends these emails straight away.

Sounds great in theory. But what if you go to your Outbox or Sent Mail folder and discover that the emails have disappeared into the never-never, somewhere between MYOB software and your email software? Don't despair. Chances are you have more than one kind of email software on your machine (maybe you've got Outlook and Outlook Express) and MYOB software is talking to the wrong chap. To fix this up, go to your computer's Control Panel, click Internet Options, followed by the Programs tab. Make sure that the default email software listed is correct.

By the way, when your customer receives their invoice, it comes in a special format called a PDF file. If your customer experiences problems opening this file, they may not have Adobe Acrobat Reader software on their computer. Don't sweat. Simply tell them they can download the software for free from Adobe at www.adobe.com.au. The other hiccup you may encounter strikes when your customer has the good sense to own an Apple Macintosh. If they can't open your attachment, get them to save it to their desktop. Then tell them to open up Acrobat Reader and from within Acrobat, go to File, then Open and select the saved file.

Jumping through the hoops (nothing is ever simple first time round)

So you've got your crash-hot invoice design that looks awesome when printed. However, when you email it to unsuspecting customers, it comes out looking kinda weird. What's going on?

✔ **Some things just won't come up on the emailed version, even though they print out fine.** Sometimes the bulk of your invoice will print just fine, but one or two fields fall off the face of the earth when emailed. The reason is usually that in the process of creating a PDF file, the font gets too big for its boots and can't fit into the field. The answer? Go to the Customise Forms menu (found under Setup) and click Customise to open up the form. Identify the culprit field and either make the font smaller or the field size larger.

✔ **The logo won't print.** Easy. You need to install Quicktime, which you'll find on your original MYOB software CD. Remember to uninstall any earlier versions first.

✔ **Things won't print, but there's no rhyme or reason to it and none of the other solutions work.** Software can be so cruel sometimes. If your sales template was created in an earlier version of MYOB software and won't play fair, then a practical approach is to customise this invoice from scratch. To do this, you go to the Customise Forms menu (found under Setup) and start afresh with a completely new form. (See Chapter 10 for more about form customisations.)

Flying with faxes

Faxing an invoice is a bit different from emailing an invoice in that you can only fax one invoice at a time. To fax an invoice, you display the sale, click the Send To button (found at the bottom next to the Print button), choose Fax, and then click Send. Wait a second or two and your fax software should pop up automatically, ready to do its stuff.

If you don't already have fax software, try WinFax (www.winfax.com) or the cheaper but less sophisticated Mighty Fax (www.rkssoftware.com).

Chapter 4

Here Comes the Money

In This Chapter

▶ Keeping track of customer payments

▶ Changing or deleting customer payments

▶ Fixing overpayments and underpayments

▶ Picking the correct tax code

▶ Recording money that doesn't come from customers

▶ Printing and emailing customer statements

▶ Seeing how much money you're owed

▶ Chasing overdue accounts

*E*ven though I've been running my own business for years, I still feel pretty chirpy when customers pay me. You will, too, especially when you find out how easy it is to record customer payments in your accounts.

In this chapter, you discover that there are two ways of recording all the money coming into your business. The first method is in Receive Payments, where you match money received from customers against the invoices they're paying. The second method is in Receive Money, where you record odd bits of income, such as bank interest, money from investors, refunds or income from insurance claims.

This chapter also talks about finding out how much you're owed, sending customer statements and how to squeeze money out of the most reluctant of customers.

Yippee! A Customer Has Paid Up

In the first part of this chapter, I assume you're using MYOB software to record sales and that before you try to record a customer payment, you've already recorded a corresponding sale. (You know, the whole cart-before-the-horse idea. Whoops, I mean horse-before-the-cart.)

Recording customer payments

It's really easy. Follow my lead:

1. **With your customer's payment in hand, go to the Sales command centre and select Receive Payments.**

   Or, if you're using MYOB BusinessBasics or MYOB FirstEdge, select Receive Payment from your Bank Register.

2. **Enter the customer's name in the Customer field, fill in the Date and write the amount in the Amount Received field.**

3. **Decide whether you want to deposit this payment straight into your bank account, or whether you want to use the undeposited funds feature.**

   In the top-left corner of each window, you can choose between depositing customer payments into your bank account or grouping customer payments with undeposited funds. This is a rather momentous decision, so if you're at all unsure, see 'Grouping Customer Payments' later in this chapter.

4. **Select the Payment Method.**

   To add a new Payment Method to this list (maybe 'Direct Deposit'), type the description in the Payment Method field, press Enter and click New when prompted. If you want to print bank deposit slips direct from MYOB software and a customer pays by cheque, click the Details button to record the BSB and Account Name.

5. **Press the Tab key again and again, with passion and abandon, until the Amount Applied column is complete.**

   To see a customer payment that's complete and ready to record, check out Figure 4-1. (If you're working with MYOB BusinessBasics or FirstEdge, you'll need to click the Split button to see this slightly more detailed Receive Payments window, listing all outstanding invoices for each customer.)

6. **Click Record.**

   That's all there is to it.

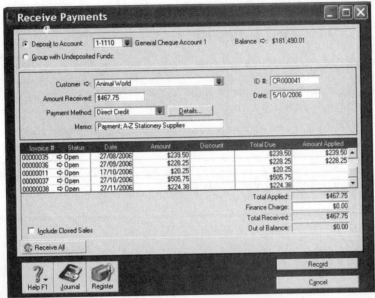

Figure 4-1:
Recording a
customer
payment.

Here are a few more illuminating comments to help you become an expert in
recording customer payments:

- ✓ Ignore the ID# field. This is just a number that keeps auditors happy.

- ✓ You can ignore the Memo field, too, if you like. Just accept whatever
  message is offered (in my book, the less typing, the better).

- ✓ If you trade regularly with a particular customer, save time by going to
  the Payment Details tab of their card and recording the customer's
  preferred payment method and, if they pay by cheque, their BSB and
  Account Name. This way, these details pop up automatically every time
  you receive a payment from the customer.

- ✓ To record payments when customers deposit dosh straight into your
  bank account, click Deposit to Account in the top left corner and select
  the correct bank account (*don't* click Group with Undeposited Funds).

- ✓ If a customer pays all outstanding invoices in one hit (don't you just love
  that?), cut a few corners by just entering their name in the Customer field
  and then clicking the Receive All button in the bottom left.

- ✓ Of course, the very easiest way to record customer payments is to
  get MYOB software to do it for you. Customers can pay you by BPAY,
  POSTbillpay or credit card. MYOB then emails you a remittance advice
  that you import into your company file to automatically record the
  payment. The hitch? For this to work, you have to register for
  M-Powered Invoices first. (See Chapter 13 for more about M-Powered
  Invoices and how they work.)

Hot keys for busy people

It gets fiddly moving around with the mouse all the time, especially for stuff that you do often, like receiving customer payments. That's why MYOB software has a whole load of cool shortcuts called hot keys.

The trick is this. If you're using a PC, you can hop directly to Receive Payments at any time from anywhere in the program simply by pressing Ctrl+B. This means you hold down the Ctrl key

and at the same time you press the letter B. If you're using a Macintosh, it's the same, except you hold down the Cmd button and then press the letter B.

Try it and see! It's simple and saves precious seconds every time you record a customer payment. Incidentally, I list this hot key, along with lots more, on the Cheat Sheet at the front of this book.

Getting up to speed

Want to use an even quicker method to record customer payments? Here's one way:

1. **From the Main menu bar, choose Setup⇨Preferences and then click the Sales tab.**

2. **Tick again Apply Customer Payments Automatically to Oldest Invoice First and then click OK.**

3. **Record a new customer payment.**

   Now, whenever you enter an amount in Amount Received, the payment is automatically allocated against outstanding invoices, putting the oldest invoice first. It's clever, it's quick and, in the unlikely event that the customer didn't pay the oldest invoice first, you can always override these figures and change them.

Finding customer payments

Some days have passed since you entered a customer payment and now you want to take another look at it.

The easiest method is to go to the Sales command centre and click Transaction Journal. When you're in the journal, click the Receipts tab, then pick a suitable date range in the Dated From and To boxes. Press the Tab key and, voilà, up comes a list of all customer payments for that period, which should look similar to Figure 4-2.

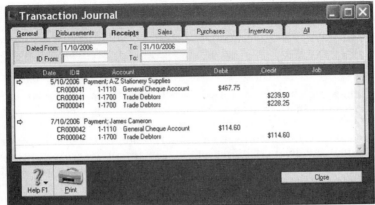

Figure 4-2:
Finding a customer payment.

Scroll down until you find the payment you're looking for and then click the zoom arrow on the left-hand side. Obligingly enough, the payment appears in all its glory. Couldn't be easier!

Printing receipts

Printing a receipt is the same as printing an invoice; the only difference is that receipts normally show a bit less detail than invoices. To print a receipt, go to Print Receipts from the Sales command centre, highlight the payment and click Print.

If a customer payment doesn't appear in the Print Receipts window for some obscure reason (yes, I know the world isn't perfect), then click the Advanced Filters button, unclick Unprinted Receipts Only, enter a date range and try again.

Oh, and one more thing while on the topic of everything-you-ever-wanted-to-know-about-receipts. If you want to change what your printed receipt looks like, go to Setup⇨Customise Forms⇨Receipts. Click Customise, fix up the formatting as you see fit, and then click OK.

Fixing up your mistakes (after all, you're human)

If you goofed up when you recorded a payment, fear not because your MYOB software is a compassionate beast. Although you can't change customer payments, you can delete them and then have another shot at fixing the problem.

To do this, first display the faulty customer payment by following the instructions in the section 'Finding customer payments' earlier in this chapter. After you've done that, go to the Edit command (tucked away on the top menu bar). If you see Delete Payment as an option here, then breathe a sign of relief and do the deed.

Things get a little tricker if you see Reverse Payment instead of Delete Payment. What this means is that the customer payment was part of a batch that you've already transferred from undeposited funds into your bank account. At this point, you can either locate the transfer in your receipts journal and delete that first, or you can accept to reverse the payment. (If you reverse a payment, it will re-appear in your Prepare Bank Deposit window, ready for you to fix up later.) For more about undeposited funds accounts, see 'Depositing funds into your bank account' later in this chapter.

One more thing. If you zoom in on a payment and you receive the message 'One or more parts of this journal entry have been reconciled', then stop and think carefully before going any further. If you delete a payment that has already been reconciled, you will throw your bank reconciliation out of balance, which, to put it mildly, is a rather dire and dreadful thing to do. So, don't.

Dealing with underpayments and overpayments

In the real world (as opposed to the perfect world assumed by most software manuals), customers don't always pay the amount they're supposed to pay. They may pay more, they may pay less, or they may pay the wrong amount completely.

When a customer underpays by a small amount

Perhaps your customer short-changes you by the princely sum of $2.50 and then runs off with a herd of camels to Woop-Woop. You realise it's not worth instigating legal action. Instead, the easiest approach is to create a credit note and write off this amount.

Here's how to create a credit note:

1. **Go to the Sales command centre and select Enter Sales.**

   (Alternatively, for MYOB BusinessBasics or MYOB FirstEdge, select New Sale from your Sales Register.)

2. Select Layout and then select Miscellaneous.

Miscellaneous-type invoices are special invoices that you don't need to print. They're ideal for adjustments, credits or fixing up odd items that you can't get rid of any other way.

3. Enter the customer's name and write a description in the Journal Memo field.

Your description should be succinct and meaningful. Revisit Ernest Hemingway if you're stuck for inspiration.

4. Allocate this credit to a sales account.

For small amounts, just pick your ordinary sales account as your allocation account.

5. Enter the amount you're writing off as a minus figure.

Because this sale is a credit, place either a minus or brackets in front of the amount. For an example, see Figure 4-3.

6. Fill in the Tax column and click Record.

Don't forget the tax code. The tax code on the original invoice is the tax code that should be on the final credit. Click Record when you're done.

7. Apply this credit against the original invoice.

Whenever you create a credit, you have to match the credit against the invoice to which it belongs. To do this, go to your Sales Register, click the Returns & Credits tab, highlight the credit and click Apply to Sale.

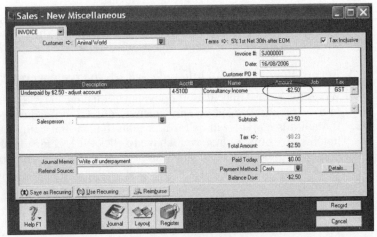

Figure 4-3:
Clearing up odd amounts on customer accounts.

Credit notes, adjustments and GST

Every time you create a credit note, I'd like you to think about two very important things.

The first thing is the tax code you select in the Tax column for the credit note. The principle is quite straightforward: The code you chose in the original invoice should be the code you choose for the credit.

The second thing is more complicated, but the idea is this: Always date credit notes or invoice adjustments with the current date. Never date them for a previous month, even if you're fixing up a mistake for that period.

The reason why? If you make changes in your accounts for a previous month, and you've already included that month's figures in your most recent Business Activity Statement, all those figures you so carefully prepared and sent to the tax office will be up the spout.

When a customer gets a little generous

You're having a boring day in the shop and Nicole Kidman walks in, buys an item for $199 and pays you $200. You're struggling to stay cool, calm and collected and succeed in recording the sale, but completely forget about her change. What should you do next?

It's simple. Find the sale in your Sales Register, zoom in on it, and change the Amount column so that it matches what was actually paid.

When a customer gets incredibly generous

Don't be tempted. There's no point in grabbing the loot and running away to deepest, darkest Peru to meet Aunt Lucy. You're going to have to come clean and send your customer a refund. Here's what to do:

1. **Record the payment in full and click OK to create a credit memo.**

   When you record the customer payment, you have to type the full amount in the Amount Applied column against an outstanding invoice (even though this invoice will be for less than the amount being paid). If no invoices are outstanding, you'll have to click the Include Closed Sales box and apply this payment against an invoice that has already been paid. A warning pops up, telling you that you're about to create a credit memo. Yeah. Yeah.

2. **Select the Returns & Credits tab located in your Sales Register.**

   The Returns & Credits window appears.

3. **Highlight the customer's name and click Pay Refund.**

   You should see the overpayment listed, next to the customer's name. Highlight the overpayment and click the Pay Refund button.

4. Make sure the refund details are hunky-dory.

When you click Pay Refund, the Settle Returns & Credits window displays the refund's details, as shown in Figure 4-4. All you have to do is check that the bank account and other payment details are correct.

5. Click Record.

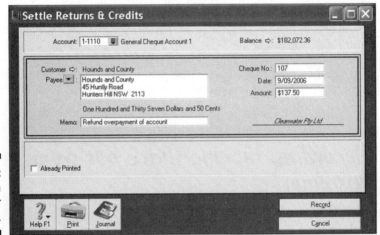

Figure 4-4:
Recording a customer refund.

When a customer pays in advance

There's nothing much sweeter than a customer who pays in advance. To record their benevolent act in your accounting records, you need to keep your wits about you.

If it's not yet appropriate to record an invoice (you probably only want to do this once the sale is complete), then you need to record a sales order instead (refer to Chapter 3 for more detail about raising sales orders). After you've generated the sales order, go to Receive Payments and record the customer payment in the same way as you would any other payment.

When recording this payment, the only hiccup may be a warning message that says something like: 'You must specify an account for customer deposits'. In this case, select a liability account — say, 'Deposits from Customers' (create a new account by this name if you need to) — to finish.

By the way, when you record a payment against a sales order, MYOB software treats this payment as if it's a customer deposit — which it is, really — and allocates the payment to a liability account. Later, when you change the sales order into a real invoice, MYOB software automatically transfers the amount of the deposit out of this liability account into your Trade Debtors account. Miracle stuff really.

Yee Haa! Someone Else Has Given You Money

Sometimes you receive money from sources other than your customers. Perhaps you receive a refund from Telstra, the bank pays you some interest or you receive a loan from Great-Aunt Thelma. In these situations, you need to make your way to the Banking command centre and click Receive Money (or, in MYOB BusinessBasics or MYOB FirstEdge, select Receive Money from your Bank Register).

You can go straight to Receive Money from anywhere in the program by pressing Ctrl+D (if you're using a PC) or Cmd+D (if you're in the Macintosh camp).

Recording income that's not from customers

Okay, if you receive money that's not a customer payment (that is, it's got nothing to do with an invoice or a sale), you still want it, right? Here's what to do next:

1. **In the Banking command centre, select Receive Money.**

   You should see a window similar to the one shown in Figure 4-5.

2. **Fill in the current Date and the Payor (called Card in MYOB BusinessBasics and FirstEdge).**

   Payor is just a complicated word that stands for the person or company who's giving you this money. Type in their name and press the Tab key.

   If you don't already have a card by this name, click New to create one. Complete the card details, then click OK.

3. **Check the bank account.**

   You have a choice between depositing money received straight into your bank account or grouping money received with undeposited funds. Only select Group with Undeposited Funds if you're using a cash drawer or you want to print your own bank deposit slips. Otherwise simply click Deposit to Account and select your business bank account from the list.

4. Enter the Amount Received and the Payment Method.

If you want to print your own bank deposit slips, don't forget to complete the Payment Method details. (Note that in MYOB BusinessBasics and FirstEdge, you can only view the Payment Method field by clicking the Split button.)

5. Write a Memo (or accept the one that's offered).

MYOB software automatically inserts a standard note in the Memo field, but I usually prefer to add a short description, such as 'Telstra refund', 'Bank interest' or 'Massive lottery win' (if only).

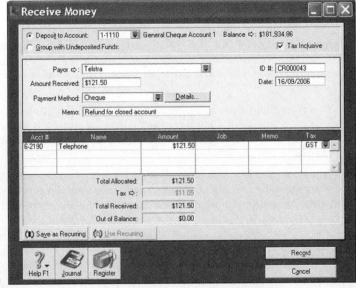

Figure 4-5: Recording deposits that don't come from customers.

6. Fill in the allocation account (Acct#) and tax code.

Ask yourself where this income came from and what it's for. (I talk more about choosing allocation accounts and tax codes in the next couple of sections.)

7. Click Record.

Always record money received from customers in Receive Payments, not in Receive Money. Otherwise, the payment won't be allocated correctly against the customer's account and their invoices will still appear as outstanding.

Figuring out which account to pick

When recording any kind of income that doesn't come from a customer, selecting the correct account can be confusing. But, never fear, help is here:

- ✔ If you're depositing your own money into your business bank account, select either Owner's Contributions (if you're a sole trader or partnership) or Loan from Directors (if you're a company) as your allocation account.

- ✔ If you don't have the foggiest where this deposit should go, create a new expense account called Suspense Account, number this account 6-9999 and use this as your allocation account. (I like the number 6-9999 because it means this account appears at the bottom of your Accounts List.) In the future, whenever you're not sure about which allocation account to choose (for any transaction, not just deposits), use your Suspense Account. Every month or so, print a report of all transactions sitting in this account and ask your accountant to help you work out the details.

- ✔ If this is a refund from a supplier, then as your allocation account select whatever expense this supplier normally gets allocated to. For example, if Telstra sends you a refund, allocate the payment to Telephone Expense.

- ✔ If this is money from an insurance or workers compensation claim, create a special income account called Insurance Recovery and use this as your allocation account. (Your accountant will be so impressed.)

Recording bank interest

You can record bank interest in the same way as you would any other deposit. However, here's an easier way.

When you're reconciling your bank account, there's a button at the bottom called Bank Entry. Click this button and a window appears where you can record bank charges and interest earned. All you have to do is enter the amount of interest received next to Interest Earned and the relevant date. Then pick your Income Account (usually Interest Income) and type a brief description as the Memo. You can see how this works in Figure 4-6, where I've recorded the princely sum of $25.20 in interest.

Click Record to include this interest in your bank reconciliation.

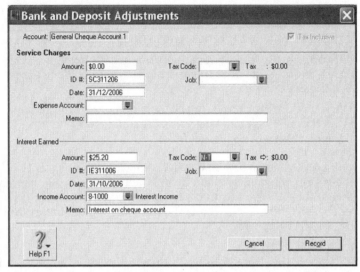

Figure 4-6:
Recording
bank
interest.

Don't forget to code any interest received with the tax code 'ITS' (ITS stands for Input Taxed Sale, just in case you're interested). Interest income is GST-free but you need to report this income separately from other GST-free income on the calculation worksheet for your Business Activity Statement.

Choosing the correct tax code

I had a dream the other night that all my tax codes were wrong and that a team of auditors, dressed in black with wide-brimmed hats and big moustaches, descended on my office at midnight to take me away . . .

Don't risk it. Instead, read through the following with care and devotion and pick the right code:

✔ If this deposit is for goods or services that you supplied to a customer, and these goods or services attract GST, select GST as your tax code.

✔ If this deposit is for goods or services that you supplied to a customer, and these goods or services are GST-free (perhaps you sell medical supplies, unprocessed food or health services), then select FRE as your tax code.

> ✔ If this deposit is for interest income or for services that are input-taxed (perhaps you're a residential landlord), select ITS as your tax code. (I talk more about this tax code in Chapter 12.)
>
> ✔ If you're in any doubt about whether something you sell attracts GST or not, remember the Australian Taxation Office's new motto, 'If it moves, tax it . . .'
>
> ✔ If you're not registered for GST, you don't need to put anything in the tax code column. Lucky you. The code N-T (standing for Not Reportable) will do just fine.

If you're recording income in Receive Money, and you know that the income includes GST, you can calculate the GST automatically. All you have to do is click the Tax Inclusive box that sits up in the top right-hand corner, then enter the full amount received in the Amount column. Before you can say 'knife', the GST appears.

Grouping Customer Payments

Before you start recording customer payments, think first about how they appear in your bank account. For example, if you receive payments from ten different customers in one day, this means that you record ten different transactions. However, the problem is that these ten payments only show up as one deposit on your bank statement, making it a tad confusing when you come to reconcile your bank account.

The ideal solution in this kind of scenario is to use a special holding account called an Undeposited Funds account. The idea is that you record all customer payments as going into this account. Later, when you deposit cash or cheques into your bank account, or you close off the Eftpos machine for the day, you create a bank deposit that transfers the money out of undeposited funds and into your bank account. Hey presto . . . the balance of your undeposited funds account returns to zero, and the deposit of all the customer payments shows up as a single amount in your bank account.

By the way, setting up an undeposited funds account makes sense if you receive several customer payments per day or if you tend to spend cash from customers before banking the money. However, if you only bank a couple of customer payments at a time and don't deal with much cash, then forget about setting up an undeposited funds account. Instead, simply record all customer payments direct into your bank account, in the way I do much earlier in this chapter (refer to Figure 4-1).

Setting up an account for undeposited funds

If you decide that you want to use an undeposited funds account, then your first step is to set up this account properly. Go to your Setup menu, choose Linked Accounts and then select Accounts & Banking Accounts. Next, make sure that the last account in this list is your Undeposited Funds account (this account always starts with the number 1), then click OK.

Now that you've set up your undeposited funds account, all you have to remember is to click the Group with Undeposited Funds button whenever you record a customer payment.

Depositing funds into your bank account

So, you've been to the bank and deposited some cash or a few cheques? Maybe you've also received some Eftpos payments, a payment by AMEX and a Diners Club voucher. Never fear, you can cope! Here's what to do:

1. **Go to the Banking command centre and click Prepare Bank Deposit.**

   You're getting ready to transfer money out of your undeposited funds account and into your regular bank account. A window appears, similar to Figure 4-7.

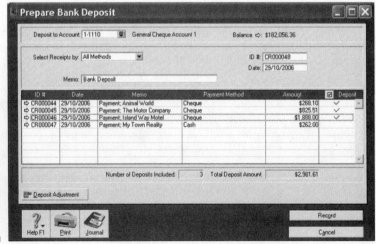

Figure 4-7: Undeposited funds accounts are handy if you receive lots of customer payments.

2. Select which bank account you want to transfer the money into.

See the Deposit to Account box in the top-left corner? Choose the bank account that you're about to deposit funds into.

3. Select a payment method, if you want.

If all your payments are a similar type, you can leave this as All Methods. However, if you receive a mixture of cash, Eftpos, cheques and so on, then you're best to select one payment method at a time (that's because different kinds of payments show up separately on your bank statement).

4. Enter the date.

You won't see any deposits with dates later than the date you enter here, so don't panic if at first you think some deposits are missing. There's method in the madness!

5. If you like, write a comment in the Memo field.

I recommend you say something meaningful like 'Eftpos payments' or 'to be or not to be, that is the question'.

6. Click off the receipts and select Record.

Go through and click in the Deposit column to select the payments you want to include on this bank deposit.

Fixing up your blunders

The theory of undeposited funds accounts is all very beautiful, but I find it incredibly easy to make mistakes, especially at first. You record a bank deposit slip and the second after you click Record you think, 'Oh no, I missed one' or '****, I keyed in a payment twice'.

The good news is you're not expected to be perfect. To fix up a mistake in a bank deposit, go to your Transaction Journal for that date and find the deposit where you transferred the batch from your undeposited funds account into your bank account. Zoom in on this deposit, go up to the Edit menu and then either delete or reverse the transaction.

When you delete or reverse a transfer from your undeposited funds account, all of the receipts for this transaction miraculously appear back in your Bank Deposit window. From here, you can zoom in and fix up any offending transactions, add more entries and then, hopefully, get it right (second time lucky!).

Pedantic housekeeping stuff

I feel a little mean being so serious and book-keeperish, but I know from experience that undeposited funds accounts can become a real pain in the neck if you're not careful about balancing every last itsy-bitsy cent.

The best way to avoid problems is to make sure that the balance of your undeposited funds account always returns to zero after each bank deposit. If you end up with any transactions sitting at the top of your Prepare Bank Deposit window that are more than a few weeks old, it usually means you've got problems and you probably need help from a friendly MYOB Certi-fied Consultant or your accountant to help fix things up.

This kind of housekeeping is like brushing your teeth. A little regular attention helps avoid huge pain and big bills later on!

Printing a bank deposit slip

So you want to print a bank deposit slip, instead of laboriously writing everything out by hand? Good move. Here's what to do:

1. **Go to Reports, click the Banking tab and highlight the Bank Deposit Slip report.**

2. **Choose Customise and then select the number of your bank account and the date.**

   You need to enter the current date in both the Dated From and To fields.

3. **Click OK and then Print.**

   Assuming you recorded the payment details correctly on the original payment, you're faced with a magnificent and beautiful deposit slip, similar to the one shown in Figure 4-8.

   Sometimes, you go to print a bank deposit slip and you get a message saying 'Nothing to Print', even when you *know* you've selected the right dates and bank account. The reason? MYOB software won't print bank deposit slips unless you record customer payments using the Prepare Bank Deposit window. That's all there is to it.

4. **Attach all cheques to the bank deposit slip and head off to the bank.**

   If you're banking cash at the same time, write a separate slip for the cash (by hand) and deposit the two slips together. If you want the bank to stamp a copy for your records, you can print a duplicate Bank Deposit Slip report, ask them to stamp it and then file it away.

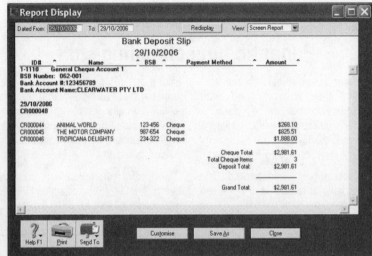

Figure 4-8:
Your
completed
Deposit Slip.

Sending Customer Statements

The next few pages of this chapter explain how to print customer statements, see how much you're owed, fire off scary reminder letters, and keep track of all those money-chasing phone calls you or your employees make. Good luck!

Getting the ball rolling

A customer is not going to pay you unless you tell them how much they owe. So, let them know that you care about them deeply by sending regular customer statements:

1. **Go to the Sales command centre and click Print/Email Statements.**

2. **Depending on your preferred poison, either click the To Be Emailed tab or the To Be Printed tab.**

   Not that I'm biased or anything, but spare a thought for the trees.

3. **Select the statement type.**

   You can choose between Invoice statements or Activity statements. I explain the difference between these two types a little later in this chapter.

4. **Click the Email Defaults button and edit the default message (for emailed statements only). Click OK when you're done.**

You can change the default email subject and message to suit yourself, maybe mentioning special offers, holiday closures or information about payment terms. Don't forget to include your 'signature' here also — your name and contact details.

5. **Click Advanced Filters and make sure that the Selected Form for Statement is the right template. When you're happy, click OK.**

   By the way, if you haven't customised your statement layout yet, this is your big chance. Select the MYOB Plain Paper Statement template, click Customise and do your stuff. (Chapter 10 explains lots more about customising forms.)

6. **Decide who's going to get a love letter this month.**

   Click against all the customers who you want to send statements to. If you're going to email these statements, make sure that every customer has a current email address. You can also customise individual customer emails by highlighting their name and changing the Message that appears at the top.

7. **Either click Print or Send Email.**

   If you click Print, your printer should spring into action. If you click Send Email, the statements should be sitting in a batch either in your Outbox or, if you're connected to the Internet at the time, in your Sent Items folder.

Choosing your statement type

When you print a customer statement, you can choose between an Activity statement or an Invoice statement.

I usually prefer Invoice statements because they're so straightforward — they simply list all invoices with any amounts outstanding. They don't include any amounts that have already been fully paid.

On the other hand, an Activity statement shows *all* transactions on a customer's account for any specified date range, starting with the opening balance outstanding and then listing every single sale and payment.

One of the drawbacks about both statement types is that they don't print a running balance down the right-hand side (the far column only shows the outstanding balance for each invoice). To get a report that *does* include a running balance — which is what you'll need if you're trying to troubleshoot a customer's account — your best bet is to choose the Customer Ledger report, found in your Sales reports menu. (***Note:*** This report isn't available in MYOB BusinessBasics or FirstEdge.)

Making your statement look magnificent

I always know when a supplier has just purchased MYOB software but hasn't quite mastered it because their statement is a jumble of fine print, columns that don't line up and boxes with nothing in them. In other words, they haven't customised their statements.

To customise your statement, go to Setup⇨Customise Forms⇨Statements. Select your Statement Layout and click Customise. Here's where the fun starts. Click the text tool (that's the letter 'A') to add new text, press the Delete key to remove any columns or text you don't want, and double-click on any field to change the font or size.

Although there's lots more information on customising forms in Chapter 10, Figure 4-9 gives you an idea of what your final statement could look like.

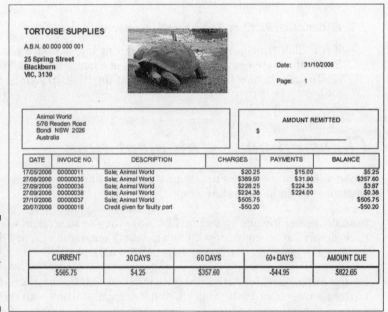

Figure 4-9:
Customise
your
statement so
it looks good.

Chasing Money

Making sales is one thing, but it's another to rake in the cash. The gentle art of extracting money from some customers can be akin to squeezing blood from a stone. In the last few pages in this chapter, I explain how to keep track of how much you're owed, as well as how to print reminder letters and keep track of money-chasing phone calls. Last of all — and most regrettably — I explain how to write off a bad debt.

Seeing how much you're owed

To see how much you're owed, go to your Analysis menu and click Receivables (or, for MYOB BusinessBasics and MYOB FirstEdge, select Analyse Receivables from the Sales command centre). A list of all the customers who owe you money pops up (similar to the one shown in Figure 4-10), grouped in columns according to how overdue the accounts are. If you want to see the individual invoices that make up a customer's total debt on this report, click the zoom arrow next to their name. To see the details of any of these invoices, click the zoom arrow next to the invoice number.

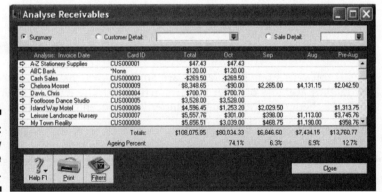

Figure 4-10:
Seeing how much you're owed.

Here are a few points to consider when looking through this report:

- ✔ Lots of statistics and well-researched studies support the theory that the older an account is, the less likely the customer is to pay. You should chase accounts as soon as they become overdue. Don't wait until months have passed.

- ✔ If a customer is overdue with their account, consider cutting their supply until they pay. You can set credit limits and put customers on credit hold by going to the Selling Details tab of their card and clicking Credit Limit & Hold.

- ✔ As your business grows, look at this report every single week. Make sure that the percentage of accounts that are way overdue doesn't increase month after month. Don't wait until it's too late and you're already strapped for cash before getting on the phone and asking your customers to cough up.

- ✔ Think of receivables as cash. Your cash. It's your money that customers are holding on to and you need it.

- ✔ If you want to print a receivables report for a date that has already passed (maybe it's already July but you want a receivables report dated June 30), then print a Receivables Reconciliation Summary report. If you want to see how much GST is included in this summary (sometimes your accountant asks for this information), print a Receivables Summary With Tax report.

Producing reminder letters in a flash

MYOB software's reminder letters are amazing, awe-inspiring, astonishing, astounding and lots of other things starting with the letter 'a'. Take the time to check them out. (Note that reminder letters aren't available in MYOB BusinessBasics or FirstEdge.)

Ageing gracefully

I prefer statements to show the month that invoices belong to, rather than the headings 30 days, 60 days, 90 days and so on. A statement showing totals for June, July and August (for example) is much more meaningful and easier for customers to understand.

If you want to do this, go to Setup, click Preferences and then select the Reports & Forms tab. Under the Ageing option, select Identify by Month Names. That's all there is to it!

1. **Go to the To Do List and click the A/R tab.**

   You see a list of all those recalcitrant customers who owe you money. By the way, A/R stands for Accounts Receivable.

2. **Click in the Action column against the customers you want to send reminders to.**

3. **Click the Mail Merge button.**

4. **Pick a template from the list and click Use Template.**

   This template list appears foreign to anyone who doesn't speak Ancient Greek (as the list in Figure 4-11 shows). However, it's not as complicated as it looks. coll_1st.dot, coll_2nd.dot, coll_3rd.dot and coll_fin.dot are all money-chasing letters. The first two are relatively sweet; the other two are more demanding. Choose one of these templates and click Use Template.

5. **Watch the magic show begin.**

   When you select your template, Microsoft Word springs into action, creating letter after letter after letter, each one personalised with the customer's name, address and how much they owe.

Figure 4-11:
Try out the standard letters for chasing money.

 The standard account reminder letters are well-written, but you can adapt them by changing the Word templates found in the Letters folder within your MYOB program folder. You can identify Word templates by the letters 'dot' at the end of their name.

Credits that won't go away

Have you ever looked at a receivables report or a customer statement and seen the same amount twice, except that one amount is positive, the other negative? (For example, a customer is flagged as owing $90 in March, followed by a $90 credit outstanding from April.) The total amount due is zero, but they still show up on the receivables report. To stop this happening, you need to match up the invoice and credit so that they belong together.

Go to your Sales Register and click the Returns and Credits tab — a list of all outstanding credits is displayed. Highlight the offending credit, click Apply to Sale, click in the Amount Applied column then select Record.

Keeping notes when you get the run-around

One of MYOB software's most awesome features is the Contact Log. This is where you record special notes about each customer and attach these notes to their card, so you can look them up whenever you need to. (Note that the Contact Log feature isn't available in MYOB BusinessBasics or FirstEdge.)

The Contact Log is ideal for keeping track of your debt collection activities. Perhaps you phone an overdue customer and the receptionist says, 'The accounts lady only comes in on Wednesdays'. You ring on Wednesday and the receptionist says, 'The accounts lady took the day off and won't be in again till next Tuesday', and on and on and on . . .

To create a log entry, go to the Card File command centre and click Cards List. Highlight the customer's name, select New Log Entry and log any phone calls or letters in relation to this account. If you want to create a reminder for yourself to follow something up, enter a Recontact Date. When this date comes around, a reminder appears under the Contact Alert tab of your To Do List (alternatively, you can print an Overdue Contacts report, found under the Card tab of your Reports menu).

Giving up and cutting your losses

You need to be both a fortune-teller and a pragmatist when chasing money. You need fortune-telling skills to help predict which customers may not pay; you need pragmatism to accept the fact that some customers, no matter how hard you try, are never going to cough up.

So, in the name of pragmatism, here's how to write off a bad debt:

1. **Click Enter Sales and key in the customer's name.**

   A blank invoice should come up, ready to go.

2. **Click Layout, select Miscellaneous, then click OK.**

   A Miscellaneous layout is the best kind of layout for any kind of customer account adjustment.

3. **In the Description, write a short story about the bad debt and why you're writing it off. Include the original invoice number.**

4. **As the allocation account, select Bad Debt Expense.**

   If you don't already have an expense account by this name, then create a new one.

5. **Enter the amount you're writing off as a *negative* figure and make sure the amount of GST comes up correctly.**

   If GST was included on the original invoice (tick the Tax Inclusive box at the top of the sale), enter the amount *including* GST.

6. **Click Record.**

7. **Go to the Returns & Credits tab in your Sales Register and apply this Miscellaneous credit to the original debt.**

   Highlight the credit you just created and click Apply to Sale. Apply this credit against the outstanding debt in the same way as you would apply a payment, and then click Record.

Before writing off a bad debt, check with your accountant that you have followed all necessary procedures. In order to claim a bad debt as a tax deduction, you need to prove that you have chased hard enough and long enough, and that you've crossed your I's and dotted your T's.

Customer payment history

Looking for a report that identifies your worst-paying customers? It's called the Customer Payments [Closed Invoices] report and you find it tucked away on the Sales tab of your reports menu.

When you print this report, notice that the Days till Paid column shows how many days, on average, it takes each customer to pay. This means that if your credit terms are 30 days from the date of the invoice and the figure in the Days till Paid column for a certain customer is 43 days, then your customer is on average 13 days late with payments.

This report works best if you print it towards the end of the financial year, when you have a greater amount of customer history to report on.

Chapter 5

There Goes Your Cash!

· ·

In This Chapter

▶ Recording expenses

▶ Selecting which accounts to use

▶ Choosing the correct tax code

▶ Finding your transactions

▶ Changing, deleting and cancelling payments

▶ Paying by credit card

▶ Sorting petty cash

▶ Setting up templates to make things go quicker

· ·

*I*t's funny that I ended up spending so much of my working life ploughing through figures and accounts. I hate finicky details, I get bored by repetitive work and I'm naturally impatient (even eating is often an unbearable distraction from the buzz of life).

So working with accounting software has taught me many lessons over the years. I'm much more careful and precise these days, and on occasions (when no-one is watching) you may even accuse me of being infuriatingly pedantic. Why? Because it's the best way to be when you're dealing with your own money and all those little expenses that nibble away at your bottom line. After all, if I don't get my expenses right I might miss out on valuable tax deductions, the mere suggestion of which makes my Scottish blood run cold.

So take your time with this chapter, especially in the sections where I cover credit cards and petty cash, as these are expenses that most often don't get the attention they deserve.

Recording Expenses

You record most expenses (other than employee pays or supplier payments) in the Spend Money window. At first, the Cheque No. field in the top right gives the false impression that the Spend Money window is only for cheques, but in fact, this is the happening spot for ATM withdrawals, credit card debits, direct debits, Eftpos payments, electronic transfers and petty cash transactions. In short, the Spend Money window is where you're going to spend a lot of your time . . .

Recording your first payment

To make your first payment, go to the Banking command centre and choose Spend Money. (Alternatively, if you're using MYOB BusinessBasics or MYOB FirstEdge, go to your Bank Register and select Spend Money as the transaction type.) Quicker still, hop straight to Spend Money by pressing Ctrl+H if you're using a PC, or Cmd+H if you're working on a Mac.

Nervous? Don't be. Take these steps to make sure you get it right:

1. **Enter a reference number in the Cheque No. field.**

   For cheques, simply enter the cheque number. For other types of payments, such as direct debits or ATM withdrawals, enter a brief description — for example, type 'debit' or 'ATM'.

2. **Select your bank account.**

   In the top left, where it says Pay from Account, select the correct bank account (if you only have one business bank account, it's probably selected already).

   However, if you want to make an electronic payment direct from your MYOB software, don't select a bank account. Instead, click Group with Electronic Payments (see also 'Making electronic payments' later in this chapter).

3. **Check that the Tax Inclusive box is selected.**

   See the little box called Tax Inclusive at the top? Click here if you intend to enter amounts including GST.

4. **Enter the date and amount.**

   If you're feeling cool, calm and collected, take note that you only have to type the part of the date that has changed. For example, if the date says 01/09/06 and you want to change it to 05/09/06, all you have to do is type the number 5 and press the Enter key.

Then, roll up your pyjama sleeves and type the amount. After all, this is business!

5. Enter the name of the person you're paying in the Card field.

If you've never recorded a payment for this person before, a list of cards pops up, asking you to select one of them. Either double-click on a name to select it from the list or click New to create a new card.

6. For electronic payments, check the Statement Text.

The Statement Text shows what will appear on the bank statement of the person you're paying. My husband always sends me little corny messages when he transfers money to my account. (You may wish to be more restrained when paying your business associates.)

7. Record a brief but illuminating description in the Memo field.

Let your literary talents run wild, describing what this payment is all about. For example, you could type, 'Aromatherapy oils to calm reception', 'Purchase of new water filter' or 'Massage for sore back'.

8. Decide which account this expense should go to.

Everything has a place. You just have to figure out which expense account you want to allocate this payment to. (See also 'Getting out of a jam — picking the right expense account' later in this chapter.) You can either press the Tab key to view your List of Accounts and then select the relevant account from the list, or if you know the name or number already, simply type either of these in the relevant field and press the Enter key.

By now, your payment should look similar to Figure 5-1.

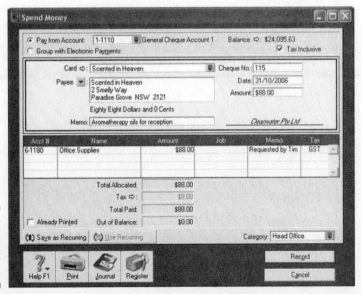

Figure 5-1: Recording your first payment.

9. **If you want to track expenses, enter a job or category code in the Job or Category field.**

   If you track expenses by particular jobs, projects or cost centres, record the relevant details in the Job or Category fields (for more details about jobs and categories, refer to Chapter 2). Otherwise, just cruise on by, pressing the Tab key to progress to the Tax column.

10. **Double-check the tax code.**

   Make sure the tax code is correct (see the sidebar, 'Brain-taxing stuff') and that the amount of GST comes up correctly in the Tax total. Most payments either have GST as the tax code (advertising, computer stuff, rent, telephone and so on) or FRE as the tax code (bank charges, donations, government charges and so on).

11. **Click Record.**

   Find your mouse, close your eyes, breathe deeply. You made it.

Brain-taxing stuff

When you record expenses, does the tax code always come up as N-T — meaning you have to remember to change it every time? If so, you haven't set up your Accounts List correctly. Save yourself heaps of time by going to your Accounts List and double-clicking on every account, one-by-one, and in the account details fix up the default tax code.

When you first install MYOB software, the default tax code for all accounts is always N-T,

but for most income and expense accounts, this code is wrong. If you're registered for GST, most income and expense accounts should have either GST or FRE as their code (although there are some exceptions, of course).

See Chapter 12 for more info if you're not sure which code to pick, or ask your accountant.

Dealing with multiple bank accounts (Bahamas, here we come)

So you've got money salted away in investment accounts, saving accounts, Swiss bank accounts and the Bahamas — not to mention a wad of credit cards and a fat overdraft. Very sensible. There's no problem setting up more than one bank account in your Accounts List. Here's what to do:

1. **Check all your bank accounts are listed in your Accounts List.**

   When you click the Asset tab in your Accounts List you should see all your bank accounts listed near the top of the list. (The only exceptions are credit cards and overdrafts, which should be listed under the Liability tab.)

2. **If a bank account is missing, work out a suitable number for it and click New.**

   If you're creating a new bank account at this point, ask yourself where you want the account to appear in the list. Think of a suitable number before you click New.

   If you're going to use this bank account more than any other, give it the lowest number possible. This way, it appears highest in your Accounts List and comes up automatically whenever you go to Spend Money or Receive Money.

3. **Enter the Account Number and Account Name.**

   Enter the Account Number you just thought of, press the Tab key with determination and type the Account Name — for example, 'Westpac Savings Account'.

4. **Choose the bank account type.**

   This bit is important so listen up. As the Account Type, select either Bank (for asset accounts) or Credit Card (for liability accounts). Or, for MYOB BusinessBasics and MYOB FirstEdge, click the button in the top left to make the account either a Detail Cheque Account (Postable) or a Detail Credit Card Account (Postable).

5. **Click OK.**

6. Test-run your Accounts List.

Repeat steps 1 to 5, if necessary, to set up all your bank accounts correctly. When you're done, go to Spend Money and click the blue arrow to the right of the account that appears in the top left corner — a list of all your bank accounts and credit cards appears, as shown in Figure 5-2. All you have to do now is to select the account you want from the list and continue on your way.

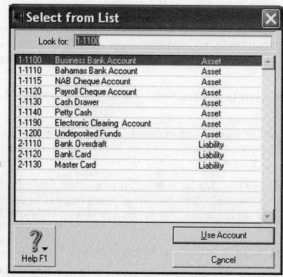

Figure 5-2:
You can have as many bank accounts as you like.

Getting out of a jam — picking the right expense account

In the bad old days of handwritten accounts, bookkeepers used a big ledger. On one side was a column for the total amount of the cheque, the other side had a range of columns, each headed with the name of an expense.

Think of *allocation accounts* as being the same as the headings in a ledger. All you have to do is work out which heading an expense belongs to.

If you sometimes get in a muddle deciding which account to pick, and you find it hard to remember account numbers, these tips should come in handy:

✔ To make the list of accounts appear, just press Tab when you arrive at the Acct # or Account Name field. Choose which account seems best and click Use Account.

✔ If you type the number 6 and then press Tab, your Accounts List pops up, starting with expenses.

✔ If you're not always sure which account to choose, create a new expense account called Suspense account and number it 6-9999. ('Suspense' is another way of saying 'I haven't a clue where this should go; maybe someone else knows'.) In the future, use this Suspense account whenever you're not sure where a transaction belongs and later — perhaps every month or so — ask someone more knowledgeable than yourself (I suggest your accountant) to re-allocate any transactions sitting in Suspense to their correct spot.

✔ Try to memorise important account numbers that you use regularly. Say them to yourself each morning when you wake up and last thing before you go to bed at night. (Say them quietly enough and you may excite your partner.)

✔ Print an Accounts List [Summary] report, without Account Balances. Reduce the size of this report on your photocopier so that you end up with a long, skinny list. Highlight important accounts and stick this somewhere near your computer.

Splitting an expense (without the headache)

What happens if you want to allocate an expense to more than one account? Simply keep typing when filling in the Acct # and Names fields, entering one line for each type of expense. Or, for MYOB BusinessBasics and MYOB FirstEdge, click the Split button at the bottom of your Bank Register.

Figure 5-3 shows how easy it is to record split expenses. In my example, a telephone bill is split between a telephone business expense account and a personal drawings account. Lovely.

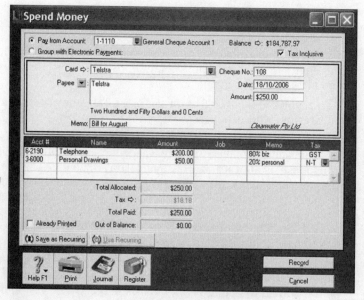

Figure 5-3:
You can split
expenses
across more
than one
account.

Making electronic payments

Most newcomers to MYOB software start out by making payments as they
normally would — by cheque, Internet transfer or credit card — and then
record these payments in Spend Money. This method works fine, but when
you're more confident you may find it more efficient to use MYOB software as
your starting point: You begin by recording the payment in your MYOB
company file and then you send the payment to your bank, ready for transfer.

When I talk about recording your first payment at the beginning of this
chapter, I note that when making electronic payments, you click the Group
with Electronic Payments button, rather than selecting a bank account from
your list. After that, you progress to the Prepare Electronic Payments
window, where you can either record an M-Powered Payment or you create a
file to send to your bank.

What happens next and much more is covered in Chapter 13.

Cards, cards and more cards

You don't have to type a name in the Card field every time you record an expense. It's quite possible to skip straight past this step and either enter a name in the Payee field or leave both the Card and Payee completely blank.

However, I can give you two reasons why it's not a good idea to leave the Card field blank. First, if you set up a Card for someone the first time you pay them, then the next time you pay this person, you only have to type the first few letters of their name and the rest completes itself, as if by magic (what more could a two-fingered typist wish for?). Second, if you enter Card field details for all your payments, later you're able to look things up, sorted by name. For example, if you always enter 'Telstra' in the Card field when paying your telephone bill, you can go to the Find Transactions menu, click the Card tab, enter 'Telstra' as the name and view all payments ever made to Telstra.

Understanding GST (You'll Be the Only One)

GST made easy? I may as well be writing a treatise on the inner workings of a guillotine. But I'm not easily discouraged, so here's my very-easy-to-swallow — oops, I mean follow — take on which tax code to choose when, and how to calculate GST backwards. If you're after more nitty-gritty GST details, try Chapter 12.

Choosing the right code

I know you'd rather be out running your own business than wasting time with bureaucratic nonsense, so I appreciate you may not be very interested in tax codes. But the rub is this: If you're registered for GST, then every time you record a payment you need to complete the Tax column.

- ✔ If the payment is for goods or services that attract GST, select GST as the tax code.

- ✔ If the payment is for a new piece of equipment or furniture, select CAP as your tax code. (CAP stands for capital acquisitions.) Depending on whether or not you're part of the Simplified Tax System — ask your accountant if you're not sure — the threshold for capital acquisitions is either $300 (if you're not part of the system) or $1,000 (if you are).

- ✔ If the payment is for goods or services that are GST-free (medical supplies, GST-free food and so on), select FRE as your tax code.

- ✔ If the payment is for goods or services that are for your own private use, select N-T as the tax code.

- ✔ If the person you're trading with isn't registered for GST but has an ABN, select FRE as your tax code.

- ✔ If the payment is for goods or services that you'll use to make input taxed sales (perhaps you're a residential landlord and you're paying for plumbing repairs), select INP as your tax code.

Whenever you pay for something and you want to claim a GST credit, make sure you obtain a proper Tax Invoice, complete with the supplier's ABN.

Calculating GST backwards

I don't know about you, but I always feel quite travel sick when I do things backwards. And calculating GST backwards makes me feel even sicker. So, what do you do when you receive an invoice or receipt that is tax inclusive (that is, you've been charged GST but the receipt doesn't show how much)?

Short of learning your eleven times table by heart, let MYOB software calculate the GST for you. If a payment includes GST, simply click the Tax Inclusive box at the top of the Spend Money window. Then whiz through the transaction and enter the tax-inclusive amount in the Amount column. Now, check that the tax code is correct (fix it if it's not!), and notice that the GST calculates automatically.

When GST doesn't come to 10 percent

Sometimes you pay a bill and the GST isn't one-eleventh of the total but something quite, quite different. What do you do?

The trick is to record your payment but split the transaction over two lines. For example, if you pay for insurance and $1,000 attracts GST, but the $250 stamp duty is free, then record the transaction's details on two lines. On the first line, select insurance expense as your allocation account, type $1,000 as the Amount and select GST as your tax code. On the next line, select insurance expense as the allocation account once more, but this time type $250 as the Amount and select FRE as your tax code.

For more details about this illuminating subject, make your way to 'Dealing with transactions when GST isn't 10 percent' in Chapter 12.

Finding an Expense After It's Been Recorded

So, you've recorded heaps of payments and now you want to have a look at them. You can do this through your Bank Register or via the Find Transactions menu.

Badgering the Bank Register

Go to the Banking command centre and click Bank Register. A list of your main bank account transactions appears on your screen (see Figure 5-4 for an example), showing all deposits and payments made over the current month.

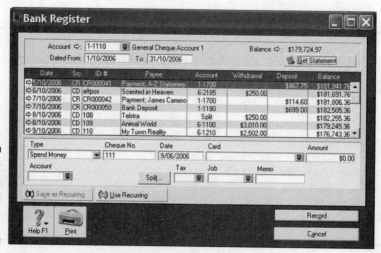

Figure 5-4:
Viewing
transactions
in your Bank
Register.

If the payment you're looking for belongs to a previous month, change the dates in the Dated From and To boxes and then press the Enter key. Quick as a flash, up come all your transactions listed in date order. Scroll down until you find the payment you're looking for and, once you've found it, click the zoom arrow to display it.

If you're hunting for a payment that came out of a different bank account, simply change the Account type in the top left corner.

Flipping out with Find Transactions

Can you see how every command centre has a menu labelled Find Transactions, with a little blue arrow pointing downwards next to it? Click this arrow and select Card from the drop-down menu that appears.

You've arrived in the Find Transactions menu, which in my book is the best place to find most transactions. Type the name of the person to whom you made the payment in the Card field and enter suitable dates in the Dated From and To fields. Press the Tab key and up pops a list of all payments made to that person in that time period. You can zoom in on any transaction that takes your fancy.

Covering Your Tracks

Before MYOB software arrived on the scene, accounting software programs were unforgiving beasts. If you made a mistake, you weren't allowed to forget it. Instead, you had to record a reversal (an entry that was the opposite of your original entry) so that the two cancelled each other out, and then start again.

This sounds fine in theory, but in practice I often found it daunting. For example, what would often happen is I'd make a mistake and try to record a reversal. But I'd make a mistake in the reversal too. Then I'd try to do a reversal of my reversal and make a mess of that. Then I'd try to do a reversal of the reversal of the reversal . . . and on and on. I usually fixed it up eventually, but all my blunderings would sit there in the audit trail forever, conspicuous evidence of my incompetence.

MYOB software is much more forgiving than this. It offers lots of ways to fix your mistakes and, better still, you can usually fix them so that no-one other than you ever knows you blundered in the first place.

Deleting payments

You've recorded a payment and you want to delete it. This is easy.

1. **Find your payment in your Bank Register or via your Find Transactions menu.**

   Refer to 'Finding an Expense After It's Been Recorded' earlier in this chapter, if you need a refresher about using these menus.

2. **Zoom in on the payment to display it.**

3. **Select Edit⇨Delete Cheque Transaction.**

   The Edit command is on the top menu bar, as shown in Figure 5-5. After you select Delete Cheque Transaction, the screen flickers for a second and your payment disappears, never to be seen again.

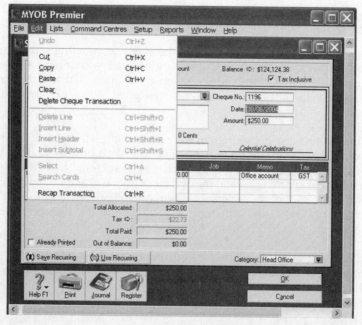

Figure 5-5:
Deleting
payments is
easy.

Sometimes, you can't (or shouldn't) delete a payment. Here's why:

✔ If you select the Edit command and it only lets you Reverse Cheque Transaction, not Delete Cheque Transaction, then you have to reverse the payment instead. Read the section called 'Reversing payments' later in this chapter to find out why.

✔ If you try to delete a payment and a warning pops up telling you that one or more parts of this journal entry have been reconciled, stop dead in your tracks and don't even think of continuing. When you delete a reconciled payment, you throw your bank reconciliation completely out of whack — something you'll bitterly regret at a later date.

Changing payments

Sometimes you may want to change a payment, rather than delete it. Perhaps you allocated an expense to the wrong account or entered the amount as $97 rather than $79. Fixing mistakes isn't a problem.

Find your payment in the Bank Register and zoom in on the payment to display it. Now, just make your changes and click Record.

Avoiding the perils of a bamboozled BAS

Sometimes changing or deleting transactions can cause problems with GST reports, especially if the transaction is more than a few weeks old. Let me explain:

Imagine that you discover in late October that a payment you recorded in September for $90 should actually have been $900. You can't just zoom in on this payment and change the amount, because you've already completed your Business Activity Statement for September. Changing the payment would change the figures that you already included on your last Business Activity Statement.

What should you do? The best solution is to reverse the payment (that is, create a payment that's exactly the opposite of the one you want to change), and then start again, recording the payment a second time. But first, you probably have to change your security preferences. Go to Setup⇨Preferences and click the Security tab. Make sure that the box Transactions CAN'T be Changed; They Must be Reversed is ticked.

Now all you have to do is reverse the payment, making sure that the reversal is dated for the current month, not the month that the mistake was made. I explain making reversals in the section 'Reversing payments', in this chapter.

If, when you try to change a payment, a warning pops up telling you that one or more parts of this journal entry have been reconciled, think very carefully. If a payment has been reconciled, you're safe to change the date, the allocation account or the Memo, but you're not safe to change the Amount. By changing the amount of a reconciled payment, you ruin your bank reconciliation, which is not a good look.

Reversing payments

If your Preferences are set so you can't delete or change entries once they're recorded, the only way you can fix incorrect payments is to reverse them.

The idea of a reversal is that you create a transaction that is exactly the opposite of the incorrect one, so the two entries cancel each other out. You can then have another stab at doing it right by entering the payment again.

To reverse a payment, first locate the payment in your Bank Register and zoom in to display it. Select Edit⇨Reverse Cheque Transaction from the top menu bar, then carefully check the date (you're usually best to change the date to the current day, rather than stick with the original date of the transaction). Click Record.

Voiding cheques

You've just bought a whizzbang tool kit from a door-to-door salesperson for $1,200, but when you open the kit you discover the bright silver case is completely empty except for a packet of jelly beans. 'Help!' you cry. And, in the nick of time, you manage to contact your bank and cancel the cheque.

Now it's three weeks later and you're wondering how to record a cancelled cheque. It's easy. Go to Spend Money, enter the number of the void cheque in the Cheque No. field, ignore all other details and click Record. A message pops up asking if you'd really, really like to void the cheque. Click OK to confirm that you most definitely do, and watch as the transaction disappears into the deep, dark void of Gollum's cave, never to be seen again.

Playing with Plastic

You record credit card transactions the same way as any other payment — in the Spend Money window.

Owning up to your credit cards

The first thing you have to do is make sure your credit card account is set up correctly. To do so, head for your Accounts List, select the Liability tab and see if your credit card appears in the list — it's usually near the top somewhere.

If you can't see it, click New to create a new account. As the Account Name, write 'Visa Card', 'AMEX card' or whatever. Make sure that the Account Type is Credit Card or, for MYOB BusinessBasics and MYOB FirstEdge, click the Detail Credit Card Account (Postable) button.

If your credit card already appears in your Accounts List, double-click it to make sure it's set up correctly. Figure 5-6 shows an example. Again, it is important to check that its Account Type is Credit Card, or it's a Detail Credit Card Account (Postable) if you're using MYOB BusinessBasics or MYOB FirstEdge. If not, change the setting.

If you already have an amount outstanding on the credit card when you create its account, you can record the balance in the Opening Balance field. However, if you do so, make a note of the amount and tell your accountant about it — the opening balance amount also appears in your special Historical Balancing account, which your accountant can sort out later.

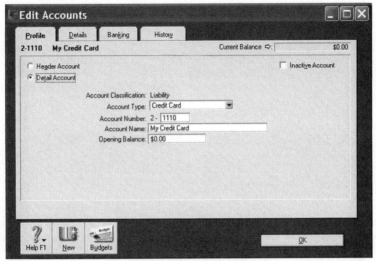

Figure 5-6:
Setting up a
credit card
account.

Confessing your spending

Sometimes when my credit card statement arrives, it sits on my desk for
a few days before I can bear to open it. But sooner or later, I face up to the
inevitable, tear open the envelope and record the day-by-day testimony of
my reckless habits. You need to do this too, every time your statement
arrives.

1. **Go to Spend Money and select your credit card account from the
   account box in the top left-hand corner.**

   If you're using MYOB BusinessBasics or FirstEdge, select your credit
   card account in the top left of your Bank Register, then choose Spend
   Money as your transaction type.

2. **Record the first debit on your statement.**

   Locate the first debit listed on your statement. Record this debit as if it
   were an ordinary payment, as explained in the beginning of this chapter.
   The only difference between a credit card debit and any other payment
   is that you select your credit card account as the bank account. Fill in
   the card, enter a Memo if you want to, choose a suitable allocation
   account (Acct#) and don't forget the tax code. (Don't worry about the
   Cheque No. field; just ignore whatever number comes up.) Click Record
   when you're done.

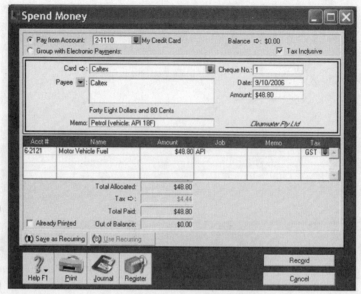

Figure 5-7:
Recording
credit card
transactions.

3. **Record transactions for each debit on the credit card, allocating them to appropriate allocation account (Acct#).**

Carry on recording a separate Spend Money transaction for each debit on your credit card statement. The idea is to think of your credit card in the same way you do any bank account, recording a separate transaction for each transaction made on the card. Continue in this way until you reach the end of your statement.

If some of the debits on the statement are for personal purchases (credit cards often end up with a mix of business and private transactions), choose a drawing account or a director's loan account as the allocation account.

Paying the price

All this spending on your credit card is very well, but the laws of Crime and Punishment state that you must pay the price. It's time to pay up and in this next section, I show you how to record your credit card payment.

1. **Go to Spend Money.**

I'm starting off with something easy, just to make you feel good.

2. Check that the account in the top left corner is your business bank account.

I assume you're paying your credit card from your business bank account, so make sure that this account is the one you select in the top left corner.

3. Fill in the date and amount, and in the Card field, write the name of your credit card.

The Card should be something like 'American Express', 'Diners Club' or 'MasterCard'. (You might need to create a new card if one doesn't already exist. Refer to 'Owning up to your credit cards' for more details.)

4. As the Memo, write 'Credit card payment'.

You don't absolutely have to write a memo here, I'm just being my thorough and pedantic self.

5. Select your credit card account as the allocation account.

Your credit card account is always a liability account and starts with the number 2. Once you enter this account, your payment should look pretty similar to the one shown in Figure 5-8.

6. Enter N-T as the tax code and then press the Record button.

N-T stands for Not Reportable, which is right for this type of transaction. All you're doing is shifting money from one bank account (your business bank account) into another (your credit card account), so GST isn't involved.

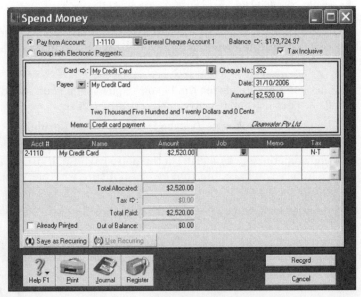

Figure 5-8:
Paying your
credit card.

Going tech-savvy with Get Statements

Did you know you can download your credit card statements directly from your bank's Web site into your MYOB company file? Go to Reconcile Accounts, enter the account number of your credit card and the current date, then click the Get Statement button. You can now add each transaction with a click of a button, simply selecting the allocation account and checking the tax code for each transaction as you go.

You can read more about downloading electronic statements in Chapter 7.

Hanging by a thread

Remember that a credit card is like any other bank account — it's just as important to keep reconciling and balancing your credit card account as it is your business bank account. The whole idea is that you compare the closing balance in your accounts against the closing balance on your credit card statement.

Don't delay. Mosey on over to Chapter 7 to find out how to reconcile your bank accounts.

It's a Petty Business

You can find as many different ways to deal with petty cash as there are to make pasta sauce. But a few things never change — no matter what type of business you run:

- ✔ Chocolate bars, roses for the beautiful girl at the train station and vet bills are not legitimate petty cash receipts. Get real.
- ✔ When someone takes petty cash from the tin and promises to come back with a receipt, they probably won't.
- ✔ When someone sticks an IOU in the petty cash tin, it means that they'd love to pay you back, but they're just not sure whether it will be this century, or the next.
- ✔ No matter how finicky you are, petty cash will never, ever balance.

In the next couple of sections, I talk about two ways to deal with petty cash. The first method is best for owner-operators paying expenses out of their own pocket. The second method is best for businesses that have employees and need a petty cash tin. Take a look and see which suits you best.

Robbing Peter to pay Paul

Recording a payment to reimburse yourself is the easiest way to deal with petty cash and works well if you're a sole operator and you tend to pay for lots of little expenses from your own pocket.

Every month or so, go on a mad Mintie hunt for your receipts. Dig through your pockets, tip out your wallet, look under the seats of your car. Then clean a patch on your desk and sort the receipts into categories: one pile for stationery, one pile for computer supplies, one pile for postage and so on. (Remember, at this point you're only wanting receipts for things that you paid for by cash; put receipts for things that you paid for by eftpos or credit card in a separate pile.)

When you're finished, use a calculator to add up the total value of each pile. Write these totals down on the front of an empty envelope. You end up with an envelope that reads something like: 'Total stationery receipts = \$42.50', 'Total postage receipts = \$35.20' and so on. Make a grand total at the bottom and stuff the receipts into the envelope and close it up.

Now it's time to pay yourself back. You can either write yourself a cash cheque for the total or transfer some money from your business account to your personal account. To record this cheque or electronic transfer in your accounts, go to Spend Money and allocate the payment to all the different expense categories, as shown in Figure 5-9.

I like this method because it is quick, blindingly simple and it fits in with the way I work.

Suppliers and your credit card

Sometimes you may decide to pay suppliers by credit card. By suppliers, I mean invoices that you've already entered as Purchases.

In this case, you record the debit on your statement in a slightly different way. Go to Pay Bills and complete the payment in the same way as you normally would. (I talk more about supplier payments in Chapter 6.)

Ignore the Cheque No., but change the bank account in the top left corner to your credit card account.

Suppliers and your credit card

Sometimes you may decide to pay suppliers by credit card. By suppliers, I mean invoices that you've already entered as Purchases.

In this case, you record the debit on your statement in a slightly different way. Go to Pay Bills and complete the payment in the same way as you normally would. (I talk more about supplier payments in Chapter 6.)

Ignore the Cheque No., but change the bank account in the top left corner to your credit card account.

Lock it up, tie it down

When your business grows, you need a more sophisticated approach to petty cash management. Here's the whole deal, from start to finish:

1. **Buy a petty cash box.**

   It's time to liberate your cash from the biscuit tin. Instead, buy a real petty cash box with a lock and key. I'm serious.

2. **Appoint a gatekeeper.**

   Put someone in charge of petty cash and make sure no-one else knows where the key is kept. This includes you. You're not allowed to raid the petty cash tin for Chinese takeaways and meat pies any more. Those days are gone.

3. **Start a float between $100 and $200.**

   Write a cash cheque for a round amount (about $100) and put the corresponding amount of cash in the tin. When you record this cheque, allocate it to an asset account called Petty Cash (there's usually one there by this name).

4. **Every time money is taken out of petty cash, it should be replaced by a receipt.**

   This is the part that requires a huge leap in psychology. Every time someone takes money from petty cash they have to come back with a receipt. This is pretty radical. It works well if the gatekeeper hassles everyone mercilessly: No receipt, no cash next time.

5. When petty cash is low, sort out the receipts.

When petty cash funds dwindle, tip all the receipts out and sort them into piles. Write a breakdown of the receipts on the back of an envelope (for example, $30 postage, $10 telephone, $15 chocolate biscuits and so on), and stick the receipts in the envelope.

6. Write a cheque to top petty cash up to the original value of the float.

It's important to get your head around this part: If you're left with $4.50 in the tin and the original float was $100, write a cash cheque for $95.50. Or, if you're left with $4.50 and the original float was $200, write a cash cheque for $195.50.

7. Enter the cheque in Spend Money, splitting it across a number of different allocation accounts.

Look at the back of your envelope for the breakdown of receipts (refer to Step 5). Enter each amount, line-by-line, selecting a different allocation account for each different kind of expense. When you're finished, your Spend Money transaction should look similar to the one shown in Figure 5-10.

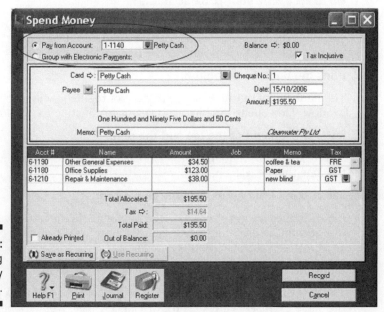

Figure 5-10:
Reimbursing the petty cash tin.

GST — when petty cash gets pettier

If petty cash receipts don't show GST separately, that doesn't mean they're GST-free. A packet of staples for $2.20 includes 20 cents GST. And even if you do feel that you've got better things to do than think about such nitpicking details, you still can't afford to lose these valuable input tax credits.

To claim the GST on these petty receipts — even if it's not shown separately — all you have to do is click the Tax Inclusive box (found above the Cheque No.) at the top of Spend Money. Assuming your tax code is correct, the GST calculates automatically.

Recording Bank Fees

Your bank statement arrives and you discover that the reason you're not making a profit is because your bank is taking it all in unscrupulous and merciless fees. Here's how to record these fees:

1. **Go to reconcile your bank account.**

   I talk more about reconciling accounts in Chapter 7, but the idea is that you click Reconcile Accounts, enter the number of your bank account at the top, and the current date as the Bank Statement Date.

2. **Click the Bank Entry button.**

   The Bank Entry button is at the bottom of the Reconcile Accounts window. This opens the Bank and Deposit Adjustments window.

3. **Enter the amount of the fee and the date.**

   Simply key in the amount of the bank fee (try not to wince), along with the date the fee was charged.

4. **Select Bank Charges as the allocation account.**

   Bank Charges always starts with the number 6. In the unlikely event that this account doesn't appear in your list, hop over to your Accounts List and create an expense by this name now.

5. **Enter the tax code (most bank charges are GST-free).**

   The government places white bread, contraceptives and bank charges in the same exclusive category; they're all GST-free. Wonders never cease. The exception to this rule is merchant fees and Eftpos fees, which do attract GST — don't forget, or you'll miss out on valuable input tax credits!

6. **Write a brief Memo and click Record.**

   By now, your transaction should look pretty similar to the one shown in Figure 5-11.

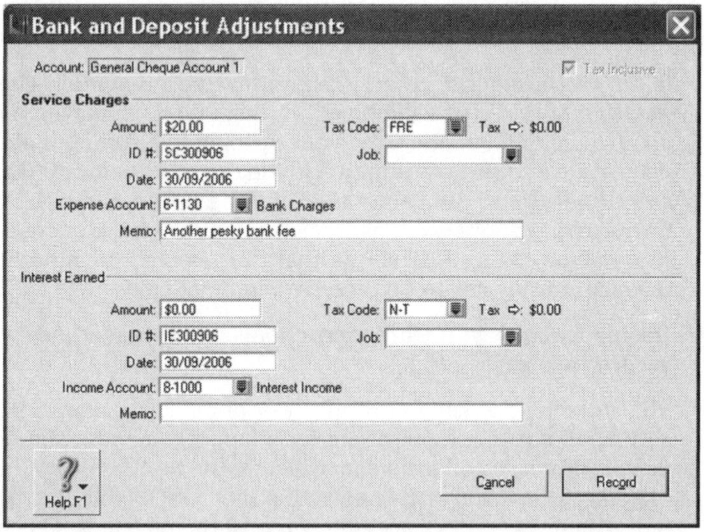

Bank and Deposit Adjustments

Account: General Cheque Account 1   ☑ Tax Inclusive

Service Charges

Amount: $20.00   Tax Code: FRE   Tax ⇨: $0.00

ID #: SC300906   Job:

Date: 30/09/2006

Expense Account: 6-1130   Bank Charges

Memo: Another pesky bank fee

Interest Earned

Amount: $0.00   Tax Code: N-T   Tax ⇨: $0.00

ID #: IE300906   Job:

Date: 30/09/2006

Income Account: 8-1000   Interest Income

Memo:

? Help F1   Cancel   Record

Figure 5-11:
Recording
bank fees.

Shortcuts for Regular Payments

If you have an expense that occurs regularly, you can save its details in a special template so that when the expense comes around again, you can record it automatically. This is an awesome feature for monthly leases, rent, direct debits and so on.

Two steps are involved in making this happen: The first is to set up a recurring payment; the second is to record it each time it comes around.

Setting up a recurring payment

To create a new recurring payment, follow these steps:

1. **Complete the payment as normal, but instead of clicking Record, click Save as Recurring.**

   Fill in the payment in the same way you normally would, but just before you reach the end, sit on your hands. Don't hit Record. Instead, click the Save as Recurring button.

2. **Give your transaction a name and say how often it occurs.**

   Create a name for this entry, such as 'lease', 'hire purchase' or 'loan'. Select how often the payment occurs in the Frequency box, then indicate the day you want the next payment to occur (this can only be a future date).

3. **Decide whether you want MYOB software to record this payment automatically, or whether you'd prefer to receive reminders.**

   In the Alerts section, you can ask to receive a reminder when this payment falls due (it will pop up as a reminder whenever you open your company file). Reminders are your best bet if the amount of the payment changes every time. Alternatively, you can choose for MYOB software to record this transaction automatically. The automatic method is excellent for recurring debits such as lease payments, fixed bank fees or loan repayments. Figure 5-12 shows that I've selected the monthly lease payment for my car to be recorded automatically.

4. **Decide whether you want your changes to be saved every time you record this transaction.**

   Think carefully when you reach this option. For example, if you're setting up a recurring payment for a monthly membership fee that usually increases once a year, selecting the box Save My Changes When I Record This Recurring Transaction tells MYOB software to update the template if you ever change the value of the payment. This ensures that future payments automatically come up at the new amount.

5. **Click Save.**

   When you click Save, you're flicked back to the payment you were working on. Don't get confused and think that nothing has happened. It has. All you have to do now is click Record one last time to record the payment.

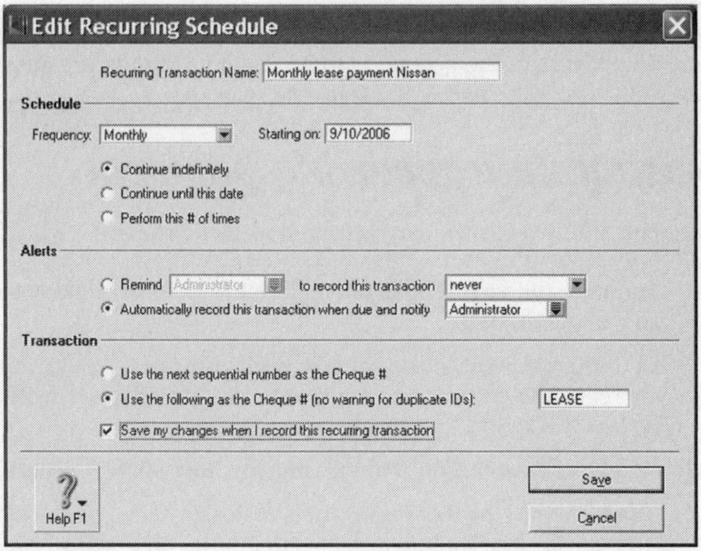

Figure 5-12:
Setting up a
template for
a recurring
payment.

Edit Recurring Schedule   ☒

Recurring Transaction Name: | Monthly lease payment Nissan |

Schedule

Frequency: [Monthly ▾]   Starting on: [9/10/2006]

    ◉ Continue indefinitely
    ○ Continue until this date
    ○ Perform this # of times

Alerts

    ○ Remind [Administrator] to record this transaction [never ▾]
    ◉ Automatically record this transaction when due and notify [Administrator ▾]

Transaction

    ○ Use the next sequential number as the Cheque #
    ◉ Use the following as the Cheque # (no warning for duplicate IDs): [LEASE]
    ☑ Save my changes when I record this recurring transaction

[? Help F1]   [Save]
                          [Cancel]

Recording a recurring payment

Next time your regular payment is due, you'll either find that MYOB software records it automatically (you'll receive notification that this has happened) or a reminder will pop up saying that the payment is due. If you receive a reminder, all you have to do is zoom in on the reminder, check whether you want to change anything, then click Record.

Everything sounds pretty simple, I admit, but here are a few possible hiccups you may encounter, along with their solutions:

- ✔ If you ask for a payment to record automatically, but you don't work on your accounts every day, MYOB software will only record this transaction when you open your company file. For example, imagine that you have a direct debit that goes out on the first day of every month. However, one month you don't work on your accounts between the end of the previous month and the 14th day of the next month. When you open up your company file on the 14th, MYOB software records the transaction, but dates it as the 14th instead of the 1st. The moral of my tale? If you don't work on your accounts every day, then don't ask for transactions to record automatically.

- ✔ If the amount of a recurring payment changes and you can't get MYOB software to 'remember' the changed amount, then you need to edit the template. Go to Lists and select Recurring Transactions. Highlight the payment, click the Edit button in the bottom right and change the details. (If you double-click on the payment itself, you *won't* change the details, you'll just end up recording a new payment.)

- ✔ To record a recurring payment when you haven't asked to receive reminders, or when the Frequency is set to Never, go to Spend Money and click Use Recurring. You can then select the template from the list.

- ✔ To delete a template, go to Lists, click Recurring Transactions, highlight the template and click Delete. This only deletes the template, and doesn't delete any transactions you recorded in the past using the template.

Chapter 6

Purchases and Supplier Payments

· ·

In This Chapter

▶ Generating purchase orders and receiving goods

▶ Recording supplier invoices

▶ Finding a purchase after it's been recorded

▶ Customising and printing purchase orders

▶ Choosing the correct tax codes

▶ Looking after supplier payments

· ·

Many people new to running a small business take a while to realise how important their suppliers are. Instead, they focus on building up relationships with their customers. But the truth of the matter is this: Suppliers are as important as customers, because without suppliers you wouldn't have any goods to sell.

A supplier needs to know what you want, when you want it and where you want it. They need to know when you'll pay them, and how. And guess what? MYOB software helps with all of these things, from churning out glamorous purchase orders to paying suppliers electronically, from keeping track of how much GST you've paid, to staying on top of backorders and price increases. And that's why, in this chapter, I tell you how to develop a fuzzy, warm relationship between you and your supplier.

Deciding if You Need This in Your Life

Before I explain how to record purchases and process supplier payments, it's worth pausing for a second to decide if you really want to get involved in a fuzzy, warm relationship with your supplier. In other words, you need to decide whether you actually want to use the Purchases command centre. It's quite possible to avoid using Purchases by recording all payments in Spend Money. Roughly two out of three businesses use MYOB software in this way.

Note: Purchase features aren't available in MYOB BusinessBasics or FirstEdge.

I can't make this decision for you, but I can explain the upsides and downsides of using Purchases.

The benefits of using Purchases (instead of using Spend Money) are:

- ✔ You can claim GST on bills that you've received, but haven't paid for yet (this only applies if you report for GST on an accruals basis). For more details, see the sidebar 'Claiming GST on unpaid supplier invoices' in this chapter.

- ✔ At the click of a button, you can see exactly how much you owe suppliers.

- ✔ You can easily see whether accounts are overdue (and by how much) before things get out of hand.

- ✔ You can see what bills you have to pay when and plan your cash flow better.

- ✔ Your monthly Profit & Loss reports are more accurate, because expenses show up in the month to which they belong, rather than showing up in the month that you pay them.

- ✔ When you're ready to pay suppliers, this method is quick, easy and efficient.

The downsides of using Purchases (instead of Spend Money) are:

- ✔ Every supplier invoice involves two entries instead of one. That's because you first record the invoice in Purchases and then the payment in Supplier Payments, instead of recording the purchase and payment as one transaction in Spend Money.

- ✔ Getting your head around Purchases can be hard, especially if you're new to MYOB software. Deciding when to use Spend Money and when to use Pay Bills also confuses some people. (Having said this, the decision is easy as pie after you've been working with purchases for a couple of months.)

Claiming GST on unpaid supplier invoices

When you first register for GST, you have to choose whether to report for GST on a cash or an accruals basis. If you choose to report for GST on an accruals basis, you have to account for GST on all outstanding supplier invoices, not just the ones you've already paid for.

This means that if you want to produce a report that claims all the GST credits due on supplier invoices (both the ones you've paid and the ones you haven't yet paid), you need to record these invoices in your accounts. To do this, you have to use the Purchases command centre.

Most of my retail clients fall into this category. Because they own shops, almost all their sales are cash, but the stock they purchase is almost always on account. (That's why it's good for them to report on an accruals basis.) To claim all the GST credits as soon as possible, they record all supplier invoices as Purchases in their accounts.

Clear as mud? For more on this fascinating topic, make your way to Chapter 12 and read about GST reports.

Recording Purchases for Inventory Items

Here's the low-down. If you want to keep track of inventory levels and costs, you need to use Item purchases.

The process of recording a purchase varies a little depending on whether you're placing an order for goods, receipting goods without a bill or recording a final bill. Read on to find out all you ever wanted to know, and more.

Placing a purchase order

In this scenario, you're using MYOB software to create a purchase order that you then email, fax or post to your supplier.

The beautiful and illustrative Figure 6-1 shows a typical Item purchase order, which includes columns for quantity, description, price, discount and so on. You may be interested to note that in my example, the business is ordering silk, thread and lace for the purpose of making hand-made lingerie — beats talking about widgets and water filters, if you ask me.

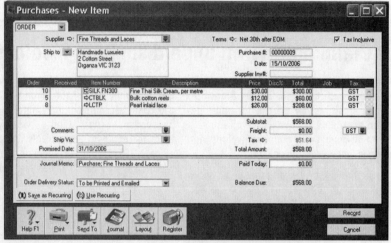

Figure 6-1:
A typical
Item
purchase
looks
something
like this.

To record the purchase of your items, follow these steps:

1. **In the Purchases command centre, choose Enter Purchases, click the Layout button and select Item as your purchase layout.**

   Easy peasy.

2. **Fill in the supplier name and press Tab.**

   If this is the first time you're using this supplier, a list of all supplier names pops up. Click New to add this supplier's name and address to your list.

3. **Select ORDER in the top left corner.**

   On your screen the colour of the Purchases window changes to yellow for orders, showing an Order column and a Received column (at this point, you can only enter figures in the Order column).

4. **Accept the purchase order number (called Purchase #) and check the date.**

   Unless you have a different kind of system, go with whatever purchase order number comes up (the number automatically increases by one with every new purchase).

5. **Enter quantities in the Order column and item codes in the Item Number column.**

   If you're ordering an item that you haven't set up in your Items List already, you can add it now. (For more details about items, go to Chapter 8.)

6. **Check the Item Description and Price and change them if necessary.**

If this is the first time you're purchasing this item, complete the Price column. If you've purchased the item before, either the last price or the standard cost comes up, depending on how you set up your inventory preferences.

7. **Fill in any other necessary information.**

All other fields on this purchase are entirely optional. For example, you can add comments, shipping information or a Promised Date for delivery. Leave the Journal Memo as it is (the default memo usually works just fine).

8. **Either click Print or, to email or fax this order, click the Send To button followed by Fax or Email.**

You'll find more illuminating and erudite text on the subject of emailing purchases orders in 'Emailing and faxing purchase orders' a little later in this chapter.

Receiving goods when there's still no bill

In this true-reflection-of-how-life-really-is scenario, the goods you ordered have arrived, you want to record them straight away so you can sell these goods to customers, but the supplier hasn't sent a bill yet. Here's how to proceed:

1. **In the Purchases command centre, choose Enter Purchases.**

2. **Enter the supplier's name and press Tab. If the original purchase order pops up, select it.**

If you already recorded a purchase order for these goods, MYOB software pops up with a window asking you to select the order from a list. Click on the original order and select Use Purchase.

3. **Either click the Receive Items button or select RECEIVE ITEM in the top left corner.**

If you already recorded a purchase order for these goods, click the Receive Items button to change from a yellow Purchase Order window to a sea-green Receive Items window. Otherwise, go to the top left corner of the purchase and select RECEIVE ITEM to cut straight to the sea-green window.

4. **If prompted, specify a liability account for item receipts and click OK.**

   If this is the first time you've ever used the Receive Items feature, you may get a warning window asking you to select an account for item receipts. All you have to do is select a liability account called something like Accounts Payable Inventory as the Liability Account for Item Receipts. If you don't already have an account by this name, then create one now.

5. **Enter quantities in the Receive column.**

   If you didn't receive the full amount of your order (maybe you ordered three items but only got two) then just enter the quantity you received. MYOB software keeps track of backordered quantities. You can also add new lines to the purchase at this point for any goods you've received that weren't on an original purchase order. If you received more than you ordered, you can click Update Order when prompted to update the original purchase order.

6. **Click Record.**

Receiving the final bill

In this last step of the process, you record the final bill for your inventory items. By the way, if you haven't yet recorded a purchase order for these goods (maybe you placed your order over the phone), then you don't need to go through the whole rigmarole of first creating a purchase order and then converting the order to a bill. You can just record the final bill when it arrives.

1. **In the Purchases command centre, choose Enter Purchases.**

2. **Enter the supplier's name and press Tab. If an original purchase order pops up, select it from the list.**

   If you already recorded a purchase order for these goods, MYOB software pops up with a window asking you to select the order from a list. Click on the original order and select Use Purchase. Alternatively, if you haven't yet recorded a purchase order for these goods, you may need to click the Layout button and select Item if the format hasn't come up correctly.

3. **Either click the Bill button or select BILL in the top-left corner.**

   If you already recorded a purchase order or receipt for these goods, click the Bill button to switch from a yellow Purchase Order window to a cool sky-blue Bill window. Otherwise, go to the top-left corner of the purchase and select BILL.

4. Check the date and enter the supplier's invoice number in the Supplier Inv# field.

Make sure the Date matches the date on the supplier's invoice and put their invoice number in the Supplier Inv# field.

5. Check all quantities are correct.

If you haven't received your full order yet (maybe you ordered 10 of something, but you've only received a bill for 6 so far), then enter the quantity that is yet to be delivered in the Backorder column. For example, in Figure 6-2, I've ordered 10 metres of silk, received 6 metres and have 4 metres still on backorder. This quantity will stay as an Order in my Purchases Register until the whole order is fulfilled.

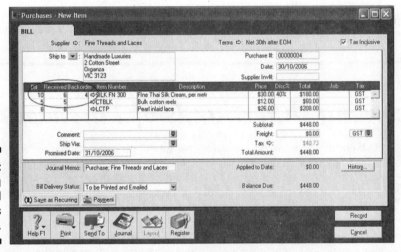

Figure 6-2:
Recording
the final bill
for goods
received.

6. Check all prices and descriptions.

Make sure all the quantities and prices are correct and that the Total Amount of your purchases matches the supplier invoice to the last cent. If you're having trouble matching up the GST amounts, you can click or unclick the Tax Inclusive button in the top right so that you're viewing prices using the same format as your supplier's invoice (some suppliers show prices exclusive of GST, others show prices inclusive of GST).

7. Click Record.

Yep, that's all there is to it. If you want to take a second look at your handiwork, make your way to the Purchases Register.

Different strokes for different folks

My clients fall into two camps when it comes to entering their purchases.

- The first camp sits down once a week or so with a pile of supplier invoices and keys these into their accounts. As soon as they record each invoice, it shows up as owing in their Payables report. That's all there is to it.

- The second camp records all their purchase orders using MYOB software, faxing or emailing these purchases direct. These purchase orders don't show up as owing in their accounts, but they do show up under the Orders tab in the Purchases Register and in the To Do List. When the goods arrive, they call up the original purchase order and record the receipt of goods. When the bill arrives, they fix up any details or price variations and change the order to a bill. Only at this point does the purchase show up in their Payables report.

Choose whichever method suits you best. (If your suppliers like to receive written purchase orders, use the second method. If not, you're better off to use the first, simpler, method.)

Recording Other Kinds of Purchases

Of course, most businesses receive lots of different kind of bills, not just ones for inventory items. In fact, your business may not buy and sell inventory at all and you may never need to record an Item purchase. So, what do you do if you get a bill for something like advertising, consultancy fees, electricity or telephone?

The answer is that you record a Service purchase. These kind of purchases are super-easy to record, so I'll just give you a quick run-down on what's important:

1. **In the Purchases command centre, choose Enter Purchases.**

2. **Enter the supplier's name and press Tab.**

   If you don't already have this supplier in your card file, click New when prompted and complete all their details.

3. **Click the Layout button and select Service as the layout.**

4. **Check the date and enter the supplier's invoice number in the Supplier Inv# field.**

   Make sure the Date matches the date on the supplier's invoice and put their invoice number in the Supplier Inv# field.

5. Complete the Description field, if desired.

For something like an electricity or telephone bill, you don't really need a description and you can keep things short and sweet, as I've done in Figure 6-3. In fact, if you want a description for this purchase to come up on your transaction reports, use the Journal Memo field, rather than the Description field.

6. Select the Acct#, enter the Amount and if you want, enter Job details.

In the Acct# column, you select what kind of expense this is. For example, you select Telephone Expense as the account for a Telephone Bill, or Travel Expense for your family holiday in New Caledonia (just kidding). Also if you want to allocate this purchase to a particular project, job or cost centre, complete the Job column.

7. Make sure the Total Amount comes up just right.

If you have problems getting the Total Amount to match the amount on your supplier's bill, chances are you're trying to enter amounts including tax when your supplier is showing amounts excluding tax, or vice versa. You can match amounts more easily by clicking or unclicking the little Tax Inclusive button in the top right of the Purchase window.

8. Click Record.

By now, you should have something pretty similar to what you can see in Figure 6-3.

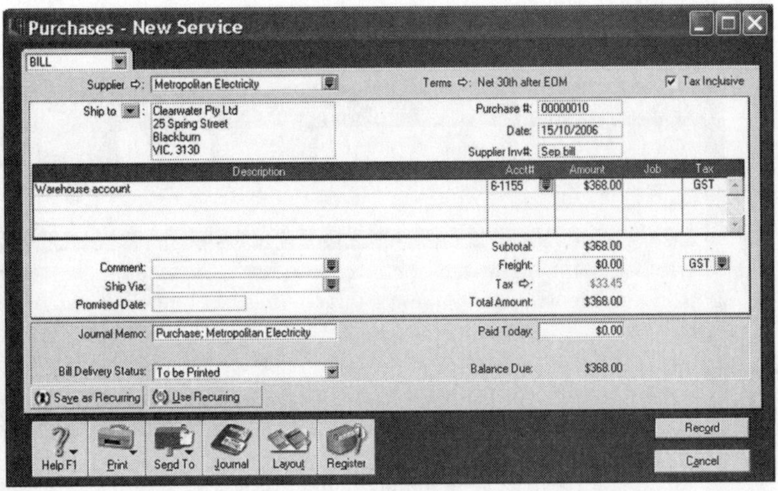

Figure 6-3:
A typical
Service
purchase.

Calling Up Your Purchase Records

You've faithfully completed your purchase order, item receipt or supplier bill and clicked Record. Now it's disappeared — or so it seems. How do you find it again? Try these ways.

Trawling through transactions

In almost every command centre, there's a button called Transaction Journal. Click here, select the Purchases tab, then enter an approximate date range for the purchase that you're looking for in the Dated From and To fields. Up pops a list of all purchases for that date range.

Every now and then I get a call from a panic-stricken client declaring, 'All my purchases have disappeared!' Don't panic. What often happens is that people forget to change the Dated From and To fields, or they change the dates but don't press Tab or Enter after they've entered the To date.

Getting smart with the Purchases Register

Your Purchases Register is the place to go to check out the status of all outstanding supplier orders, backorders or accounts. (You can find the Purchases Register in the Purchases command centre — it should look kind of similar to Figure 6-4.)

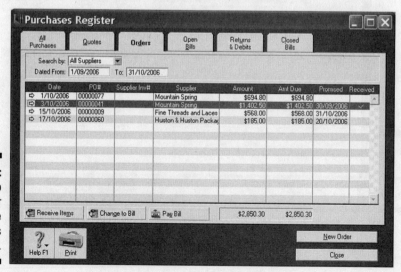

Figure 6-4: Looking up supplier orders in the Purchases Register.

Have a play with your Purchases Register to see how it works. Choose whether you want to search by all suppliers or by one particular supplier, and change the date range, if necessary. Click All Purchases to view bills and orders in the one spot. Click the Orders tab to view all outstanding orders or to convert orders to final bills. Click the Returns & Debits tab to view all credit notes that haven't yet been applied against a supplier invoice. Or if you're feeling brave, click Open Bills to see a disconcerting list of all the money you owe.

Looking up all transactions for a particular supplier

Sophisticated and rather stylish, the Find Transactions menu is my favourite way to view *all* transactions for a particular supplier. (The Purchases Register is a good way to view orders and bills, but it doesn't show payments.)

Go to the Find Transactions menu (at the bottom of any command centre) and click the Card tab. Enter the supplier's name and, if relevant, change the dates. You should see a list of all transactions relating to that supplier over your specified date range.

Sending Purchase Orders

It's one thing to type your purchase orders into your company file. But it's another thing to get them looking good, and something else altogether to discover how to email, fax and print them.

Giving your purchase order a make-over

It's Monday morning. You look glorious, sitting in your home office dressed in spotty pyjamas and fluffy rabbit slippers. It's time to dress up your purchase order so it looks good too.

To customise your purchase order, go to your Setup menu and select Customise Forms⇨Purchase Orders. Select your Purchase Layout and the template you want to use as your base. Then click Customise. I talk lots about the basic techniques for designing forms in Chapter 10, but here are a few points that apply specifically to purchase orders:

    ✔ You can show prices either as tax-exclusive or tax-inclusive. By this I mean you can include the GST in the price of each item, or you can leave the GST out and show it as a lump sum at the bottom. Choose the method that suits you best.

✔ You'll find a lot of details on the standard purchase order that you probably don't need. Feel free to get rid of information such as shipping details, page number and memo. Keep it clean and lean.

✔ Click the first icon on the Forms toolbar (at the top of the Customise Purchases window) to see a list of all available fields. Here you find lots of fields that don't print automatically but that you may find useful — such as the supplier's fax number, contact name, job codes and so on.

✔ Consider adding your own standard blurb to the bottom of purchase orders, similar to the way I have in Figure 6-5, where I state that if the order isn't delivered within five working days, any deliveries may not be accepted. To add text in this way, click the text icon on the Forms toolbar.

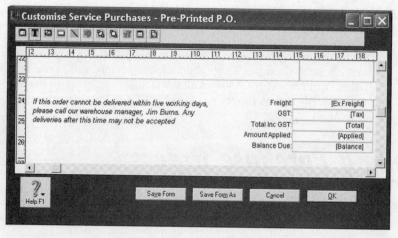

Figure 6-5: Add standard messages to your purchase orders.

Printing purchase orders

The easy way to print a purchase order is to click the Print button (found at the bottom of the purchase order) just before you record the order.

If you prefer to print purchase orders in batches, then you record your orders as you're working and then, when you're ready to print, you click Print/Email Purchases. You'll see a list of unprinted purchase orders. Select those you want and click Print.

If you want to reprint a purchase order, click the Advanced Filters button that appears on the right-hand side of the Print/Email Purchases window. Unclick the button that says Unprinted or Unsent Purchases Only, select a date range and click OK.

A problem you may encounter when printing purchase orders is that the order always defaults to a standard MYOB template, rather than one you've previously customised. The solution is to go to Print/Email Purchases and click Advanced Filters. Choose the form that you need from the Selected Form for Purchase and click OK.

Emailing and faxing purchase orders

The most efficient way to send a supplier a purchase order is not to print it at all, but to email or fax the order direct. MYOB software gets really smart and refers to the supplier's card to get their email address or fax details, so the process is as quick as can be.

To email a purchase order, first display the purchase, then click the Send To button (found at the bottom next to the Print button). Choose Email, click Send and before you know it, the order attaches itself to an email that sits in your Outbox until you're ready to log on and send it. (See Figure 6-6.)

To fax a purchase order, first display the purchase, then click the Send To button, choose Fax and click Send. Wait a second or two and your fax software should pop up automatically, ready to do its stuff.

I'm aware that I'm making this whole email and fax process sound easy as pie, and that in real life things don't always go too smoothly. If you're having problems, refer to Chapter 3, where you'll find lots more detail about emailing and faxing using MYOB software and the kind of hiccups you may encounter when getting everything going.

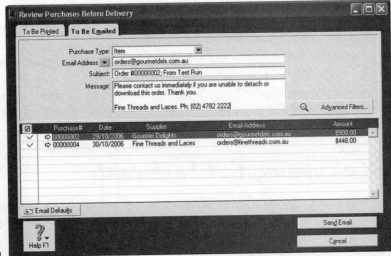

Figure 6-6: You can email purchase orders direct to suppliers.

Understanding GST

I'm not entirely sure why I wrote 'Understanding GST'. If our senior politicians can't understand GST, how do we mere mortals have a hope?

What I can tell you about GST is how to make it work with your MYOB software. The good news is that when it comes to purchases, everything is pretty straightforward. Choose the right code and you're away.

Make sure you receive an invoice complete with an ABN for everything you buy. If any supplier fails to supply you with their ABN, you not only have to withhold 48.5 percent tax from their payment but you have to complete mounds of paperwork for the tax office as well. It's simply not worth it.

Tax codes — a real guessing game

Every time you record a purchase you must complete the Tax column. Here are some tips in case you're not sure which code to use when:

- If the purchase is for goods or services that attract GST, select GST as your tax code.
- If the purchase is for a new piece of equipment or furniture, select CAP as your tax code (CAP stands for Capital Acquisitions). Depending on whether or not you're part of the Simplified Tax System (ask your accountant if you're not sure) the threshold for capital acquisitions is either $300 (if you're not part of the system) or $1,000 (if you are).
- If the purchase is for goods or services that are GST-free (medical supplies, GST-free food, etc.) select FRE as your tax code.
- If the purchase is for goods or services that are for your own private use, pick N-T as your tax code.
- If the person you're trading with isn't registered for GST, select FRE as your tax code.
- If the purchase is for goods or services that you'll use to make input taxed sales (perhaps you're a residential landlord and you're paying for plumbing repairs), then select INP as your tax code.

Calculating GST backwards

Sometimes a supplier provides an invoice or receipt that is tax-inclusive (that is, you've been charged GST, but the invoice doesn't show how much).

If this happens, all you have to do is select the Tax Inclusive box at the top of the purchase window. Then, simply enter the tax-inclusive amount in the Amount column of the purchase. Press the Enter key and voilà! The GST calculates correctly.

When GST doesn't quite add up

Occasionally MYOB software calculates the amount of GST on a purchase slightly differently to your supplier and the GST total differs by a cent or two.

Don't tear your hair out wondering why this is (although I can tell you now that it's due to the way different software packages deal with rounding cents up and down). Instead, be pragmatic and ignore the difference. After all, two cents doesn't mean much in the grand scheme of things.

If you find that the tax is out by more than a few cents, use a different strategy. In all likelihood, the difference won't be due to rounding errors but will be because the purchase has a mixture of taxable and non-taxable goods. What you need to do is split the purchase across two or more lines. See Chapter 12 for more details.

Getting Everything Just Right

If you're anything like me, you sometimes make mistakes. In fact, if you're anything like me, you often make mistakes. Fortunately, you can cover your tracks so that no-one need ever know a thing.

However, before you start deleting or changing things willy-nilly, one word of caution. If a purchase belongs to a previous period and you've already completed your Business Activity Statement for that period, please don't delete the purchase or make any changes that affect the GST. Instead, change your security preferences so that you can reverse the purchase, then date the reversal with the current date. (I talk more about reversals in the section, 'Doing it all again'.) This way you won't stuff up the GST totals on your Business Activity Statements, and even better, you save your accountant from having a nervous breakdown.

Destroying the evidence

You've recorded a purchase and now you want to delete it. Doing so is easy.

1. **Locate your purchase in the Transaction Journal or in your Purchases Register (refer to 'Calling Up Your Purchase Records' earlier in this chapter), then zoom in to display it.**

2. **From the main menu bar, choose Edit➪Delete Purchase.**

   Figure 6-7 shows how it's done.

Your purchase has now gone to live in the land of odd socks and ballpoint pens, never to be seen again.

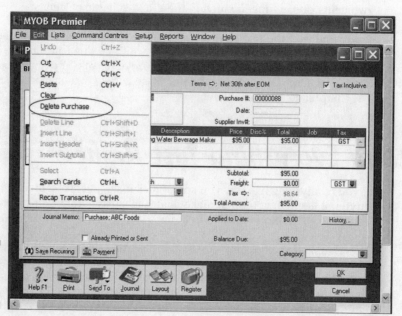

Figure 6-7: Deleting a purchase.

Changing your mind

Sometimes you may want to change a purchase, instead of deleting it. Perhaps you want to fix up a quantity or price or perhaps you selected the wrong tax code. This is no problem.

Find your purchase in the Transaction Journal or Purchases Register (refer to 'Calling Up Your Purchase Records' earlier in this chapter), and zoom in on the purchase to display it. Make any necessary changes and click Record.

Doing it all again

If you've set your preferences so that you can't delete or change entries once they've been recorded, or if a purchase belongs to the previous financial year, the only way you can change or delete purchases is to reverse them. (This is obvious when you display a purchase and then go to the Edit menu. You don't have the option to Delete Purchase, rather it says Reverse Purchase.)

The idea of a reversal is that you create a purchase that is exactly the opposite of the incorrect one, so the two entries cancel each other out. (Think of it as two wrongs making a right.) You can then enter the purchase again, hopefully getting it right this time.

To reverse a purchase, first find it in the Transaction Journal or Purchases Register (refer to 'Calling Up Your Purchase Records' earlier in this chapter), then zoom in to display it. From the Main menu toolbar, choose Edit⇨Reverse Purchase. Check all the details of the reversal carefully, making sure the reversal has the correct date (you're usually best to enter the current rather than the date of the original purchase), then click the Record Reversal button.

Paying the Piper

Shakespeare wrote, 'He who dies pays all debts'. I really hope you don't have to resort to anything this drastic in order to do the right thing by your suppliers. Here's the clean-living, happy-go-lucky method with no blood or guts involved.

Recording supplier payments

MYOB software lets you square up with your suppliers in two different ways. Go with the method you like best:

- ✔ Pay suppliers using cash, a chequebook or maybe via Internet banking, then record the payments into your MYOB company file at a later time — maybe days, weeks or even months later.

- ✔ Use MYOB software as the starting point for paying your suppliers. You record the payment in your company file *first*, then you either generate a payments file to import into your banking software or you process the payments direct using MYOB's M-Powered Payments facility (see the following section, 'Understanding where M-Powered Payments fit in' for more details).

Regardless of whether you're recording supplier payments before or after the financial transaction has taken place, the way you record a supplier payment is much the same. Here's how it works:

1. **Go to the Purchases command centre and select Pay Bills.**

   The shortcut for Pay Bills is Ctrl+M (if you're a PC person) or Cmd+M (if you're from Macintosh land).

2. **Enter the supplier's name in the Supplier field.**

3. **Select your bank account.**

   In the top-left corner, where it says Pay from Account, select the correct bank account (if you only have one business bank account, this selection is probably correct already). If you haven't made this payment yet, and you want to make an electronic payment direct from your MYOB software, don't select a bank account. Instead, click Group with Electronic Payments.

4. **Leave the Memo as is, and fill in the Cheque No. and Date.**

   Rather than make extra work for yourself, it's usually best to leave the Memo field as it is. The cheque number comes up automatically, adding one to the last number entered. If this is incorrect, you can override it, or for electronic payments, ignore it.

5. **For electronic payments, check the Statement Text.**

   The Statement Text shows what will appear on the bank statement of the supplier. You may want to include your customer number or the invoice number, whatever is most practical.

6. **Fill in the Amount of the payment.**

   If you've already paid this supplier, then enter the amount now. Otherwise, to calculate how much you should be paying, click the Pay All button to calculate the total Amount due.

7. **Press the Tab key to complete the Amount Applied column.**

   Depending on your settings in Preferences, you may need to press the Tab key to apply your payment against the outstanding purchases. You can see how this looks in Figure 6-8.

   If you're settling a number of invoices with one payment, it's preferable to maximise the Pay Bills window. If you're using a PC, go to the far top right-hand corner where you should see a hyphen, a box and a cross. Click the box and the Pay Bills window expands, allowing you to see more information. Or, if you're using a Mac, drag out the bottom corner of the Pay Bills window to make it bigger.

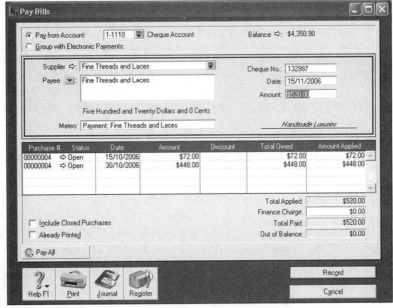

Understanding where M-Powered Payments fit in

Most newcomers to MYOB software start out by making payments as they normally would (by cheque, Internet transfer or credit card) and then later, they record these payments in their accounts. This method works fine but once you're confident, you may find it more efficient to use MYOB software to make your payments.

Using MYOB M-Powered Payments, you can make electronic payments to your suppliers directly from your MYOB software. When you pay a supplier, MYOB software sends the payment electronically to its M-Powered Services Centre, and from there the payment goes to your supplier, along with a remittance advice (sent either by fax or email — whatever your preference). All through this process, you can log on and monitor the progress of your payments, including when payments are sent, when they're processed, if they fail due to insufficient funds and so on.

Sure, you pay transaction fees (see Chapter 13 for these details), but if you pay more than five suppliers per week, I reckon that M-Powered Payments is well worth the fees. If you were to put a value on your own time (or on your bookkeeper's time) and calculate how long it takes you to pay a supplier the old way (including writing a cheque, printing a remittance advice, writing their address on an envelope, entering the payment into your MYOB company file, and so on) as well as work out the costs (the envelope, the stamp and the petrol to the post office), then chances are the true 'transaction cost' of paying a supplier is much more expensive than you think.

For lots more about M-Powered Payments, make your way to Chapter 13.

Taking the short road home

When it comes to paying suppliers, anything that saves me time and money makes me happy. Here are my favourite shortcuts:

- ✔ Hide your mouse. (Sit on it if necessary — I know some habits die hard.) Instead, move around by using the Tab key.

- ✔ Change your settings in Preferences so that you automatically apply payments against outstanding purchases, starting with the oldest one first. Go to Setup and click Preferences and then click the Purchases tab. Select the box Apply Supplier Payments Automatically to Oldest Purchase First.

- ✔ At the end of each month, print an Aged Payables report and match the totals on this report against your suppliers' statements. This simple act of checking that you have the same figures as your suppliers means you can be confident when writing cheques.

- ✔ Pay suppliers by electronic transfer, either using MYOB M-Powered Payments or your bank's direct fund transfer services. (I talk more about electronic transactions in Chapter 13.) Electronic payments save more time than you could ever imagine.

- ✔ Don't pay your bills. This is really quick. (Just kidding.)

- ✔ If you don't use window envelopes, print mailing labels — it's much, much quicker than copying addresses out by hand. (I deal with printing mailing labels in Chapter 10.)

Fixing up supplier payments

Have you made a mistake with a supplier payment? (Maybe the cheque number is wrong, the amount is wrong or maybe you've applied the payment to the wrong invoice.) The bad news is that you can't change a supplier payment after it's been recorded. However, the good news is that you can delete or reverse this payment and then have another stab at getting it right.

Here's what to do:

1. **Go to your Transaction Journal and click the Disbursements tab.**

   To delete a payment, you first need to find it. The Disbursements Journal is your best bet.

2. **Enter an approximate date range for the payment you're looking for.**

   Enter suitable dates in the Dated From and To fields. The smaller this date range, the fewer transactions you have to search through to find the one you're looking for.

3. **When you find the correct supplier payment, zoom in on it.**

   Zooming in makes me think of tabloid journalists with long-range cameras checking out unsuspecting pop stars. In MYOB software, zooming in means clicking the little white arrow next to the transaction.

   At this point, you may encounter the message, 'One or more parts of this journal entry have been reconciled'. Don't go any further. Click OK and then Cancel. (If you delete the payment, you throw your bank reconciliation out of balance, which is not a good idea.)

4. **From the Main toolbar, choose Edit⇨Delete Payment or Edit⇨Reverse Payment.**

   Go to the Edit command on the top menu bar. Whether you can see Delete Payment or Reverse Payment at this point depends on how you set your preferences. Either method is okay. However, if this is a payment you made electronically using MYOB M-Powered payments, you'll need to make your way to Chapter 13 for more details about reversing transactions that are part of a batch.

Facing the music (how much do you owe?)

You've done all the hard work — generating your purchase orders, recording purchases and entering supplier payments. Now you can enjoy the fruits of your labours.

Go to your Analysis menu and click Payables. In a second, up comes a magnificent list, similar to the one shown in Figure 6-9, showing everyone you owe money to, grouped neatly by month and complete with totals and ageing details. (I don't know about you, but for me it's such a relief to be able to keep track of what I owe and when it's due.)

Analyse Payables

Analysis: Bill Date	Card ID	Total	Oct	Sep	Aug	Pre-Aug
⇨ Clear & Bright Filters	SUPP000002	$3,056.78	$129.75	$502.20	$2,424.83	
⇨ Curbys Super Stands	SUPP000003	$6,602.80	-$328.50	$988.65	$677.25	$5,265.40
⇨ Huston & Huston Packaging	SUPP000004	$2,626.97	$240.20	$152.30	$181.75	$2,052.72
⇨ Metropolitan Electricity	SUPP000005	$385.00	$385.00			
⇨ Mojo Advertising	SUPP000006	$1,059.30	$379.00	$475.80		$204.50
⇨ Mountain Spring	SUPP000007	-$475.63	-$475.63			
⇨ Outreach Real Estate	SUPP000008	$3,231.76				$3,231.76
⇨ Sven Horsky	*None	$20.00	$20.00			
⇨ Underwater Springs Pty Ltd	SUPP000009	$4,811.56	$5,491.46	-$679.90		
	Totals:	$22,013.54	$6,536.28	$1,439.05	$3,283.83	$10,754.38
	Ageing Percent:		29.7%	6.5%	14.9%	48.9%

Help F1   Print   Filters   Close

Figure 6-9:
Seeing how
much you
owe.

This is a simple report, but I'd like to share a few things with you before going any further (some of these things I learnt the hard way):

✔ If you click Filters you can choose to age Payables as of a certain date. There's not much point in using any other date than the current date because the whole idea of a Payables report is to see where you're up to right now.

✔ If you do want to see what you owed on a date that's already passed (perhaps your accountant wants a Payables report for a previous month) then the regular Analyse Payables report isn't the one for you. Instead, go to Reports and print a Payables Reconciliation Summary.

✔ If your report lists accounts in 30-day periods (0–30, 31–60, 61–90 and so on), don't be fooled into thinking these days correspond to months, because most months don't have exactly 30 days.

✔ If you want your report to group accounts month by month (which is usually the best way to work), go to Setup, click Preferences and then hit the Reports & Forms tab. Under the Ageing option, select Monthly Ageing Periods.

Keeping things in tune

Using the Purchases command centre is like keeping a car on the road — doing so requires a certain amount of maintenance. Odd amounts crop up that you can't delete, credits appear that won't go away, or accounts show up as owing when you know they're not. Here's the practical mechanic's guide to a six-month service and tune.

When you know you don't owe money but the report says you do

If your Aged Payables report says you owe a supplier money and you're positive that you've paid the account, you almost certainly used Spend Money when recording the payment, instead of Pay Bills. Just like putting diesel in an unleaded car, this upsets the works.

To fix this problem, simply remove the outstanding purchase, either by deleting or reversing it, depending on your Preference settings. (I explain deletions and reversals earlier in this chapter, in the section 'Getting Everything Just Right'.)

Occasionally, when you try to delete a purchase you get a message saying you can't, either because the purchase belongs to a previous financial year or because payments have already been applied. In this case, you should create a credit purchase. See 'Odd amounts and fiddly stuff' later in this chapter.

Credits that stick around like a bad smell

Sometimes you get an amount showing up twice for a particular supplier on your Payables report, the first time as a positive amount, the next time as a minus amount. The total amount due is zero, but the Aged Payables report keeps listing both amounts.

Change into fourth gear, head for your Purchases Register and click the Returns & Debits tab, where a list of all outstanding credit purchases appears. Highlight the offending credit and click Apply to Purchase. Click in the Amount Applied column then hit Record. Problem fixed.

Odd amounts and fiddly stuff

No matter how meticulous you are, odd amounts inevitably creep into your supplier accounts. Here are a few maintenance tricks:

- ✔ For most credits, go to Purchases and create a new purchase, entering a minus quantity in the Received column for an Item purchase or a minus figure in the Amount column for a Service purchase.

- ✔ To get rid of odd little amounts (perhaps there's five cents outstanding on an account), go to Purchases and select Miscellaneous as your purchase format. Create a credit purchase for this amount and then apply it in the Returns & Debits tab of your Purchases Register. (Don't forget to select the same tax code as you chose in the original Purchase!) For an example of a miscellaneous credit, see Figure 6-10.

- ✔ To spring-clean your credits, go to the Returns & Debits tab in your Purchases Register and look at every credit listed. Wherever possible, apply these credits to outstanding purchases.

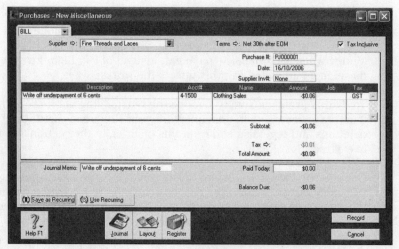

Figure 6-10:
Use Miscellaneous purchases to fix up odd amounts.

Chapter 7

Reconcile Yourself

In This Chapter

▶ Picking up mistakes (and why you should reconcile accounts)

▶ Deciding which accounts you need to reconcile

▶ Reconciling the first time

▶ Reconciling the next time

▶ Fixing up those annoying glitches

▶ Getting M-Powered with electronic statements

*Y*ou have to reconcile yourself to a lot in this life. When you go for a picnic, it always rains. When your computer crashes, it's the one time you didn't back up your system. When you drop a piece of toast, it always lands jam-side down.

One more fact of life that you have to reconcile yourself to is this: If you're going to use MYOB software, you have to reconcile your bank account. You have to do this — there's no escape.

Why You Need to Reconcile Accounts

Reconciling a bank account means comparing the transactions you enter in your MYOB company file to those on your bank statement. You tick these entries off one by one and check that you and your bank agree, down to the very last cent.

Reconciling bank accounts isn't an activity that only boring bookkeepers with nothing more exciting in their life engage in. Instead, it's one of those necessary evils we all have to face up to, sooner or later. In fact, reconciling accounts is the only way to pick up mistakes, such as a payment entered as $900 instead of $90, a deposit entered twice, or a missing bank charge.

The good news is that reconciling bank accounts is surprisingly quick and easy and, although you may find it hard to believe, it can even be satisfying in a weird, nerdish kind of way.

Which Accounts to Reconcile

Most businesses have lots of bank accounts, from savings accounts and term deposits to credit cards and loans. Although you don't have to reconcile all these accounts, if you don't, your accountant probably will. An easy way is to divide these accounts into three categories:

> ✔ **The absolute minimum you should reconcile:** As the absolute bottom line, you should reconcile your business bank account. If you don't do this, you can't rely on any of your financial reports, as you can't be sure that the information you've entered is correct.
>
> ✔ **Accounts you should reconcile if you have time:** It's a good idea to reconcile all credit card and savings accounts, as well as your business bank account. These accounts are pretty straightforward and it's one less job for your accountant.
>
> ✔ **Accounts you should reconcile if you're conscientious and want to save money:** It's fantastic if you can reconcile all your loan accounts as well as all other bank accounts. Loan accounts can be tricky (you often have to split up interest and principal on each loan repayment). But, again, if you don't do it, your accountant will. Perhaps you can ask your accountant to reconcile your loan accounts with you the first time and then you can follow the same procedure next time.

How to Reconcile for the Very First Time

Reconciling your bank account for the first time is like learning to ride a bicycle. It's a bit scary when you start, but fun when you're finally zooming at what feels like a million miles an hour down the driveway.

Seriously though, the first time you reconcile your bank account is definitely the hardest. That's because you have to allow for all those unpresented payments and deposits that existed before you started using MYOB software for your accounting. This can be tricky, but don't worry. I guide you safely through the whole kit and caboodle.

Step one — Get ready to rock

The first time you reconcile your bank account, you need to draw up a list of all unpresented payments and deposits as at the date you started recording your accounts. (This list is usually called a bank reconciliation report.) You can see how a typical bank reconciliation report looks in Figure 7-1. (I typed mine up on a word processor, but it's also fine to write this report by hand.)

Bank Reconciliation for Business Account 30 June

Balance of bank statement			$6,600.00
Less: uncleared cheques	00471	30.00	
	00482	65.00	
	00493	195.00	290.00
			$6,310.00
Add: uncleared deposits			$1,020.00
Cashbook Balance			**$7,330.00**

Figure 7-1: A typical bank reconciliation report.

It's okay if you don't have this report because you can create one. What I'm about to explain sounds pretty technical, but don't stress out. Go slowly and everything will be just fine. Here's what to do:

1. **Find out the balance of your opening bank statement.**

   For example, if you first started recording transactions from 1 July 2006, dig out the bank statement for this period. Write the balance of your account as at this date on a scrap of paper.

2. **Make a list of payments that were unpresented as at this starting date and write down the total amount.**

   By unpresented, I mean all those payments you made before this date, but haven't yet cleared through your bank account. For example, if you started recording transactions on 1 July 2006, make a list of all the payments you made before 1 July that didn't go through your account until after 1 July. Unpresented payments are usually cheques that your suppliers haven't banked yet, but occasionally an unpresented payment could be an online transaction you recorded in your accounts on 30 June but that didn't clear until 1 July.

3. **Make a list of deposits that were unpresented as at your starting date and write down the total amount.**

   Look at your deposit book for this period to see if there are any deposits that didn't clear immediately. An example may be a deposit dated 30 June that didn't clear through your account until 1 July, or Eftpos payments received from customers on 30 June that didn't appear on your bank statement until 1 July.

4. **Work out what your real bank account balance was as at your starting date.**

   Your real bank account balance is what you would have in your account if all unpresented payments and deposits cleared immediately.

In other words, the real bank balance is the amount you wrote down in Step 1 (the balance from your bank statement), less the amount you wrote down in Step 2 (total unpresented payments), plus the amount you wrote down in Step 3 (total unpresented deposits).

5. **When you're done, write this information neatly as a report.**

   I know I'm sounding like a schoolteacher, but your accountant may ask for this report later on. (To see how it should look, refer to Figure 7-1.)

Step two — Clarify your starting point

As part of getting your bank reconciliation happening, you have to record how much money you had in your bank account when you first started. You may have already done this when you worked your way through the Easy Setup Assistant (refer to Chapter 1), but it's a good idea to check this figure before going any further.

Go to Setup, then Balances, followed by Account Opening Balances. Look at the Opening Balance column next to your bank account. This balance should be the same as the balance you worked out in Step 4 in the preceding section, 'Get ready to rock' (what I call your real bank account balance). If not, change it now.

Step three — Record any unpresented payments

Your next move is to record any unpresented payments. To do so, follow my lead (these steps may seem a bit weird, but believe me, there's method in my madness):

1. **Go to Spend Money in the Banking command centre.**

2. **Select the first payment from your list of unpresented payments and enter the Cheque No., Date and Amount.**

   Complete the Cheque No. and Amount as you would with any other payment (ignore the Cheque No. if the payment isn't a cheque), but for the Date, don't write the actual date of the payment. Instead, use your starting date (usually 1 July).

3. **Leave the Card and Payee blank and write a description in the Memo.**

   You don't need to fill in the Card or Payee fields for this payment, so leave these fields blank. In the Memo field you could write 'Unpresented payment as at your start date' (see Figure 7-2).

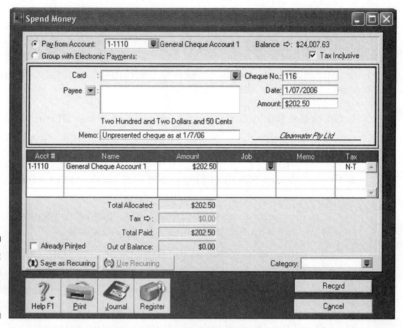

Figure 7-2:
Recording
unpresented
payments.

4. **Choose the bank account you're reconciling as your allocation account.**

   I know this means you're taking money out of your bank account and sticking it back in again, but as I said before, there's method in my madness.

5. **Leave the Tax column blank and click Record.**

   Even if the original transaction included GST, don't put GST in the Tax column or you'll throw out the GST reports for the year. Instead, leave the Tax column blank or select N-T (standing for Not Reportable) as your code.

6. **Repeat this process for every payment in your list.**

   Do this again and again, until every payment in your list of unpresented payments has been recorded. If you've got this far, you're doing great!

Step four — Record any unpresented deposits

If you had any unpresented deposits in your list, you have to record these in the same way you entered the unpresented payments. Go to Receive Money in the Banking command centre and record any unpresented deposits, one by one. Again, date these deposits with your starting date and select your bank account as the allocation account.

Step five — Throw a party, success is in reach!

Fantastic! You're almost there. This is the last stage and the one where, with fingers crossed, everything balances.

1. **Go to the Banking command centre and select Reconcile Accounts.**

   You're now looking at a funny window with lots of blank lines and not a lot else.

2. **Press Tab to see a list of accounts and choose your account from the list.**

   A list of all your accounts appears. Pick your bank account from this list (it's usually near the top) and click Use Account.

3. **Enter your starting date as the Bank Statement Date and press the Tab key again.**

   When you do this, all the transactions you have just entered should appear like magic.

4. **Click off the Deposit side of all unpresented payments.**

   All being well, you should now see all the payments and deposits you just entered, going in and out of the account. Wherever you see a payment listed in the Deposit column, click it, as shown in Figure 7-3. Don't click the Withdrawal side of these unpresented payments.

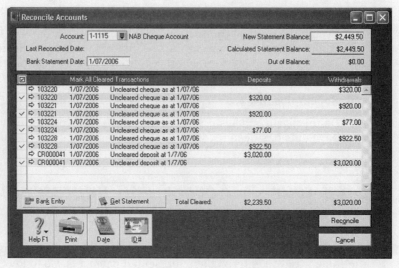

Figure 7-3: Your first bank reconciliation looks something like this.

5. Click the Withdrawal side of all unpresented deposits.

Now click off all deposits that you see listed in the Withdrawal column. (I know this seems back-to-front, but it all comes out in the wash.)

6. Enter the opening bank statement amount against New Statement Balance.

This is the amount of your bank statement that you wrote down in Step 1 of 'Get ready to rock'.

7. Now comes the big moment. Click Reconcile and wait for the message telling you that your account reconciles.

Stick your head out the window and look for flying pigs. Hopefully, yours are airborne and you receive a comforting message similar to the one shown in Figure 7-4, telling you that your account reconciles.

If by any chance your bank account doesn't balance first time, don't be discouraged. Work through these instructions one more time, checking each step as you go, and you should be able to find where you went wrong. (I'm not being discouraging saying this; I'm just being realistic. It often takes a couple of goes to get your first bank reconciliation to balance.)

8. When you get the message saying your account reconciles, click Reconcile one more time.

Clicking Reconcile again clears your marked payments and deposits off the screen, ready for your next bank reconciliation.

Congratulations, you've done it!

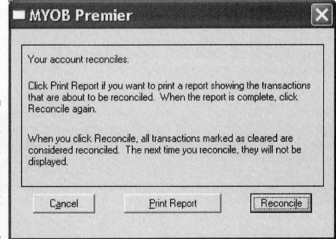

Figure 7-4:
When your account reconciles, a message tells you that everything balances.

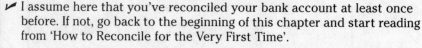

The bigger, the better

Reconciling accounts is much quicker and easier if you make the Reconcile Accounts window as big as possible on your screen, so that you can see lots of transactions at one time.

If you're using a PC, maximise the window by clicking on the square sitting at the top right of the Reconcile Accounts window (between the hyphen and the cross). If you're using a Mac, drag the corners out as far as you can.

Reconciling Again and Again

Once you've done your very first reconciliation, it gets much, much easier. Sure, there are a few things you still need to know, but at least I can stop sticking technical icons down the left-hand margin.

Figuring out where to start

Before you reconcile your bank account again, you need to figure out where you finished working the last time. If you're like me, and only sit down to reconcile your account every few weeks or so, it can be tricky remembering where you were up to.

Try this idea: Go to Reconcile Accounts as normal and select your bank account in the Account box. But before you do anything else, write down the amount sitting in the Calculated Statement Balance field. Now enter the current date as the Bank Statement Date and note which month is the first month listed for most of the payments at the top. This gives you a rough indication of where you were up to in your last reconciliation.

Rummage through your bank statements for this period, scanning the running balance column. Sooner or later (hopefully sooner), you find the amount you just wrote down when you looked at the Calculated Statement Balance. Yippee! You've found it. This is the spot you need to start from.

✔ I assume here that you've reconciled your bank account at least once before. If not, go back to the beginning of this chapter and start reading from 'How to Reconcile for the Very First Time'.

✔ You can avoid losing your 'reconciling' place in future if you use a highlighter pen to mark the spot you last worked on in your bank statement.

Reconciling your bank account (when you've done it before)

So, you've pinpointed when you last reconciled your bank account (as discussed in the preceding section). You're now ready to continue. Make yourself a cup of coffee, find a bar of chocolate and grab your mouse.

1. **In the Banking command centre, select Reconcile Accounts.**

2. **Press Tab, select your bank account, then click Use Account.**

   When you press Tab a list of accounts appears. Pick your bank account from the list — it's near the top.

3. **Check your Calculated Statement Balance.**

   If you're starting off from where you finished working the last time (and it's always a good idea to check this), then the Calculated Statement Balance should equal the balance at the top of your bank statement.

4. **Enter the date you're reconciling up to in the Bank Statement Date field.**

   Enter the date that your bank statement goes up to.

5. **Click off your payments and deposits, one by one.**

   Work down your bank statement and, one by one, find each transaction and click against it. The result should look something like Figure 7-5.

6. **After half a page or so, enter the running balance from your statement in the New Statement Balance field, then press Tab.**

   When you first work on reconciling, don't try to do a whole page at a time. Instead, work in small, bite-sized chunks of a third, or half of a page. When you complete a stage, look at the running balance on your bank statement and stick this in the New Statement Balance at the top, then press Tab . . .

7. **Cross your fingers and check that the Out of Balance amount is zero.**

   If the Out of Balance amount is zero, give yourself a pat on the back and eat some chocolate. If it's not zero, read the section 'When Your Bank Account Just Won't Balance' later in this chapter.

8. **Click Reconcile and then Reconcile once more.**

   Yippee! You receive a message saying 'Your account reconciles'. It's a good feeling, isn't it? All you have to do now is click Reconcile to continue or click Print Report to print a summary report of everything you've done. Chocolate time!

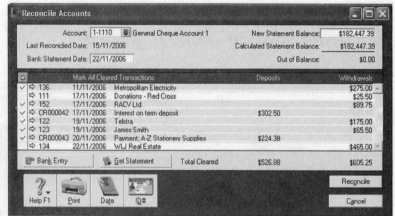

Troubleshooting Tricks

Once you know how to reconcile your bank account, you can progress to the more fiddly bits, which you need to know sooner or later. These troubleshooting tips explain how to enter missing transactions, fix up wrong transactions and look for a particular cheque number.

When you're faced with a big, black hole

It's amazing how often a client phones me and says, 'I've gone to Reconcile Accounts, entered my account number and nothing's there!'

Stay cool! Don't panic! All you have to do is enter a date in the Bank Statement Date field, press your Tab key and, lo and behold, all your transactions appear.

If you've forgotten bank charges or interest

You're happily reconciling away and you come across some bank charges, interest payments or direct debits. What should you do?

The good news is that you don't have to quit from where you are. Simply click the Bank Entry button to pop direct to the Service Charges window, where you can record bank charges or interest earned.

If you're not sure of what GST code to pick, don't get too bamboozled. Remember that most bank fees are GST-free (select FRE as your code) but merchant fees and Eftpos fees are taxable (select GST as your code). Interest income is an input-taxed sale, so select ITS as your code. (For more about recording bank fees, refer to Chapter 5.)

When stuff disappears but you know it's there

You're absolutely, totally, 100 percent positive that you recorded a particular transaction (perhaps only a few minutes before). Yet when you go to Reconcile Accounts, the darned thing won't show up on the screen. Where's it gone?

Don your detective hat and try the following:

✔ Make the Bank Statement Date a month or so in the future. (Whenever you reconcile an account, you only see transactions that have a date on or before the Bank Statement Date. By changing the date to sometime in the future, more transactions often show up on screen.)

✔ Perhaps you accidentally sent the missing transaction to a different bank account. Go to your Find Transactions menu, click the Card tab and enter the name of whoever you made the payment to, or received the deposit from. When you find the transaction, zoom in to display it and check you selected the correct bank account in the top left corner.

✔ Look for the button at the bottom called ID#. Click here to sort transactions in cheque number or transaction number order, rather than date order. You can see an example of this in Figure 7-6. This is a fab way to look for a particular cheque.

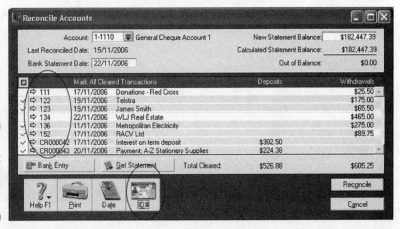

Figure 7-6: You can sort cheques in number order.

Hot keys to stop you sweating

I find that when I'm reconciling bank accounts, I often want to hop to somewhere else in the program without having to quit from where I am.

This is where shortcut keys are so useful. Press Ctrl+H (if you're using a PC) or Cmd+H (if you're using a Macintosh) and you arrive in an instant at Spend Money. Record your payment, then press Escape or click Close and you're back at your bank reconciliation.

It's the same idea with deposits. Press Ctrl+D (if you're using a PC) or Cmd+D (if you're using a Macintosh). In the blink of an eye, you arrive at Receive Money.

If you're using Windows, you can even cycle though all the windows you have open without having to close them. To do this, while holding down the Ctrl button with one finger, press Tab again and again and watch as you cycle through the open windows.

Entering missing transactions on the fly

If you're in the middle of reconciling and realise you've forgotten to enter a transaction, you don't need to close Reconcile Accounts. All you have to do is go to Command Centres on the top menu bar and select the function you need (for example, Banking followed by Spend Money, as shown in Figure 7-7).

Go ahead and record your missing entry. When you're finished, click Cancel and you arrive back at Reconcile Accounts.

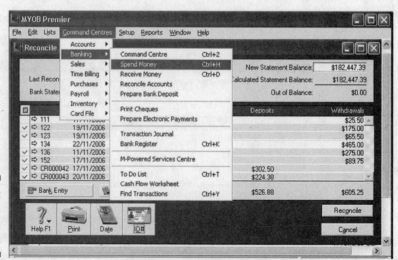

Figure 7-7: Adding a missing transaction.

If you can't get your head around going off to do something different in another command centre without closing Reconcile Accounts, it's fine to quit out of Reconcile Accounts in the middle of doing a reconciliation. The transactions you marked are still checked off when you return.

Zooming in to fix mistakes

However brilliant you are, sooner or later you're in the middle of reconciling and discover that you've made a mistake. Perhaps you entered a payment as $800 instead of $80, or perhaps you recorded a deposit as $78 instead of $87. Whatever you've done, it's easy enough to fix.

See the zoom arrow next to every transaction in your bank reconciliation? Click the relevant arrow to see the original transaction displayed in all its glory. For most transactions, change any details that you need to, such as the date, amount or cheque number, then click Record.

When zooming in doesn't work

Did I just mention that when you discover a mistake, all you have to do is zoom in and fix it? Well, this works for most things, but some transactions just can't be changed (like employee pays, supplier payments and customer payments). No amount of clicking on the grey screen changes a thing!

Instead, try one of these solutions:

✔ Go to the Edit menu at the top, delete the transaction and then enter it again, but correctly this time.

✔ If deleting doesn't appear as an option, your only choice is to reverse the offending transaction, then re-do the entry. (I explain how to reverse transactions in Chapters 5 and 6.)

When Your Bank Account Just Won't Balance

Nothing is more irritating than reading a computer book that explains step-by-step what to do, and tells you not to eat the chocolate till you get the steps right (like I did earlier in this chapter). It's especially irritating if you faithfully follow the instructions, reach the end and your reconciliation just doesn't work!

It would be embarrassing if I owned up to the number of times I've had trouble reconciling a bank account (and how many times I've snuck in the chocolate bars anyway). But the upside of this is that my troublesome times have taught me a few tricks. And I'm really happy to share them with you.

Tricks to try before you kick the cat

When your bank account doesn't balance, stay calm and try the following:

- ✔ Have you missed something on your bank statement that should have been ticked in the Reconcile Accounts window? Look at every line on the statement and check that there's a tick next to the corresponding entry.

- ✔ Have you ticked something in the Reconcile Accounts window that isn't on your bank statement? If your eyes are going crooked looking from the statement to the screen and back to the statement again, try counting the number of ticks in your Reconcile Accounts window and then the number of lines on your bank statement. They should be the same!

- ✔ Do all the amounts match? For example, it's not enough simply to match cheque numbers on the statement against cheque numbers in the Reconcile Accounts window. Make sure that the amount of the cheque is the same in both places.

- ✔ How much are you out by? Does this amount ring a bell?

Tricks to try before you kick the computer

If you've tried all the above suggestions with no success, turn the computer off, take a walk around the block and think about something totally different for a while . . . When you're energised and your shoulders have recovered from computer cramp, try the following ideas:

- ✔ If your bank account is an overdraft but you're actually in credit, you need to enter the New Statement Balance as a minus amount. (This seems weird, but it's true.) Figure 7-8 shows an example of how this works — note the overdraft account has gone into credit by $1629.39.

- ✔ Did you start off from the right spot in your bank statement? It's easy to accidentally skip a page or part of a page.

- ✔ Somewhere on your bank statement you can usually find a summary of total debits and total credits. This corresponds to the bottom of the Reconcile Accounts window, where you see totals for Deposits and Withdrawals. Try comparing these totals with your bank statement's totals to see whether the problem lies with deposits or withdrawals (or both!).

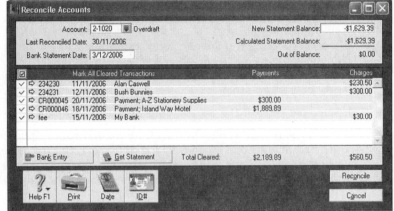

Figure 7-8:
Beware of
how you
enter the
balance of
overdraft
accounts.

✔ If your Out of Balance amount is a multiple of nine, look to see if you put in two numbers back to front — for example, you entered 43 instead of 34, or 685 instead of 658. (It's a curious thing, but if you turn a number back to front and subtract your result from the original number, the difference is always exactly divisible by nine.)

✔ Try dividing your Out of Balance amount by two, and look for a transaction for this amount. In other words, if your Out of Balance amount is $90, look for a transaction equalling $45. This trick helps locate transactions that have been entered the wrong way round (a debit instead of a credit, a payment instead of a deposit and so on).

✔ If your bank account is normally in credit, but you're overdrawn, be sure to enter the New Statement Balance as a minus amount.

Tricks to try before you kick the bucket

You've tried all of the above suggestions and it still doesn't balance. Don't abandon ship yet, there's still hope. Here's my sure-fire, last-resort approach, which always, always works.

1. Unclick all transactions to take you right back to the beginning.

Edit the Bank Statement Date so that it's several months into the future, then remove the ticks from every transaction on your reconciliation. I know this undoes all your work, but it's time for some radical action.

2. Check that your opening balance was right.

I talk a lot about checking your opening balance earlier in this chapter, in the section 'Figuring out where to start'. If you don't start off from the right spot, you're never going to get anything to balance. Go back and check this one more time.

If you find that your opening balance is wrong, you're in trouble, as the offending transaction can be very hard to find. For help, visit my Web site at www.veechicurtis.com.au, go to the Forum Board, click the Troubleshooting and Reconciliations forum and you'll find a free document you can download called 'How to Reconcile Your Bank Account When the Opening Balance is Wrong'. This document should get you back on track.

3. Start marking off the transactions again, but only do a few at a time.

When you're sure you're starting from the right spot, start marking off the transactions one by one, as you did before. But this time, only do a few at once (perhaps five or ten at the most), working your way down to the next balance on your bank statement. (Bank statements usually have a closing balance for the end of each day.)

Whatever you do, don't try to reconcile a whole page at a time, as this makes it so much harder to pinpoint your problem.

4. When you get to the next balance on your bank statement, enter this in the New Statement Balance field, then press Tab.

Enter the next balance on your statement in the New Statement Balance field, close your eyes and cross your fingers. When you press Tab you should find that your Out of Balance amount is now zero. (The trick to this method is that by doing small bits at a time, you narrow down the problem, making it really easy to spot.) Yippee!

5. Click Reconcile and then Reconcile again. Continue till you're done.

You're returned to your Reconcile Accounts window. Now, continue in the same way, working down your bank statement section by section, until your final balance reconciles.

Fantastic plastic

Reconciling a credit card account is the same as reconciling any other bank account. Simply go to Reconcile Accounts, select your credit card account as the Account and you're away. You should see the individual debits of your credit card purchases in the Withdrawals column and your monthly payment in the Deposits column. Mark them off, one by one, and check that the closing balance on your credit card matches the closing balance in the Reconcile Accounts window.

As soon as you get the hang of reconciling your credit card this way, you may want to get really smart and try downloading credit card transactions automatically from your electronic bank statement. For more details, see 'Downloading transactions directly' later in this chapter.

Deciding When to Print

Whenever you reconcile your bank account, you have the option of printing a reconciliation report. Should you or shouldn't you?

✔ If you're new to reconciling, I recommend you print a Bank Reconciliation report (as shown Figure 7-9) at the end of every statement. Once you're accustomed to the whole deal, you can get away with printing a Bank Reconciliation report at the end of each month. Or, if you hate printing reports and keep forgetting to do so, at the very least, print a Bank Reconciliation report when 30 June rolls around (or whatever the last day of your financial year is). Your accountant won't be happy if you don't.

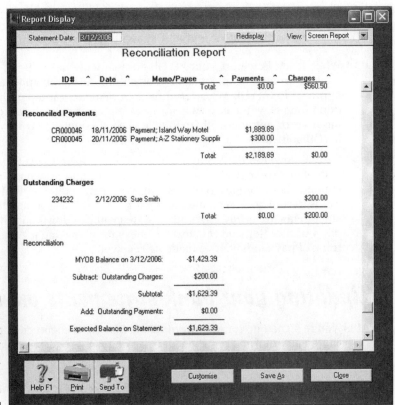

Figure 7-9: Don't forget to print your Bank Reconciliation report.

✔ If 30 June has passed and you're cursing because you forgot to print the Bank Reconciliation, you can still do it at a later date. Go to the Banking tab on your Reports menu and highlight the Reconciliation Report. Click Customise, select your bank account number, enter 30 June as the Bank Statement Date and Bob's your uncle (or auntie or whoever).

✔ When you decide to print a Reconciliation Report from the Reconcile Accounts window, you end up stopping the reconciliation process. The solution? Once your Reconciliation Report has finished printing, click the Reconcile button one more time from the Reconcile Accounts window to complete reconciling your bank account.

Getting M-Powered with Bank Statements

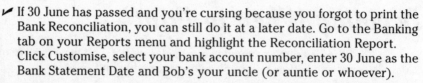

If you bank with the Commonwealth Bank, then M-Powered Bank Statements are a good way to keep all your banking information in one place (in your MYOB company file, that is) and to stay right up to date.

✔ When it's M-Powered, your MYOB company file talks directly to your bank, downloading all kinds of information. After you apply and receive approval for MYOB M-Powered Bank Statements (and pay the fees, don't forget), you can view your bank statements, make account inquiries or automatically reconcile bank accounts, all from within your MYOB software.

✔ With M-Powered Bank Statements, you don't have to wait for bank statements to arrive in the mail, or fiddle around downloading statements off the Internet. Instead, your bank statement information forms part of your accounts, ready for you to access at any time. These statements are always right up to date (you can download the previous day's transactions on the next business day), making it easy to keep track of payments you've made or received.

Updating your bank statements online

After you're signed up for M-Powered Bank Statements, you can update your bank statement information whenever you choose — once a week, once a day or once a millisecond. Here's what to do:

1. In any command centre, click the M-Powered Services Centre icon.

The MYOB M-Powered Services Centre appears. (If you haven't applied for M-Powered Bank Statements yet, click the M-Powered Service Setup button and follow the prompts to complete the relevant applications.)

2. Click Send/Receive.

This takes you straight to the M-Powered Services Centre. Wait a few moments — count the flies on the wall — as your MYOB software downloads the latest and greatest information regarding your personal wealth (or lack of it) and the Transmission Summary window appears.

3. Check your Transmission Summary.

4. Click OK.

This returns you to the M-Powered Services Centre, at which point you can click Close.

Your update is now complete. You can now go to the Banking tab on your Reports menu to view the fruits of your labour.

Downloading transactions directly

When you're confident with reconciling bank statements, you may want to go the whole hog and download your bank statements directly into your MYOB company file, paving the way not only for the automatic transaction entry but for automatic bank reconciliations. Here's how it's done:

1. Go to your bank's Web site and download your statement.

How this step works in practice depends on your bank. If the bank offers you a choice of formats for your statement file, select OFX, QFX, QIF or OFC, because these formats are the only types that MYOB supports.

By the way, I find it easiest to download my statements one small date range at a time. That way, if my bank balance doesn't reconcile first go, the mistake is easier to spot.

2. Save the statement file in your MYOB folder.

If you like, change the file name so that it includes the date. For example, rename the file 'Mar01to07.qif'. This helps you choose the right file if you regularly download statement files.

3. Go to Reconcile Accounts and select your bank account.

I suggest you try this whole lark with a credit card account first — if you have one — because credit cards are the easiest account types to reconcile.

4. Enter the Bank Statement Date.

Be careful here. If you open a statement file with a date range that goes *beyond* the date you enter here, transactions that occur after this date may get matched. You won't see that these transactions are matched (because later transactions are hidden from view), but your Calculated Statement Balance will be up the spout. The solution? Always make sure your Bank Statement Date goes right up to the end of the date range of the statement file you're working with.

5. Click the Get Statement button, find your statement file and click Open.

6. Watch with wonderment as everything matches up automatically.

When you open your statement file, the transactions in your statement file match up with any identical transactions in your company file, using the cheque number and amount to match cheques, and the amount only to match deposits.

7. Add any transactions that you know you haven't recorded.

As part of the reconciliation process, you'll get a list of *unmatched transactions*. If you know there's a transaction you haven't recorded in your accounts yet, highlight the amount and click Add Transaction. MYOB then obligingly pops up with the Spend or Receive Money window, with most details complete. All you have to do is complete any missing information, such as the allocation account number or tax code.

By the way, if you decide to enter *all* transactions by working from your bank statements rather than working from cheque stubs and deposit books, remember that you won't pick up on any uncleared cheques or deposits. You have to add these transactions separately in order for your financial statements to be correct.

8. Match up any transactions that you know you've recorded, but which didn't find their mate automatically.

If a transaction appears as unmatched but you think you've recorded it already, click the Match Transaction button, find the transaction you want to match and click Match.

9. Click Done and finish your bank reconciliation as normal.

When you finish matching and adding transactions, click Done to skip any transactions that haven't found a home and to return to the bank reconciliation. You can now finish your bank reconciliation as normal, entering the New Statement Balance and checking that the Out of Balance amount is zero.

Chapter 8

Stocking Up

· ·

In This Chapter

▶ Finding out if you need to use inventory

▶ Entering your first stock counts

▶ Attending to your Items List

▶ Selecting tax codes

▶ Pricing, pricing, pricing

▶ Making inventory adjustments

▶ Completing the perfect stocktake

· ·

*1*f inventory gives you a headache, think of this chapter as your pain relief. No more running out the back to see if there's stock on the shelf; no more random guessing of a price because you can't be bothered to dig out the supplier's invoice. And no more stocktakes where all you do is dream up a figure similar to last year and hope your accountant doesn't notice.

MYOB software transforms the task of managing inventory from a nightmare into one that's laughably straightforward. In this chapter, not only do I explain Einstein's theory of relativity in a way your three-year-old could understand it, but I also tell you how to set up inventory so that it works just the way you want it to.

By the way, inventory features are not included in either MYOB BusinessBasics or FirstEdge. In order to take advantage of any of the splendiferous features discussed in this chapter, you first need to upgrade your software to MYOB Accounting, MYOB Premier or MYOB AccountEdge.

Deciding Whether to Use Inventory

Before you plough through a whole chapter about inventory, spare a few seconds to consider whether you actually need inventory at all. (There's no right or wrong way to use MYOB software. It's all horses for courses . . . your black stallion may be another person's Shetland pony.)

So browse through the next two sections and ponder your options. I provide three reasons to read this chapter and then three reasons to skip it. All you have to do is decide which path to take.

Three reasons to read this chapter . . .

- ✔ If you buy goods for resale, chances are you need to use inventory (unless you purchase a point-of-sale system instead).

- ✔ If you manufacture certain goods over and over again, then you need to use inventory (although you may not choose to track the building of each item).

- ✔ If you charge by the hour, you may want to set up your time as an item using the Inventory command centre.

. . . and three reasons to skip this chapter

- ✔ If you're a service business and you always use Professional or Service-style invoices, then you really don't need to use inventory. An amazing number of Australian small businesses (about 60 percent) fall into this category.

- ✔ If you're a busy retailer, you probably need to use a point-of-sale system (such as MYOB RetailManager) rather than the inventory features in your MYOB accounting software.

- ✔ If you manufacture one-off custom goods (anything from stained glass windows to custom-built kitchens), you probably won't need to use inventory — it gets too fiddly and time-consuming for these types of jobs.

Creating a New Item

So you're ready to create your first inventory item? Follow my erudite instructions and you're on your way:

1. **Go to the Inventory command centre, click the Items List button, followed by the New button that appears at the bottom of the Items List window.**

2. **Enter an Item Number for this item, then press the Tab or Enter key.**

The Item Number doesn't have to be a number. In fact, it often makes more sense to use letters instead of (or as well as) numbers. For example, a penguin fridge magnet could have FM-Penguin1 as its number, or a small black T-shirt could be TS-SmBl. Above all, be consistent with item numbers — follow a pattern from one inventory item to the next.

3. Enter a Name for the item.

Enter a brief description as the Name for this item, such as 'Fridge Magnet, Penguin Design No1'. You're limited to 30 characters, so be concise.

4. Click the buy, sell or inventory boxes for the item.

If you buy this item for resale, and you want to track how many you have in stock at any one time, then click all three boxes. If you don't buy this item for resale and you're not sure which boxes to tick, check out the section, 'Pick a box' later in this chapter.

5. Select the income, cost of sales and asset accounts, where prompted.

When you click the I Buy, I Sell and I Inventory boxes, MYOB software prompts you to complete the corresponding income, cost of sales and asset accounts, as shown in Figure 8-1. It's MYOB software's way of saying, 'You've told me that you sell this item, now tell me what kind of income account this sale should go to' or 'You've told me that you buy this item, what's the cost of sales account?'

For example, you could specify that sales of fridge magnets should go to 'Income-Gifts', or that T-shirt sales could go to 'Income-Clothing'. (I talk more about selecting these accounts in the section, 'Telling things where to go' later in this chapter.)

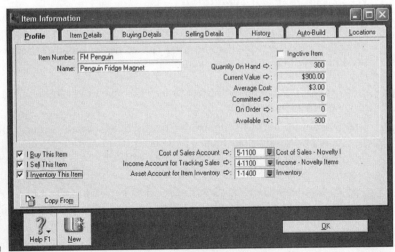

Figure 8-1:
Creating a new inventory item.

6. **Click OK to record your new item's main details, then select tax codes if prompted.**

   You may be prompted for a Tax Code When Bought and a Tax Code When Sold. Usually, the tax code is either FRE or GST (depending on the item), but if you're not sure, see 'Checking Up on GST', later in this chapter.

7. **Click OK again.**

   Your new item is now added to your Items List.

   If you like, you can add even more information to your new item — such as prices or supplier info — by opening it again and clicking the Item Details, Buying Details or Selling Details tabs. (I talk about these settings later in this chapter.)

Pick a box

Those three little innocent boxes, I Buy This Item, I Sell This Item and I Inventory This Item, can cause such confusion. Which boxes you tick depends on the kind of business you have and how you manage your inventory. Here goes . . .

When you buy something and then sell it

If you buy items for resale, whether they're clothes or medicines, books or shoes, tick all three boxes: I Buy This Item, I Sell This Item and I Inventory This Item.

When you just sell something

If you sell things that you don't buy, the only box you have to tick is I Sell This Item (leave the other boxes unticked). 'Hang on,' I hear you cry. 'How is it possible to sell something you've never bought?' Believe me, it is possible and here are some examples:

- ✔ Lots of my clients sell their time. They create an item called 'Labour' and price it with their hourly rate.

- ✔ I've set up MYOB software for heaps of associations and clubs that charge membership fees. They set up annual subscriptions in their Items List, creating different items with different prices for each membership type.

- ✔ Backpacker hostels, guesthouses and caravan parks often create items for Nightly Rates, Weekend Rates, Linen Hire and so on, similar to the example shown in Figure 8-2.

- ✔ My local computer shop offers photocopying services and Internet access. They set up items for copy charges per page or Internet access per hour.

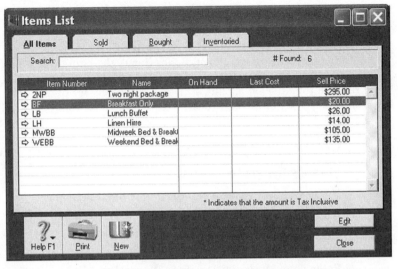

Figure 8-2:
Your Items
List can
inventory
services you
provide, not
just items
you buy for
resale.

When you make something with your own fair hands

If you buy separate items and then join them together to make something else (maybe you buy vegetable oil, perfume essences and bottles and combine these products to make massage oil), then tick all three boxes — I Buy This Item, I Sell This Item and I Inventory This Item.

When you buy something but don't sell it

Sometimes you only want something in your Items List so that you can print up purchase orders. Lots of things fall into this category — for example, office stationery, packaging for sending out goods, or miscellaneous manufacturing supplies, such as rags, oil or gas.

For these types of items, only click the box I Buy This Item.

Copy and paste

Do you stock a lot of similar items? Perhaps you sell a range of hats that are all the same except for their colour, or a range of pots that only differ by size.

If you do, give your weary fingers a typing holiday and make friends with the Copy From command.

In the Inventory command centre, click New, type an Item Number, press Tab, and then click Copy From. Select a similar item from the list and, before you can say knife, all the details from this item copy across to the new one you're creating. All you have to do now is fix up any information that's different.

Setting up supplier details

If you want to, you can record supplier details for all your items. Although entering supplier details is entirely optional, the cool thing about setting up supplier details is that if stock levels run low, you can generate new purchase orders automatically, making sure you never run out of any item ever again (er, is that a pig or an emu I see flying overhead?). Sound good? Then hit the road, Jack:

1. **Open your Items List, select the item you want and click Edit.**

2. **Click the Buying Details tab.**

3. **If you want to, enter a standard cost for this item.**

   If you're not sure whether you want to run with standard costs for inventory items, see the sidebar 'When cost price isn't quite what it seems' later in this chapter.

4. **Enter your Minimum Level for Restocking Alert.**

   Think about how low you're prepared to let the stock fall before you buy more. For example, if you know that you always want to keep at least 10 units in stock, enter 10 as the Minimum Level.

5. **Enter the supplier's name in Primary Supplier for Reorders.**

   Enter the usual supplier for this item. It doesn't matter if you occasionally buy this item from someone else.

6. **Enter your supplier's code for this item in the Supplier Item Number field.**

   Sometimes this is useful, sometimes it isn't. If you think your supplier likes to see their own item codes on purchase orders, enter their code here. Otherwise don't bother; it's only another time-consuming job.

7. **Enter the quantity you normally order as the Default Reorder Quantity.**

   If you normally order 20 of these items at a time, enter 20 as your Default Reorder Quantity. This means that when your stock falls below minimum levels, a purchase order comes up for this quantity.

   For example, say your minimum stock level for something is 10 units and you normally order the item in lots of 20. If your stock level falls to 8, a purchase order comes up for 20 units, not for 2.

8. **Check your details, then click OK.**

   Your screen should look similar to the one shown in Figure 8-3. Go ahead, click OK if you feel ecstatically happy with your work.

Item Information

| Profile | Item Details | **Buying Details** | Selling Details | History | Auto-Build | Locations |

120   **Icelandic Bikinis**

Last Purchase Price: $50.22   Including Tax
Standard Cost: $55.00   Tax Code When Bought ⇨: | GST | Goods & Serv
Buying Unit of Measure: 1
Number of Items per Buying Unit: 1

Optional Restocking Information for the To Do List

Minimum Level for Restocking Alert: 2
Primary Supplier for Reorders ⇨: | Sven Horsky |
Supplier Item Number: CB120
Default Reorder Quantity: 5

Help F1   New   OK

Figure 8-3: Setting up supplier details to generate purchase orders automatically when stock runs low.

Telling things where to go

Whenever you create a new item, you have to select corresponding income, cost of sales and inventory accounts. Careful selection of these accounts is important, because they affect how your Profit & Loss report comes out.

Income accounts

If you click I Sell This Item when you create a new item, MYOB software prompts you to select an income account. Take care to select an income account that makes sense, creating a new account if an appropriate one doesn't exist already.

As I explain in Chapter 2, it usually works well to create several income accounts in your Accounts List so you can track your different revenue sources. You can then mirror this arrangement by organising your items in a similar way, so that items are grouped into departments. Working in this manner allows you to see at a glance from your Profit & Loss report how different product groups are performing.

Sometimes clients protest when I ask them to do this, saying, 'It's not practical to split my products into groups.' But when I persist, they almost always agree it's a good idea. Here are some real-life examples:

✔ A client of mine is a gift wholesaler and has separate income accounts in their Accounts List for Glassware Sales, Pottery Sales and Textile Sales. They group their items in the same way, linking each item to the appropriate income code.

✔ Another client has a small retail computer store and organises both their income accounts and their items list into five groups: hardware, software, accessories, repairs and miscellaneous.

✔ A fast-food store splits income into junk food, really junky food and cardboard (just kidding).

Cost of sales accounts

If you click I Buy This Item and I Inventory This Item when you create a new item, MYOB software prompts you to select a cost of sales account.

Probably the simplest method is just to have one account called Cost of Goods Sold (sometimes also called Purchases). Alternatively, if you've divided your income accounts into a few groups, then you may want to mirror these income accounts by creating cost of sales accounts with the same name. For example, if you have an account called Income-Shoe Sales, create a corresponding account called Cost of Sales-Shoes. The Profit & Loss report in Figure 8-4 shows how this setup works in practice. I like it because not only can I see the income for each group of products, I can also see at a glance each one's profitability.

When you've figured out your cost of sales accounts, it's easy to pick the right account for tracking the cost of sales for each item in your Items List.

Figure 8-4:
If you link items to separate income accounts, you can see how each product range performs.

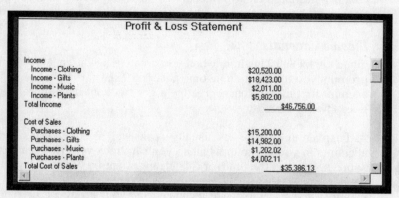

Inventory accounts

If you click I Inventory This Item when you create a new item, MYOB software prompts you to select an inventory account.

Don't get tied up creating lots of different inventory accounts. Unlike income or cost of sales accounts, you only need one inventory account to keep track of the stock you have on hand.

Surprisingly enough, this account is called Inventory and you find it sitting in the Assets section of your Accounts List.

Expense accounts

If you buy some items that are not for resale, then you only need to tick the box I Buy This Item. If you do so, MYOB software prompts you to select an Expense Account for Tracking Costs.

You can pick either a cost of sales or an expense account here. If the item is a supply you use for manufacturing (whether it be a sheet of steel, a metre of cloth or a drum of oil), then select a cost of sales account. But if the item is a supply that relates to administration (maybe stationery or computer supplies), then choose an expense account.

Getting items organised

Sometimes you need to record more information about items, maybe organising them into groups, detailing colour or size, or recording additional buying information. This is where custom lists work a treat.

In your Items List, every item has three Custom List fields, shown under the Item Details tab. Here's how to customise these lists so they work for you:

1. **From the top menu bar, choose Lists⇨Custom List & Field Names and then select Items.**

2. **Enter descriptions for your item groups or categories and click OK.**

   Your choice of description will vary, depending on the kind of products you sell. For example, if you sell clothing and you want to categorise items according to colour and size, you might enter Colour and Size as the names of Custom Lists #1 and #2. Or, if you sell CDs, you could enter Artist and Distribution Method as the names of Custom Lists #1 and #2.

3. **Back at the top menu bar, choose Lists⇨Custom Lists, then select Items.**

   Spot the subtle difference between this step and Step 1? This time you navigate to the Custom Lists menu, not the Custom List & Field Names menu.

4. **Add new entries for each Custom List and click OK.**

   For example, if the description for your Custom List #1 was Colour, you might add entries for Blue, Red and Yellow. If the description was Distribution Method, you might add entries for Account Sales, Sale or Return and Consignment.

5. **Go to your Items List, highlight an item you want to add custom information to, then click the Item Details tab.**

6. **Select the appropriate custom list info.**

   Figure 8-5 shows an example of a finished item, complete with custom information.

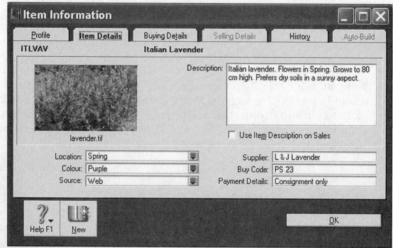

Figure 8-5: Organising items using custom lists.

Doing Your First Head Count

To get opening inventory balances up and running, first set up descriptions for all your items in the Items List, as I explain earlier this chapter. When you're done, pick a date (the last day of a month is usually the best) and get ready for the truly thrilling activity of entering your opening inventory counts and costs.

Counting is as easy as 1, 2, 3 . . .

In order to enter your opening inventory balances, you need to know the opening counts and costs for each item. With this information in hand, get ready . . . get set . . .

1. **Go! Head for the Inventory command centre and click Count Inventory.**

   A list of all your items appears.

2. **In the Counted column, enter stock counts for the first 20 or so items in your list.**

   I recommend you enter opening inventory counts in short batches, rather than all at once, because if you accidentally press the wrong key, you won't lose a whole heap of work.

   After you've entered the first 20 or so items, you should end up with a list of items and counts, similar to the list shown in Figure 8-6.

3. **Click Adjust Inventory.**

Count Inventory

Item Number	Name	On Hand	Counted	Difference
101	Caramel Fudge	0	3,453	3,453
120	Cooler Filter Large	0	1,324	1,324
200	Cooler Medium	0	345	345
220	Cooler Filter Medium	0	44	44
300	Cooler Small	0	0	0
320	Cooler Filter Small	0	33	33
400	Pottery Crock	0	55	55
410	Glass Crock	0	46	46
500	Spring Water Beverage	0	879	879
550	Coffee Powder	0	45	45
560	Tea	0	2,343	2,343
600	20 Litres North Spring	0	0	0

Help F1   Print   Adjust Inventory

Cancel

Figure 8-6:
Here's how
to record
inventory
counts.

4. Select your Inventory account as your Default Adjustment Account, then click Continue.

At this point, the rather complicated-looking Default Expense Account window pops up. Don't stress out about the fine print; simply enter the number of your Inventory asset account as the Default Adjustment Account. (Inventory always starts with the number 1.)

5. Click Opening Balances and, if prompted, click Adjust Balances.

MYOB software gets terribly psychic at this point and asks if you're entering opening inventory balances. Indeed, this is exactly what you're doing, so just click Opening Balances to continue.

An extra window may also pop up, asking if you want to adjust your balances so that your asset accounts match with inventory balances. It's a good idea, so click Adjust Balances.

6. Check the Date and write a suitable memo.

Aha! You've arrived at the Adjust Inventory window. Check the Date (it should be the date of stocktake, not the current date) put something short and sweet in the Memo field (for example, 'Opening stock counts').

7. Complete the Unit Cost column for each item.

Steady, now. One by one, fill in the item costs for each line of this window, like I have in Figure 8-7.

At this stage, you've headed into serious accounting-land and you need to be meticulous. When filling in item costs, don't change the Account column under any circumstance and be very careful that you use the correct costs (remember that you're entering costs, not selling prices, and that these cost prices should be tax-exclusive, before GST).

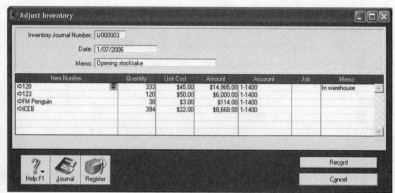

Figure 8-7:
Recording
how much
each item
costs.

8. Click Record.

After you click Record, repeat the entire process again and again, in batches of 20 or so items, until you've entered opening quantities and costs for all your items.

By the way, if you go to view the Buying Details of an item after recording the opening balance for that item, you may be surprised to see that the Last Purchase Price shows up as zero. Don't worry — that's because you haven't recorded a purchase for this item yet! If you click the Profile for that item instead, you'll be able to see the Average Cost, which should be the cost price that you entered when doing the opening stock count.

Making sure you got it right

As you know by now, entering inventory counts and unit costs is a fairly involved process. That's why it's a good idea to check your work, before you record any item sales or purchases.

Now I'm going to be unashamedly technical. After all, there's a limit to how much you can simplify quantum physics.

1. Go to Reports, click the Inventory tab, highlight the Items List Summary report and click Print.

2. Check that this report matches your original records.

Check through each line of the Items List Summary report, particularly the Units on Hand and Average Cost columns.

3. Circle the Grand Total at the bottom of the Total Value column on your Items List Summary report.

The Grand Total represents the total dollar value of your inventory (the cost of each item multiplied by the quantity of each item).

4. **Go to the Reports menu again, click the Accounts tab and highlight the Standard Balance Sheet report.**

5. **Click Customise and select the date of the stocktake as the date. Click OK and then click Print.**

6. **Look at the balance of Inventory and check that this matches the total from your Items List Summary report.**

   Pick up the Balance Sheet you printed in Step 5 and look up the balance of your Inventory account (it will be somewhere near the top, included in Current Assets). Then pick up the Items List Summary report you printed in Step 1 and look at the Grand Total you circled at the bottom.

7. **If the two balances match, yell yippee! You are truly brilliant.**

8. **If the two balances don't match, contemplate the meaning of life.**

   If the two balances don't match, then something is astray. You've either entered a wrong quantity or cost in your opening inventory journals, or the opening balance of Inventory is wrong. It's probably time to talk to your accountant and ask for some help.

Bleep, bleep, bleep

If you're a retailer, you probably need a point-of-sale system. Chances are that you need . . . drum roll . . . MYOB software's very own point-of-sale software.

As with any point-of-sale system, the idea is that you hurl your old-fashioned cash register out the window (first making sure that there are no dachshunds taking a stroll underneath) and replace it with your computer. You put bar codes on all your items, and replace the peaceful tap, tap, kerchunk of your cash register with the not-quite-so-peaceful beep, beep, ping of your scanner and cash drawer.

MYOB software has a range of point-of-sale products, starting with MYOB RetailBasics (that will set you back a modest $314) to MYOB RetailManager (a more handsome $2,005). Depending on what level of software you buy, you can potentially run stock control for thousands of items, manage lay-bys, keep a record of account sales, print barcode labels and much more.

One of the best things about using MYOB point-of-sale solutions is that they speak the same language as everyone else in the MYOB software family. Daily sales summaries, account updates and banking details all automatically travel across from your point-of-sale system into your accounting system, so you never have to enter information twice.

Find out more about MYOB point-of-sale products, visit www.myob.com.au and follow the links for Point of Sale.

Giving Your Items List the Once-Over

Regardless of whether your Items List is short or long, thin or fat, spotted or striped, it needs a certain amount of tender loving care. In the next few sections, I provide the ultimate set of care and feeding instructions.

Finding items

After you find the item you need you can do with it what you will. But first . . .

- ✔ The easiest way to find an item is to go to your Items List and type the first letters or numbers of the Item Number in the Search field. Press the Tab key and you go straight to the section of the list where the item lives.

- ✔ If you remember the name of an item but forget the number, then change your settings in Preferences so you can view the items by name. Take a look at the sidebar, 'Viewing by name, not by number', later in this chapter to find out how.

- ✔ If you're one of those people who prefer printed lists (old habits die hard), then go to Reports, click Inventory and highlight your Items List Summary report. Click Customise and note how you can print this report in lots of different ways, sorting by item number, item name or by a selected supplier. Play with these settings until you get the information you're looking for.

- ✔ One way to find items quickly is to make sure each one's Item Number (or Name) begins with a letter that indicates its product group. For example, a mail-order business that sells hats might start all hat Item Numbers with the letter H, all sloppy joes with the letters SJ and all T-shirts with the letters TS. See Figure 8-8 for an example.

- ✔ If you have a huge Items List, looking for stuff gets much easier if you organise items into groups. Refer to 'Getting items organised' earlier in this chapter to find out more about how this works.

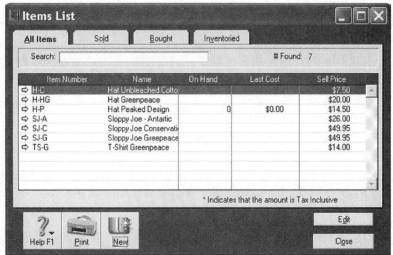

Figure 8-8:
Identify your
items quickly
by assigning
them a letter
or letters
that indicate
their product
group.

Changing items

It's easy to change an item. All you have to do is find it in your Items List, double-click on it and make your changes. Unlike lots of other accounting software programs (which shall remain nameless), MYOB software is extremely flexible and lets you change whatever you like — item numbers, descriptions, linked accounts and so on.

TIP

Viewing by name, not by number

Did you know you can sort your Items List either by name or by number? To sort by name, go to Setup⇨Preferences and then click the Windows tab. Click the option Select Items by Item Name, Not Item Number.

Whenever you're creating an invoice or a purchase order, or you're searching through your Items List, type the first letters of the item name and hey presto, there you have it.

Deleting items

To delete an item, look for it in your Items List and double-click on it. Go to the Edit menu on the top menu bar (as shown in Figure 8-9) and choose Delete Inventory Item.

This works fine, unless you have current invoices or purchase orders for this item still in the system. In this case, a warning appears stating you can't delete the item yet. If this happens to you, your best bet is to make this item inactive for the time being. The idea is that inactive items are hidden so that they don't pop up and irritate you all the time (if only one could do the same with the tax office). To make an item inactive, first highlight the item in your list, click Edit, then select the Inactive Item check box.

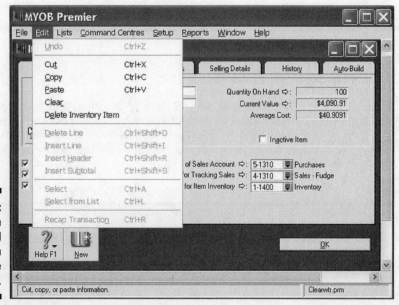

Figure 8-9:
You can delete old items when they've done their dash.

Checking Up on GST

Does the stuff you buy and sell attract GST? If so, you need to pick your GST codes pretty carefully, or you'll end up in the soup. And the soup won't be a yummy, clear consommé that you get out of easily. No, it will be a murky minestrone from which it's hard to return.

Selecting GST on items you buy

To check the GST for any item in your list (or to set GST for the first time), highlight the item and click Edit. Then click the Buying Details tab and look at the Tax Code When Bought.

If you're not sure what the correct code should be, read the following checklist and take your pick:

- ✔ If the item has GST on it, select GST as the tax code.
- ✔ If the item is GST-free (medical supplies, GST-free food and so on), select FRE as the tax code.
- ✔ If the supplier you buy the item from isn't registered for GST (but has an ABN), then pick FRE as your tax code.
- ✔ If you're not registered for GST, enter N-T (standing for Not Reportable) as your code.

Selecting GST on items you sell

To check the GST for an item in your list, highlight the item and click Edit. Then click the Selling Details tab and look at the Tax Code When Sold and select one of the following options:

- ✔ If the item attracts GST, select GST as your tax code.
- ✔ If the item is GST-free (medical supplies, GST-free food and so on), then select FRE as your tax code.

It's up to you whether your Base Selling Price includes GST or not. If it includes GST, then click the box Prices are Tax Inclusive. If it doesn't, then leave this box unclicked.

While you're lurking in the Selling Details tab of an item, I'd like to point out something pretty important. Can you see that you can choose to either calculate GST on the Actual Selling Price, or calculate GST on the Base Selling Price? For GST to calculate correctly, make sure you select to calculate GST on the Actual Selling Price.

Pricing to Sell

It's time to price your goods. Whether it's a market price, standard price, retail price, wholesale price, discount price, list price, rate for the job, fee for a service, fare, quoted price, flat charge or some other exotic beast, the time has come to do the deed.

So, in order of complexity, I explain how to price a single item, how to price a few items and how to price a whole lot of items at once.

Pricing one item at a time

Do you want to change the price for something? If so, double-click on the item in your Items List, select the Selling Details tab, change the Base Selling Price and click OK. That's all there is to it.

Pricing a few items at a time

If you want to update prices for a few items (maybe a supplier has just increased prices on all its products), go to the Inventory command centre

---

Different strokes for different folks

Do you sometimes charge different prices depending on the customer — maybe offering trade or staff discounts? MYOB Premier and AccountEdge both allow for up to six pricing levels for each item, with prices linking back to whatever Price Level you select in each customer's card.

You can also set up discounts for volume sales, creating up to five quantity breaks for each item. You may have one price for sales of 25 to 49 units, another price for sales of 50 to 99 units and so on. Combine six pricing levels with five

quantity breaks and there you have it — a whopping choice of 30 different prices per item.

Upgrading to MYOB Premier costs around $1,099 if you have MYOB Accounting Plus (these prices include GST) or, if you're using a Macintosh, upgrading to MYOB AccountEdge from MYOB FirstEdge costs around $429. The upgrade process is painless, with all your existing company data transferring across seamlessly. For more info about product upgrades, visit the upgrades page at www.myob.com.au.

and click Set Item Prices. A list appears showing item numbers and names, average costs and prices, similar to the one shown in Figure 8-10.

☑	Item Number	Name	Avg. Cost	Current Price
	500	Spring Water Beverage I		$362.73
	550	Coffee Powder		$27.50
	560	Tea		$37.50
✓	600	20 Litres North Spring		$25.00
✓	610	20 Litres South Spring	$12.9653	$25.00
✓	630	20 Litres Clear Carbon	$15.6594	$30.00
✓	640	20 Litres Orange Carbon	$10.104	$30.00
✓	650	12 Litres North Spring	$1.8938	$18.50
✓	670	12 Litres Clear Carbon	$8.7728	$17.50
✓	680	12 Litres Orange Carbon	$10.90	$17.50
	700	Pine Stand	$19.9534	$50.00
	710	Steel Stand	$69.2647	$76.00
	730	Pine Stand - 1Month Rei		$10.00
	740	Steel Stand - 1 Month Ri		$14.00
	850	Misc. Service		$14.00

Help F1   Print   Shortcuts   Last Cost   Avg Cost   OK

Figure 8-10: Pricing a few items at a time.

Scroll down to find the items you want to change and fix up the price in the Current Price column. If you want to check out the last price you paid for this item, click the Last Cost button. To return to view average costs, click the Avg Cost button.

Pricing lots of items in one hit

Sometimes you may want to update a large number of selling prices all at once — for example, if you're reviewing profit margins, or if all your supply prices suddenly change. In either case, you should get MYOB software to do the legwork.

From the Inventory command centre, select Set Item Prices and click in the Shortcut column against all the items you want to update, then click the Shortcuts button (it's the one with all those dollar signs and the pencil). This opens the Pricing Shortcuts window, as shown in Figure 8-11.

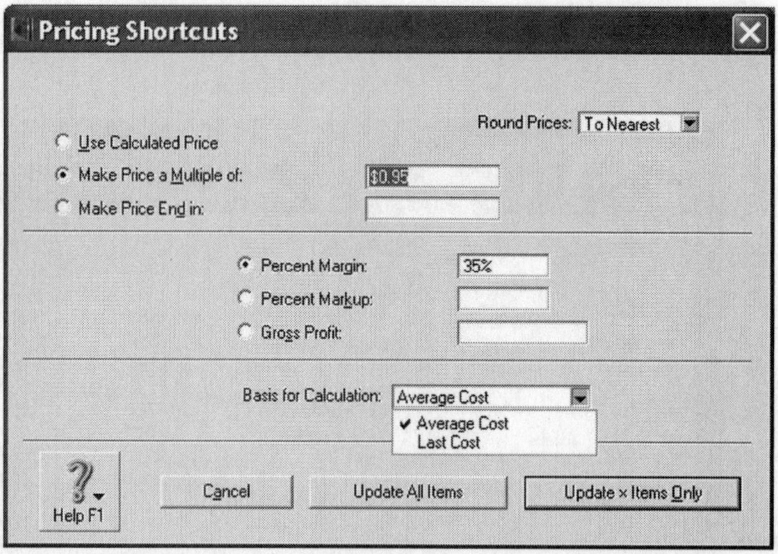

Pricing Shortcuts   [X]

Round Prices: [To Nearest ▼]

○ Use Calculated Price
● Make Price a Multiple of: [$0.95]
○ Make Price End in: [   ]

_____

○ Percent Margin: [35%]
○ Percent Markup: [   ]
○ Gross Profit: [   ]

_____

Basis for Calculation: [Average Cost ▼]
                        ✔ Average Cost
                          Last Cost

[? Help F1]   [Cancel]   [Update All Items]   [Update × Items Only]

Figure 8-11:
Pricing
Shortcuts
are handy for
updating lots
of prices at
once.

You could probably follow your nose and use your profiteering instinct to complete your choices, but just in case you need a hand, here are a couple of examples:

- You have an item that costs $19.50. You want to round the price up to the nearest dollar and mark it up 100 percent. To do so, opt to Round Prices up, Make Price a Multiple of $1 and enter 100 as the Percent Markup. (The final price is $40.00.)

- You have an item that costs $20.00. You want to make 33 percent gross profit and round the price to the nearest 50c. To do this, select Round Prices to Nearest, Make Price a Multiple of $0.50 and enter 50 as the Percent Markup. (The final price would be $30.00.)

If you find that the Set Item Prices menu doesn't really work for you — updating prices this way can get a bit cumbersome if you have hundreds of items because it's so easy to lose your place — then an alternative is to export your Items List out of your MYOB company file and into a spreadsheet such as Excel. You then fix up the prices in Excel, save the spreadsheet as a text file, and import this text file back into your MYOB company file. If you think this sounds a bit scary — and it is a little daunting first time you do it — get an MYOB Certified Consultant to help you with the process the first time around.

When cost price isn't quite what it seems

The pricing menus refer to Average Cost and Last Cost quite a lot. If you're going to rely on either of these to set your sales prices, it's important to understand what each expression means.

Average Cost divides the total dollar value for an item by the quantity on hand. Average Cost doesn't include GST, early payment discounts or freight. Last Cost is the amount in the Price column for the last purchase of this item. Last Cost includes GST, but doesn't include supplier discounts, early payment discounts or freight.

The other figure that you'll see under the Buying Details tab is something called 'Standard Cost'. The Standard Cost is a figure you can enter yourself, rather than a figure that the system generates automatically. Some businesses like to record standard costs in their systems so they have a benchmark price they can refer to, especially if the actual purchase price varies from week to week. Other businesses choose to record standard costs that include both materials and labour, so they can generate custom reports that allow for the cost of manufacturing. The whole concept of standard costs gets a bit technical, so you may want to talk to your accountant before you spend time recording costs in this way.

You can set your preferences so that standard cost comes up whenever you generate a purchase order or record a supplier invoice. To do this, go to Preferences, click the Inventory tab and click Use Standard Cost as the Default Price on Purchase Orders and Bills.

Fixing Things Up When Stuff Goes Wrong

I always know a person has not had a great deal to do with computers when they talk about computers in terms of logic and reason. This person has yet to discover that computers are sensitive, temperamental, unpredictable and highly strung animals.

Put together, computers and humans open up endless possibilities for disaster. Therefore, it's not surprising that sometimes your inventory costs or counts go completely out of whack. However, you can make inventory adjustments to fix things up.

Adjusting the quantity of an item

What do you do if you know you have three stuffed bears on the shelf but your Items List says you have four? Or, perhaps you can see that you're completely sold out of lemonade but your Items List says you have 50 crates left?

Follow these steps:

1. **In the Inventory command centre, choose Count Inventory.**

2. **Enter the quantity you have on hand in the Counted column and click Adjust Inventory.**

   As you enter your quantities, the difference between the On Hand column and the Counted column calculates automatically.

3. **Select your Default Adjustment Account and click Continue.**

   Your best bet is to choose the cost of sales account that this item normally goes to as the Default Adjustment Account.

4. **In the Adjust Inventory window, check the Date and type a Memo.**

   Look at Figure 8-12 to see an example inventory Memo. Note that although you can fit a whole essay in the Memo field, only the first seven words or so appear on reports.

5. **Check that you're happy with the journal and click Record.**

   Check that the Quantity and Amount columns make sense before you click the Record button.

Figure 8-12: Changing item quantities using Adjust Inventory.

Adjusting the cost of an item

Oscar Wilde once said that experience is the name that people give to their mistakes. I think he had some insight into how easy it is to really mess things up, especially when you're first working with inventory.

There's no quick explanation for why, one day, you look up the average cost for an item and it's completely out the window. You know that a box of CDs doesn't cost $1,500 or that a new laptop costs more than $50, but suddenly your Items List says that this is the case.

Don't con yourself into thinking MYOB software has made a mistake — the cause is always human error, somewhere!

One way to fix unit costs is to go to your Items Register, select the item in question and double-check the cost price for every purchase for that item. Hopefully, you can see where the mistake is and fix it.

An alternative approach that's more practical if there are lots of purchases to look through is simply to fix the average cost so that it's correct. Here's how:

1. **Calculate the difference between what the average cost should be and what it is.**

   For example, if you know a box of blank CDs costs $5 to buy, but the unit cost comes up as $12, then the difference is $7.

2. **Go to your Analysis menu, click Inventory and check out how many of this item you have in stock.**

3. **Multiply the quantity you have in stock by the difference in unit cost.**

   For example, if I had 20 boxes of CDs in stock, I'd multiply $7 by 20 to arrive at $140.

4. **In the Inventory command centre, select Adjust Inventory.**

5. **Enter the date and write a clear, concise Memo.**

   Use the Memo field to explain why you're adjusting inventory value. Then, if someone asks you months later why you did this, you're able to justify your actions.

6. **Enter zero in the Quantity column and your dollar difference in the Amount column.**

   Figure 8-13 shows how your inventory adjustment should look. The dollar difference should be the amount you calculated in Step 3. You can ignore the Unit Cost column.

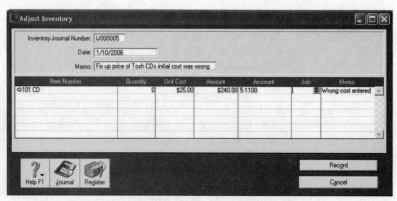

Figure 8-13: Fixing up inventory costs.

7. Select an expense account for this adjustment.

Select the cost of sales account that this item or these items normally go to. For example, to adjust the stock count for CDs, I adjust an account called Cost of Sales-Accessories.

When working with any inventory adjustment, never select Inventory as your expense account or adjustment account. This throws your reports out of whack and turns your accountant into a dribbling, moaning, nervous wreck.

8. Click Record.

Phew! It's over and done with. Don't forget to go straight to your Items List Summary report and check that the average cost is now correct.

Troubleshooting transactions

To find any transaction relating to a particular item (including stock counts and adjustments), go to your Items Register and choose to Search By Item. Select the item in question, followed by a suitable date range, and the Items Register displays every sale, purchase and inventory adjustment for that item, as shown in Figure 8-14. If you like, you can then double-click on any transaction to view it in all its glory.

The Current Value column shows the running balance for the cost value of that item. Occasionally, this running balance may seem to do the impossible and show up as a minus figure. Don't stress. Minus figures pop up if you record the purchase of an item, then record the sale of an item but give the sale an earlier date than the purchase.

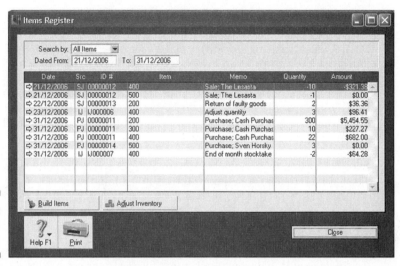

Figure 8-14:
Your Items
Register.

If you want to see only cash transactions for a particular item — without being confused by inventory counts and other adjustments — go to your Find Transactions menu and click the Item tab. Enter the item code, followed by a suitable date range, and a list appears, showing all sales and purchases for this item.

Standing Up and Counting Down

Yeeeah! It's time to do a stocktake. As if there aren't enough problems to worry about for 30 June, without counting, counting and counting . . .

I've done oodles and oodles of stocktakes over the years. The one I remember best was years ago in a huge warehouse when the stocktake took about ten hours, with eight staff counting all day. Then the manager and I stayed up till 2 a.m., typing the counts into the computer one by one.

Things seemed fine until two days later when the computer crashed. Stay calm, I declared, we can restore the information from our backup. This we did, restoring the data from the day just before the stocktake. Never mind, I said, we'll just type in the stock counts from the stocktake sheets one more time.

This is where the trouble hit. We looked high and low, far and wide, but the stocktake sheets had disappeared forever — through the shredder, I suspect. And so we did the stocktake all over again. What a way to spend a weekend!

Getting ready for D-Day

Before you start your stocktake, make your way to Reports, click the Inventory tab and print an Inventory Count Sheet.

Use the count sheet to complete your stocktake. As you go, keep an eye open for any item counts that look odd, or where they're significantly different from what you should have — you can see how much you should have by referring to the On Hand column.

Avoid complete bamboozlement by making sure that no stock goes out for sales and no stock arrives until the count is complete.

Doing the grand reckoning

On the face of it, entering stock counts is pretty simple. Go to Count Inventory in the Inventory command centre, enter your counts from your count sheet in the Counted column and record your adjustment.

However, here are a few tips to make sure things go swimmingly:

- ✔ Only enter counts for 10 or 20 items at a time. It's easier to see what you're doing this way, and if you (or your computer) do something silly, you won't lose too much work in one hit.

- ✔ When prompted for a Default Expense Account, pick the cost of sales account the items you're adjusting normally go into. Cost of sales accounts always start with the number 5.

- ✔ Never, ever, ever select Inventory as your Default Expense Account. If you do, you'll throw everything out of balance and make your accountant catatonic.

- ✔ To see the dollar effect of stocktakes separately in your Profit & Loss report (perhaps you do stocktakes every month and you want to see if counts are always under and by how much), create a special cost of sales account called Stocktake Adjustments. Use this as your Default Expense Account.

- ✔ Get the date right. If you do a stocktake on 30 June, date the journal 30 June. (Even if you enter the stock counts a week later, this has to be the date, otherwise nothing makes sense in your financial reports.)

✔ When you're done, print an Items List Summary report and compare the final counts with your handwritten stock count sheets. This way you can spot if you've made a blunder.

✔ Don't enter any item sales or item purchases until you've completed your stocktake, entered the count and checked your work. If you ignore this step, you won't know which way is up.

✔ In the final wash-up, staple your original Inventory Count pages and your final Items List Summary report together. Keep these final records in a safe place.

Assessing the aftermath

Your stocktake adjustments complete, the last job on your list is to make sure everything balances. The theory is that the total value of inventory according to your Items List (that is, quantities multiplied by average cost) equals the value of the inventory account (or accounts) in your Balance Sheet.

Ready to take the test?

1. **Go to your Reports menu, select the Inventory Value Reconciliation report and then click Print.**

   Make sure to select the stocktake date as the date for this report before you print it.

2. **Check that the Out of Balance amount equals zero.**

   At the bottom of your Inventory Value Reconciliation report is the total Inventory Value, the corresponding Account Balance of your inventory account and an Out of Balance amount. Check that the Out of Balance amount equals zero. (In the ideal world, the first two amounts should equal one another. The Out of Balance amount only appears as anything other than $0.00 if they don't.)

3. **If the Out of Balance amount doesn't equal zero, get help.**

   Out of Balance amounts in your inventory can be tricky. I suggest your first port of call is a support document called Inventory Value Reconciliation, which you can download for free from www.myob.com.au/support. (If you have trouble locating this support note, try searching on the document number, which is '9169'.) Alternatively, ask your accountant or an MYOB Certified Consultant for assistance.

Going on location

If you run your business across several locations (maybe you have warehouses in each state, or perhaps sales representatives who each have their own stock), then you should probably consider upgrading to MYOB Premier Enterprise. Premier Enterprise has the most sophisticated inventory control in the MYOB software range, allowing you to keep track of what stock you have in each location, as well as what stock you have overall. With Premier Enterprise, you can define locations in any way that you choose (from separate aisles in a warehouse to separate buildings in different countries), process sales from any location and move items between locations.

To find out more about MYOB Premier Enterprise, visit www.myob.com.au or contact your local MYOB Certified Consultant.

Chapter 9

Saving Money on Payday

· ·

In This Chapter

▶ Preparing to pay up

▶ Organising employee card files

▶ Getting your wages categories organised

▶ Calculating holiday and sick leave entitlements

▶ Salting it away with super

▶ Paying your taxes

· ·

*I*f you have a few employees, chances are you also have a mound of paperwork that takes up more room than the State Library archives. And the ATO sends an endless roll of information that defies comprehension and that's guaranteed to give you recurring nightmares about being back at school, memorising logarithmic tables and doing long division.

Take heart. Instead of pounding your head against a brick wall and tearing out your fingernails, switch over to MYOB Accounting Plus, MYOB Premier or MYOB AccountEdge and keep sane, saving yourself hours of precious time every week.

In this chapter, I talk about setting up payroll for your business, and talk about PAYG tax, super, holidays and more. Reading this chapter may not be the most enthralling way to spend a sunny afternoon, I admit, but without some pain, there's no gain.

First Things First

Before you head to the Easy Setup Assistant to set up Payroll, it's a good idea to organise a few things. The first is to decide on a payroll start date.

Although, in theory, you can start at any time, you should try to start using Payroll on 1 July. (I've learnt this the hard way.) This way you can enter a whole year's pays in the one spot without a problem, making it easy to balance tax and print payment summaries.

If you can't start on 1 July, at least try to start on the first day of a quarter — for example, 1 October, 1 January or 1 April. Never start Payroll in the middle of the month. It's too confusing and it's likely to throw your super calculations out of whack.

After you decide when you want to start, carve yourself out some quiet time and assemble all your pay records in one spot. You need your wages books, employee cards, employment declarations and so on. With these treasured but now archaic items at hand, you're ready to begin.

The Easy Setup Assistant

Use the Easy Setup Assistant to set up your payroll. To do so, go to Setup on the top menu bar and select Easy Setup Assistant. Then click the Payroll button to continue, as shown in Figure 9-1.

I could write a whole essay about all 101 steps involved in setting up Payroll, but I know you don't need me to explain every teensy bit. Instead, I'm going to give you a few tricks to make things easier and point out a couple of traps that you don't want to fall into.

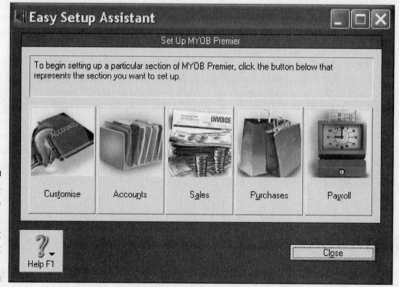

Figure 9-1:
The Easy
Setup
Assistant
helps you get
started.

Some tricks to help along the way . . .

Look out for these items when you're making your way through Payroll in the Easy Setup Assistant:

- ✔ The Payroll Information menu asks about the number of hours in a Full Work Week. Look up your award if you're not sure about how many hours this is. If you have multiple awards within your business, check the award or agreement that relates to the majority of your employees.

- ✔ The Linked Accounts menu asks you to what accounts you want to use to pay your employees. It's usually best to select a Cash Drawer or Undeposited Funds account for Cash Payments, your regular business bank account for Cheque Payments, and your Electronic Clearing Account for Electronic Payments.

- ✔ Setting up Payroll Categories is probably the most complex part of setting up payroll. If you're not a payroll expert and you're just getting started, you probably need to review only the Wages categories at this stage (you can review Entitlements and Superannuation categories a little later). See 'Way to Go with Wages' for more details about setting up Wages categories.

- ✔ The Employee Cards menu involves setting up employee cards. When doing so, don't forget to click the Payroll Details tab on each employee card and select the correct payroll categories, and then click the Payment Details tab to select the correct payment method.

. . . and some pitfalls to avoid

Here are some pitfalls to look out for when setting up Payroll (I've learnt these the hard way too!):

- ✔ The Payroll Year menu asks you to select your Current Payroll Year. Your Current Payroll Year is the year that it will be when you next complete payment summaries. (For example, if it's July 2006 now, it will be June 2007 by the time you next complete payment summaries.) Choose your payroll year carefully, because after you make a selection, you can't go back.

- ✔ In the Employee Cards menu, you have to pick tax scales for each employee. The default is the Tax Free Threshold setting, which is good because most employees fall into this category. But . . . don't forget to change the tax scale for any employees who have a second job or who have not yet given you an employment declaration.

✔ The step most likely to cause trouble is the History section of the Employee Cards menu, where you enter pay histories. (You only need to do this part if you're starting Payroll after 1 July.) Don't enter figures in this section until you're absolutely sure they're 100 percent completely and totally perfect. If you're not sure, skip this section for now and give yourself some time to settle in. You can come back and complete the pay histories later.

Hiring and Firing

Every employee has their own card in the Card File. The idea is that you list each employee's name, address and phone number in the Profile window (this is the first screen you come to when creating a new card) and then you complete their payroll information by clicking the Payroll Details tab.

Figure 9-2 shows a typical Payroll Details view. At the top you list personal details, such as Date of Birth, Gender and Start Date. Then you click the left-hand side menus to enter more details. Click Wages to record pay rates and pay frequencies, Superannuation to enter fund details, Entitlements to select holiday and sick leave info and Taxes to select the appropriate tax scale.

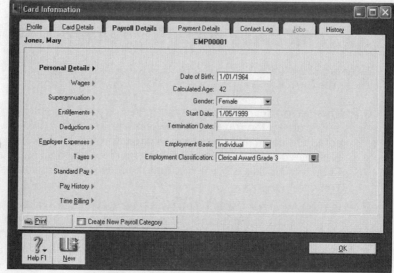

Figure 9-2:
You store most payroll information on the Payroll Details tab.

Taking on a new employee

Every time you hire an employee, you need to create a new card. Here goes:

1. **From the Card File command centre, select Cards List, click the Employee tab, then New.**

   This instruction applies if you want to enter a new employee. However, if you're setting up payroll for the first time, you can reach this spot in the Easy Setup Assistant by selecting Payroll⇨Employee Cards.

2. **Fill in the name, address, phone number and so on.**

3. **Click the Card Details tab.**

   You can do whizzbang stuff here like insert mugshots of employees or add extra info in the Custom Fields or Custom Lists.

4. **Click the Payroll Details tab and complete all Personal Details.**

   You're required to type a Date of Birth (often surprising); Gender (usually obvious) and a Start Date. Unless the employee is a subcontractor, select Individual as their Employment Basis. You also need to enter an Employment Classification to show what award or agreement this employee is employed under.

5. **Click the Wages side menu and choose either Salary or Hourly as the Pay Basis.**

   The Pay Basis needs to be either Salary or Hourly. Hourly works best if the employee's hours vary from week to week or they receive any kind of loadings or penalties. Also, choosing Hourly as the Pay Basis makes sense if an employee earns less than $55,000 per year, as you need to track start and finish times under the WorkChoice provisions.

6. **Still in the Wages side menu, check the Pay Frequency and Hours in Weekly Pay Period.**

   Be careful with these settings, because one wrong click now can mean big trouble later.

7. **Still in the Wages side menu, decide an expense type for this employee for your Profit & Loss.**

   Choose a Wages Expense Account that reflects the type of work the employee does. For example, if you employ office staff, factory staff and management, I recommend you create different expense accounts for each category of staff. You then link each employee to the right kind of expense account, similar to the way I've done in Figure 9-3.

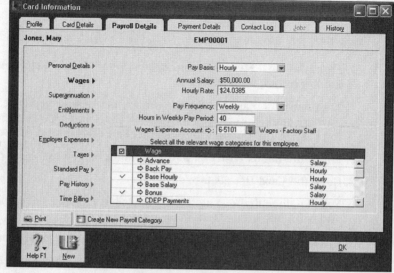

Figure 9-3:
Completing
payroll
details on
your
employee's
card.

8. **Still in the Wages side menu, select all wages categories that apply to this employee.**

   You're feeling daunted? Don't be. Instead, ask yourself what wages categories apply to this employee. Often, you only need to click Base Hourly or Base Salary, but sometimes other categories apply, such as Overtime, Holiday Pay and Sick Pay.

9. **Click the Superannuation side menu and set up superannuation details for this employee.**

   Unless the employee isn't eligible for super (and beware, almost every employee is!), then enter the name of their Superannuation Fund and their Employee Membership #. If you don't have this info yet, make a note to get it as soon as you can. Then, in the list of superannuation categories, select the category that applies to this employee. Unless the employee has something unusual, such as additional superannuation or salary sacrifice, your best bet is simply to click against the Superannuation Guarantee category.

10. **Figure out what you're going to do about holiday and sick leave.**

    Yep, I know I'm being vague here. However, first check out 'Siesta Time' later on in this chapter — it covers holiday and sick leave in detail — before you proceed. Then, when you've figured out what you want to do, go to the Entitlements side menu on the Payroll Details tab for this new employee and click off the appropriate categories.

11. **Click the Taxes side menu and set up the employee's tax info and record any rebates.**

This is where you record the employee's Tax File Number and select the appropriate Tax Table. For most full-time or part-time employees, the Tax Free Threshold setting works fine, but for casual employees, select Tax Free Threshold/No LL as the Tax Scale (check with your accountant if you're not sure about tax scales). Also, if the employee is entitled to any rebates, put the amount they're owed for the whole year in Total Rebates.

12. **Go to the Standard Pay side menu and make a stab at completing the employee's standard pay.**

    I'm chickening out of explaining everything about standard pays here. Make your way to the section 'Setting up standard pays' later in this chapter to get the whole picture.

13. **Click the Payment Details tab and fill in the employee's banking details.**

    Take your pick for the Payment Method: cash, cheque or electronic. You need to get this right now or things fall in a heap when you go to process the pays.

14. **Heave a huge sigh of relief and click OK, then OK again.**

    It's pretty awesome the first time you set up a new employee, isn't it? But, again, it's like riding a bike. Once you've done it the first time, you never forget.

Changing employee details

Nothing in life stays the same. The receptionist gets married and changes her name from Miss Wren to Mrs Finch. The technician goes religious and changes his name from John Smith to Swami Vahriswati. The bookkeeper runs off with the gardener and changes her address to Fly By Night Motel, Vanuatu.

The short way home

If you're using a PC and you press the Ctrl key and the letter F at the same time, you go directly to Cards from wherever you are in the software. Or, if you're using a Mac, press the Cmd key and the letter F at the same time. From here, simply click the Employee tab to see a list of all employees.

Shortcut keys save heaps of time, so try to memorise one a week, starting now. Oh yes, and after you have the shortcut keys under your belt, why not keep up the momentum and move on to poetry? The world would probably be a better place if we could all recite a few stirring poems off by heart.

The good news is it's easy to change information about an employee. Make your way to the Card File command centre, click Cards List, and double-click on the employee's name. Make your changes, click OK and you're done. It couldn't be simpler.

Biting the bullet

Were they pushed or did they jump?

Whether an employee got the chop or just left, after an employee has gone you probably want to get rid of the person from your company file. You can't completely remove an employee until you've started both a new payroll year and a new financial year. However, in the meantime you can hide ex-employees from your drop-down lists. To do so, click Cards List, double-click on the employee's name and then click the little box in the corner called Inactive Card. Making employees inactive also prevents their names appearing when you go to process payroll.

After you've completed your end-of-year rollovers, return to the card for the long-gone employee, but this time double-click on their name, go to the top menu bar and choose Edit⇨Delete Card, then stare wide-eyed at the screen and say 'You're terminated' when the record is zapped.

Way to Go with Wages

Wage categories cover everything you pay to your employees. These include their salaries, holiday pay, sick pay, allowances, penalty loadings, bonuses and so on. The idea is that you need to allocate a separate wages category for every type of payment you give an employee.

Creating categories for wages

Your Payroll Categories List comes well stocked with lots of wages categories. These categories fit the bill for most businesses, but you may need to add one from time to time. Here's what to do:

1. **Select Payroll Categories, click the Wages tab and then click New.**

2. **Give the new category a name and select whether it's Salary or Hourly.**

   You can name the category anything you like, such as Overtime, Leave Loading, Allowance or Slush Money. If it's a regular sum to be included with each pay (most allowances and loadings are like this), then pick Salary. If it's based on the number of hours worked (such as overtime or penalty rates), choose Hourly.

3. **If you choose Hourly, select how you want to calculate the rate.**

   You can choose between multiplying the regular rate by a number (for example, enter 2.0 in the field for double-time), or choose a Fixed Hourly Rate.

4. **If you want these wages to be reported separately, click Optional Account.**

   Selecting an Optional Account enables you to report payroll categories separately on your Profit & Loss report. For example, instead of including motor vehicle allowances as part of ordinary wage expenses, you can click the Optional Account button in the Motor Vehicle Allowance payroll category, selecting Motor Vehicle Allowance as the account in the Override Account box, as shown in Figure 9-4. Motor Vehicle Allowance then appears as a separate line on your Profit & Loss report. (I recommend you do this for allowances and reimbursements.)

5. **If the new category is exempt from PAYG, click Exempt.**

   Sadly, there is not much left in life that is exempt from tax. But, reimbursements are normally exempt, and so is the first $320 of holiday leave loading. If you're sure a wage category is exempt from PAYG, choose Exempt and then click against PAYG Withholding, then click OK.

6. **Save your incredibly fantastic work by clicking OK again.**

   You've done it!

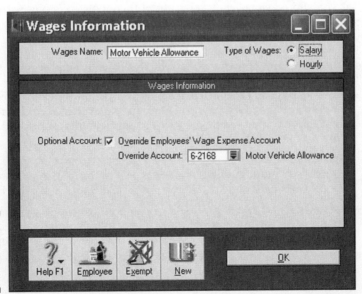

Figure 9-4: Setting up optional accounts.

Setting up allowances

There are a lot of different types of employee allowances — most of which you probably wish you didn't have to pay — including motor vehicle allowance, tool allowance, uniform allowance and so on. Although the standard payroll category list doesn't include any allowances, it's not difficult to add them.

Follow the instructions for creating a new wages category as I explain in the preceding section. Click Salary as the Type of Wages and, if you want the allowance to show up as a separate item to wages expense on your Profit & Loss report, click the Optional Account box and select the relevant expense account.

Setting up standard pays

The idea of a standard pay is you can set up a default for each employee's regular pay, specifying how many hours an employee works each week, what allowances they receive, whether the employees contribute additional superannuation and so on. These details then flow through to the Process Payroll window, ready to record each employee's pay automatically.

Of course, you can still edit an employee's pay before you record it (for example, if they get holiday pay or sick pay), but the idea is that the default makes a good starting point. To view an employee's standard pay, go to their card, click the Payroll Details tab and head for the Standard Pay side menu. What you should see is every element of the employee's pay, with amounts against each payroll category that applies, similar to what comes up in Figure 9-5.

Here are tips about applying standard pays to your employees:

- ✔ **Missing payroll categories.** If a payroll category doesn't show up in the employee's standard pay, you need to mark off all payroll categories that apply to that employee (wages, entitlements, super and so on). You do that under the relevant side menus.

- ✔ **Part-timers.** If the Hours Per Pay Frequency doesn't come up right in an employee's standard pay, you need to go to the Wages side menu of that employee's card and change the number of Hours in Weekly Pay Period.

- ✔ **Casuals.** If you employ casuals whose hours vary every week, get wise and change the number of hours in the Hours column of their standard pay to zero hours. That way you don't risk accidentally paying a casual for hours that they didn't work.

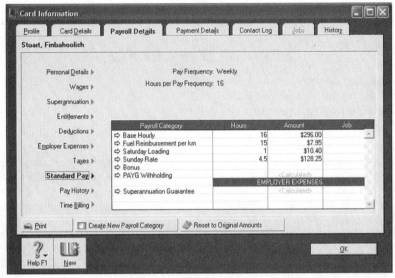

Figure 9-5:
A standard
pay for a
casual
employee
who
regularly
works
weekends.

By the way, if you're not sure whether your standard pays are all set up correctly, the proof of the pudding is this: If you find yourself making the same change to an employee's pay every pay period (for example, changing the amount of an allowance or deduction), then this means that their standard pay isn't right and you need to fix it.

Multi-tasking gone mad

It's not only wonderful mid-30s women like myself who are so magnificent at multi-tasking No, in these days of harsh economic rationalism, a tram driver has to hand out tickets as well as take money, a waiter works as a higher-paid breakfast chef on the weekends, and a receptionist may have to cover for the bookkeeper from time to time. So, how do you cater for employees who do different work at different rates?

The trick is to enter the rate the employee most often earns as the Hourly Base Pay in their card. Then create additional payroll categories for each different rate they earn. For example, to properly account for my fictitious waiter-turned-chef, I would create an extra wages category called Breakfast Chef, and enter the hourly rate as a Fixed Hourly Rate. Then two payroll categories would pop up on the pay for this employee, each with a different hourly rate.

Keeping a log of events

The Contact Log is a handy place to store info about your employees. To see how it works, go to the Contact Log, highlight an employee's name in the Card File, click Log and then New.

This log works like a notebook, providing a space to record an employee's holidays, sick leave, employment anniversary or any other important events. I find that, as the years go by, the log builds up a complete picture of important info about an employee, and is the ideal record if there's ever any confusion about how much holiday or sick leave is due.

The only thing that sometimes clutters up the Contact Log is if your Preferences are set up so that every pay transaction appears in the log. To avoid this, go to Setup⇨Preferences, then click the Banking tab. Remove the tick from Make a Contact Log Entry for Every Spend Money Transaction. Then purge any existing contact logs for a clean start (see your MYOB software user guide for more details about purging contact logs).

Pay Time

Open wide, come inside, it's play time. Sorry, I mean *pay time*. Follow the instructions below to record your first employee pay.

Doing your first pay run

When I describe how to enter your first employee pay, I assume that you've already set up the employee's card, along with their basic payroll categories (as explained earlier in this chapter). With this underway, you're ready to record your first pay run:

1. **From the Payroll command centre, click Process Payroll.**

2. **Decide whether you want to pay all employees in the one hit, or pay one employee only.**

   Usually, it's best to process all pays as a single batch. The only reason you would pay one employee separately is if you were processing a pay adjustment or termination pay.

3. **Select the Pay Frequency, pick your dates and click Next.**

   The Pay Frequency refers to whatever you chose as the Pay Frequency in each employee's card. You have to do pays as separate batches (weekly, fortnightly, monthly and so on). For example, even if payday falls due on the same day for both your weekly and fortnightly employees, you do two separate batches.

With dates, be careful to get them right. The Payment Date is usually one day after the Pay Period End date.

4. **Make sure that all employees you want to pay are on this list, and that employees who have left or resigned aren't on this list.**

The Select & Edit Employee's Pay window shows a summary of all the employees in this pay run, similar to Figure 9-6.

If an employee is missing from this list, it's probably because you set up their Pay Frequency incorrectly (for example, selecting Monthly instead of Weekly). Go to the Payroll Details tab of their card to fix this up. On the other hand, if you get an employee who has long since departed showing up in the list, fix this error by going to that employee's card and making it inactive.

5. **Edit the pays for any employees whose standard pay was different from normal. Then click Record and OK.**

If any employees have variations to their standard pay for this period (maybe they did some overtime, went on leave or had a sickie), zoom in on their pay and fix it up. You can see how an individual pay looks in Figure 9-7.

The first section of each pay shows wages. It's here that you change the hours; for example, adding overtime hours, inserting hours next to Sick Pay and reducing the number of hours next to Base Hourly, or adding reimbursements.

The second and third sections of an employee's pay shows entitlements and superannuation. If you've set up these payroll categories properly, both sections should calculate automatically.

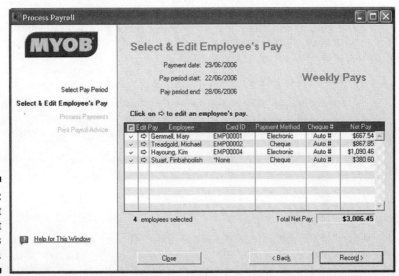

Figure 9-6:
The Select & Edit Employee's Pay window.

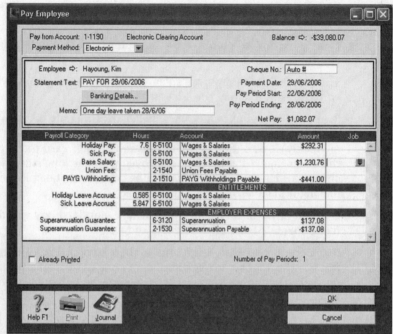

Figure 9-7:
An individual
employee
pay.

6. **Depending on what payment method or methods apply, click Print Paycheques, Prepare Electronic Payments or Spend Money to process the payment batch. Then click Next.**

   Eek! I wish I could make this sound less technical. But here's the rub: If you pay employees by cheque, click Print Paycheques; if you pay employees electronically, click Prepare Electronic Payments; if you draw a single cash cheque once a week or you pay direct from your cash drawer, click Spend Money. (For more detail about electronic payments, make your way to Chapter 13.)

7. **Print your pay advices.**

   You're almost there. You can either click Display Payroll Advice to view and print payslips for all employees, or, if you've created a special customised form for payslips, click Print Customised Payslips.

8. **Click Finish.**

Working with timesheets

When MYOB software released versions 9 (Premier) and 15 (Accounting Plus) and payroll switched to batch processing (rather than recording one employee pay at a time), employers with lots of casuals protested that this new system was a nightmare, because every employee's pay varied from week to week. In response to these howls of complaint, Version 10 (Premier) and 16 (Accounting Plus) offer the elegant solution of entering employees' times into a timesheet, and these timesheets then carry across into payroll.

I like this new way of working because it offers the best of both worlds. You get to record timesheets for casual employees, but you don't have to re-enter details for employees whose pay stays the same each week.

If you employ casuals, check out how the whole system works: Go to Enter Timesheet in the Payroll command centre and for each employee, create a new timesheet with their name and how many hours they worked. (If this is the first time you're viewing the Timesheet menu, you're prompted to click the Preference called 'I use Timesheets for Payroll'.) You can see how a timesheet looks in Figure 9-8.

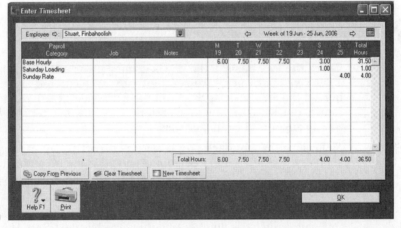

Figure 9-8: Timesheets work well if you employ lots of casuals.

You'll probably find you can follow your nose and make it all work, but here are some tips that may help out:

✔ For most employees, you can save time with future pays by clicking the Copy From Previous button on the bottom-left of the Enter Timesheet window. This way all the payroll categories come up automatically and all you have to do is change the number of hours against each category.

✔ If the pay week starts on the wrong day (for example, a Monday rather than a Tuesday), you need to go to Setup⇨Preferences, click the System tab, then select the day your pay week starts.

✔ Always press Tab or Enter after entering figures in the Hours columns. (If you just type the figure in the column and click OK, your changes don't go through.)

✔ You can use timesheets to adjust standard pays for salaried employees. For example, if a salaried employee takes 8 hours' sick leave one pay period, you can record a timesheet that shows how many hours of sick leave were taken and when. This info then carries across into their pay (you'll still need to manually adjust their Salary, however).

✔ Remember to enter hours as decimals. For example, if an employee works 8 hours and 15 minutes, this actually means they worked eight and a quarter hours. You should key this in as 8.25 hours, not 8.15 hours. (Maybe now you'll regret all those times when you went surfin' instead of going to maths class . . .)

Keeping everything sweet

If you're having problems getting an employee's pay to calculate correctly, here are some tricks:

✔ **Check the tax.** If the tax doesn't come up right, check the tax scale you selected for this employee in the Taxes side menu, found under the Payroll Details tab of their card.

✔ **Check the Pay Basis.** If the pay is coming up as a ridiculous amount of a few cents per week, chances are that you've entered an hourly rate but set the Pay Basis as Salary in the employee's card. No matter how radical our industrial relations reform is, you won't get away with paying anyone 35 cents per week.

✔ **Make sure the standard pay is set up correctly.** Regular payments such as allowances and deductions should come up automatically — if they don't, go to the employee's card and change their standard pay.

✔ **Remember to record entitlements.** If you paid holiday or sick pay on this pay, reduce the number of hours listed against Base Hourly and then fill in the hours against Holiday Pay or Sick Pay instead.

✔ **Check super is calculating correctly.** Make sure that the Superannuation Guarantee category appears on every pay (even if the amount next to this category is zero). The only reason for this category not to appear is if you forget to select superannuation in the employee's setup — a big mistake! However, don't worry if super comes up as zero in the first or second pay period of the month. That's because MYOB software (with true brilliance) doesn't calculate super until employees hit the $450 monthly threshold.

✔ **Make sure the working week is the right number of hours.** Always make sure the total hours come up correctly. You don't want a 40-hour week to show up on each employee's pay if the standard working week according to their award is actually 38 hours.

Deleting and reversing pays

Employee pays differ from most other transactions in MYOB software in that after you record them, you can't change them. Your only solution is to delete or reverse the pay completely and start again:

1. **Go to the Payroll command centre and choose Transaction Journal.**

2. **Scroll up and down to find the offending pay and then click the zoom arrow on the left to display it.**

3. **On the top menu bar, choose either Edit⇨Delete Transaction or Edit⇨Reverse Transaction (depending on what option comes up).**

Sounds kinda easy, but things get a little trickier if you get a warning saying *'One or more parts of this journal entry have been reconciled'* when you zoom in on the transaction. Although reversing this transaction would be okay, things aren't so straightforward if your only option under the Edit menu is to delete the transaction (if you delete a transaction that has already been reconciled, you'll throw your bank or payroll clearing account out of kilter).

In this kind of situation, I usually prefer to leave the pay as is instead of deleting it. However, if the mistake is fundamental (maybe the total amount was right but the wrong pay categories or the leave accruals were wrong), then what I do is temporarily change my preferences so that that the option appears to *reverse* the offending pay transaction.

Here's how you get a reversal to happen:

1. **Go to Setup⇨Preferences and click the Security tab. Click against Transactions CAN'T be Changed; They Must be Reversed.**

2. **Zoom in on the pay transaction you want to reverse. Go to Edit on the top menu bar and select Reverse Transaction.**

   Aha! What was black is now white, what was positive is now a minus.

3. **Click Record.**

4. **Re-enter the pay transaction, correctly this time.**

5. **Go to Reconcile Accounts as if you're about to reconcile your bank account and check that the reversal appears in the Deposits column and your re-entered transaction in the Withdrawal column.**

   See, in the real world, the two transactions cancel one another out.

6. **Return to Setup⇨Preferences and click the Security tab. Unclick Transactions CAN'T be Changed; They Must be Reversed.**

   Don't skip this last step. Before continuing with other work, you must reset your preferences!

Payment summaries in a flash

It may seem pretty radical the first time you do it, but by far the easiest and quickest way to produce payment summaries is to print them on plain paper and then send a disk or CD to the Australian Taxation Office.

All you have to do is click Print Payment Summaries and follow the prompts. For plain paper certificates, you'll be prompted to save a special file that it calls 'Empdupe.a01'.

This doesn't refer to dupes or dopes, and although it may seem a rather bizarre title, don't change the file name — you'll send the tax office into total confusion. I recommend you save this file first into your MYOB program folder and then onto a disk or CD.

Don't worry; this Empdupe file doesn't contain any confidential business information. It's not a backup or summary of your company data, rather it only contains the information that is on any ordinary payment summary.

As part of this process, MYOB software prompts you to print a special form called a Magnetic Media Information form. This is the form that you send to the tax office's processing centre along with your Empdupe disk.

The form also asks for a weird code called a Media Identifier. This is kind of like your own password to make sure they don't confuse your disk with someone else's disk — in the same way newborn babes are tagged with plastic bracelets in hospitals so they don't get them mixed up. I always use the first six digits of my phone number for this code.

When you're finished with these forms, all you have to do is photocopy the payment summaries so that you have copies for your own records and distribute the original copies to your employees.

Siesta Time

I reckon that tracking holidays and sick days is the trickiest part of managing payroll. That's not to say that it isn't straightforward, it's just that your success rate relies on how you set up the whole thing.

Setting up for holidays

Before you can be sure holidays are going to work properly, you need to check that Holiday Leave Accrual is set up correctly. Here's what you do:

1. **Choose Payroll Categories, click the Entitlements tab and double-click the Holiday Leave Accrual category.**

2. **If you have hourly employees, check that the entitlement is calculated on a percentage basis.**

   If your employees work on an hourly rate, click against Equals 7.6923 Percent of Gross Hours. (This sounds like a weird figure, but it translates into 20 days of holiday per year. This is the standard amount of holiday leave most employees receive.) To see how this looks, see Figure 9-9.

3. **If you have salaried employees, create a new entitlement called Holiday Leave Acc Salaried.**

   If you have both hourly and salaried employees on your payroll, then you're going to need two Holiday Leave Accrual categories. Change the name of the Holiday Leave Accrual category so it's called Hol Leave Accrual Hrly and call the new category Hol Leave Accrual Slry.

4. **For salaried employees, calculate how many hours entitlement they receive each pay period and then edit the Hol Leave Accrual Slry category so that it calculates this number of hours per pay period.**

   Here's an example. Suppose a salaried employee is due four weeks per year. If they work a 38-hour week, that's 4 x 38, which equals 152 hours per year. If they get paid fortnightly, work with 152 divided by 26. So the answer is 5.846 hours per Pay Period. (Ah, don't you just love maths?)

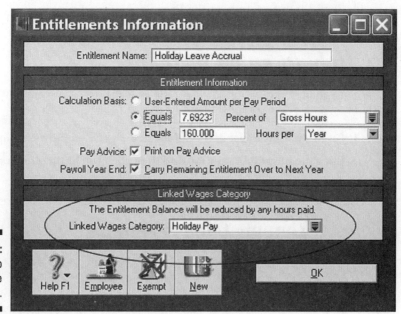

Figure 9-9:
Setting up holiday leave entitlements.

5. **For each holiday category, click the check boxes Print on Pay Advice and Carry Remaining Entitlement Over to Next Year.**

I find it works best if you print how much holiday time employees are due on their pay advices. Certainly, you need to click Carry Remaining Entitlement Over to Next Year, otherwise holiday leave goes back to zero when you hit 30 June.

6. **Make sure the Linked Wages Category is Holiday Pay.**

The Linked Wages Category for each holiday leave entitlement category should be Holiday Pay, as shown in Figure 9-9. If it's not, change it now.

7. **For each holiday leave entitlement category, click the Employee button, select which employees receive that kind of entitlement, then click OK.**

To select employees, click in the column against their names.

8. **For hourly employees, click Exempt to select any wages categories that are exempt from accruing holiday pay.**

I talk more about avoiding overpayments in the section 'Making sure you don't overpay' later in this chapter.

9. **Click OK to record and save your changes.**

10. **Click Close to return to the Payroll command centre.**

Catching up on holidays

When you first set up holiday leave, don't forget to set up employees who already have leave owed to them.

1. **Go to the Cards List and double-click on the employee's name.**

2. **Click the Payroll Details tab and then click the Entitlements side menu.**

Keeping things to yourself

Payroll information is sensitive. There's no better way to create friction between employees than have them compare wages with one another, especially with family businesses (where the children of the employers so often end up with a sweetheart deal). However, not only is payroll information sensitive, some of it is actually protected by the Privacy Act and, in particular, you're obliged to keep employee tax file numbers secure.

The only sure way to do this is to password-protect the whole of your company file and then set up sub-passwords with restricted access to the payroll section of your file. I talk all about passwords in Chapter 14.

3. Enter the total number of hours of leave due in the Carry Over column.

Remember to express these figures in hours — not dollars or weeks. For example, if you're setting up an employee who is owed two weeks' holiday and that person works a 38-hour week, the number of hours in the Carry Over column should be 76.

Making sure you don't overpay

Does this heading make your day? Okay, read on . . .

If you accrue holiday or sick leave on a percentage of wages paid, then you need to be careful that employees don't build up leave on miscellaneous payments, such as allowances, bonuses, holiday leave loading, overtime or reimbursements. (Otherwise, they'll end up taking one week's holiday for every four week's work, a privilege normally reserved for public servants.)

To check you're not paying more holidays or sick days than you should be, go to Payroll Categories, click the Entitlements tab and one by one, open up any Leave Accrual categories that calculate on a percentage basis. Click the Exempt button at the bottom of each category and mark off all the different wages categories that are exempt from accruing leave, as shown in Figure 9-10.

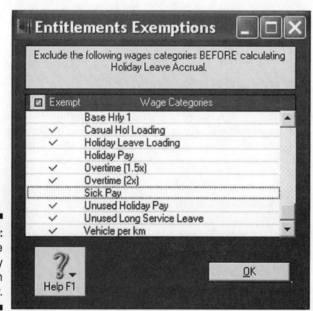

Figure 9-10: Making sure you don't pay too much holiday pay.

Chucking a sickie

Dawn breaks to the sight of blue skies, a touch of wind and the perfect surf. Life is too sweet to spend working and so it's time to chuck a sickie. It's another great Australian institution (if you're not an employer, that is).

Setting up sick pay and sick leave accrual is exactly the same as setting up holiday pay and holiday leave accrual, which I cover in the preceding sections of this chapter. So, I won't bore you to death by explaining it all again here. Instead I bring you back to life by pointing out some salient things that relate only to sick leave:

- As I explain in 'Setting up for holidays' earlier in this chapter, 20 days of holiday works out as 7.6923 percent of gross hours. So, ten days of sick leave works out as 3.846 percent, five days works out as 1.923 percent and so on. (I hope you love maths as much as I do.) Note that under the new WorkChoices legislation, the standard amount of sick leave is 10 days per year.

- I don't normally select the box Print on Pay Advice. I reckon that if employees aren't told how much sick leave they're due on every pay slip, this is probably a good thing.

- Sick Leave Accrual gets linked to Sick Pay, just as Holiday Leave Accrual gets linked to Holiday Pay.

- When an employee rings in with double pneumonia, a broken leg and a fractured skull, this is not a good enough excuse. They must work, work, work! (Oh dear, my Calvinistic discipline doesn't die easily.)

Celebrating anniversaries

Employee anniversaries are important things to remember. Maybe an employee's sick leave accrual increases from five days to eight days per year; maybe you've agreed to give an employee a pay rise after one year; maybe you schedule performance appraisals at each anniversary.

Here's how to create a contact alert so that you get a reminder whenever an employee anniversary comes around:

1. Create a contact alert for each employee's hiring date anniversary.

I'm not talking about weddings or romantic assignations — I'm talking about the date you hired the employee. Go to each employee's card, one by one, and click Log. Click New to create a new log for this employee and then, in Notes for this log, type the memo 'Employment Anniversary'.

As the Recontact Date, enter the date of this employee's next anniversary.

2. **Throughout the year, keep checking the Contact Alert tab in your To Do List.**

   When employee anniversaries come around, a reminder appears under the Contact Alert tab of your To Do List.

3. **After you've done whatever it is you have to do, change the Recontact Date to the next year.**

   To do this, you go to the log entry in that employee's card and change the Recontact Date to another year in advance.

How Super, It's Super . . .

Superannuation is a big deal, not just in terms of how much money is involved, but also because of the onus on small business to get super payments right. The superannuation audits I've experienced are sombre indeed and auditors aren't shy about delivering hefty fines for the slightest transgression.

Even the date when you have to pay superannuation is crucial. If your super payments don't reach employees' funds by 30 June, then you can't claim them as a tax deduction for that year. And if they don't reach the funds by 28 July, you will never be able to claim them as a tax deduction. You will also be fined.

So the moral of the tale is this: Be diligent, set up superannuation in MYOB software correctly and pay up frequently.

Setting up super

In order to be certain that superannuation works correctly, you should double-check your settings. Here's how:

1. **Choose Payroll Categories, click the Superannuation tab and double-click the Superannuation Guarantee category.**

2. **Check that the Linked Expense Account is an account called Superannuation Expense.**

If it isn't, select Superannuation Expense as your Linked Expense account (this account starts with the number 6). If you don't see this account in your list, head over to your Accounts List and create one now.

3. Check the Linked Payable Account is an account called Superannuation Payable.

This bit is important to get right, so be careful. Pick Superannuation Payable as your Linked Payable account (this account starts with the number 2). Again, if you don't see this account in your list, go to your Accounts List and add it.

4. Check that the Contribution Type shows up as Superannuation Guarantee (expense).

5. Click Print on Pay Advice.

When you click here, the amount of superannuation prints on employee pay slips. (I recommend you do this, because it's the law.)

6. Enter the current percentage in the Calculation Basis field.

Enter the current super percentage as a Percent of Gross Wages (usually 9 percent, unless your arrangement with your employees specifies otherwise).

7. Make sure the Limit is set to No Limit and that the minimum wages threshold is $450.

If an employee earns less than $450 a month, you usually don't have to pay super. However, some awards have a lower threshold than this, so you may want to double-check the fine print of the relevant award before completing this step.

8. Click Exempt to mark off any wages categories that are exempt from super.

Make sure that you mark off all the wages categories that are exempt from superannuation, such as bonuses or overtime. Take a look at 'Making sure you don't pay too much super' later in this chapter to find out more.

9. Check your work and click OK.

Finally! I don't know about you, but I'm exhausted. But hey, before you click OK, check your screen against Figure 9-11 to make sure everything looks fine.

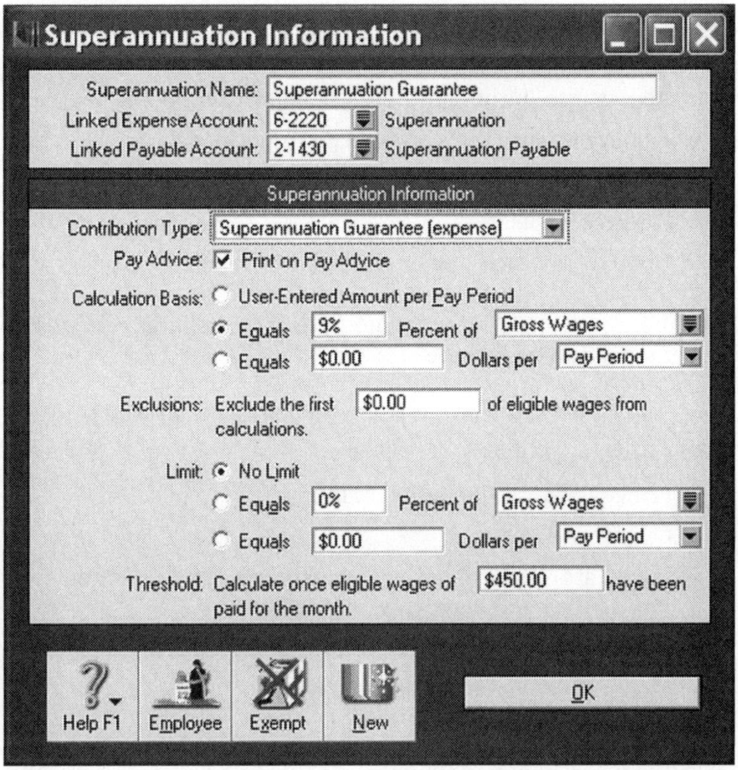

Superannuation Information

Superannuation Name: Superannuation Guarantee
Linked Expense Account: 6-2220 ▼ Superannuation
Linked Payable Account: 2-1430 ▼ Superannuation Payable

Superannuation Information

Contribution Type: Superannuation Guarantee [expense] ▼
Pay Advice: ☑ Print on Pay Advice
Calculation Basis: ○ User-Entered Amount per Pay Period
⊙ Equals 9% Percent of Gross Wages ▼
○ Equals $0.00 Dollars per Pay Period ▼

Exclusions: Exclude the first $0.00 of eligible wages from calculations.

Limit: ⊙ No Limit
○ Equals 0% Percent of Gross Wages ▼
○ Equals $0.00 Dollars per Pay Period ▼

Threshold: Calculate once eligible wages of $450.00 have been paid for the month.

Help F1   Employee   Exempt   New   OK

Figure 9-11:
Setting up super-annuation.

Making sure you don't pay too much super

Maybe it's my Scottish blood, but I hate paying more than I have to. I especially hate seeing my clients do the same. It's astounding how often I come across clients who pay too much super on behalf of their employees.

The trick is to remember this: Superannuation is only due on what is termed ordinary time earnings (OTE). If you like, you can contact the Australian Taxation Office for a detailed document explaining what OTE is all about. However, this fine example of English double-speak might be more understandable were it written in Swahili, and so in the interests of your blood pressure, I summarise the main points in this section.

In most cases (with the exception of a few obscure awards), wages categories that you do need to pay superannuation on include:

- Allowances (although there are some exceptions)
- Regular bonuses that are linked to performance
- Casual loadings
- Director's fees
- Holiday pay, sick pay or long service leave.

Now here's the good news. In most cases, wages that you *don't* need to pay superannuation on include:

- Annual holiday leave loading (usually 17.5 percent)
- Christmas bonuses
- Fringe benefits (including hair cuts)
- Overtime payments
- Payments in lieu of notice (for example, if you offer an employee $1,000 just so they will leave now, not later)
- Payments for any holiday or long service leave owing at termination
- Maternity or paternity leave payments
- Redundancy payments
- Reimbursement of expenses (includes mileage, travel, food and so on)
- Workers comp payments.

To make sure that you're not paying super when you don't have to:

1. **Go to your Payroll Categories list.**

2. **Click the Superannuation tab and double-click your Superannuation Guarantee category.**

3. **Click the Exempt button and make sure that all wages categories that don't attract super are marked.**

Giving your employees a Super Choice

Under the Super Choice legislation, you need to give your employees a choice about what super fund they subscribe to. To do this, you need to give all eligible employees a *Standard choice form* within 28 days of starting employment.

You may find that Super Choice doesn't apply to your workplace. Ineligible employees include certain public sector employees, employees working under a Federal workplace agreement, and in certain circumstances, employees who *aren't* employed by a corporation and who work under a state award. For more information about Super Choice and how it affects your obligations as an employer, visit www.superchoice.gov.au.

The outcome of this legislation for you as an employer is that you may end up paying super on behalf of your employees into lots of different funds. If this happens to you, you'll probably find that subscribing to MYOB M-Powered Superannuation works best. For more about this service, see the following section 'Subscribing to M-Powered Superannuation'.

By the way, MYOB software offers you a quick way to print a Standard choice form for an employee, complete with your own details as well as their details. Just go to the Payroll Details tab of the employee's card, click the Superannuation side menu and click Print Superannuation Choice Form.

Subscribing to M-Powered Superannuation

The idea behind M-Powered Superannuation is that you can go to Pay Superannuation, see how much super you owe, click a few buttons to confirm these amounts and within a couple of minutes, complete the process that electronically transfers funds from your bank account to the bank accounts of the various superannuation funds to which your employees belong, complete with electronic remittance advices for each payment. Pretty amazing.

Whether M-Powered Superannuation is the way to go for your business depends partly on how many employees you have and how many different funds you have to make payments to. Currently, the cost of this service is a modest $1 per employee per month (it's the same cost whether you pay monthly or quarterly). Your initial reaction may be 'Why incur this extra expense when it doesn't take long to do it myself?' Fair enough, but if you pay wages to a bookkeeper, do your sums to see how long it takes them to report for and pay superannuation every month or quarter. Chances are the $1 fee is quite a bargain.

To subscribe to M-Powered Superannuation, click Pay Superannuation, followed by Tell Me More. Follow the prompts to complete your online application. The process takes a couple of weeks to finalise (banks are involved, after all) so don't expect to get everything to happen in an instant. After your application is processed, you're asked to activate the service and fix up a couple of settings in your company file. And that's all you have to do.

By the way, although M-Powered Superannuation supports most Australian super funds, it doesn't support self-managed super funds (otherwise knows as DIY funds). You'll have to send off super payments for employees with DIY funds using your trusty old-fashioned chequebook.

Reporting on how much super you owe

One of the neat things about using the payroll part of MYOB software is that you can print reports saying how much super you owe at the drop of a hat. How you print this report varies, depending on whether you subscribe to M-Powered Superannuation, or not.

The best report to see how much super you owe is the Superannuation Accrual by Fund [Summary] report, found under the Payroll tab of your Reports menu. Simply pick your date range and click Print (if you want to print a separate page for each fund, go to the Finishing tab on the report customisation window and click Separate Pages). You can see how this report looks in Figure 9-12.

If you subscribe to M-Powered Superannuation, this report is all you need. When you're ready to pay super, MYOB software handles the rest of the reporting side of things, informing the super fund of how much you're paying, who the payments are for, and so on.

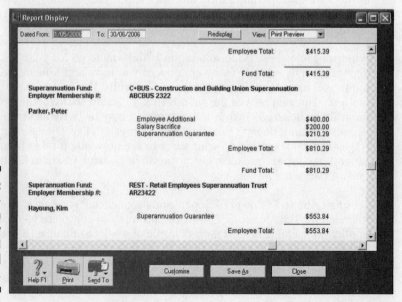

Figure 9-12: The Super-annuation Accrual by Fund [Summary] report.

If you *don't* subscribe to M-Powered Superannuation, you may find that the Superannuation Accrual by Fund [Summary] report falls short in that it doesn't include the employee's membership number. That's okay if your employees only subscribe to one fund, because you can print an Employee Advice Summary report and use this report as your remittance when paying super (this report *does* include employee membership numbers). However, if your employees belong to more than fund, you have three choices:

- ✔ Print an Employee Advice Summary report (which includes employee membership numbers) and copy the information by hand onto the forms the super fund (or funds) send you.
- ✔ Display the Superannuation Accrual by Fund [Summary] report and then send it to Excel. In Excel, insert the employee membership numbers. Then use this report as your remittance when sending off payments to the super fund (or funds).
- ✔ Print the Superannuation Accrual by Fund [Summary] report and then write the employee membership numbers on by hand.

Remembering those who come and go

When you print your superannuation report, you may even find a tiny amount of super outstanding for someone who has long since gone. But guess what? Even that Irish student who came one Monday and left the following Tuesday should have signed up for a superannuation fund. Seems ridiculous, but then think of the people making up these laws.

Don't be tempted to forget these passing souls. If someone has earned more than $450 with you in any one month, you have to pay super for them. Send it to the ATO Super Guarantee Holding Fund and they'll gladly take it for safekeeping.

When you've paid up your super, store a copy of your Superannuation Remittance report in a safe place, so that you have a record of how much you've paid, and why.

Paying super (if you're M-Powered)

The best way to record your superannuation payments depends on whether you subscribe to M-Powered Superannuation or not. If you subscribe to M-Powered Superannuation, read on. Otherwise, skip to the heading entitled 'Paying super (if you're not M-Powered)'.

Choosing a fund for your employees

Sooner or later you'll strike an employee who doesn't belong to a super fund or an employee who chooses not to nominate their own fund on their super choice form. What this means for you is that you're meant to send this employee's super to your 'default' employer fund. That's fine if you're already signed up with a fund. However, if you're not, you have to go through the process of applying to a fund, which means doing the research, looking at the returns different funds give and filling in all the forms.

If you find yourself in this position, then MYOB's Default Superannuation Fund may be the way to

go. In order to cut down on the hassle and extra paperwork of applying to a new fund, MYOB software made an alliance with a fund called Spectrum Superannuation. The performance of Spectrum Superannuation compares pretty well against other funds, and the application process is straightforward.

To apply to Spectrum Superannuation, go to www.myob.com.au and search on 'MYOB Default Fund Application Form'.

Assuming you've already got M-Powered Superannuation up and running, here's how to process your superannuation payments at the end of each month or quarter:

1. **Go to your Reports menu and print a Superannuation Accrual by Category report.**

   This report gives totals for all super categories, including salary sacrifice and superannuation guarantee. Add up the category totals to see how much you owe in total.

2. **Go to the Payroll command centre and click Pay Superannuation. Select the account you want to pay the super from and enter the date range.**

   Remember that the bank account you choose has to the one that you authorised for M-Powered Superannuation. Also, be precise with your dates: Make sure you enter the first and last dates of the month or quarter for which you're paying super in the Dated From and Dated To fields, but stick the current date in the Date field.

3. **Confirm which payments you want to process by clicking in the far right-hand column next to each Amount.**

   Unless you have a good reason otherwise, click against every name and amount that shows up. You can see how this might look in Figure 9-13.

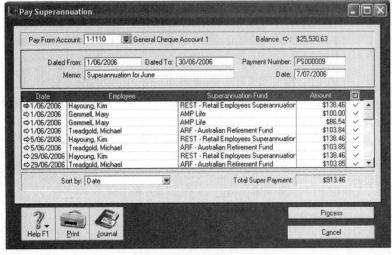

Figure 9-13:
Paying your
super-
annuation
obligations
using
M-Powered
Super-
annuation.

4. **Check that the total payment you're about to process matches the total of your Superannuation Accrual by Category report that you printed in Step 1. If not, figure out the cause of the difference.**

   Watch out. If you haven't selected a fund name for every employee, your totals won't match. If an employee doesn't have a super fund specified in their card, their name simply doesn't appear in the Pay Superannuation window. Scary stuff.

5. **Everything looks hunky-dory? Then click Process, come up with your password when prompted and authorise the payment.**

   This bit is pretty straightforward. Do make sure that you're connected to the Internet though, otherwise your payment won't go through.

Paying super (if you're not M-Powered)

As I explain in the preceding section, the best way to record your superannuation payments depends on whether you subscribe to M-Powered Superannuation. Here I'm assuming that you *don't* subscribe to M-Powered Superannuation and that you've already sent off cheques to your employees' superannuation funds.

To record your superannuation payment or payments, go to the Payroll command centre and click Pay Liabilities. You then see a window that looks very similar to the regular Spend Money window. Now follow these steps:

1. Enter the cheque details in the same way you do for a regular Spend Money transaction.

Use your instincts. Complete the Cheque No., Payment Date, Supplier (the name of the superannuation fund) and Memo fields.

2. Select Superannuation as your Liability Type.

3. Ask to Sort by Superannuation Fund and select the date range.

Pick your date range carefully. For example, if you're in October 06 and you're paying superannuation for the first quarter, the date range needs to be 01/07/06 to 30/09/06. You should be able to see all superannuation amounts that were due for that date range, grouped by fund.

4. Select all employees you're going to pay.

You want to record a separate transaction for each fund, so only click against employee names for one fund at a time. Your transaction should look something like mine, shown in Figure 9-14.

5. Click Record and then repeat this process for each fund.

When you click Record, the employees who have been paid disappear from the Pay Liabilities window. You can then repeat the process for each fund until no more names appear. (If an employee's name does still show up, this almost certainly means you forgot to pay their super or you've missed recording a payment.)

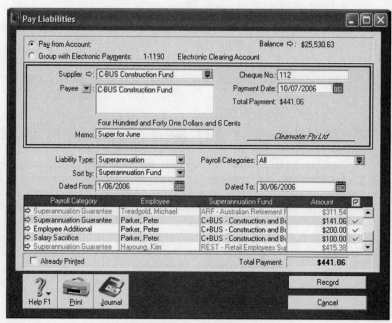

Figure 9-14: Recording your superannuation payment using the Pay Liabilities window.

Getting super to balance

In theory, if you pay super from either the Pay Superannuation or the Pay Liabilities windows, then your super will always balance. However, because I'm a persnickety fusspot kind of person, I like to make sure it really, really does balance.

The quick and dirty way to do this check is to display your Balance Sheet for the month or quarter you just paid and look at the balance of your Superannuation Payable account. This balance represents the amount you actually paid. For example, if you paid $2,010 superannuation in October for the months July, August and September, then you can expect the balance of Superannuation Payable in your September Balance Sheet to be $2,010 as well.

If super doesn't seem to balance, then return to Pay Superannuation (if you use M-Powered Super) or Pay Liabilities (if you don't use M-Powered Super). This time, as the date range, enter 1 July for Dated From and the date up to which you've just paid as your Dated To. See if any old super payments for previous months pop up. If they do, chances are you missed these payments and that's why your superannuation isn't balancing.

By the way, if you do all this and you still can't get super to balance, it's probably time to call the cavalry. Your accountant or an MYOB Certified Consultant is your best bet to save the day.

The Joy of Taxes

I tossed up whether to call this section 'Death by Taxes' or instead 'The Joy of Taxes'. I settled on the latter, despite my reservations.

Why? Because even though Albert Einstein once said, 'The hardest thing in the world to understand is income tax', this complexity is the very reason why everyone loves MYOB software so much. Throw away those tax tables, hurl your wages book in the bin and arrange a party for 30 June.

Checking your tax tables

Tax tables don't have anything to do with tax executives sitting in a flash boardroom. Rather they're special formulas for calculating Pay As You Go (otherwise known as Pay All You've Got) on employee wages. Generally, tax tables stay relatively static from one year to the next but sometimes they include major changes.

✔ If you subscribe to MYOB Cover, you receive tax table updates or product upgrades automatically every time tax tables change.

✔ If you don't subscribe, you either have to upgrade to the latest version of MYOB software or, if the option exists, purchase the tax tables only. (Whether you're able to purchase tax tables only or you have to upgrade to a new version seems to depend partly on the extent of changes and partly on MYOB company strategy. Your guess is as good as mine as to what will happen in years to come.)

✔ To check whether your tax tables are current, go to your Company Data Auditor and look at the Payroll Tax Tables Date.

✔ To load new tax tables, click Load Tax Tables from the Company Data Auditor.

Paying as you go

As you approach the 28th day of each month or each quarter, it's time to pay your PAYG tax (this is part of your Business Activity Statement, if you're registered for GST). Here's what to do to see how much you have to pay:

1. **Go to Reports, click Payroll and highlight the Employees Register Summary report.**

2. **Click Customise to specify which month or quarter you want figures for.**

3. **Click Print.**

   Your report should look something like the one shown in Figure 9-15.

4. **Look at the total of the Taxes column to see how much tax you need to pay.**

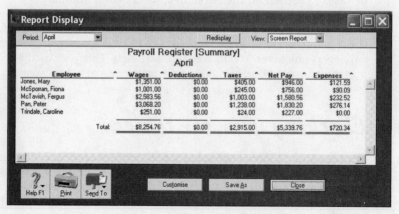

Figure 9-15: Your Employees Register Summary report.

The Register Summary report is important, and one of the few reports I recommend you print out and keep in a safe place. (You may need to refer to it when it comes time to reconcile wages and payment summaries at the end of the year.)

Recording tax payments

If you're registered for GST, then your PAYG tax payment is now part of your monthly or quarterly tax payment that you submit with each Business Activity Statement. I explain how to record this tax payment in Chapter 12.

If you're not registered for GST or you lodge Instalment Activity Statements separately on the first and second months of each quarter, record your PAYG tax payment in Spend Money. Complete the payment as normal, selecting the ATO as the Card, but select PAYG Payable as your Allocation Account. Detail the period you're paying for in the Memo field.

Part III
Moving On

Glenn Lumsden

The new version of MYOB software for people who say they'll back up their files 'tomorrow'.

In this part . . .

In the third part of this book, I assume you're already up and running. Hopefully, you've set up your accounts, made a few sales, recorded some expenses and maybe even had a go at reconciling your bank account. And so now, it's time to get down to some more serious stuff. You're going to find out how to fill in your first Business Activity Statement (oh joy of joys), how to back up your data (lightning can strike at any time) and how to get your business forms looking good.

In this part I also discuss a few things that should make your life much easier, such as M-Powered Payments, online banking and how to knock up whizzbang custom reports. I also dedicate an entire chapter to the topic of understanding your Profit & Loss and Balance Sheet reports, and how to analyse where you're making (or losing!) money in your business.

Chapter 10

Looking Good with Forms

- -

In This Chapter

▶ Understanding what forms are all about

▶ Adding new text and formatting it

▶ Getting creative with boxes, lines and pictures

▶ Mastering templates

▶ Arming yourself with some tips and tricks (discovered the hard way)

- -

*W*orking with figures can be a little dull sometimes. It's a rare person who gets a kick out of audit trails and bank reconciliations (although I confess to having met a few people who get their excitement that way). So, if you've been finding all this accounting stuff pretty boring until now, it's time to cheer up.

Customising forms is not only pretty easy, but also lots of fun. Forget about searching for numbers and totals, balancing your tax or sweating over your inventory. Instead, this is the chapter where your artistic side can blossom.

So sit back, relax and enjoy!

What Forms Are and How They Work

The idea is this: For every bit of stationery in your business, MYOB software has a corresponding form. You'll find different forms for invoices, mailing labels, purchase orders, customer statements and printed cheques. Although the standard format for all these forms is okay, most people like to refine the formats by adding comments, inserting logos, changing fonts and so on.

If you're wondering why you would bother customising your standard forms, remember that invoices and customer statements are one of the main ways you project your business image to customers. Sending out the standard invoice format without doing a thing to it is rather like turning up at a customer's office in your pyjamas. Not a good look.

So, here's how to dress things up. I show you how to customise forms and make your business stationery look spiffing, spectacular, splendiferous and lots of other things beginning with 'sp'.

Customising Your First Form

Ready to customise your first form? Here goes:

1. **Go to Setup⇨Customise Forms and select the form that you want to customise.**

   You can choose between cheques, paycheques, receipts, invoices, statements and purchase orders.

2. **If relevant, select the version of the form you want to customise from the Layout menu at the top.**

   Most forms have more than one version. For example, when customising invoices, you can choose between several layouts (Service, Professional, Item and so on), and with statements you can choose between Activity or Invoice layouts.

3. **As the Form to Customise, select the template that's closest to what you're looking for.**

   With invoices, purchases and statements, you can pick whether you want to customise a Pre-Printed or a Plain Paper version of this form. Pre-printed layouts don't include lines, boxes or headers (the assumption is that you're using a pre-printed form) but plain paper layouts do.

   If you subscribe to M-Powered Invoices, you'll need to select an M-Powered template when customising invoices or statements. These templates always start with the letters 'MP'.

4. **Click Customise.**

   You're away! You arrive at the rather odd customising window — similar to the one shown in Figure 10-1 — ready for you to do your stuff. (I explain the fiddly details of customising, such as inserting new text, adjusting fonts and adding logos, later in this chapter.)

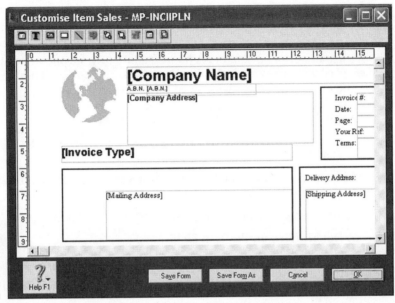

Figure 10-1:
Customising
forms is easy
when you
know how.

5. Experiment with the forms toolbar to find out what each icon does.

See the strip of icons top-left in Figure 10-1? This pretty little darling is
the forms toolbar. Click each icon in turn and see what it does. Try adding
new data fields, inserting new text, adding logos or changing fonts. (For
the moment, I'm suggesting you follow your nose and experiment; you
can get stuck into the mechanics of finetuning later in the chapter.) Don't
worry if you mess something up; it's easy to fix. Once you get the hang
of the different commands, start customising your form so that it includes
your business details and looks the way you want it to.

Whenever you're customising a form, click the Save Form button every
few minutes. This means that you're saving as you go and if your
computer crashes, you won't lose all your work. Alternatively, if you
want to create a new form based on a pre-existing template — and you
don't want to lose what's on the template — then click Save As. You'll be
prompted to enter a short Form File Name made up of a few letters,
followed by a more detailed Description.

6. When you're happy with your changes, click OK.

Click OK to save your changes and leave the customisation window.
Now try printing a sample of the form you just customised so that you
can see it in real life and check out your magnificent work of art.

Inserting new text

If you want to insert text into a form — maybe you want to stick a standard disclaimer at the bottom of each invoice or add your phone number to the top of customer statements — here's what to do (I'm assuming you're already in the Customise Forms window at this point):

1. **Click the capital 'T' on your forms toolbar.**

   The forms toolbar is the row of icons that appears at the top of every customisation window, as shown in Figure 10-1.

2. **Click on the form that you're customising, roughly in the spot where you want the text to appear.**

   When you click on the form, the Text Field box pops up.

3. **Double-click on the Text Field.**

   You arrive at the Field Information window.

4. **Enter the words you want to include on your form in the Text box.**

   Don't worry about running out of room when typing in the Text box. Although it may seem as if there's not much room here, you can actually write your entire life history in this box because the text wraps around.

5. **Click on Text Format to adjust the font and size of your new text, then click OK.**

   You can change the font, size or colour of your text, and even make it bold, underlined or italicised. If you want to get really tricky (and use up dozens of colour ink cartridges), you can also add a Background Colour.

6. **Drag the Text box to wherever you want it to appear in your form.**

   Position your mouse over the Text box and click once so that a box appears around it. Hold your mouse button down until a little white hand appears, drag the Text box to the correct spot on your form and then release the mouse button.

   Splat! (Do it again if this makes you feel good — or if you want to move the Text box some more.)

Making things bigger or smaller

You want to make a field bigger or smaller? Alice had a caterpillar, you've got a mouse. Grab your furry friend and click once on the field so that a black box appears around it. Magic! Can you see the tiny little black square in the bottom right of this box? Persuade your mouse to sit on top of this black square, then click and hold down your mouse button. A little cross icon appears and, with your mouse button still held down, you can either drag the corner of the box downwards and to the right to make it bigger, or upwards and to the left to make it smaller.

By the way, making a field bigger or smaller doesn't make what prints out bigger or smaller. To do that, you need to adjust the size of the font. Read on to find out more . . .

Getting your form to look good

Inspiration strikes. You've had enough of those boring old fonts and you need to change them now. It's easy. Just double-click on any field to be transported straight to the Field Information window, as shown in Figure 10-2. From here, you can click the Text Format button to choose different fonts, font sizes and whether they're justified to the left, middle, right or on the decimal (you should always justify amounts on the decimal). One trick to remember, however: If you choose a font larger than the one you had before, it may well be too tall or too wide to fit into the field. If this happens to you, enlarge the field by dragging out the bottom corner with your mouse.

To make things a little more glam, click Font Colour from within the Text Format window to change the colour of text. However, do be realistic. For example, if you're customising an invoice and you print lots of sales every day, you probably want to stick with black text for everything except logos or business details.

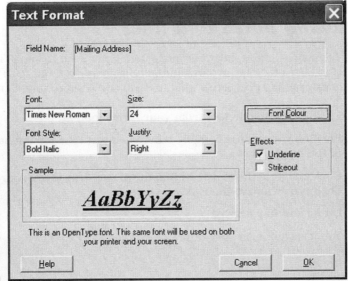

Figure 10-2:
Play with fonts to get the look you want.

If you find that all the fonts on your form are different to what you'd like, you can change the *default font* (a much more efficient process than manually changing every single field, one by one). Here's how it's done:

1. **Go to the File menu.**

   It's on the top menu bar.

2. **Choose Default Fonts.**

3. **Click the Forms button and select a font and the size.**

   This changes the font for all forms that you haven't customised yet. (Sorry, if you've already started customising a form, you won't be able to change the default font for that particular form.)

4. **Click OK.**

Moving stuff around

To move a field to a different spot, grab your mouse and position it over the item you want to move. Click once so that a box appears around the item and then hold the mouse button down until a little white hand appears. It's not drowning, just waving.

Drag the item to its new spot and let go of the mouse button. The white hand disappears, sinking back into the innards of your form.

Drawing boxes and lines

Your life may be chaos, but your customers don't need to know. Try adding boxes and lines to your invoices and purchase orders to make them look lean, mean and hungry. Here's what to do to add a box around a piece of text:

1. **Click the rectangle tool from your forms toolbar.**

2. **Position your mouse roughly where you want the top left-hand corner of the box to be.**

3. **Click and hold the mouse button down and drag the corner of the box downwards and to the right.**

4. **Let go and hey presto!**

   You have a box on your form.

Now for some pins and tucks . . .

- ✔ **Move the box again.** Grab your mouse again and position it over the box. Click once, holding the mouse button down and adjust the position of the box.

- ✔ **Add a line to your form.** Click the line tool on your forms toolbar (the one that's a diagonal line). Position your mouse roughly where you want one end of the line to be. Click and hold the mouse button down and drag the line downwards (for a vertical line) or sideways (for a horizontal line). Let go and the line magically appears.

- ✔ **Adjust the thickness of boxes or lines.** Double-click on the box or line to call up the Field Information settings, then adjust the Line Size. Size 1 is the thinnest; Size 6 is the thickest.

Of course, you may find that the easiest way to add a box to a form isn't to use the rectangle tool at all. If you only want a box around a single field, then the easiest method is to double-click on that field, select the Border tab and click Left, Right, Bottom and Top to have a border wrap all the way around.

Adding logos

Invoices and receipts aren't exactly the most exciting documents in the world, so spicing them up with a company logo is a good idea.

Here's how to insert a logo into any of your business forms:

1. **Scan the logo and make sure it's an appropriate size and format.**

   Your logo file can be in any one of five formats: bmp, gif, jpg, png or tif. Whatever the format, make sure the file is no bigger than 1,000 kilobytes — you may have to lower the resolution or *greyscale* the image (make it black and white) in order to meet this condition. (Big picture files are like carrying a typewriter on a marathon — they slow things down unreasonably.)

2. **Copy the logo into your MYOB program folder.**

3. **Open the form you want to add the logo to.**

   Go to your Setup menu, click Customise Forms, select the form that you want to insert the logo into, then click Customise.

4. **Click the picture tool on your forms toolbar and then click on the form where you want the logo to appear.**

5. Double-click the Picture field and click Load Picture.

6. Find your logo file and click Open, followed by OK.

Highlight your logo file (it should be sitting in your MYOB program folder) and click Open. You should see what your logo looks like in the Preview Picture box, as shown in Figure 10-3.

7. Adjust the size of the image.

Drag the bottom corner upwards to make the graphic smaller or drag the bottom corner downwards to make it bigger. Curiouser and curiouser — the magic never stops!

I feel a little bit guilty writing these instructions — I've made it sound oh so easy — when in fact adding logos is sometimes a bit like negotiating with a teenager (it takes a few goes before you get your own way). Here's some negotiation tactics, learnt at the coalface:

- If logos are refusing to load or don't print out the correct size, try displaying the image first in another program (Microsoft Word will do just fine), resize the image so it's just the size you need it to be on your form, and click Copy. Then, return to your Customise Forms window and click the picture icon on your forms toolbar. However, instead of clicking Load Picture, click Paste Picture.

- If the logo refuses to print, however hard you beg, make sure you have Quicktime installed. You can find this software on your MYOB software installation CD.

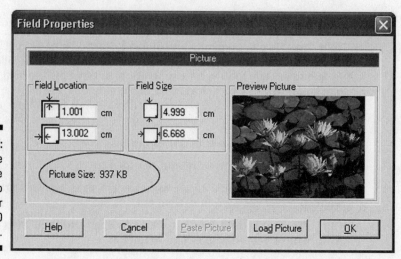

Figure 10-3:
Make sure the file size of your logo isn't greater than 1,000 kilobytes.

- As I mention earlier in this chapter, the last thing you want is a logo file that's so big it grinds everything to a halt. Lowering the resolution usually does the trick, but you don't want to go lower than 72 dpi — your logo will look like it has a 6 o'clock shadow. Anything around 100 dpi is fine.

- If reducing the file size of your image proves difficult (maybe you're adamant about printing a detailed logo in full colour), you can always resort to printing your forms on business letterhead.

Finetuning Tricks and Tips

Maybe I'm a little too particular, but I really like my forms to be absolutely, totally perfect.

Lining everything up

If you have lots of information on a form, it's sometimes hard to make it line up perfectly. Yeah, it may look okay on the screen, but when you print it out, you find that it's not quite right.

Try these tips to solve the problem:

- **Use a ruler:** Grab a piece of paper that's the same size as the form you want to print. Sketch roughly on this paper where you want things to appear, drawing boxes, columns, totals and so on. Then get a ruler and measure how far these items are from the top of the page and the left of the page. Compare these measurements to the rulers that appear along the top and the side of the customisation window on your screen.

- **Align headings or rows:** If you want to align headings or rows of text, double-click on each one and check out the Field Location. The first box with the up and down arrows shows you how far this field is from the top of the page; the second box shows you far this field is from the left hand side of the page. For example, if one heading is 9.35 centimetres from the top of the page and you want another heading to sit next to it, edit the Field Location of this heading so that it's also 9.35 centimetres from the top.

- **Change the size of a field:** As I explain earlier in this chapter, you can drag out the corners of a field to make it larger or smaller. Alternatively, be more precise by double-clicking on the field and, in the Field Size, specify exactly how high and how wide you want it to be. (It's easier to line up headers if they're all exactly the same height.)

Backing up to go forward

You may think that you are a peculiarly blessed and lucky person, but that doesn't mean that calamity can't come knocking at your door. So make sure you back up all your customised forms, not just your company file. Normally, backing up forms is pretty easy: Simply select Backup All Data (as opposed to selecting Backup Company File Only) when exiting your company file. Do this, and your sanity is guaranteed (well, almost).

However, if you're working on a network or you don't back up using the Backup command from within MYOB software, you need to be careful that whoever is responsible for backups knows that it's not enough just to backup your MYOB company file. All the customised forms that live inside the Forms folder, which sits inside your MYOB program folder, need to be backed up as well. (Depending on how your network is set up, this Forms folder could be a shared folder sitting on the server, or it could be a separate folder on each user's local machine.)

Deleting stuff you don't need

One of the hassles about MYOB software's standard forms is the way they include everything you might ever need and a bit more besides. It's a bit like going on holidays with the kitchen sink and 150 rubber plants. I bet if you look carefully, you find information you don't need: salesperson details, shipping information, tax breakdowns or whatever.

When you spot a field you don't need, get rid of it. To do this, click just once on the field to highlight it and then press the Delete button.

Adding new fields

I find that when my forms have evolved somewhat, I often end up wanting to undelete something I deleted earlier. Or I decide that I want to make use of a field that doesn't normally print, such as a job column or a memo.

To add a new field, go to your Forms Toolbar and click the data fields tool (the first icon on the left). A long list of available fields appears (similar to what you can see in Figure 10-4) covering everything from additional addresses to customer ABNs, due dates, custom fields and so on. Click to the left of any name to insert this field into your form and then drag and drop it into position.

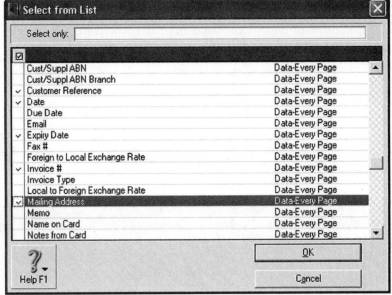

Figure 10-4:
The data
fields tool
lets you
select from a
whole range
of fields for
use on
forms.

Picking your page size and form size

If you want to print forms trouble-free, then you need to make sure that your page size and form size are perfect. Here's how:

1. **Go to Print Setup (Windows) or Page Setup (Mac) and select the size paper you use.**

    A box called Paper appears, with the word Size below it. Simply select your paper size. (It's almost always A4 unless you're doing something unusual.)

2. **From within the Customise Forms window, double-click the form properties tool on the forms toolbar, then select your paper size one more time.**

    On the forms toolbar, the forms properties tool is the second-last icon from the right. When the Form Properties window opens, select your paper size from the Paper menu.

3. **While you're at it, double-check the size of your form.**

At first, the difference between form size and paper size is tricky to get your head around. Form size means the size of whatever it is you're printing; paper size means the size of the paper you're printing it on. So if you decide to print two sales per page, and the form size is 21 centimetres wide by 15 centimetres high, the paper size would be 21 centimetres wide by 30 centimetres high. Figure 10-5 shows an example.

4. Specify how many forms you want to print per page.

If you want to print three receipts per A4 page, select 3 as the Number of Sales per Page. If you want to print two remittance advices per A4 page, select 2 as the Number of Sales per Page.

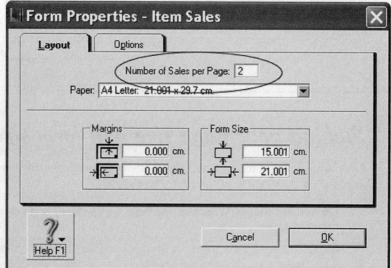

Figure 10-5: In the Form Properties Item Sales window you can print two or more receipts per A4 page.

5. Now fix up your margins.

You're almost there. If you want to add margins (maybe you're printing mailing labels and you can't print on the top 5 millimetres of the page), do this now.

6. Click OK when you're done.

This action closes the Forms Properties window and returns you to the main Customise Forms window.

7. Click OK once more to save your changes.

Print preview heebie-jeebies

You're customising away — la, la, la-de-da — then you wonder what your form looks like, so you click the print preview button that sits on your forms toolbar (it's the last icon on the right). Oh. Surprise, surprise, it doesn't make much sense.

Actually, print preview doesn't give you a true picture of how your final form will look. Instead, the best way to see how your customisation is

shaping up is to create a real-life example then print it out. For example, if you're customising an invoice, create a dummy invoice (you can always delete it later on) and then print it.

Sometimes you have to print this dummy form several times as you work on your customisation before you arrive at the result you want. Just try to block out images of native forests being wood-chipped and you should be fine.

Working with Several Different Templates

One of the things I love about customising forms is that the possibilities are endless. Clubs adapt invoices to become annual subscription reminders, colleges adapt invoices to become course enrolment forms and factories change purchase orders into production run lists. The only limit is your imagination.

One of the tricks with all this is that you can customise forms more than once. With one standard invoice and one company file, you can create lots of different forms for different situations. It's cool, it's fun and it works.

Calling a spade a spade

As I explain at Step 1 in 'Customising Your First Form' earlier in this chapter, the first time you customise a form you find the template that's closest to what you're looking for, then you click Customise. You make your changes, click OK and you're done.

However, if you want to customise a form further but keep your original customisation so that you've got two versions of the form, then things are a little different. Select the form you want to create a second version of and click Customise. Make your changes, but this time don't click OK, click Save Form As.

You'll be prompted to enter a Form File Name and a Description. If you need multiple layouts of a particular form (maybe you're running three different businesses and need different sales invoices for each business), then be careful when recording a new Form File Name. This is the name by which you (or anyone else working with your company file) will identify this form in the future. Make this name something easy to recognise and ensure the first letter of the name is such that the form appears in a logical place in your list of forms (forms are always listed in alphabetical order). You can see how a possible list of forms could look in Figure 10-6.

When you've chosen your Form File Name and a suitable Description, click OK and then OK once more to save your new form. That's all there is to it.

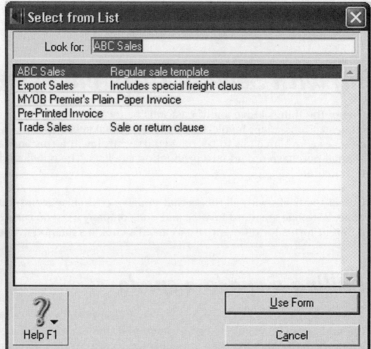

Figure 10-6:
You can save lots of versions of the same form, each with minor variations.

Getting the right form first time around

Forms are fickle things. One of the cries of complaint I hear quite often is 'Why does the form layout always default to the wrong one, so that I have to change it every time I print?'

The answer is quite simple. In order to change the default, you have to go to the Print menu for that form (such as Print/Email Invoices, Print/Email Statements or whatever) and click the Advanced Filters button. You choose the customised form layout that you want as your default from the Selected Form menu and then click OK.

That's all you have to do, but remember that your default form choices are *user-specific*. What this means is that your choice of default form won't carry across if anyone else logs into the company file. In other words, every employee has to log in with their own user ID and set up their own form defaults.

Making a silk purse from a sow's ear

The key to versatile forms is to think of what information you'd like to print on your form and, if any of this information doesn't print out as standard, recycle a field that's not being used for anything else.

Figure 10-7 shows how a firewood company has applied this principle, adapting a regular sales template to become a delivery docket. The Salesperson field has become the driver's name, the Comments field now provides special delivery instructions, the Due Date field has become the Delivery Date and the Customer PO field now covers the customer's first name. The result? A practical delivery docket that fits the bill exactly.

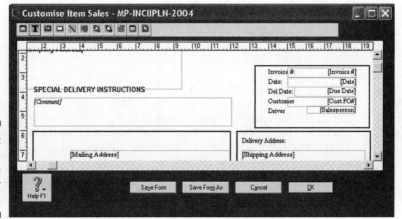

Figure 10-7: Adapting fields to meet your own needs.

Where forms are stored

All of your customised forms live in a special folder called Forms, which sits inside your MYOB program folder. Mostly, they mind their own business quietly and happily and you're none the wiser.

However, if you ever have to shift your company file from one computer to another, then you need to know where your customised forms reside. That's because as well as installing the MYOB program on the other computer and moving your company file across, you also need to copy the contents of the Forms folder onto the new computer.

To do this, simply open up Windows Explorer or your Macintosh Finder on the original computer and whack all the files sitting in the Forms folder onto a disk or CD. Then hop to the new computer and copy all these files from the disk or CD into the new Forms folder.

Smart, Smarter, Smartest

Dumb, Dumber, Dumbest worked for the movie world, but it has no place in the management of small businesses. Smart is the way to go with these tips that you won't find in any user guide. I've discovered this lot through persistence, pig-headedness and many years of practise and now I'd love to share them with you.

Imaginative invoices

Remember, the way you present your invoices is the way you represent your company to your clients:

✔ **Use your letterhead:** If you don't print hundreds of invoices every week, my number one tip is to print them on your letterhead. Chances are your letterhead already looks pretty good (it's probably professionally printed and designed) and so using it for invoices is not only smart, it also makes customising a quick and easy job.

✔ **Spring-clean:** Delete any fields you don't need, such as the Memo or Salesperson fields, or Shipping info. The less rubbish, the better.

✔ **Bring the dead back to life:** Click the data fields icon (the first on the left on your forms toolbar) and check out all the available fields for this form. If you think one of these fields would be useful (the Contact Name is a good example), then find it and drag it into the main part of the form.

✔ **Spell out GST so everyone can see:** If you sell a mixture of taxable and non-taxable goods, then your customers will love it if you show the GST amount as a separate figure on each line of your invoice. To do this, go to customise your sales form and select the data field icon from the forms toolbar (it's the first one on the left). Click next to the Line Tax field to include it on your form and then drag this field into position so that it appears next to the Amount column.

✔ **Keep forms simple:** At the bottom of most standard invoice templates are tax codes, rates and totals. If you only charge one rate of tax, these other boxes cause more confusion than anything else. You should give them the heave-ho.

Peachy purchase orders

Just because your suppliers are the only ones who see your purchase orders, it doesn't mean these forms need to look like something your partner designed on a typewriter. Here's how to get them ship shape:

✔ **Tidy up:** There are bound to be a few fields you don't need. The Ship Via, Supplier Invoice #, Amount Applied and Discount fields are just some that are usually irrelevant. Give them the chop and your purchase order will look much tidier.

✔ **Include item numbers:** I can't tell you how often clients call asking why Item Numbers don't print on purchase orders. The answer is to customise your purchase order by clicking the data field tool on the forms toolbar (the first icon on the left). When the list of available fields appears, scroll down till you see the field called My Item #. Click this field so that it appears on your purchase order, then drag it into position.

✔ **Fax or email purchase orders:** If you want to fax or email purchase orders straight from MYOB software without printing them first, you can. Before recording your purchase order, simply click the Send To button and select either Email or Fax. In the blink of eye, these orders appear in your email outbox, ready to send, or as a pending fax in your fax queue.

Magnificent mailing labels

In years gone by, setting up mailing labels in almost any software program was like some weird initiation rite. Many hours and curses and mashed bits of paper later, you'd finally get there.

Expressway to heaven

If you want, you can use pre-printed stationery (as opposed to plain paper stationery) for your business invoices, statements or purchase orders. MYOB Software has a special relationship with a company called Forms Express, which provides a range of stationery designed to fit with all MYOB products. Forms Express can also supply you with printed cheques that comply with Australian banking regulations.

The easiest way to order stationery from Forms Express is via the company's Web site at www.formsexpress.com.au. Alternatively, you can phone 1800 808 862 or fax 1800 676 641.

But I'm not fibbing even a little bit when I say that setting up mailing labels is like falling off a log. Here's what to do:

1. **Write down your mailing label's vital statistics.**

   Grab your mailing label sheet and a ruler and get ready to measure up. Write down the size of the sheet itself, the size of each label and the size of the margins (if any).

2. **Go to the Card File command centre and click Print Mailing Labels.**

3. **Click Customise, then head to the forms toolbar and double-click on the form properties icon.**

   The form properties icon is second-last from the right on the forms toolbar.

4. **Specify how many rows and columns you have on your mailing label sheet, as well as the size of the sheet itself and the margins.**

   Start by detailing how many rows and columns you have on each mailing label sheet. Then complete the Paper size of the sheet itself (it's usually A4) and specify how big the margins are. (The margins are the little blank bits at the top and at the left of many mailing label sheets, before the first label starts.)

5. **Enter the dimensions of the mailing label itself.**

   Specify how tall your mailing label is, plus how wide. This complete, your Form Properties window should look pretty similar to Figure 10-8. In this example, I've set up mailing labels to print on an A4 sheet. My sheet has three mailing labels on each row and seven mailing labels in each column, making a total of 21 labels per sheet.

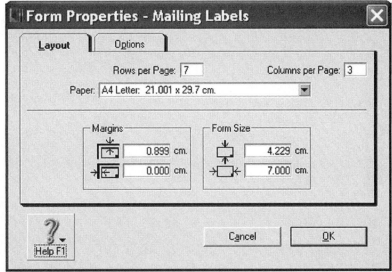

Figure 10-8:
Mailing
labels are a
piece of
cake.

6. **Click OK once to return to Customise Mailing Labels, then click OK one more time.**

Could it be easier? I don't think so.

Chapter 11

Relishing Reports

· ·

In This Chapter

▶ Finding reports and seeing what they do

▶ Finding transactions: Some tips and tricks

▶ Creating your first report

▶ Making your reports look good

▶ Saving your settings

▶ Designing bar charts and pie graphs

▶ Sending reports to Excel

▶ Creating custom reports

▶ Persuading your printer to co-operate

· ·

*B*eneath its cool, calm exterior, your MYOB company file is a seething mass of information, and offers reports so that you can tap into almost anything you can think of — from budget analysis reports to inventory forecasts, from salesperson totals to address list details. You get lots of different ways to print every report, too. You can add splendiferous colours to headings, choose wild and crazy fonts or even swap columns around.

There's no need to be overwhelmed by the number of choices. In this chapter, I take you on a journey through the ups and downs of report-land, showing you how to work out which reports you need each month, figure out what they're actually about, then make them look really good.

Getting Started With Reports

This book isn't meant to be like a course or a tutorial, but sometimes the best way to get your head around something is to sit down and try it out.

So, before you create your first reports, check out the differences between each of the methods I describe in the following sections, and experiment by trying a few things yourself.

Choosing from a select range

If you think of your MYOB company file as being a restaurant, and reports as food, then your Analysis menu is the upmarket à la carte section where you can dine on the best tucker. That's because the Analysis menu only includes a few select reports in its offerings, but these reports are all the ones you can't afford to be without.

Note: The Analysis menu isn't available in MYOB BusinessBasics and FirstEdge.

The Analysis menu sits in the bottom right-hand corner of every command centre. Click the blue arrow that appears to the right of the Analysis button to see a list of several reports.

When you have time, I suggest you look at each of these reports, but for the time being, start with the Analyse Sales report:

1. **Go to the Analysis menu and click Sales.**

2. **Click Filters and select your date range.**

   If you want to report on more than one month at a time, drag your trusty mouse along the months from left to right. If you want to report on last year's figures, click the Last Years Actuals Only button (rather than This Years Actuals Only).

3. **Click OK.**

4. **Click either of the Sales buttons to view the report as a pie or bar chart.**

   Your report should look similar to the one shown in Figure 11-1. I talk more about creating charts later in this chapter, but for the moment, it's good just to know that this feature exists. Looks pretty impressive, don't you reckon? (I'm assuming that you've been making unprecedented sales, of course.)

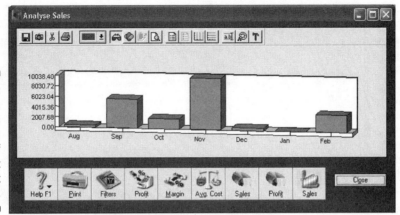

Figure 11-1:
Go to the
Analysis
menu for a
selection of
your most
important
reports.

Reporting on individual accounts or cards

Don't want a full meal — just a quick bite? Then your Find Transactions menu is the place to go. The Find Transactions menu is just the ticket for unusual inquiries, such as troubleshooting and reporting on individual accounts or cards. Follow these steps to check out how the menu works:

1. **Go to any command centre and click the arrow next to the Find Transactions button.**

   You can choose to inquire by Account, Card, Item, Invoice, Bill, Job or Payroll Category.

2. **Click the Card tab and enter the name of one of your suppliers or customers.**

   When you click the Card tab, the Find Transactions window pops up, with an empty field above the date range. Type the name of a supplier you've made a few payments to, or a customer who you have invoiced a few times.

3. **Enter a suitable date range in the Dated From and To fields, then press the Tab key.**

   When you press the Tab key, every transaction associated with this supplier or customer during the selected date range pops up. In Figure 11-2, for example, the Find Transactions window lists every purchase and every payment I've made to the fictitious Mojo Advertising.

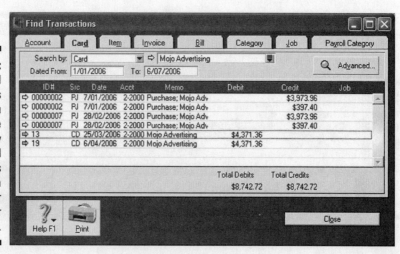

Figure 11-2:
The Find
Transactions
menu
provides the
fastest way
to locate all
transactions
for a
particular
supplier or
customer.

4. **Now click the Account tab and enter an expense account that you know contains transactions. Fill in the Dated From and To fields, then press the Tab key.**

   For this step, I enter my telephone expense account because I know it has transactions allocated to it. The Find Transactions window then lists every payment I've allocated to this expense account.

5. **Experiment with the other tabs and see what you can discover.**

   Hang out in the Find Transactions window for a while and have a play. Click Invoice to search by invoice number, Bill to search by purchase order number or supplier invoice number, and so on. As fast food goes, the Find Transactions window is hard to beat.

Too much on your plate?

I read the other day that in the land where smorgasbords come from, Swedes pick delicately and carefully at their meals, eating small amounts at a time. Australians, on the other hand, tend to heap their plates as high as possible, fearful that, even in the all-you-can-eat joints, the offer will soon be withdrawn.

So take heed. MYOB software may offer a plethora of reports, but that doesn't mean that you have to gobble them all in one go. Instead, browse through the reports menu carefully and only print the ones you absolutely need. Digest these first and try to understand what they're about before printing more. It's much better to print one report every month that you read and understand than to print ten reports that end up rotting in a filing cabinet. Such restraint also saves paper, saves time and saves trees.

Going the whole hog

Why go à la carte when you can have the entire smorgasbord? For the mother lode, head to the Reports menu (found along the bottom of every MYOB command centre) and click the arrow next to it. You can choose any category of report you want, but for the moment, select Accounts.

Rather surprisingly, you're not immediately transported to an island in the South Seas. Instead, you arrive at the Index To Reports window, similar to the one shown in Figure 11-3. Check out how you can click the little tabs along the top to see different groups of reports. For example, you can click the Sales tab to see a list of all the sales reports, the Card tab to see a list of card file reports and so on.

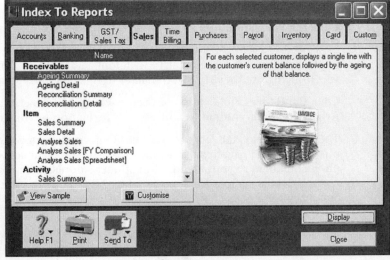

Figure 11-3:
The main reports menu offers a great selection of reports.

All you have to do now is select the report you want, click Customise to specify a date range for the report and then either click Display to view the report on screen or Print to produce it on paper. In the next few sections of this chapter I go into the finer details of this process.

Giving Reports a Facelift

Here's how to create reports — that is, how to customise reports by selecting dates, changing fonts, adding columns and finally, saving your settings when you're done.

Creating your first report

Creating a great-looking report takes about eight steps and, because things often make more sense when you work with a real-life example, I show you how to produce your very first Sales Summary report. After all, it's a report that every business needs to print, sooner or later.

1. **Go to your Reports menu, click the Sales tab and select the Customer Sales Summary report.**

2. **Click the Customise button and review the settings for this report.**

    Like most reports in MYOB software, you can filter this report in many different ways, including by date range; by amount (for example, only reporting on sales greater than $1,000); by employee (employee usually means salesperson in this context); by referral source (how that customer heard about you); and much more.

3. **Click the Format button. Experiment with different fonts and colours, clicking OK when you're done.**

    Here's your chance to be creative with fonts and colours. For pointers, see 'Bringing out the artist within' later in this chapter.

4. **Click the Report Fields tab and then click against descriptions in the Available Fields column to add more information to your report.**

    The Report Fields tab lets you add extra information to your report, other than what usually appears as standard. For example, you can add phone numbers to your standard Customer Addresses report or add custom details such as Customer Name or Buy Code to your Sales Summary report (as shown in Figure 11-4).

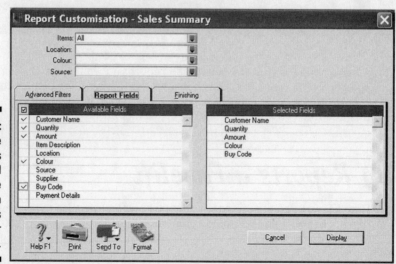

Figure 11-4:
Use the Report Fields tab to add to the information that appears on your reports.

5. Click the Finishing tab and review your selections.

The stuff that appears on the Finishing tab depends on the report type itself. But it's here that you can choose whether to round to the nearest dollar, include account numbers, print your company name and lots of other fiddly, not particularly important, things.

6. Click Display to view the report on screen.

Display your report before you print it — it's amazing how often you'll realise that what you've selected isn't quite right. You can then go back and fiddle with the settings a bit more before printing.

By the way, if you want to narrow or widen a column, you can. Look for the ˆ symbol that appears between each column header. Rest your mouse on this symbol until a cross-bow symbol appears. Then drag your mouse gently to the left or right to narrow or widen the column.

7. Click either the Send To or the Print button to email, fax or print your report.

When you click the Send To button, you have the rather phenomenal choice to email or fax your report to someone, send your report to Excel or create a PDF or HTML version of your report. Of course, you can always be incredibly old-fashioned and click the Print button instead. (For more about printing, see 'Getting everything to fit' later in this chapter.)

8. Read your report.

Yep, I know I'm stating the obvious. But it's amazing how many reams of reports lie around offices, lonely and unloved, without anybody giving them as much as a second glance.

Serving up what's on the screen

Want to print exactly what you can see on the screen at the moment? You can. And it's easy!

If you're a PC person, press the Print Screen key on your keyboard (often called PrtSc or Prnt Scrn). Then select Start⇨Programs⇨Accessories⇨Paint. Go up to the Edit menu in your Paint program and click Paste. Aha! Your picture appears, ready to print.

If you're a Macintosh person, you need to press three keys simultaneously: Command (⌘), Shift and 4. See how your cursor turns into a tiny cross? Drag this cross diagonally across the window you want to capture and then let go. Snap! A new file pops up called Picture 1. Double-click on this Picture file to open it and then select File⇨Print.

Bringing out the artist within

Have you always fancied yourself as an artist? Then here's your chance. Use the Report Format window to let your creative impulses run wild:

1. **Go to the main reports menu, select the report you want to format and click the Customise button.**

2. **Click the Format button.**

   The Report Format window opens.

3. **In the Report Line menu, choose which section of the report you want to format. Then select a font and size for the section's text.**

   Reports are divided into sections — such as Company, Address, Report, Headers and Subtotals — which you select in the Report Line menu if you want to change the font and size of its text.

   Figure 11-5 shows an example.

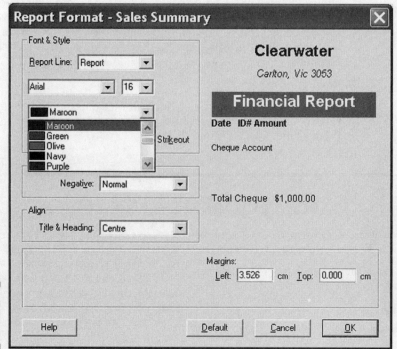

Figure 11-5:
Formatting
your reports.

4. Consider whether you want the text to appear in colour or just in black.

Sure, colours look funky and everything, but if you want to save on colour cartridges, it's probably best to keep most office reports to black ink only.

5. Muse about margins and consider your political allegiances.

If you're feeling picky, fiddle with the margin settings in the Left Margin and Top Margin fields. And, depending on your political preferences, choose whether to align your report headings to the left, the centre or the right.

6. Click OK.

You're back at the Report Customisation window again.

Getting everything to fit

Sometimes when you go to print a report, you get a warning saying that your report is too wide to fit on the paper. Never fear, here are some alternatives to a crash diet:

- **Reduce the font size.** Click the Format button in the Report Customisation window and then select Body (how come that sounds so enticing?) from the Report Line menu. Reduce the font size (sizes 8 or 9 work pretty well for most reports).

- **Change the orientation.** Change the way the report prints on the paper. To do this, go to your File menu and click Print Setup (Windows) or Page Setup (Macintosh) and change the orientation of the paper from Portrait (tall) to Landscape (wide).

- **Scale down the report.** When you're in the Print Setup or Page Setup menu, you may be able to scale the report down to, say, 80 percent (whether you can do this depends on your printer driver).

- **Trim unnecessary data.** From the Report Customisation window, click the Report Fields tab and remove any columns you don't need.

- **Narrow columns where possible.** Display the report and make sure the View setting at the top says Screen Report (and not Print Preview). Then look for the ^ symbol that appears between each column header. Rest your mouse on this symbol until a cross-bow symbol appears. Then drag your mouse gently to the left or right to narrow or widen the column.

To check how the report will look when printed, change the View settings at the top of your report display from Screen Report to Print Preview.

Saving your custom settings

One thing that gets irritating is the way report settings only last for the current session — you quit out of MYOB software, but the next time you open your company file, your selected report fields and advanced filters have returned to their default settings. The solution to this problem is to create a custom report. Here's what to do:

1. **Create the report of your dreams.**

   Refer to the section 'Creating your first report' earlier in this chapter. Never mind if the final report is tall, dark and handsome or if it's small, fair and intelligent (like yours truly, although the intelligent bit is always up for debate).

2. **Display the report of your dreams.**

   Click the Display button and check out your magnificent creation.

3. **Click the Save As button and give your new report a name and description.**

   Make the Report Name short and sweet and the Description something meaningful, so you know later why you created the report in the first place.

4. **Click OK and then Close to return to the main reports menu.**

5. **Click the Custom tab on the reports menu and ponder your brilliance.**

   When you click the Custom tab on the main reports menu, a list of all your custom reports appears, including the report just created. Select this report, click Display and note how all your custom settings have been saved. What more could one wish for.

 Custom reports are stored in a folder called Custom that lives inside your MYOB program folder. Deleting, moving or renaming this folder means you lose access to all of your custom reports! So, hey, don't do it.

 By the way, if you've got a report that you use heaps, a smart idea is to go to customise this report, then click the Finishing tab and tick the option Add to Reports Menu. Now, whenever you want to print this report, go to your top menu bar and click Reports. Your report will appear here, listed separately.

Cooking Up Graphs and Pies

I love graphs because they show me at a glance what's going on with my business. It's so much quicker than poring over rows and rows of figures. And I love pies because they are so satisfying, especially those great chicken and leek ones they have at my local deli.

Charting events

You can print both Profit & Loss reports and Analyse Sales reports as bar charts (although bar charts aren't available in MYOB BusinessBasics or FirstEdge).

To view a bar chart of your final profit (or loss) over the past few months, follow these steps:

1. **Go to the Analysis menu and click Profit and Loss.**

2. **Click Filters and select your date range.**

   If you want to report on more than one month at a time, drag your mouse along the months from left to right. If you want to report on last year's figures, click the Last Years Actuals Only button (rather than This Years Actuals Only).

3. **Click OK.**

4. **Click the Net P&L button.**

   This turns your report into a bar chart! Hopefully your profit and loss shows a lovely steady trend upwards, upwards, upwards . . .

Making a graph of your sales is pretty much the same process as graphing your profit and loss. Go to your Analysis menu, click Sales and then click Filters. Choose your dates and decide whether you want to chart Items, Customers or Salespeople. Click OK, followed by the Sales button to arrive at a pretty smart-looking graph of your sales results.

Slicing it up

I like pie charts best for showing sales figures (although you can print pie charts for your assets and liabilities, too). To see a pie chart, go to your Analysis menu, click Sales and then click Filters. (Note that pie charts aren't available in MYOB BusinessBasics or FirstEdge.) Next, select All Items, the month or months you want to report on and click OK.

Now you can either click the Profit button or the Sales button (choose the buttons with the flash frisbee icons) to see a pie chart. The Profit button shows how much profit you made on each different stock line you sold; the Sales button shows the percentages of how each item sold, as shown in Figure 11-6.

If you like, try highlighting important parts of a pie chart by separating slices from the rest of the graph. To do this, grab your mouse and position it over the slice of the pie you want to separate. Then hold down the mouse button and drag the slice of the graph away from the rest of the graph.

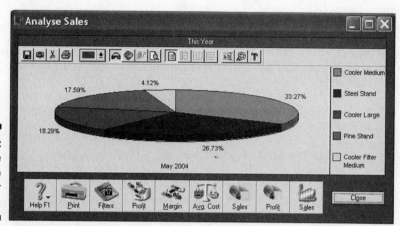

Figure 11-6:
Create pie
charts to
analyse your
sales.

Pie charts work best if you don't have too many different stock items (or in the case of Balance Sheet pie charts, if you don't have too many different asset or liability accounts). Otherwise the information gets rather jumbled and you can't see what's what.

Prettying everything up

When you create graphs and pie charts using your Analysis menu and display them on your screen, a tools menu appears along the top, which you can use to pretty up your pies and graphs. However, rather than drag you through a long page of instructions about how to use this tools menu, I suggest you follow these pointers and just go ahead and play with it on your own:

- **Printing:** Can you see the little Print icon at the top? This is the most important button because it's the only way you can print the graph. (Clicking the big Print button doesn't work for some strange reason.)

- **Copying:** Click the little camera icon if you want to copy the graph into another graphics program so that you can fiddle with it a bit more.

- **Editing:** Click the icon with the letters 'a' and 'b' to edit the graph's titles. You can insert titles at the top, the bottom, the left or the right.

- **Options:** Click the hammer icon for more ways to tweak the graph's legend, the pattern and colours used in the graph and so on.

Don't forget that this creation of yours is temporary. As soon as you close the graph, you lose all the changes you made. For this reason, if the graph you want is really important, it's best to send the report to Microsoft Excel and create a graph there. See the following section 'Closing the Communication Gap' for more about sending information to Excel.

Closing the Communication Gap

Imagine that you're working in an office and the receptionist speaks German, the bookkeeper speaks Turkish and the manager speaks Japanese. They struggle along doing their separate jobs and then one day a translator, who speaks all three languages, arrives in the office. Suddenly, everyone can communicate with one another and work goes along much more efficiently.

Think of the business software in your office as being a group of individuals, all trying to communicate with one another. Your job (and MYOB software is here to help, of course!) is to get them talking to one another. You can hook MYOB software up with Microsoft Excel, create reports you can read in your Web browser and generate custom reports using third-party software.

Making magic with Excel

If you have a report that almost does everything you want, but not quite (and isn't that often the case?), then the solution is to send the report out of MYOB software into Excel. Once the report is in Excel, you can change headings, cut and paste columns, convert figures into graphs and much, much more.

Sending reports to Excel is a piece of cake (so long as you don't have MYOB BusinessBasics or FirstEdge, that is). Go to your main Reports menu and select the report you want to send to Excel. Click the Send To button, followed by Excel, then watch as Excel opens up automatically, displaying your report in all its finery (as shown in Figure 11-7).

Printing without procrastinating!

If you're in a transaction journal and you have the information you want to print in front of you, then take a shortcut. Hold down the Ctrl button and press the letter P (for the PC guys and gals) or hold down the Cmd button and press the letter P (for the Macintosh lads and lassies). This keyboard shortcut takes you straight to the Print menu where all you have to do is click OK to print the information you're looking at.

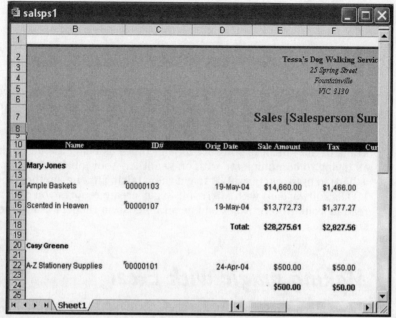

Figure 11-7:
You can send all reports to Microsoft Excel.

The spreadsheet shows:

	B	C	D	E	F
				Tessa's Dog Walking Servic	
				25 Spring Street	
				Fountainville	
				VIC 3130	
			Sales [Salesperson Sun		
	Name	ID#	Orig Date	Sale Amount	Tax	Cur
	Mary Jones				
	Ample Baskets	'00000103	19-May-04	$14,660.00	$1,466.00
	Scented in Heaven	'00000107	19-May-04	$13,772.73	$1,377.27
			Total:	$28,275.61	$2,827.56
	Casy Greene				
	A-Z Stationery Supplies	'00000101	24-Apr-04	$500.00	$50.00
				$500.00	$50.00

Keeping Excel cooking

The relationship between Microsoft Excel and MYOB software is a lot like any other relationship. Sometimes the two stop talking to one another and you've got to engage in a bit of counselling to make them happy again.

✔ **Excel icon is dimmed:** If the Excel icon is dimmed, it usually means you've installed Excel after you've installed your MYOB software. The solution? Reinstall your MYOB software.

✔ **Run-time errors:** Sometimes you get a really nerdy message when you try to send a report to Excel, telling you that you have a Run-Time Error. The solution? Contact MYOB technical support (call 1300 555 151) and tell them you've received the Run-Time Error 1826/5922. (Don't forget to include your serial number and contact details.) They will then email you a small but magic file called myobmain.dot that fixes the problem.

✔ **Lost templates:** If you get a message saying the MYOB software can't find the report template, it's probably because you've changed the template's name or moved the spreadsheet folder (called Spredsht) that sits inside your MYOB program folder.

✔ **Formulas not totalling:** Another problem you may encounter is that the column totals don't update automatically in your Excel reports, even though the formulas all look perfect. You can fix this in Excel by navigating to Tools⇨Options and clicking the Calculation tab. Make sure that all calculations are set to Automatic, not Manual.

Viewing your reports on the Net

You can save any report in HTML format so that you can then view it with a Web browser (such as Mozilla's Firefox or Microsoft's Internet Explorer), or store it on a file server so that it's available on the Web for others to read.

To save a report in HTML format, first select the report in your Reports menu and click Send To. Select HTML and when prompted, save the file with the 'htm' file extension.

Creating specialised custom reports

Sometimes, customising standard reports within MYOB software or sending standard reports to Excel isn't enough. You need a report that gets a bit of information from one place, a bit of information from another place, multiplies one column by another and so on.

Happily, these days you have plenty of reporting solutions available:

- ✔ **Get a report custom-written.** If you don't have any programming experience, or you're only looking for one or two custom reports, the best approach is to employ an MYOB Certified Consultant to create a custom report for you. You can find a complete list of Certified Consultants at www.myob.com.au/support/ccmembers. Read the business description for each consultant carefully, as only a small proportion specialise in custom reporting.

- ✔ **Purchase MYOB ReportWriter.** ReportWriter is a reporting tool designed to help you generate your own custom reports, working with the data in your MYOB company file. The good thing about ReportWriter is the wonderful visual reports you can create. The bad thing is you need to be either one very smart chicken or have previous programming experience in order to make the most of your investment. Go to www.myob.com.au and search on ReportWriter to find out more.

- ✔ **Check out MYOB BusinessAnalyst.** MYOB BusinessAnalyst is the software that lets you view reports that have been written in ReportWriter. (Quite a few of the custom reports available from Certified Consultants require you to purchase MYOB BusinessAnalyst first.)

- ✔ **Visit MYOB Solution Store.** The MYOB Solution Store at www.myob.com.au/webstore has a list of third-party developers who have created add-on solutions and advanced reports that link to MYOB software. You may find that the custom report you're looking has been written already and there's no need to re-invent the wheel.

- ✔ **Visit my Web site.** If you're looking for a geeky propeller-head kind of person, then that's not me. However, if you go to the Links page on my Web site (visit www.veechicurtis.com.au), I list several businesses that provide custom reporting solutions.

When the Printer Plays Possum

I know how it is. It's six o'clock on a Friday evening and you promised your partner/girlfriend/boyfriend/spouse that you would be there in time for the latest exciting social engagement. You have to print a report before leaving work and at the crucial moment the printer plays possum.

What should you do next? Read on and (hopefully) you'll get a life.

What to do before you swear

Maybe you've used a few choice swear words already. Now you can cool down and try these possibilities:

- ✔ **Power:** Check that the printer is plugged in, warmed up and happy. Have a talk to it, give it a pat and double-check the socket.

- ✔ **Connection:** Is there a cable connecting the computer to the printer and is it plugged in at both ends? Wiggle each end of the cable a little to make sure both are secure.

- ✔ **Paper:** Have you stuck some paper in the printer? (Just like my good self, printers don't work unless they're fed.)

- ✔ **Toner:** If the paper obediently spits out of the printer, but it's completely blank, check your toner, ink or printer cartridge.

What to do before you scream

So you tried all my suggestions in the preceding section and your report still isn't printing? It's time to get serious:

- ✔ **Power:** Switch off your computer and your printer and wait a couple of minutes. Read a short novel. Then switch everything back on again and try once more.

- ✔ **Printer driver:** Reinstall your printer driver. (I talk more about this in the sidebar 'The magic printing file' later in this chapter.)

- ✔ **Fax software:** Do you have fax software running? Danger, danger, danger! If you do, close it down and try printing again.

- ✔ **Printer port:** Maybe you haven't got the right printer port selected for your printer. (This is nothing to do with fortified wine. A *port* is an overly romantic term for the socket at the back of your computer where the printer cable plugs in.) For PCs, check this by clicking the Printers and Faxes icon in the Control Panel (the port should be listed under printer properties). For Macs, go to your System Preferences, click Print & Fax and then click Printer Setup.

- ✔ **Reinstall your MYOB program:** If you can print from your word processor but you can't print from your MYOB company file, then reinstall your MYOB program from your CD. (Don't worry, doing this reinstalls the program only; you won't lose any of your precious data.)

- ✔ **Hard disk space:** If your computer crashes after only printing a few lines (or nothing at all), then check how much space you've got on your hard disk. You should always have at least 30 megabytes free. (If you get 'error –4' as your error message, this almost always relates to lack of hard disk space.)

- ✔ **Printer cable:** If your printer is toying with you, being good some of the time but garbled the rest of the time, then you may have a faulty printer cable. Try using another one.

- ✔ **Last resort:** Check your cupboard for ammunition. You could always do away with your printer.

What to do before giving up

Now it's challenge time! I hate giving up. Here's what to do next:

- ✔ **The methodical approach:** Try the Windows Print Troubleshooter tool. Go to the Start button, click Help and under the Contents tab, click Troubleshooting. Click Print and follow the instructions.

- ✔ **The cosmic approach:** Phone your mother. She'll say you can do it. A little psychology is invaluable when engaging in technological warfare.

- ✔ **The charming and enigmatic approach:** Ring a friend who knows more about computers than you do. Be very nice to them.

- ✔ **The life-is-too-short-to-waste-it-on-this-rubbish approach:** Try someone else's printer and see if it works.

The magic printing file

Every printer comes with its own special file that lets it communicate with your computer. This file is called a *printer driver*. Sick printer drivers are by far the most common cause of printing problems, throwing up lots of horrible things like garbled documents, missing pages, or a failure to print anything at all.

If you've got a PC, check your printer driver by going to the Start button, clicking Settings and then Printers. Click Add Printer and follow the instructions to reinstall your printer driver. If you've got a Macintosh, first check the Chooser to be sure your printer is selected. If it is, find the original CD that came with your printer and reinstall the driver.

If you can't find the original CD that came with the printer, you can usually download drivers from the Internet (www.driverguide.com is a handy Web site that contains a fair few). Otherwise, go to Search, type in the name of the manufacturer and the model of your printer and you should be able to find something that will save the day.

Chapter 12

The Gist of GST

*T*hey don't it call it the Gouge and Screw Tax for nothing. If it moves, tax it. If it makes a noise, tax it. If it's cash, tax it extra, just for revenge. (Unless it's a life essential, of course.)

I'm not cynical, just bewildered by the chaos that this tax has brought and by how so incredibly human it is to create this complex labyrinth of rules. A croissant is exempt from GST, except when it's got a chocolate filling. A coffee is exempt from GST, as long as you drink it outside. A book has GST on it, unless it's educational (and since when is any book not educational?).

But I'm not here to lecture you about the politics of GST. Instead, I'm here to explain how MYOB software makes this complicated beast really quite simple and how you can make the paperwork as painless as possible.

Understanding Where Everything Fits

In order to master this chapter, you need to understand three basic terms:

✔ **Taxable supplies:** Taxable supplies are any goods or services that attract GST. Examples include computers, consultancy fees, electrical goods and clothes. Our beloved politicians have also added GST to everything that's bad for us (like alcohol, chocolate and junk food) as well as everything that's fun (like eating out, going to the movies and bungy-jumping).

✔ **GST-free supplies:** GST-free supplies are goods or services that are GST-free. Examples include fresh food, many medical services and products, many educational courses, child care within the Childcare Rebate Act, 1993, exports and a range of religious supplies. If you're not sure whether something you sell has GST on it or not, contact the ATO for a ruling. (How the government could have taken something so simple as a Goods and Services Tax and made it into something more complex than rocket science beats me, but there you have it.)

If you sell GST-free goods or services, you can still claim input tax credits for GST you pay on your supplies.

✔ **Input-taxed supplies:** Input-taxed supplies are supplies that do not have GST added to the final selling price. Examples include bank charges, residential rents and income from unit trusts.

If your business sells an input-taxed supply (maybe you're a landlord of residential property), then you can't claim input tax credits for the GST you pay on your supplies.

Setting Up Your Tax Codes

Before you start recording transactions, I recommend you give your Tax Code List a good spring-clean, checking that your tax codes are set up correctly and adding codes where necessary.

Looking for speed? Three's all you need

When you first create your MYOB company file, you find that your Tax Code List comes with codes for all types of businesses and includes everything from Wine Equalisation Tax to Luxury Car Tax. But the good news is that, 95 percent of the time, most businesses need only three codes. Here's how to check that they're set up correctly:

1. From the top menu bar, choose Lists⇨Tax Codes.

Your Tax Code List pops up, as shown in Figure 12-1.

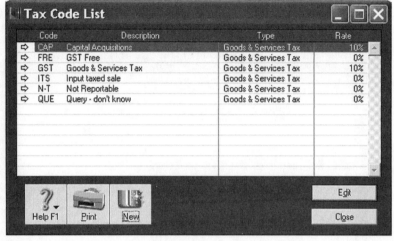

2. **Make sure that the rate for GST is 10% and that this code is linked to GST Collected and GST Paid.**

   Double-click your main GST code, the one called GST — wonders never cease! Check that the Rate is 10 percent and that the linked accounts are liability accounts called GST Collected and GST Paid, as shown in Figure 12-2.

3. **Make sure that the rate for FRE is 0% and that this code is linked to GST Collected and GST Paid.**

   Double-click your GST-free code, the one called FRE in your list. Similar to your main GST code, make sure the linked accounts are GST Collected and GST Paid. The only difference is that the Rate is 0 percent, not 10 percent.

4. **Make sure that the rate for CAP is 10% and that this code is linked to GST Collected and GST Paid.**

   The CAP code stands for 'capital acquisitions', meaning capital purchases such as new equipment, new furniture, new motor vehicles and so on. (You have to show capital acquisitions separately on your Business Activity Statement so this code is important.)

   Double-click your capital acquisitions code and check that the Rate is 10 percent and the linked accounts are GST Collected and GST Paid. (See Figure 12-3 for an example.)

5. **Consider whether your business needs any additional tax codes.**

   After you have checked the setup for these three essential tax codes, browse through the following sections of this chapter to see whether your business needs any additional codes.

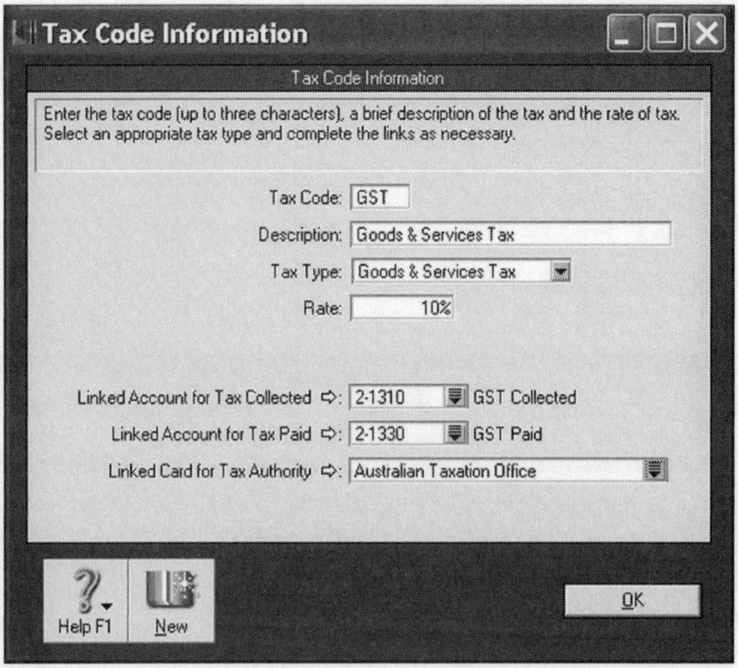

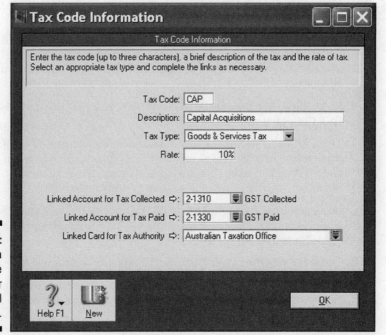

Figure 12-2: Your run-of-the-mill GST code.

Figure 12-3: Applying a separate code for capital acquisitions.

Dealing with input-taxed sales or purchases

If you earn income from dividends, interest, financial services or residential rentals, you need an additional tax code called ITS (standing for input-taxed sale). If you have expenses that relate to input-taxed income (such as expenses on your residential investment property), then you need an additional tax code called INP (standing for input-taxed purchase).

Here's how to create these codes, from go to whoa:

1. **From the top menu bar, choose Lists⇨Tax Codes.**

2. **Click New.**

3. **Enter ITS as the Tax Code and Input-Taxed Sale as the Description.**

   Actually, you can enter something more meaningful for the Description if you like, such as Interest Income or Rental Property Income.

4. **Select Goods & Services Tax as the Tax Type and enter 0% as the Rate.**

   Seems bizarre, doesn't it? You're selecting Goods & Services Tax as the Tax Type, rather than Input Taxed.

   No, I haven't lost my marbles; rather, this is one of MYOB software's delightful idiosyncrasies.

5. **Link this account to GST Collected and GST Paid.**

   Simply select these accounts from the drop-down lists next to the fields Linked Account for Tax Collected and Linked Account for Tax Paid, as shown in Figure 12-4.

6. **Click OK to save your tax code.**

7. **Repeat this process (if necessary) to create a code for input-taxed purchases, selecting INP as the code (not ITS) and Input Taxed Purchases as the Description.**

   You only need the INP code if you have expenses that relate directly to input-taxed sales. For example, if you only use the ITS tax code for interest income (and usually, you won't have expenses relating to interest income), then you don't need the INP code. However, if you use the ITS tax code for residential rental income, then you need to use the INP code to track all expenses relating to the property.

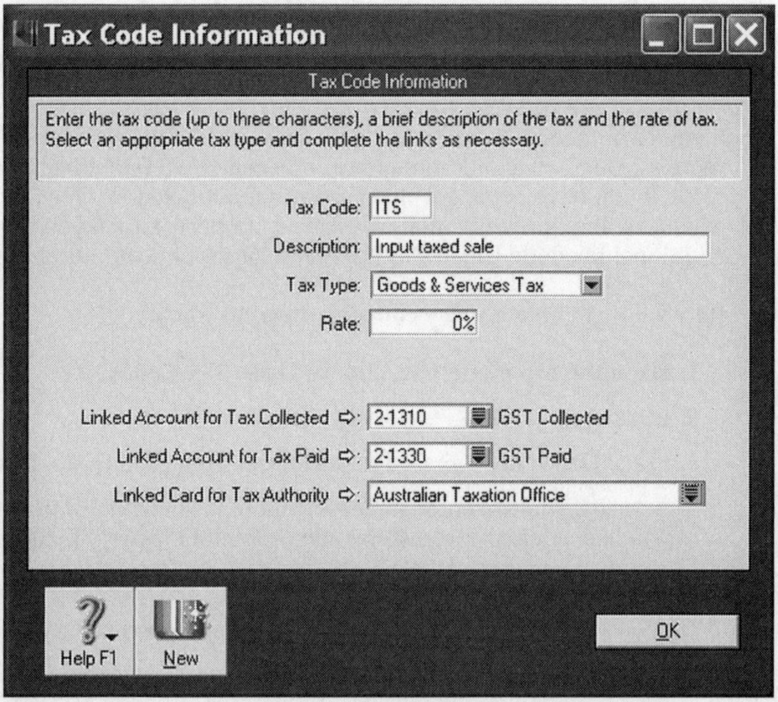

Figure 12-4:
Setting up a
tax code for
input-taxed
sales.

Exporting goods to foreign lands

If you export goods overseas, then you need an additional tax code called
EXP (which stands for export sales).

In this scenario, go to Lists⇨Tax Codes and create a new tax code called EXP.
This code is set up exactly the same way as your FRE tax code, with a
0 percent rate. As the Description, enter something like Export Sales.

Deleting unwanted tax codes

As you progress, if you spot a code in your Tax Code List that you're sure you
don't need, then I suggest you delete it (the old sales tax codes are an
excellent example of codes ripe for the chop). To do this, double-click the tax
code, go up to the Edit menu and select Delete Tax Code.

Picking the Right Code

The secret to producing an accurate Business Activity Statement is to get the tax codes right on every transaction. Fortunately, this is pretty easy once you know how, as I explain in the next few sections.

Getting it right every time

Every account in your Accounts List is linked to a tax code. (To see what I mean, go to your Accounts List, double-click on any account and click the Details tab. There, as in Figure 12-5, you see the Tax Code for this account.)

This Tax Code comes up as the default code every time you select an account on a transaction. For example, if the tax code for your Advertising Expense account is GST, then every time you allocate a Spend Money transaction to Advertising Expense, GST pops up automatically as the Tax Code.

The implications are huge: If you set up the Tax Code for every account in your Accounts List correctly, right from the start, you're almost guaranteed of coding all your transactions right, every time. Perfection and nirvana are but moments away.

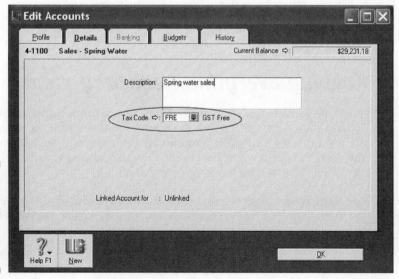

Figure 12-5:
Every account has a corresponding Tax Code.

Setting up tax codes in your Accounts List

As I explain in the preceding section, the secret to coding transactions correctly is to set up the linked Tax Codes in your Accounts List correctly. Here's an indication of which codes to use for each account, although I do suggest you double-check all of these settings with your accountant before you begin.

- ✔ **Accounts with GST as the tax code:** Use GST as the tax code for most expense accounts, including things such as advertising, commercial rent, electricity, merchant fees, postage, telephone and travel within Australia.

- ✔ **Accounts with FRE as the tax code:** Use FRE as the tax code for accounts relating to bank charges (with the exception of merchant fees), government charges, interest expense, medical supplies, motor vehicle registration, rates, residential rent and stamp duty.

- ✔ **Accounts with CAP as the tax code:** Use CAP as the tax code for all fixed asset accounts such as furniture and fittings, motor vehicles and tools.

- ✔ **Accounts with N-T as the tax code:** Use N-T as the tax code for all asset and liability accounts (with the exception of fixed asset accounts), private drawings accounts, superannuation and wages.

- ✔ **Accounts with QUE as the tax code — the query code:** Use QUE as the tax code for all hire purchase expense accounts, insurance expense, lease payments and subcontractor expense accounts. Then, make sure you double-check the correct GST treatment with your accountant or supplier. (See 'Putting off the inevitable' later in this chapter for more about setting up this code.)

Keeping everything squeaky-clean

I mention earlier in this chapter that the secret to producing accurate Business Activity Statements is to select the right tax codes for all transactions. I'm going to take this a step further now and talk about the most common coding mistakes. And guess what? Because they're so common, these are the mistakes the ATO will be watching out for in any audit . . .

- ✔ **Bank fees and merchant fees:** Bank fees are almost always GST-free, but merchant fees (for credit cards and hire of Eftpos machines) are not.

- ✔ **Government charges:** Council rates, filing fees, land tax, licence renewals, motor vehicle rego and stamp duty are all GST-free. So don't get tempted to claim back 10 percent!

✔ **Insurance:** Insurance is tricky because almost every insurance policy is a mixture of being taxable and GST-free (stamp duty doesn't have GST on it). Don't get caught out. Instead, double-check the exact amount of GST on every single insurance payment.

✔ **Overseas travel:** Overseas travel is GST-free.

✔ **Personal stuff:** You can't claim the full amount of GST on expenses that are partly personal — motor vehicle and home office expenses are the obvious culprits.

✔ **Petty cash:** Another trap for the unwary, petty cash is usually a mixed bag. Coffee and tea are GST-free, biscuits and sticky-tape aren't.

✔ **Small suppliers:** Watch out for small suppliers who have an ABN, but aren't registered for GST. Record these purchases as GST-free.

Putting off the inevitable

Sometimes you may not be sure whether or not an expense has GST on it. Although it's pretty tempting just to pick any old code and ignore the problem, you're best to use a special query code called QUE instead. Using this code means you can still record the expense and continue working on your accounts, but later on, you can print a GST Detail report listing all transactions allocated to the QUE tax code and ask your accountant to help you fix them up.

Here's how to create a QUE tax code:

1. **From the top menu bar, choose Lists⇨Tax Codes.**

2. **Click New.**

3. **Enter QUE as the tax code and Don't Know in the Description area.**

4. **Select Goods & Services Tax as the Tax Type and enter 0% as the Rate.**

   I suggest you enter 0% as the Rate, because it's better to under-claim GST, rather than over-claim. You can always make an adjustment if this query ends up having GST on it.

5. **Link this account to GST Collected and GST Paid.**

   Simply select these accounts from the drop-down lists next to the fields Linked Account for Tax Collected and Linked Account for Tax Paid.

6. **Click OK to save your tax code.**

Knowing what not to touch

You've probably noticed that there's an extra code you can't delete or change that sits in your Tax Code List. This code is called N-T and stands for non-reportable (yes, I know that logically the code should be called N-R, but it isn't!).

The distinction between the FRE tax code and the N-T tax code is that transactions coded FRE are reported on your Business Activity Statement, whereas transactions coded N-T are not.

Use N-T as the tax code for any transactions you allocate to an asset, liability or equity account — such as tax payments, loan settlements, private drawings or transfers between bank accounts. (The only exception is when you purchase new capital items, in which case you need to use the CAP code, as I explain earlier in this chapter.)

Also, use N-T as the tax code for all wages and superannuation payments. (Although you do report wages on your Business Activity Statement, they appear separately from other expenses.)

Dealing with transactions when GST isn't 10 percent

Okay, let me get one thing straight. GST is *always* 10 percent. That's the rate set by our wonderful federal government. However, sometimes you come across a transaction where it seems like the GST *isn't* 10 percent. Then, when you look closer, you find that the transaction is actually a combination of taxable items (which of course are 10%) and non-taxable items (which are 0%).

An example may help. You get an insurance bill for $550 and you enter the payment. MYOB software calculates the GST to be $50 but when you look at the bill, you notice that GST is actually $49.09. That's because there's $10 stamp duty in the insurance bill and stamp duty is GST-free.

What some people do when faced with this icky situation is they zoom in on the arrow next to the GST amount and they edit it. 'No, no, no,' I cry. Why? Because although MYOB software lets you do this (why I'm not quite sure), if you edit the GST amount you knock your Business Activity Statement out of balance.

The solution to this kind of situation, although a bit convoluted, is this: You record the insurance bill in Spend Money or Purchases, but you split the transaction over two lines. With the insurance example (assuming you've ticked the Tax Inclusive button), that means you'd allocate $540 to Insurance Expense with GST as the Tax Code, and you'd then allocate $10 to Insurance Expense with FRE as the Tax Code. Clear as mud? You can see in the illustrious Figure 12-6 how it all works.

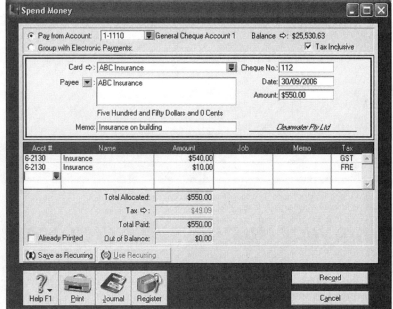

Figure 12-6: When GST doesn't come out at 10 percent.

Getting personal

If your business purchases goods or services that you use partly for private purposes, then be careful not to claim the GST on the private component.

For example, if you run your motor vehicle as a business expense but your log book shows that 20 percent of use is actually personal, then only claim 80 percent of the GST when you record the transaction. You can see how this works in Figure 12-7, where Maryanne pays for motor vehicle repairs on her Mercedes sports car. The total bill is for $1,000 but when she records this payment, she only allocates $800 to Motor Vehicle Repairs, allocating the remaining $200 to Personal Drawings.

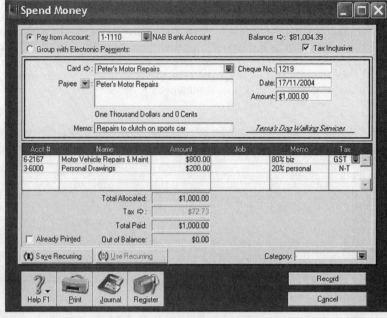

Figure 12-7:
Don't claim
GST on
personal
expenses.

Printing Your Business Activity Statement

Okay, so you have set up your tax codes and made sure you've coded your transactions correctly. Now I want to show you how to print your Business Activity Statement and make sure that it's correct.

Auditing your own accounts

The first thing you want to do before cooking up a Business Activity Statement is check that the figures you've got in the system are as perfect as a ripe mango in mid-summer. To help you in your quest for perfection, MYOB software comes with its very own auditor, ready to spot every single mistake.

1. **Go to your Accounts command centre and click the Company Data Auditor button.**

   The Company File Overview window pops up and on the left-hand side you'll see four side menus: Company File Overview, Account Reconciliation, Transaction Review and Tax Exception Review.

2. Click the Tax Exception Review side menu.

You'll see a list of five reports. The first two reports check for tax amount variances; the second two reports check for tax code exceptions and the last report reconciles linked accounts.

3. Enter a Date Range and click Run Review.

I usually go the whole hog and use 1 July as my Start Date and the current date as my End Date. In theory I only need to check errors for the current month or quarter, but I reckon that if the review picks up any errors that happened before that, so much the better.

4. If any red crosses appear against a report name, click Display to view what's wrong.

If everything's hunky-dory, you get a green tick. If something is amiss, you get a fearsome red cross. Click Display to check any reports where you failed the grade. (Read on to find out more about these reports and what they mean.)

Tax amount variances

The tax amount variance reports pick up if you (or anyone else) have zoomed in on any tax amounts and changed them (there's one report for sales transactions, and another report for purchases). I talk about this insidious sin a little earlier in this chapter, in the section 'Dealing with transactions when GST isn't 10 percent'. If any transactions come up with tax amount variances, zoom in and fix 'em up. This may mean splitting the transaction across two lines: one line for the taxable bit and another line for the tax-free bit.

Tax code exceptions

The tax-exception reports pick up any transactions where the tax code for an account differs from the code on the transaction. For example, if you have GST as the Tax Code for Telephone Expense, but you record the payment of a telephone bill with the FRE code, then this transaction will come up on your Tax Code Exceptions report.

Obviously, just because something appears on a Tax Code Exceptions report, that doesn't mean to say you've made a mistake. For example, you may have GST as the Tax Code for Staff Amenities Expense and most staff amenities really will have GST. However, every now and then you buy coffee and tea and these beverages, being defined by the powers-that-be as a *necessity* (how wise for once), are GST-free. The fact that you allocate this purchase to Staff Amenities and it's GST-free doesn't mean you got it wrong.

What I generally do with the Tax Code Exceptions report is display the report and look through for mistakes. If I zoom in on a transaction and I can see that it really is a tax exception, I stick an asterisk (*) in front of the memo. That way, if myself or anyone else displays a Tax Code Exceptions report in the future, they know that all transactions with an asterisk in front of them are okay and have been checked.

One more thing. You may find that the problem is that the Tax Code for the account itself is wrong in your Accounts List. To fix this up, go to your Accounts List, double-click on the offending account, click the Details tab and change the tax code. Easy as pie.

Tax code reconciliations

The Tax Code Reconciliation report is a bit of a weird old thing that picks up if anyone has done a journal directly to a linked tax code account, such as your GST Collected or GST Paid account. Unless someone has been doing some pretty creative accounting, this report usually comes up clean. If you find there are errors, you can usually zoom in on the offending transaction and re-allocate it quickly enough.

Getting your final reports ready

Before printing your GST reports and Business Activity Statement, don't forget to reconcile your bank account right up to the last day of the period for which you're reporting. Your accountant is the best person to ask about printing reports for your Business Activity Statement, but here are the reports I suggest you print, along with why they're important:

- ✔ **GST [Summary–Accrual] or GST [Summary–Cash] report:** Choose either the GST [Summary–Accrual] report, or the GST [Summary–Cash] report, depending on your reporting basis. (To find these reports, click the GST tab on your Reports menu.)

- ✔ **Profit & Loss report:** Your Profit & Loss is a vital reference. Read this report and ensure it makes sense! (You can find the Profit & Loss report on the Accounts tab of your Reports menu.)

- ✔ **Balance Sheet report:** Your Balance Sheet is the litmus test for whether your GST accounts reconcile. See the sidebar called 'Hanging in the balance' for more details on reconciling these accounts. (You can find the Balance Sheet report on the Accounts tab of your Reports menu.)

- ✔ **Employees Register Summary report (MYOB Accounting Plus, MYOB Premier and MYOB AccountEdge only):** This report is important because it provides a double-check for Questions W1 (total wages) and W2 (total PAYG tax) on your Business Activity Statement. (You can find this report on the Payroll tab of your Reports menu.)

TIP

Cash is king

Lots of people ask me whether they can use accrual accounting for their finances, but cash accounting for GST. The answer is yes, of course. It's fine to record supplier invoices as Purchases and to record customer invoices as Sales (that's what I mean by accrual accounting, in case you're wondering). But then, when you're ready to report for GST, you ask for the GST [Summary Cash] or the GST [Detail Cash] report.

And, miraculously enough, even though you've already recorded customer sales and supplier invoices, the GST for these transactions doesn't come up on these reports until your customers pay you or you've paid your suppliers.

Creating your Business Activity Statement

MYOB software comes with a special feature called BASlink, which is designed to make the horrible job of completing your Business Activity Statement not quite so horrible. Set up correctly, you can generate a report that looks almost identical to the pink Business Activity Statement form you receive from the ATO (except that your version comes complete with the correct figures, of course).

Here's what you do:

1. **Go to the Accounts command centre and click the BASlink button.**

2. **Select the period you want to report for.**

   Select the last month of your reporting period. So, if you're reporting for the period July to September, select September as the month.

3. **Click the BAS Info button and complete your selections, then click OK.**

   If you're registered for GST, make sure you select the report Business Activity Statement. (If you're not registered, select Instalment Activity Statement as your report.) Then choose your GST calculation method — Calculation Sheet is usually best — then either Accruals or Cash as your accounting basis, plus your reporting frequency (select Monthly or Quarterly). Ask your accountant if you're not sure about any of these settings.

4. **Click Prepare Statement and then press OK to continue.**

5. Click Setup (or, if you've used this report before, click Complete).

At this step you get to choose between setting up your tax codes for your BASlink report or simply moving on to complete the form. Click Setup if this is the first time you've used this BASlink report; otherwise, click Complete. A window then pops up, similar to the one shown in Figure 12-8, which looks exactly like the paper BAS form you know and love.

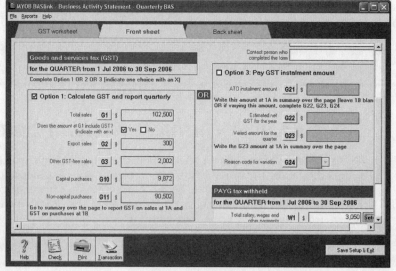

Figure 12-8: The BASlink report looks just like your regular Business Activity Statement.

6. Work through the GST worksheet, clicking the Setup buttons next to each question and selecting the corresponding tax codes.

Note: You don't need to click the Setup buttons if you've used this report before. However, the first time you generate this report, you need to click the Setup button that appears to the right of each question on the form, selecting the tax codes that belong to each question. If you're not sure which code to pick, see 'Setting up tax codes for your BAS' later in this chapter.

7. Click the Front Sheet and the Back Sheet tabs at the top of the report and click the Setup buttons, if necessary.

Again, if this is the first time you're generating this report, you need to click the Setup button that appears to the right of each question on the form, selecting a tax code for each question.

8. Click the Back Sheet tab, then click the Link button that appears next to questions and select the appropriate accounts depending on the type of tax being paid.

On the Back Sheet, some questions have a Link button next to them (rather than a Setup button). For these questions, pick the relevant account from your Accounts List, depending on the type of tax being paid — usually Income Tax Expense, Fringe Benefits Tax Expense or Provision for Income Tax. Ask your accountant if you're not sure which account to select.

9. **When you think everything is hunky-dory, click the Check button on the bottom left.**

   The Check button allows you to double-check all your work and, if you forgot something, it tells you. Kind of like having a fairy godmother, right on tap.

10. **Click the Print button, then copy the information onto the printed form that the ATO sends you.**

    Although MYOB software prints out a form that looks almost identical to the Business Activity Statement, you can't actually lodge this form. Instead, copy the figures onto the Business Activity Statement form that the Australian Taxation Office sends you.

11. **Click Transaction and then Print to find out how to record your tax payment or refund.**

    This step produces a handy help-sheet, showing you how to record your tax payment or refund. The transaction is often quite complex and split across several accounts, so store this help sheet carefully — you're going to need it all too soon!

12. **Click Save Setup & Exit, backup when prompted, then congratulate yourself on a job well done.**

    I seriously suggest you back up your Business Activity Statement when prompted. MYOB software stores this backup on your hard disk in a special BAS backup folder, but if you want to make an additional backup onto a removable disk or CD, then do so now.

Setting up tax codes for your BAS

At Step 6 in the preceding section, 'Creating your Business Activity Statement', I explain that when you first set up your BASlink report, you need to select the relevant tax code or codes at every question using the Setup button that appears to the right of each question. Daunting?

It need not be. Here are lots of hints about which tax codes to use where — but please, if you're at all unsure, talk to your accountant.

Sales: The first (and quite easy) section

Here's my simple guide to help you through the maze:

- ✔ **Question G1:** You report all sales in this question, so select every tax code you ever use for sales. Usually, this is simply GST, ITS and FRE, but if you export goods overseas or sell liquor wholesale, you also require the EXP or WET codes.

- ✔ **Question G2:** You report all export sales here, so use the EXP code.

- ✔ **Question G3:** You report all GST-free sales here, so use the FRE code.

- ✔ **Question G4:** Here's the spot for any input-taxed sales (including interest or residential rental income). ITS is the code to select here.

Purchases: The second (not quite so easy) section

Again, it's just a case of clicking the Setup buttons next to each question and selecting the right codes. Never fear, help is here:

- ✔ **Question G10:** You report all capital acquisitions here. CAP is the code.

- ✔ **Question G11:** You report all other expenses (with the exception of capital acquisitions) here. Select every tax code other than CAP that you use for purchases and expenses, such as FRE, INP and GST.

- ✔ **Question G13:** You report all purchases that relate to input-taxed sales here. INP is the darling that you're looking for.

- ✔ **Question G14:** You report all GST-free purchases here. FRE is your code.

PAYG Withholdings: The third (and fairly easy) section

When you click the Front sheet tab on your BASlink report you see a section called PAYG tax withheld. This is the where you specify the total value of wages paid to employees, along with how much tax you withheld. How you answer these questions depends on your version of MYOB software:

- ✔ **If you use MYOB Accounting Plus, MYOB Premier or MYOB AccountEdge:** Click the Setup button next to W1 and check out the list of payroll categories. Mark off all Wages categories, with the exception of Employee Advances. All done? Now, click the Setup button next to W2 and select PAYG Withholding.

- ✔ **If you use a version of MYOB software that doesn't include payroll:** Click the Setup button next to W1 and check out the list of tax codes. Select Y as your code and, when prompted, select this code for box W2 as well. (See MYOB software's online help if you need more info on the Y tax code and how it works.) Alternatively, if you don't use tax codes to track wages, you can manually type in figures for total wages and total PAYG tax.

Hanging in the balance

If you report for GST on an accruals basis, it's pretty easy to see whether your GST accounts balance, or not. Simply print a Balance Sheet for the last day of the reporting period printed on your BAS, and look at the balance of your GST Collected and GST Paid accounts. In the perfect world (hey, who said it wasn't?), whatever amounts appear here should be the amounts that appear on your BAS for the same period.

Things get a little trickier if you report on a cash basis, because you have to allow for the GST that you don't have to send to the ATO yet (because you haven't received payments from customers for outstanding invoices or you haven't paid suppliers). In this situation, you first print up three reports for the last day of your reporting period: a Receivables With Tax report, a Payables With Tax report and a Balance Sheet. The amounts for GST Collected and GST Paid on your Balance Sheet, *less* the balance of Tax Outstanding on the Receivables and Payables reports, should equal the amounts that appear on your BAS for the same period.

Confused? Yes, I know I've been unashamedly technical. If you're feeling bamboozled an alternative approach is to ask your accountant to help set up a system so you can balance your GST.

PAYG Instalments: The home stretch

As if things aren't confusing enough, the tax office uses the expression PAYG to refer to two entirely different types of tax. First, there's PAYG Withholding tax, which is the tax you take out of employees' pays, and then there's PAYG Instalment tax, which is really just the old much-hated provisional tax dressed up in a new frock.

Have a look at your pink Business Activity Statement form and see if you have to pay PAYG Instalment tax. If you do, here's how to set up BASlink so it calculates automatically:

1. **Go to the Accounts command centre and click the BASlink button.**

2. **Click the BAS Info button and under the PAYG Instalments section, select your Instalment reporting frequency.**

   Your reporting frequency may come up correctly already, but if it doesn't, change it to either Quarterly or Monthly — whatever is appropriate.

3. **Select your Instalment Option.**

   If you're paying a fixed instalment, select Option 1. If you're paying a percentage, select Option 2.

4. **Enter your PAYG Instalment Rate and click OK.**

If you selected Option 1, enter your PAYG percentage. If you selected Option 2, enter your PAYG instalment amount.

5. **If you're paying on a percentage basis, click Prepare BAS and go to the Back Sheet tab.**

6. **Click the Setup button next to question T1 and select all your income accounts.**

Click against all your income accounts, including the accounts that start with the number 8, as well as the accounts that start with the number 4.

7. **Click Save Setup & Exit to save your changes.**

Making Up for Your Mistakes

I remember being ditched by a boyfriend once who, listing my failures, recounted that I could never admit to my mistakes. He looked surprised as I replied that I'd made one with him.

And in this spirit of confession, you'll be delighted to know that I now readily admit to my mistakes, especially when it comes to accounts. It's so easy to muddle debits with credits, choose the wrong expense account or enter a payment twice. I freely admit it. And, assuming that you're not perfect either, I now discuss what to do when this happens to you . . .

Fixing up mistakes

Don't despair if you find you've made a mistake with GST on a BAS that you've already lodged. Usually, the easiest approach is to simply reverse the offending transaction (I talk more about reversing transactions in earlier chapters), dating your reversal in the current period, and then re-enter your transaction, recording it correctly this time! This way, the impact of your mistake comes up in the current BAS and you end up adjusting it automatically.

However, be aware there are time and dollar limits on what corrections you're allowed to make in your current BAS for mistakes made in a previous period. If you're not sure what these limits are, ask your accountant for the latest info. Also, regardless of what method you use to make adjustments, remember to keep notes about when mistakes were made as well as when they were corrected.

By the way, if you're not eligible to make an adjustment on your existing BAS, then your only option is to revise your earlier BAS. Contact the ATO or your accountant and ask them to walk you through this process.

Safeguarding against accidents

One way to protect yourself (or others) from accidentally changing transactions for a previous month or quarter is to use the Lock Periods feature in MYOB software (see Figure 12-9). After a period has been locked, you can't inadvertently add or change any transactions that belong to that period, or earlier.

To lock a previous period, go to the top menu bar, select Setup⇨Preferences, followed by the Security tab. Click against Lock Periods and select the month up to which you want to close off the accounts. Click OK and you're done!

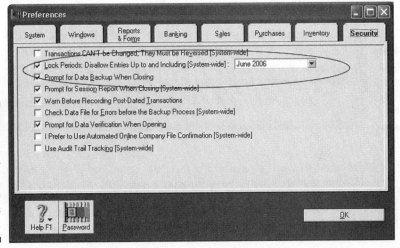

Figure 12-9: Locked periods are handy for preventing changes to previous periods.

Time to Pay Up

After you've completed your Business Activity Statement, you need to record your payment or refund. See the little button at the bottom of your BASlink report called Transaction? Click here and, rather obligingly, up pops a picture of how to record your GST payment or refund. Then, click Print — it's easier to read this way.

The whole idea is this: When you send in your BAS, you report on a whole range of taxes — GST Collected, GST Paid, PAYG Withholding tax and PAYG Instalment tax, to name but a few. Therefore, when you pay your tax (or receive a refund), you need to allocate this payment or deposit to all the different tax accounts. Figure 12-10 shows this transaction.

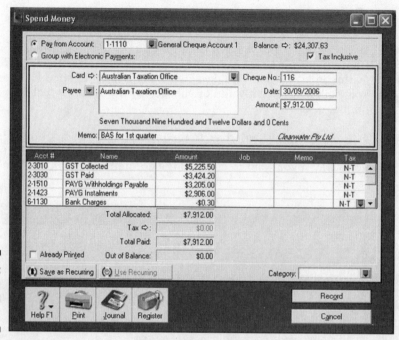

Figure 12-10:
Recording
your BAS
payment.

And one last pearl of wisdom before this delightful chapter comes to a close. However miraculously everything balances, you'll always end up with a few cents gone astray, because the BAS rounds every field to the nearest dollar. Simply allocate these few cents to your Bank Charges account and everything will be just fine.

Your BAS Checklist

When you send in your BAS, it doesn't get read by a real, live person with warm skin, the occasional pimple and an irrational desire to be loved. No, your BAS gets read by a beige scanner that communicates to the outside world in a series of forlorn beeps. Have compassion for this computer and remember that the days of insight, common-sense and initiative are completely over.

- Use the form the ATO sends to you, not the BAS form that MYOB software prints out, even if the two do look virtually identical. Without those diddly-squat barcodes at the top of the ATO form, the poor tax office computer won't know what's what.

- Write your answers in pencil first. This stuff is so mind-numbingly fiddly, it's almost impossible not to make a blunder.

- When you do finalise your answers, use black pen, because the poor darlin' computers (or should I say scanners) at the ATO can't read any other colours.

- Copy the totals from the back of your BAS onto the front of your BAS. (It wouldn't be the government if you didn't write it twice.)

- Ignore any cents. If you write down you have to pay $1,285.23 in GST, you could end up with a bill from the tax office for $128,523.00. Yucky in anyone's language.

- Keep a copy of your BAS. It's amazing how often you have to refer back to this pesky form.

- Don't include things like dollar signs or minus signs, even if the amount is negative. Seems incredible, but that's the way the cookie crumbles.

Chapter 13

M-Powering Yourself and Going Online

*Y*ou may feel a bit hesitant about embracing online technology (after all, there are more interesting things to embrace). However, as you get into it, you'll find that paying employees and suppliers by electronic transfer isn't only easy, it's even kind of fun.

The whole idea is that you switch on your computer, decide how much you want to pay someone and then send a message down the wire from your computer to your bank. After a few seconds of whirring and humming, rather miraculously, the balance in your bank account goes down and the balance in the other person's bank account goes up. And the whole procedure is done without counting cash, writing a cheque or sending a carrier pigeon. Awesome.

By the way, this chapter talks about M-Powered Payments, M-Powered Invoices, M-Powered Bank Statements and M-Powered MoneyController, but *doesn't* provide details about M-Powered Superannuation, a delightful topic I cover in the illustrious Chapter 9.

Getting Ready for Electronic Payments

You can pay people electronically two different ways.

- **Regular electronic payments.** With this method you record the payment in your MYOB company file, create a summary payment file, open this summary file using your bank's Internet banking service and then send your payment to suppliers and employees.

- **MYOB M-Powered Payments.** This method lets you pay suppliers and employees electronically direct from your MYOB company file — without using your bank as an intermediary.

Setting up employee and supplier details

In order to pay suppliers and employees electronically (no matter which method you use), you first need to enter their bank account details in your MYOB company file.

1. **Go to Cards List in the Card File command centre.**

   (I thought you'd like to start off with something easy.)

2. **Double-click on the name of the company or person you plan to pay electronically and click the card's Payment Details tab.**

3. **If you're paying an employee, specify how many accounts you want the pay between.**

   For example, some employees like to split their pay across a couple of accounts, maybe paying $200 against a mortgage, $100 into a savings account and the balance into a cheque account.

4. **Complete the account details.**

   Complete the BSB Number, Bank Account Number and Bank Acct Name, as shown in Figure 13-1. (The BSB Number is a special six-digit code that stands for the bank's name and branch.)

5. **Complete the Statement Text for suppliers, but leave the Statement Text for employees blank.**

For suppliers, detail what you want the suppliers to see on their statements when you pay them — maybe your customer reference ID or something similar. For employees, simply leave the Statement Text blank. This way, the default message on their statement appears as 'PAY for', followed by the pay period (for example, PAY for 25/12/06), which is about as clear a message as you can get.

6. **Optional: Click Send Automatic M-Powered Payment Remittances to this Supplier if you want to take advantage of this service.**

See 'Letting Suppliers Know You've Paid Them' later in this chapter for more about sending remittance advices. If you click this option (and you have to sign up for M-Powered Payments in order to do so), you're prompted to enter either email or fax details for this supplier.

7. **Double-check the banking details, then click OK.**

I know I may strike you as Fixated, Insecure, Neurotic and Emotional (otherwise known as FINE), but be ultra-careful when recording banking details. Even if you only enter one teensy-weensy figure incorrectly, your bank happily transfers money to the wrong bank account! Random acts of kindness are one thing, but donating funds to completely unknown individuals is pretty extreme.

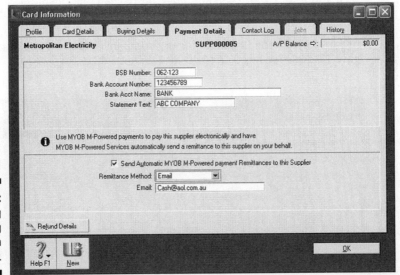

Figure 13-1:
Entering banking details for a supplier.

Hooking up your bank account

Head to your Accounts List and double-click on the name of the bank account from which you want to make electronic payments. Click the Banking tab and complete your banking details, bearing in mind the following:

TIP

- ✔ Your BSB Number is a special six-digit code that stands for your bank and branch. This number is listed just before your account number on any bank statement or chequebook.

- ✔ If you want the option to pay by regular electronic payments (not just by M-Powered Payments), click I Create Bank Files [ABA] for This Account.

- ✔ The Bank Code is a three-letter code that stands for your bank (NAB, CBA, WBC and so on).

- ✔ Your Direct Entry User ID is a special code that your bank gives you when you register your online banking software. (You don't need this code for M-Powered Payments.)

- ✔ You only need to tick Include a Self-Balancing Transaction if your bank requires a self-balancing transaction for each electronic payment you lodge.

- ✔ If you want to, you can nominate more than one business bank account for M-Powered Payments.

You can see how the Bank Info for my company looks by checking out Figure 13-2 (please feel free to credit this account at any time).

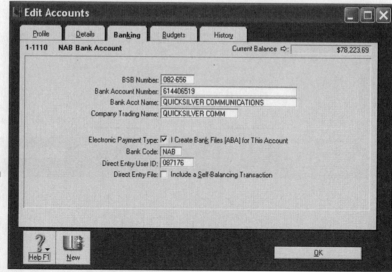

Figure 13-2:
Completed bank account details.

M-Powering yourself — ready or not?

Throughout this chapter, I make the distinction between MYOB M-Powered Payments (where you make electronic payments directly out of your MYOB company file) and regular electronic payments (where you send a payment batch out of your company file into your Internet banking software).

Although using MYOB M-Powered Payments is much more efficient and almost always more cost-effective than making regular electronic payments, there are still some valid reasons why I continue to explain both options. First, M-Powered Payments isn't available for all versions of MYOB software; second, M-Powered Payments isn't available to all banks; third, you still need to make sure this way of working is cost-effective for your business. Finally, the application process takes a while, so you may want to use regular electronic payments while you're waiting for your M-Powered application to go through.

Understanding when M-Powered Payments is an option

Although the M-Powered Payments option is a wonderful thing, not all MYOB software users can access it.

- ✔ MYOB M-Powered Payments isn't available in MYOB software versions earlier than 2004, nor in MYOB BusinessBasics or FirstEdge.

- ✔ If you have a Macintosh, M-Powered Payments isn't an option, in the same way that making regular electronic payments via Macs isn't available at many banks either. (It's a wonder the Anti-Discrimination legislation in this country doesn't address the persecution of Apple Macs, but there you go.)

- ✔ At the time of writing, the only banks that have a direct facility with MYOB software are the Commonwealth Bank and Westpac. Other banks are still going through the negotiation process — the ANZ is pretty close — so it's best to ring MYOB customer service on 1300 555 111 for the latest news on what your bank is up to. (For more about your options if your bank doesn't have a direct facility, skip to the section 'What to do when your bank won't play'.)

The cost (and hidden savings) of M-Powered Payments

The current M-Powered Payments fees are as follows:

- ✔ $10 per month access fee to MYOB M-Powered services (this fee covers all services, including M-Powered Invoices and Superannuation). This fee is waived if you subscribe to a current support plan.

- ✔ 25 cents per electronic payment.

- ✔ 25 cents per remittance advice sent by fax. Remittance advices sent by email are free.

Not so obvious as the M-Powered Payments fees are the hidden savings. When you pay suppliers or employees the old-fashioned way, you need to put a value on your own time and calculate how long it takes to write a cheque, do a remittance advice, address an envelope, lick the envelope (oh, that wonderful taste) and record the payment in your accounts. You also need to factor in postage and the bank fees for processing a cheque (usually about 50 cents a pop). If your maths is anything like mine, you'll likely arrive at the conclusion that M-Powered Payments is one of those very rare beasts: A genuine bargain.

M-Powered Payments also works out cheaper than most electronic banking facilities, especially if you choose to send remittance advices by email, rather than by fax. If you make a batch of payments to suppliers using M-Powered Payments, these go out of your bank account as a single transaction, incurring only one electronic transaction fee from your bank for the whole batch.

What to do when your bank won't play

As I mention earlier in this chapter (see 'Understanding when M-Powered Payments is an option'), only the Commonwealth Bank and Westpac offer direct facilities with M-Powered Payments. If you bank with any other institution, your only option is to apply for a TNA (Transaction Negotiation Authority). The idea of a TNA is that your bank agrees to reimburse MYOB for all payments made, regardless of whether or not you have sufficient funds in your account. This surprising degree of trust comes with a small fee, normally around $100 for setting up the whole TNA rigmarole (this fee does vary from bank to bank).

Although you can theoretically apply for a TNA with any bank, building society or credit union, MYOB already has agreements in place with the following banks: Adelaide Bank; Bank of Queensland; BankSA; Bank of Western Australia; Bendigo Bank; St George Bank and Suncorp-Metway Bank. With these banks, you don't have to approach the bank yourself to apply for a TNA. Instead, you simply submit an M-Powered Payments application and MYOB arranges for your bank to send you a 'letter of offer' for a TNA facility.

Applying for M-Powered Payments

In truth, MYOB software is so keen that you apply for M-Powered Payments that it's hard to avoid the pesky Help window that asks if you'd like to click that innocent 'Tell Me More' button. However, you can cut to the chase by going to www.myob.com.au/m-powered and clicking Apply Now. (You need your software serial number handy.) The application form is rather daunting, but don't be deterred. Tell yourself it's easier than climbing Mt Everest (not that I've ever tried).

The whole application process takes anywhere between two and six weeks, depending on how well you dance the paperwork polka (I always seem to do something wrong and make the whole process drag on much longer) and also on whether your bank has a direct facility with MYOB or you need to apply for a TNA. When your application is approved, you'll be asked to go to the M-Powered Service Centre and activate your service. This complete, you'll be ready to go.

Making Your First Electronic Payment

Suppose you're ready to record your first electronic payment. You can process this payment either via MYOB M-Powered Payments or via regular electronic banking. This section explains both methods and how they work.

Preparing to pay suppliers electronically

With both M-Powered Payments and regular electronic payments, creating an electronic payments file ready to send to the bank is easy. Here's how to get started:

1. Record supplier payments in your MYOB software.

Record your supplier payments the same way you normally do, either in Spend Money or Pay Bills, depending on your preference (refer to Chapter 6 for more details). Complete the date and the transaction details as per any other transaction, but ignore the Cheque No. field ('cos guess what, this payment isn't a cheque).

2. Click the Group with Electronic Payments button.

You find this button in the top-left corner of the Spend Money or Pay Bills windows. When you click this button, you group this electronic payment in a batch with any other electronic payments you make that day. You can see how this works in Figure 13-3.

3. Check the reference in the Statement Text field.

This reference appears on your supplier's bank statement, so make sure you're at least a little bit coherent. That way your supplier can identify that your company is making the payment.

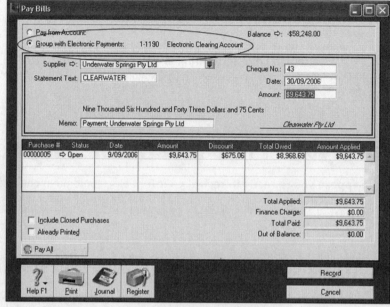

Figure 13-3:
Click Group
with
Electronic
Payments to
make a batch
of electronic
payments.

4. Record your payment as normal and repeat this process for anybody else you plan to pay electronically that day.

After you record your first electronic payment, record any other payments that you want to make electronically, so that you can combine all your payments into the one batch.

You're now ready to process all electronic payments. To find out what to do next, see the section 'Preparing your electronic payments file' later in this chapter.

Paying employees electronically

Before you try to pay employees electronically, first go to each employee's card, select Electronic as the Payment Method, and complete all their banking info. (Refer to the section 'Setting up employee and supplier details' earlier in this chapter for more details.)

With your setup complete, recording employee payments is easy-peasy. Simply record pays in the normal way, as described in Chapter 9, until you reach the Process Payments window. At this point, click the Prepare Electronic Payments button. This takes you to the Prepare Electronic Payments window, from where you can make your selections to send electronic payments to the bank. Read on to find out more . . .

Preparing your electronic payments file

If you record a supplier or employee payment and select Electronic as the Payment Method, then that payment goes into a batch with all other payments that you mark for electronic processing. When you're ready to process these payments, this is what you do:

1. **Click the Prepare Electronic Payments button.**

   If you're paying suppliers, go to Prepare Electronic Payments from either the Banking or the Purchases command centre. If you're paying employees, you arrive at Prepare Electronic Payments in the third step of the payroll process.

2. **Look at what comes up and consider whether it's reasonable.**

   If no transactions appear, or you can't see all the transactions that you know should be there, choose or tweak the selection using the Select Payment By menu. I find the easiest and quickest method is to select All Payment Types here.

   If you find that a whole swag of transactions appear, dating back to the Dark Ages, it's probably because you've been using MYOB software for a while and other transactions were allocated to your Electronic Clearing account in the past. See the sidebar 'When clearing accounts need clearing' for details of how to extricate yourself from this particular pickle.

3. **In the Pay From Account box select which bank account to make the payment from.**

   This is usually your business cheque account or something similar.

4. **Update the message in Your Bank Statement Text.**

   The Your Bank Statement Text box shows what is going to appear on your bank statement — not your suppliers' or employees' statements. The suggested text that MYOB software offers at this point is usually rather obscure (what does IDEP 0010 mean to you?), so change this text to something more meaningful.

5. **Check the Bank Processing Date.**

   As the Bank Processing Date, choose the date that you want these payments to go out of your bank account. If you're creating this file after-hours, choose the next day as your date, otherwise your bank gets nasty and rejects the file. You can even choose to process payments to be made at a future date — great if you're going away on hols — so long as the date isn't more than 45 days into the future.

6. **Select the payments you want to process.**

Select all payments you want to process in this batch by clicking in the far right column, as shown in Figure 13-4.

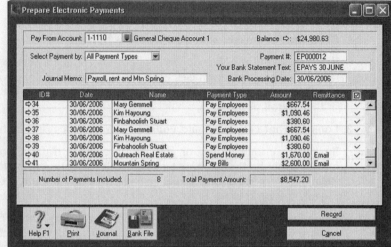

Figure 13-4:
Processing
your first
electronic
payments
batch.

7. **To pay this batch using M-Powered Payments, click Record.**

The Authorisation window appears.

8. **Select either Authorise Now or Authorise Later.**

It's up to you, but even if you select Authorise Later you're basically ready to send your M-Powered Payments batch now. (See 'Transmitting an M-Powered Payments file' later in this chapter.)

9. **To pay this batch using regular electronic payments, click the Bank File button, and then click Save.**

When you click the Bank File button, you're prompted to save your electronic payment file. Note the folder where this file is stored — you need to know this information later, when you're in your Internet banking software — and click Save. See 'Transmitting a regular electronic payments file' for more details about what happens next.

Here's a frugal way to ensure that your first attempt at electronic payments isn't a disaster: On your first go, pick three suppliers or employees and pay them (electronically) ten cents each. If the payment works, they'll go wild with gratitude. If the thing is a flop, you haven't lost much. I reckon this experiment is much better than waiting till crunch time — like payday for employees, and having to deal with 15 irate staff when the whole thing stuffs up.

When clearing accounts need clearing

Sometimes when you first try to process electronic payments, you find that a whole bunch of transactions appear, dating months or even years back. Don't sweat. You can get rid of these old transactions by heading to your Accounts List and creating a new Electronic Payments account (make sure to select Bank as the Account Type). Then go to your Linked Accounts menu (found under Setup) and click Accounts & Banking Accounts. Select this new account as your Bank Account for Electronic Payments.

Transmitting an M-Powered Payments file

If you're using MYOB M-Powered Payments, after you create your electronic payment using Prepare Electronic Payments (refer to your choices in the preceding section, 'Creating your electronic payments file'), your next step is to transmit this payment to your bank.

1. **Click the M-Powered Services Centre button that appears on the bottom-right of every command centre.**

2. **Check the Status column, authorising payments if necessary.**

   If the status of any payments is To Be Authorised or Partially Authorised, zoom in on these payments and authorise them.

3. **Click Send/Receive.**

   All electronic payments with To Be Sent as their status fly off into the ether, fattening other people's accounts (usually the next day).

4. **Read the Transmission Summary and click OK.**

   Assuming your payment instructions go through successfully (and they should do if you're currently online!), a Transmission Summary pops up. Check that all your payments were processed successfully and click OK to return to the M-Powered Services Centre.

Transmitting a regular electronic payments file

After you record your payments and create your payments batch (refer to 'Paying suppliers electronically', 'Paying employees electronically' and 'Preparing your electronic payments file' earlier in this chapter), you're ready to send your payments down the wire to your bank.

The symmetry of this line dance depends on which bank you're with, but the essential process is always the same:

1. **Fire up your online banking software or Internet banking.**

   Depending on your bank, you either have special online business banking software or you simply fire up regular Internet banking (with some banks, the limitation of Internet banking is that you can't import payment batches).

2. **Open your electronic payments file.**

   Your electronic payments file is the file you created in 'Preparing your electronic payments file'. If it's not obvious how to open this file, contact your bank and ask for help — let your bank earn those hefty fees. *Hint:* Banks often describe this procedure as importing a file or direct funds transfer.

3. **Check your payments and send them off into the wild unknown.**

   When you open up your electronic payments file, you should see each payment listed one by one, complete with banking details. Check these payments one last time and then send the file. The deed is done!

Letting Suppliers Know You've Paid Them

So you've benevolently sent money electronically to all your suppliers! Now you need to inform them of your good work. It seems a bit futile to send remittance advices by snail mail when you've gone to all the trouble of electronic transfer, so your best bet is to send remittance advices by fax or email.

If you subscribe to M-Powered Payments, then sending remittance advices is a walk in the park. Simply go to the Payment Details tab in each supplier's card and click Send Automatic M-Powered Payment Remittances to this Supplier, then select whether you want to send remittances by email or fax.

Now, whenever you process a supplier payment, your supplier automatically receives a remittance advice, complete with invoice numbers, dates and amounts. (Note that sending remittance advices by email is free of charge, but faxes currently cost 25 cents each.)

If you don't subscribe to M-Powered Payments, then there's no simple solution to the remittance advice dilemma. With some trickery and imagination, you can customise the standard cheques template (go to Setup, click Customise Forms, then Cheques) so that this template prints out looking like a remittance advice, not a cheque. However, you still have to go through the high jinks of emailing these remittance advices, one by one.

The mysterious electronic clearing account

Whenever you record an electronic payment, you click the button in the top-left corner called Group with Electronic Payments. But have you noticed that this payment doesn't come out of your business bank account? Nay, it comes out of a special electronic clearing account.

When you're ready to process these payments, you go to Prepare Electronic Payments. After they're processed, the combined total of these electronic payments comes out of your business bank account and goes into your electronic clearing account. The balance of your electronic clearing account (which doesn't exist in reality and is just a mythical creation) always starts with zero and returns to zero.

The moral of the story? If you see that the balance of your electronic clearing account isn't zero (assuming you've processed all electronic payments at that point), then you have a problem. See if you can figure out when it went out of balance; account inquiries are helpful for this process. This will usually identify the culprit transaction.

Keeping Track of the Dosh

One of the magnificent things about MYOB M-Powered services is the way you can keep track of where your payments are up to. You can see payments you've authorised; payments you haven't; payments that have been sent but not cleared yet or payments that have been rejected. For the person who likes to be in control, it's heaven on a stick.

Getting status conscious

To review the status of your M-Powered Payments, click the M-Powered Services Centre button in any command centre, then click Send/Receive to go online. After you're connected, a Transmission Summary pops up, confirming how many messages have been sent or received. Click OK.

Back in the M-Powered Services Centre, you see a list of all outstanding payments, along with their status. Here's what the different status messages mean:

- ✔ **To Be Authorised:** You've chosen to authorise this payment later.
- ✔ **Partially Authorised:** You need a second authorisation for this payment.
- ✔ **To Be Sent:** You've authorised this payment but haven't sent it yet.
- ✔ **Sent:** You've sent this payment but it hasn't cleared out of your bank account yet.

- ✔ **Processed:** This payment has already been sent and has been cleared by your bank.
- ✔ **Future Dated:** This payment will be processed at a future date.
- ✔ **Cancelled:** This future-dated payment has been cancelled at your request.
- ✔ **Awaiting Approval:** Your bank has received this payment but, due to insufficient funds in your account, it hasn't been processed yet.
- ✔ **Failed:** This payment has been rejected, probably due to insufficient funds. (Better luck next time.)

Changing your mind

With M-Powered Payments, although you can't change payments after you've sent them, you can sometimes delete them and start again from scratch.

You can only delete a payment if the status is To Be Authorised, Partially Authorised, To Be Sent or Cancelled. (I guess it's a bit optimistic to think you could change a payment after it's already hit someone else's bank account.) However, if the status of your payment is Sent, Awaiting Approval or Processed, you won't be able to delete it. The only way to stop a payment is to contact the MYOB M-Powered Services support team on 1300 555 931 or email m-powered@myob.com.au.

Going back on your word

If you need to cancel a future-dated payment, contact MYOB M-Powered Services on 1300 555 931 or send an email to m-powered@myob.com.au. Ask for a *Change Request Form*. You can cancel this payment if you manage to return this form to MYOB M-Powered Services by close of business on the business day before the requested processing date.

If your cancellation instructions are successful, MYOB M-Powered Services sends you confirmation of the cancellation. Likewise, the status of this payment changes from Future Dated to Cancelled.

Dealing with rejection

Rejection is hard enough to deal with at the best of times, but when the bank starts knocking you back you know it's time to get a therapist. Trouble is, therapy gets kind of expensive, so I feel obliged to offer an alternative course of action.

1. **Contemplate the nature of your failure.**

   With M-Powered Payments, you know when a payment has been rejected because the Status comes up as Failed (you can zoom in on this payment to view more details to find out why this happened). With regular electronic payments, you usually have to wait until the bank notifies you to discover that a payment has been rejected. The most common reasons for rejection are insufficient funds (forgive the irony) or wrong account numbers.

2. **Go to your Bank Register and display the payment batch that includes the rejected payment. Zoom in on the rejected transaction.**

3. **From the Edit menu, select Reverse Transaction and click Record.**

   When you ask to reverse the transaction, MYOB software obligingly comes up with a transaction that's the exact opposite of the one you recorded initially. You may want to change the date of this reversal so that it matches the date that the transaction actually bounced.

4. **Click the Prepare Electronic Payments button.**

   You should see the reversal that you just recorded appearing in the list of electronic payments, similar to Figure 13-5. It's easy to spot reversals because they're negative amounts.

5. **Select the rejected transaction and click Process, then OK.**

   A scary warning message pops up, saying that continuing may result in bank reconciliation problems. Don't hesitate, you're strong and fearless!

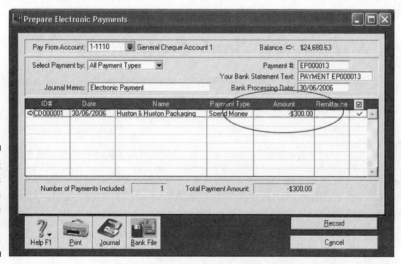

Figure 13-5:
Reversals show up as negative electronic payments.

6. **Either click Record (for M-Powered Payments) or click Bank File (for regular electronic payments).**

   A warning message tells you that this transaction will be recorded, but no bank file created. This is absolutely fine.

7. **Click OK.**

8. **Double-check that everything is as it should be in the world.**

   Head over to your Bank Register and make sure that the rejected transaction appears as a deposit in your account.

Signing Up for Other M-Powered Services

Although most of this chapter talks about M-Powered Payments, some other M-Powered services warrant a mention. In this section I talk about M-Powered Bank Statements, M-Powered MoneyController and M-Powered Invoices. (However, I don't cover M-Powered Superannuation in this chapter because it's part of the whole payroll deal in Chapter 9.)

By the way, the $10 M-Powered monthly access fee is a single fee that covers *all* M-Powered services. This coverage means that if you already subscribe to M-Powered Payments, you don't have to pay an extra $10 a month when you sign up for a different M-Powered service. (Actually, most people don't end up paying anything at all, because MYOB waives the monthly fee if you subscribe to a current support plan.)

M-Powered Bank Statements

With M-Powered Bank Statements, you can download bank statement information directly into your company file. In practice, this means you can view your bank statements and make account inquiries from within MYOB software.

After you have M-Powered Bank Statements up and running, click the Banking tab of your Reports menu and explore the new M-Powered reports:

- ✔ The Bank Statements report looks similar to a regular bank statement, listing the bank details of every cheque, deposit and withdrawal, as well as a closing balance.

- ✔ The Transaction Enquiry report searches on transactions for any date range, cheque number or amount.

- ✔ The Bank Account Balance report gives a daily summary of total deposits and withdrawals, as well as a closing balance for each day.

Currently, M-Powered Bank Statements is only available to Commonwealth Bank and Westpac customers. A fee of 10 cents per transaction applies (after all, there's no such thing as a free lunch), but the upside is that your bank statement information forms part of your accounts and that your bank statements are always up to date, making it easy to keep track of payments you've made or received. Of course, whether or not these fees outweigh the benefits depends partly on how many transactions you make per month. For more details about M-Powered Bank Statements, refer to Chapter 7.

M-Powered MoneyController

Put simply, M-Powered MoneyController does two things. The first is that it analyses how much money you need to put aside into investment accounts. The second is that it makes it easy for you to transfer money back and forth between your regular bank accounts and investment accounts.

Although no fees are attached to this service, the whole MoneyController deal rests on an agreement between MYOB Software and Macquarie Bank. So, in order to use these whizzbang MoneyController features, you first need to open up a special investment account with Macquarie Bank.

If you're thinking about using M-Powered MoneyController, the easiest way to see how it works is to open up the Clearwater demonstration file (to do this, click the Explore button on the MYOB Welcome window). Go to the Accounts command centre and click MoneyController.

Figure 13-6 shows what MoneyController looks like. The Analyse Provisions tabs looks at how much you owe in GST and PAYG Withholding, and tells you how much money you should have put aside at any time. The Analyse Investment Capacity tab shows your Bank Accounts and Trade Debtors and compares the total of these assets against your current liabilities, such as credit cards and Trade Creditors. The difference, if it's a positive amount, is the amount you can safely salt away in an investment account.

When you've figured out how much money you need to transfer into an investment account, you don't have to then fire up your Internet banking software and do a transfer. Instead, you simply click the Prepare Money Transfer button. The Transfer Money window then confirms how much money you want to transfer, what accounts you want to transfer the money to and from, and what's going to appear on the statement. All you have to do is check these settings and click Record.

For more information about M-Powered MoneyController, visit www.myob.com.au/m-powered.

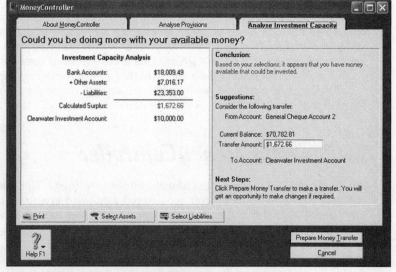

Figure 13-6:
M-Powered
Money-
Controller
helps you
manage your
surplus cash
efficiently.

M-Powered Invoices

If you subscribe to MYOB M-Powered Invoices, you can offer your customers the choice of paying invoices by BPAY, POSTbillpay or by credit card over the phone.

The advantages of subscribing to M-Powered Invoices include that you'll probably get paid quicker (don't people just love their Frequent Flyer points?), your invoices will look pretty swish (not everyone can offer 24-hour a day pay-by-phone facilities) and you can spend more time at the beach (the whole process is blindingly efficient).

Weighed up against these advantages, probably the only disadvantage of M-Powered Invoices is the fees, which can become pretty hefty. You incur a transaction fee of $2 per payment, along with normal credit card merchant fees (which at the time of writing are approximately 1.65 percent, plus 8 cents per transaction). Oh yes, and the process of applying for M-Powered Invoices can be a bit of a rigmarole.

Of course, whether M-Powered Invoices is going to work out well for you depends on your total sales, how many payments you process every month, how much you value your own time (or that of your bookkeeper's) and the average value of your invoices. (If your average sale is only $50, a $2 fee per invoice is kind of punitive; but if your average sale is $500, then $2 doesn't seem so bad.)

Understanding Your M-Powered Box File

In the more recent versions of MYOB software, whenever you create a new company file, MYOB software automatically creates a box file using the same name. For example, if you create a new company file called Peachy Veechi.dat, MYOB software automatically creates a box file called Peachy Veechi.box as well.

The function of this box file is to keep track of your M-Powered transactions, and as such, it's crucial to keep your company file and box file together at all times. If you do separate the two files — maybe by moving your company file to a new computer or by changing the folder in which it's stored — you lose a record of all the electronic payments you've made, or worse still, payments you've sent to be processed may not go through correctly.

In a similar vein, never rename your company file without renaming your box file at the same time. Think of your box file and your company file as mating swans, who will pine away if they are separated or can't find one another. Similarly, when backing up or restoring files, make sure you back up or restore both the company file and its related box file. (This process happens automatically if you back up using the commands from within MYOB software, but doesn't happen automatically if you back up using some other method.)

Chapter 14

Looking After Your Files

. . . .

In This Chapter

▶ Backing up, backing up, backing up

▶ Restoring your backup when you have to

▶ Verifying files to keep 'em clean

▶ Optimising files to keep 'em happy

▶ Staying cool when you strike an error message

▶ Keeping stuff private with passwords

. . . .

My mother once gave me the sage advice that no-one ever goes to their deathbed bemoaning that they never did enough housework. There are many, many better things to do with one's life, she said.

I've had a pretty interesting life so far, getting by with doing as little housework as possible. But the one area where I reckon a little tidiness doesn't go astray is inside my computer. That's because as soon as I get lazy and forget to back up or organise my files, my cantankerous laptop chucks a wobbly and I end up losing work, having to do stuff all over again, or struggling for hours begging my laptop to make up and be friends.

So tie on your apron, grab your broom, wet your mop and read this chapter to get a run-down on all you need to know to keep everything spick and span.

The Backup Bible

What does all this talk about backing up mean? Put simply, a backup is when you make an extra copy of your business data and store the copy somewhere other than on your computer, usually on a CD, DVD or external hard drive. The reason why this extra copy is so important is that it can save your bacon if anything ever happens to your computer (which undoubtedly will happen, sooner or later).

Many things can put your computer out of action. Your hard disk could come down with a virus and take to its bed; your computer could be struck by lightning and lose its marbles, or your whole system could just curl up its toes and die. Alternatively, your office could be burnt to the ground (taking your computer with it), or you could be burgled — I'm such a sunny and optimistic kind of person, aren't I?

If you wouldn't go on a long trip without checking the oil in your car, or take a parachute jump without an emergency chute, then don't even think about not backing up.

Deciding how often to back up

So you're running a small business, you've got hours of leisure time and you're looking for something else to do . . .

No? The irony of backing up is that the busier you are, the more often you need to do it. If you work on your accounts every day, you should do a backup once a day. If you work on your accounts every week, then you should back up once a week.

Another important trick to backing up is to make extra archival backups and keep them separate from your ordinary backups. The idea behind the archival backup is that if corruption sneaks into your company file and it takes you a while to discover it, you can always go back to the previous month or quarter's archival backup and use it as a clean copy. If you have a thousand or more transactions a month, make an archival backup at the end of each month. Otherwise, make an archival backup at the end of each quarter.

Don't forget that many networks are set up so only information stored on the main server is backed up. If your company file is located on a local workstation, you *must* remember to devise special backup procedures for this file.

Backing up your company file

Okay, are you ready to rock? Here goes:

1. **Insert a CD or DVD into the relevant drive, or plug your external flash drive or hard drive into the USB port.**

   In order to back up onto a CD or DVD, you need a CD or DVD burner (which is a bit different from a regular CD or DVD drive). If you're not sure what you've got, ask the nearest propeller-head.

Also, when buying CDs, you have the choice between CD-RW disks and CD-R disks. CD-RW disks let you write to them again and again, meaning that you can delete or add more data to the CD as often as you like. CD-R disks let you write to them once only, which means you can't delete or update them once you're done.

2. **Choose File from the top menu bar and then select Backup.**

I'm assuming you have your company file open at this point.

3. **Choose either to Backup all Data or to Backup Company File and M-Powered Services Centre only.**

Unless you have a pressing reason otherwise, always choose to Backup all Data. This selection takes very little extra storage space and you can sleep easy knowing that you've backed up everything to do with your MYOB company file — including custom reports, customised forms and your BAS templates.

4. **Select the Check Company File for Errors button and click Continue.**

You can skip this step if you're really running short of time; however, I don't recommend you do.

MYOB software then verifies your data and (hopefully) gives you a message that 'no errors were found in your company file'.

5. **Click OK.**

6. **Check the location of your backup, changing it if necessary.**

If you're using a PC, don't forget to select the correct Drive in the Save In field, as shown in Figure 14-1. For example, if you're backing up onto CD or DVD, that's usually the D: or E: drive. External hard drives could come up as the E: drive or F: drive. If you don't change the drive, you may end up backing up onto your hard disk (usually the C: drive), which is where your actual company file resides, thereby defeating the whole purpose of backing up!

If you're using a Mac, click the Desktop folder and double-click on your backup drive. Then click Open if you want to store your file in a particular folder on your backup or simply click Save.

7. **Check the file name and click Save.**

The file name that comes up automatically is always something like MYOB1230.zip (if you're using a PC) or Backup 30/12/06 accounts.sit (if you're using a Mac). The numbers stand for the date (for example, 1230 stands for 30 December) and the extensions *zip* or *sit* mean that your information is compressed so that it takes up the least room possible. Usually, this file name is fine and you can leave it as is.

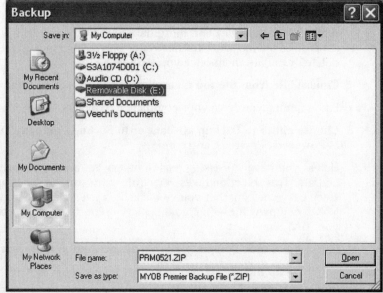

Figure 14-1:
When
backing up,
make sure
you select a
removable
drive, such
as a CD or
DVD.

8. Check that the file actually copied onto your backup, then eject it.

I know I'm neurotic, but I always like to go into My Computer (if using a PC) or my Finder (if using a Mac) and check that the file is sitting on my backup before I eject the CD or DVD, or unplug the removable hard drive. You can see this action in all its glory in Figure 14-2.

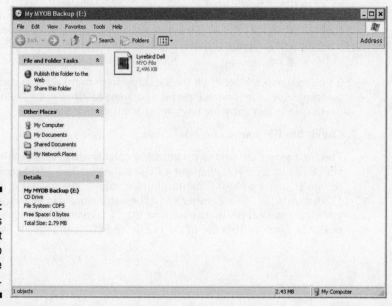

Figure 14-2:
Always
check that
your backup
file is where
it should be.

9. **Label your backup and store it in a cool, dry place away from the office.**

Remember that computer data is sensitive to magnetic fields (such as sound-system speakers, microwaves and incredibly beautiful people of the opposite sex). Also, if you want your backup to live a full and healthy life, don't store it on the dashboard of your car, underneath the rabbit cage or, worse still, on top of the computer. Take it away from the office and put it somewhere where it won't be disturbed.

If you're making an archival backup (such as an end-of-year backup), consider writing your password on the backup label. That way, if you need to restore this backup several years later, maybe in the event of an audit, you won't be scratching your head trying to remember what password you used all those years ago.

Restoration Rave

Now that you have a backup of your company file, maybe you want to use it; perhaps even on another computer? However, you can't just copy the file across from the backup and simply open it. No such luck. When you back up a file, all the information is automatically compressed so that it takes up less space. To get at your backup file, you first have to *restore* it.

I explain how to restore a backup in the following section. Then — because I'm nothing if not a realist — I leap to your aid and tell you what to do if restoring your file fails.

Backup blues

Okay, tell me truthfully: Where do you store your backups? If your answer is that you store them in the office somewhere (or if you work from home, at home somewhere), then my reply to you is that you may as well not bother making backups.

Why? Because if you store your backups anywhere near the computer, you're not protected against fire or theft. Last year, a client rang to tell me that they had come in to the office one day to find the whole place stripped. The desks, phones, filing cabinets and shelves had all been lifted. All that was left were the telephone cables sticking out of the walls. Worse still, their nightly backups, stored so faithfully in their filing cabinets, were gone.

This client is still struggling to reconstruct the business. They've had to build everything up from scratch again, trying to remember who their customers are and trying to figure out who owes them money.

So, take your backups off-site, away from where you work. If you work from home, ask a close relative or friend to look after your backups at their house. If you work in an office, take your backups home, ideally every night. If you know that you won't ever be this efficient, delegate the job to someone else.

Restoring your file

So, disaster has struck and you want to restore your company file from the backups that you've so faithfully maintained. Cross your fingers, curl up your toes and follow my lead:

1. **Insert your backup CD or DVD into the computer's drive, or plug in your removable hard drive or flash drive.**

2. **Open your company file or the sample company file on your computer.**

   You can either open your normal company file or click Explore from MYOB's initial Welcome window to get into the sample company. Either file will do.

3. **Select Restore from the File menu.**

   Depending on how you've set up your security preferences, you may receive a message asking if you want to back up. Click No to continue restoring your backup file.

   However, if you're in your company file and you haven't backed up recently, click Yes to backup now.

4. **Locate your backup company file and click Open.**

   If you're using a PC, the Select File to Restore window pops up, similar to the one shown in Figure 14-3. In the Look In menu, double-click the drive where your backup is stored. Select your backup file and click Open.

   If you're using a Macintosh, go to your desktop and double-click the location where your backup is stored. A list of all the files on this backup pops up. Select the one you want to restore and click Open.

5. **Select a destination folder for your restored company file.**

   If any part of restoring a file is going to confuse you, this is it. When the Save As window appears, you have to decide where you want your restored company file to live. In 99 out of 100 cases, you restore your company file into the MYOB program folder on your hard drive. You may need to change the drive name or the folder name that appears in the Save In menu to navigate to this folder.

6. **Accept the suggested file name and click Save (or click Restore if you're using a Mac) then click OK.**

   At this point, MYOB software is clever enough to suggest a new name for the file you're restoring. This is good, because you don't want your restored file to wipe out any other company files living on your hard disk.

Figure 14-3:
You need to
select your
backup file
from the
place where
it's stored.

On your PC click Save and then OK or, if you're a Mac user, click Restore and then OK. Your backup file is uncompressed and restored with the new file name.

7. **Open your restored file and check that everything is cool.**

   Whenever you restore a backup file, it's worth browsing through the transaction journals and checking that it's the right file.

Shortcomings of shortcuts

Whenever you restore a file, MYOB software automatically renames it. This is good, because it protects you from accidentally copying over any old files.

However, if you normally open up your file using a shortcut that sits on your desktop, don't forget to update this shortcut so it points to your new file, not to your old file.

To do this, highlight the shortcut and click with your right mouse button (not your left mouse button). Go to Properties and change the Target file to update it with the name of your new company file.

Incidentally, this only applies to PCs. Macintosh computers are so clever, you can rename and move files as many times as you like, but the alias stays intact.

Panic! The black hole beckons

So, your computer died, you have tried to restore a file from the backup and, for one reason or another, the restore process didn't work. Or maybe — could this possibly be true? — you never had a backup in the first place.

Stay cool, there's no need to flee into exile quite yet. There are a few things you can try before packing your suitcase:

- **Search for a backup:** Even if you think you may have no other backups, dig around for one that you or someone else may have made in the past. Even if they're a couple of months old (the backups, not your co-workers), they're better than nothing.

- **Fix the backup data:** If you had a backup, but for some reason the restoration process failed, you can try to fix the data using a repair program such as Norton Utilities, which comes with Norton SystemWorks. (It's sometimes possible to resurrect seemingly dead data and bring it back to life this way.)

- **Change the file attributes:** Sometimes when you back up onto CD, the attributes of your file automatically change to read-only status, meaning that you can't open or restore the file. The solution is to copy the backup from your CD onto your hard disk, and then, from either My Computer (Windows) or your Finder (Mac), select the backup file, go to your File menu and select Properties. Untick the Read Only box and everything should be sweet as.

- **Call the MYOB Technical Support team:** If you think your backup is all right, but you can't get your head around how to restore your file — I can't imagine how this could be the case after you've read my flawless instructions — phone MYOB Tech Support (see Appendix A for details) and get them to walk you through the process, step by step.

- **Look on your hard disk:** It's possible that either you or someone else has accidentally backed up onto your hard disk sometime in the past. Go to My Computer (if you're using a PC) or your Finder (if you're using a Macintosh) and look in your MYOB program folder (or the Backup folder that sometimes sits within your program folder) for backup files.

- **Fix the original cause of the error message:** If you were restoring a backup because your existing file had come up with error messages, and your restore hasn't worked, then it's possible that the MYOB Company File Repair team can repair your file (for a modest charge, of course). Call 1300 555 151 and ask for a Datafile Submission Request form.

Save yourself from sorrow

If you have more than one company file, you can store your backups onto the same CD, DVD or removable hard drive. However, watch out for this trap:

If you back up more than one company file onto the same location on the same day, the second backup overwrites the first, because MYOB software always chooses the date as the name of the file when it's backing up. To avoid this calamity, change the default file name in the Backup window so that the name not only indicates the date, but the company name.

Looking After Your Data

Your company file is a sensitive and impressionable creature. It needs a stable home life, occasional counselling and a lot of love and affection.

Taking the truth test

MYOB software is as prone to corruption as any politician. Whether it's caused by a power surge, by someone pulling out the plug of the computer when you're working in your company file or a virus, it's possible that you end up with missing links or corrupt data.

The best way to detect corruption as soon as it happens is to verify your company file regularly. Think of file verification as a kind of truth test — you're the interrogator and you put your company file through a special routine, asking it lots of questions. If the file is corrupt in any way, the test results scream out an alert.

I recommend you set up your Preferences so that they remind you to verify your file. Go to Setup⇨Preferences and select the Security tab. Then select the check box Prompt for Data Verification When Opening, as shown in Figure 14-4. Now, every time you open your company file, you receive a prompt to verify it.

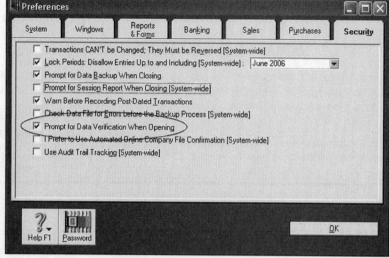

Figure 14-4:
Set up
Preferences
so that
you're
prompted to
verify your
company file.

Discovering corruption and blowing the whistle

When verifying your file, if you receive an unnerving message stating that your file has a problem, follow this plan of attack:

1. **If you're working on a network, either move to the computer where your company file is located, or copy your company file onto your local machine.**

   This step avoids further corruption problems from occurring.

2. **Optimise your company file.**

   The optimisation process often fixes up errors. I explain how to optimise files in 'Keeping your company file lean and clean' later in this chapter.

3. **Try verifying your file again to see if the error still exists.**

   If your file is clean, thank your lucky stars. If it's not, read on . . .

4. **Restore your company file from your most recent backup until you find a file that's okay.**

   Using your most recent backup, go through the restoring process, which I explain earlier in this chapter in 'Restoring your file'. Then verify the file before doing anything else. If your backup is clean, then you're out of the woods. If your backup is corrupt, then restore a previous backup. If that backup is corrupt, restore the backup before that one and so on.

5. **If your backups have errors, send your file off for repair.**

    If all your restored files come up with data verification errors — or if the most recent clean file is too long ago and it's impractical to re-enter so much information — your best bet is to send a copy of your damaged file to the MYOB Company File Repair Team. Call 1300 555 151 and ask for a Datafile Submission Request form.

Keeping your company file lean and clean

Every time you delete or change entries in your company file, you create holes inside your file that take up space — kind of like the way your brain fills up with trivial information that's of no use to anyone. It's a good idea to clean out these holes every now and then so that your company file takes up less room on your hard drive and runs a bit faster. This process is called *optimising*. Here's the low-down:

1. **MYOB Premier and MYOB AccountEdge only: Chuck any other users off the system if they're logged on and use the machine where your company file is stored.**

    These multi-user versions of MYOB software are great, but if someone else in the office has the temerity to be using MYOB software when you want to optimise your company file, tell that person to log out and take a break.

2. **Go to File⇨Optimise Company File.**

    A message pops up explaining that MYOB software will create an automatic backup.

3. **Click OK to continue and OK once more when optimising has finished.**

    The optimisation process can take anywhere from a few seconds to 20 minutes to complete, depending on the size of your company file.

After you've optimised your file successfully the first time, you'll realise that optimising is no big drama. If you're using MYOB Premier or MYOB AccountEdge, I suggest that to keep things speedy, optimise every week. Otherwise, try optimising your file at least once a month. Failing this — at least I'm being realistic about human nature here! — optimise your file whenever you start a new financial year or a new payroll year.

Avoiding corruption in the first place

As a citizen of New South Wales, I can claim to know all there is to know about avoiding corruption. And so, in the interests of the public, here are some tips for staying squeaky clean:

- **Steer clear of international wheat deals.** Need I say more.

- **Quit correctly.** When you've had enough of working on your accounts (I know how you feel), go to the File menu and select either Exit (for Windows) or Quit (for Macs).

- **Mind your manners.** If you work on the 'host' machine (in other words, the machine where your MYOB company file lives), don't turn off the power on your machine while other innocents are still working in the company file. Such behaviour is the modern-day equivalent of pulling the chair out from someone when they try to sit down.

- **Scare away the bogey-men.** If you live in an area with lots of storms or you work in a factory environment where heavy equipment makes for a dirty power supply, get a UPS (uninterruptible power supply). Power supply spikes are but an invitation for bogey-men and data corruption.

- **Check your installation.** If you're running MYOB software over a network, install the software on all local machines. Any program shortcuts should point to this local installation (never to the server).

- **Keep up the vitamin C.** Install virus-checking software and scan your emails for viruses before opening them.

- **Cut everyone some slack.** Always make sure you've got ample hard disk space free (say, 100 megabytes). Files are much more likely to fall over if they don't have enough room to breathe.

- **Get an engineer to give your network the once-over.** Things that cause problems include electrical cables running over network cables, fluoro lights next to network cables, faulty network adapter cards, poor network connections, out-of-date network drivers, fast machines with slow network cards and slow machines with fast network cards.

- **Keep verifying and optimising your file.** Refer to 'Discovering corruption and blowing the whistle' for more about verifying, and 'Keeping your company file lean and clean' for more about optimising.

Diagnosing error messages

There's nothing so unnerving as an incomprehensible error message —
I mean, just what does Error-47 stand for? Sometimes, error messages appear
out of the blue and then disappear like a stranger in the night, never to be
seen again. Other times, error messages persist and return to haunt you,
eventually bringing MYOB software to its knees.

I don't have enough room in this chapter to list all the possible error
messages that can occur, along with their solutions. However, I can tell you
where to look for help:

- ✔ **Ring the MYOB Technical Support Team:** If you subscribe to MYOB
  Technical Support or MYOB Cover, call them. Why struggle when
  there's an expert waiting to help?

- ✔ **Read the help file:** Press F1 to open the Help menu. Look for the
  Troubleshooting Topics list (you can usually navigate to it from the
  Maintenance Topics list, but it does depend on what version you have).

- ✔ **Hop online:** Visit `www.myob.com.au/support/notes` and do a Category
  search for 'Errors and Warnings'. You're greeted by a pretty scary list of
  over 200 support documents. Be brave, hopefully one of these docs will
  have the answer to your prayers.

Sssh! It's a Secret

I don't know about you, but I feel quite private about my finances. And just as
I wouldn't leave my tax return lying around on the coffee table when friends
are visiting, I like to protect my company file from uninvited inspection.

Protecting the privacy of your company file is easy because all you have to
do is create an administrator password.

Creating an administrator password

Your main password is called the administrator password. If you haven't
already created a password for your MYOB company file, here's how to set
one up the first time:

1. **Open your company file, typing Administrator for the User ID.**

   Whoever has Administrator as their user ID automatically has unlimited access to the company file. Only the Administrator can create new user IDs and set restrictions for other users.

2. **Leave the Password field blank and click Change Password.**

3. **Enter your password in the New Password field and then again in the Confirm Password field. Leave the Existing Password field blank.**

   Try to avoid using the names of your pets or children, it's sooo obvious.

4. **Click Record and then OK.**

   Your company file should open.

5. **Remember your password!**

   Next time you open up your company file, you'll need this password. So guess what? Don't forget it! By the way, if you're going to manage security effectively, only the business owner or manager should know the password that's associated with the Administrator ID.

Creating sub-passwords for employees

Whenever you open your company file using Administrator as the user ID, you gain unlimited access to all areas, including the ability to create new user IDs, set up sub-passwords and create restrictions for each user.

However, take time to consider what you want each employee (or user) to do in your company file. This helps you work out whether it's appropriate to create restrictions and in which areas.

One of the common restrictions that employers place on employees is to prevent them from viewing everyone else's pay rates and personal details. To do this, you create a sub-password for each employee, then select the restrictions. Here's how:

1. **Go to Setup⇨Preferences, click the Security tab and then click Password.**

The Password button sits at the bottom-left — see the graphic of the bad guy dressed in black with an overcoat and a big hat?

2. **Select the employee's User ID from the left-hand column of the User Access window (or click New to create new user IDs and passwords, if necessary).**

   In case I haven't made this clear already, every employee needs their own user ID and password. Don't let employees log on as Administrator and don't tell them the administrator password.

3. **In the Not Allowed column, click against activities or menus that you don't want the employee to access.**

   Figure 14-5 shows the activities and menu areas that you can you restrict the user from accessing.

4. **Click OK to save your password changes.**

   After you save your changes, tell the employee why you're giving them a password and, if you've restricted them from some areas in your company file, explain why. People can become curious (and sometimes even resentful) if they think you're trying to hide something from them, so it's a good idea to explain your reasoning.

Figure 14-5:
You can restrict employees so that they can only access certain sections of your file.

User Access

To restrict a user's access, choose the user from the list on the left, then mark the restricted function on the right.

If you restrict a user's access to a function that's marked with an asterisk (*), the user won't be able to view or report on the transactions created by that function.

User ID	Not Allowed	Available Functions
Annie		**Receivables & Payables**
Clarabel		Credit Terms
Edward		Sales & Purchases Information
Henry		Add/Edit a Comment
James		Add/Edit a Shipping Method
Thomas		Add/Edit a Referral Source
		Add/Edit a Payment Method
	X	**Payroll**
	X	Payroll Categories List
	X	Wages Information
	X	Wages Exemptions

Help F1   [New]   [Edit]   [Delete]   [Cancel]   [OK]

What to do if you forget your password

If you forget your administrator password, try free-associating for a while (you can meet a lot of new people that way). Didn't work? Try every password that you have ever used, the names of your kids, your pets or obscure rugby league teams. It's amazing what you can retrieve from the dark and dusty shadows of your brain.

If this fails, you can either throw yourself off the nearest cliff — don't do it! There is life beyond technology! — or you can send your file off to the MYOB Technical Support team, who can hack into it for you and reset your password. But be warned, this service usually takes a couple of days and there's a small charge.

By the way, if you haven't ever created a password in your MYOB company file, and you've found your way to this part of the book because you're desperately trying to open up some data, then try logging in with the user ID 'Administrator' (and leave the password blank).

Chapter 15

Understanding Your Business

. . . .

In This Chapter

▶ Tracking jobs and projects to find out how profitable they are

▶ Using business categories as cost centres

▶ Giving your Balance Sheet the once over

▶ Working with Profit & Loss reports

▶ Going the whole hog with budgets

. . . .

*B*efore computers gave us the ability to analyse information with such ease, many businesses led a precarious existence where optimism and intuition played a bigger part than the analysis of facts and figures. To some extent this still happens, especially in smaller businesses.

Without information at their fingertips, many businesses operate in the dark. For example, a builder knows that only some jobs make money, but he's not sure which ones; a hairdresser suspects that one of her branches is profitable, the other isn't; and a guesthouse owner wonders whether the expenses from the restaurant eat into the profits made by accommodation.

What if we could switch the light on? If the builder knew for sure what kind of jobs brought the money in, he'd probably be more selective with his clients; if the hairdresser could see just how much she was losing in her second shop, she'd probably close it down; and if the guesthouse owner could really analyse the restaurant figures, he'd make some big changes, and quick.

Fortunately, MYOB software gives you the ability to cast as much light on any situation that you could ever wish for. In this chapter, I explain how you can use MYOB software to analyse where you make money, and where you don't.

Seeing Where the Money's Made

One of the fascinating facts about small businesses is that so many of them are really a collection of businesses bundled under the one name — like the newsagency that doubles as a post office and drycleaning agent, or the handyman who fixes your cupboard doors and also mows the lawn. The secret of success with these kinds of businesses is to find out which part of the business is bringing in the dough, and how much profit it's making.

MYOB software's ability to help you find out where your business is making money is one of its best-kept secrets. It's a cinch! You simply use the Jobs List.

The Jobs List can be used for lots of different things — cost centres, profit centres, projects, ventures, locations or any other identifiable arm of your business. I talk lots about this in the next couple of sections.

Finding out how jobs work

Every transaction you record includes the following information:

- ✔ **The name of the customer, supplier or employee.**

- ✔ **An allocation account.** This information is an account number or name in your Accounts List and refers to the type of income or type of expense it is. A payment for electricity may be allocated to Electricity Expense, and a payment for rent may be allocated to Rent Expense.

- ✔ **A job number (optional).** Ah, here we are! This is where you can record a job number, if you like, selecting what part of your business (whether it's a project, a location or an arm of your business) this income or expense belongs to.

- ✔ **A tax code.** Select whatever code applies.

The Spend Money window shown in Figure 15-1 illustrates how this concept works. The Card field shows the name of the supplier; the Account Name field shows the type of expense it is; the Job column shows the project code; and the Tax column shows the tax code.

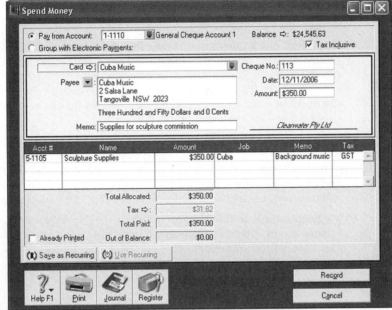

Figure 15-1:
Use the Jobs feature to track where you make a profit.

Figuring out how job reporting can work for you

Make yourself a drink, sit back and have a think about how your business could use jobs. Contemplate the different projects you do, and consider whether your business is made up of different enterprises.

Everything has its place

When you're working with jobs, sooner or later you'll come across expenses that are difficult to allocate to any one particular job. Things such as accounting fees, bank charges, legal fees, merchant fees and even telephone bills are often hard to pigeonhole. I've got a neat solution to this dilemma: Create an additional job called 'Admin' and use this job for all expenses that don't belong to a particular job. Then, you can generate a Profit & Loss report for each job, as well as a Profit & Loss report that shows all shared overheads.

In case all this navel-gazing doesn't make sense to you, here are a few of my own examples, which show how I've set up jobs for different clients:

✔ One client has a guesthouse that offers both accommodation and dining facilities. All accommodation income and expenses are given the job code 'A' and all dining income and expenses are given the job code 'D'. This allows my client to produce a monthly Profit & Loss for the accommodation business, a Profit & Loss for the restaurant and a Profit & Loss for the combination of both.

✔ A hairdresser friend has two salons in different suburbs of Sydney — one in Paddington and one in Rose Bay. She codes the income and expenses from each salon with a different job code ('P' for Paddington and 'R' for Rose Bay) so that she can print up a Profit & Loss for each salon separately, as well as a Profit & Loss for the two salons combined.

✔ My neighbour is a builder who builds several houses every year. He creates a new job code for every house and codes all income and expenses with these codes. This allows my neighbour to see how much profit (or sometimes how much loss) he makes on each house.

By the way, when working with jobs, the reports you rely on are the Jobs Profit & Loss reports tucked away on the Accounts tab of the Reports menu. Another place to look up job info on the run is to go to your Analysis menu and click Jobs.

Creating a new job

After you've got your head around jobs and how they work, you're ripe to create your first new job. (Note that all job features are limited in MYOB BusinessBasics and FirstEdge.)

1. **From the main menu, choose Lists⇨Jobs, then click New.**

2. **Decide whether the job is a Header Job or a Detail Job.**

   Header jobs are the headings under which detail jobs are grouped. For example, a builder may have a header job called Renovations. Then, under Renovations, he lists separate detail jobs for each renovation job that he's doing.

3. **Enter a Job Number and, if it's a detail job, indicate it's position in your list.**

   If you only have a few jobs, avoid using numbers — use letters of the alphabet instead. Numbers are hard to remember and you're more likely to make a mistake with them. Also, make the job number short (a single letter is often fine), because the fewer keyboard strokes you have to type the better. If you want this job to sit under a particular header, select its header in the Sub-job field.

4. Insert a Job Name.

Enter the name of the job in the Job Name field. This may be the name of a job, a project, a location or an arm of the business.

5. Optional: Enter a Job Description and a Contact.

These two fields are entirely optional and to be honest, hardly ever useful. Feel free to ignore them!

6. Optional: If you've already started the job, enter the Percent Complete.

Another optional field, the Percent Complete box is only meaningful if you're going to enter budgets for this job, and track actuals against budgets as the job progresses. It's up to you.

7. Fill in some other fairly unnecessary details (again, optional).

If you're feeling incredibly enthusiastic, complete the Start Date, Finish Date and name of the Manager. (I usually find most businesses are too busy doing the job to spend time recording all these details.)

8. If you want to track expenses for reimbursement, complete the Linked Customer field.

If you're likely to have any job-related expenses that you want to on-bill to a particular customer, you need to specify the customer's name in the Linked Customer field. You also need to click the Track Reimbursables check box in the top-right corner of the New Job window.

9. Click OK.

This adds the job to your Job List, as shown in Figure 15-2 — my, that was quick!

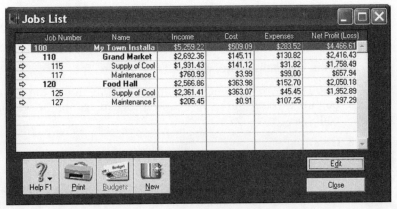

Figure 15-2:
A completed
Jobs List.

Where categories fit into the picture

If you have several business divisions, you may prefer to analyse your cost centres using categories, rather than jobs. (Note that categories aren't available in MYOB BusinessBasics or FirstEdge.)

Categories work in almost the same way as jobs, but with two important differences. The first difference (and here's the good news) is that you can print a Balance Sheet report for each category (which you can't do for jobs), making categories ideal for businesses with distinct divisions. The second difference (and this is the bad news) is that you can't split a single transaction across more than one category, whereas you can split a single transaction across several jobs.

So, if your business has individual payments that need to be split across more than one cost centre, you're better off using jobs to analyse your cost centres, rather than categories. On the other hand, if you have separate bank accounts and business divisions that operate relatively independently, category tracking is your best bet.

To switch on category tracking and see how it works, go to your Setup menu, select Preferences and click the System tab. Tick the option to Turn On Category Tracking and select Required if you want it to be compulsory for every single transaction to have a category allocated to it. Finally, go to your Lists menu, select Categories and click New to create your category names.

Getting rid of jobs

Jobs tend to come and go, and from time to time it's good to give your Jobs List a good spring clean.

Here's how to delete a job:

1. **Go to your Jobs List and double-click the job you want to remove.**

   A dialogue box appears showing information for that particular job.

2. **From the main menu, choose Edit⇨Delete Job.**

   If you still have current transactions relating to this job, a warning may pop up. If you're sure you want to proceed, ignore the warning and continue.

3. **Gloat!**

Incidentally, you can exclude finished jobs from your Jobs List report. Just enter 100% in the Percent Complete field in the Job Information window for finished jobs and then click Exclude 100% Complete Jobs in the report filters.

Understanding Financial Statements

You've probably read a hundred business books telling you how to understand your Profit & Loss, interpret your Balance Sheet, go crazy with ratio analysis and print out enough budget reports to sink a battleship. What I do in the following sections is put this learned theory into the context of MYOB software, explaining how to produce these reports and ensure they make sense.

Checking out your bottom line

I'm always amazed at the number of clients who work for hours and hours every week, punching information into their company file, without taking the time to print out any reports and look at them.

When you have MYOB software up and running, printing a Profit & Loss report is as easy (quite literally) as clicking a couple of buttons. So there's no reason for not looking at your Profit & Loss report every single month. Did you make a profit? If not, why? What happened with your expenses? Can you save money on anything? How did sales compare to last month, last year or the year before that? What trends can you see in these figures?

The quickest way to churn out a Profit & Loss report is to open the Analysis menu (on the bottom right corner of all windows) and . . . guess what . . . choose the Profit & Loss menu. I then play with the Filters, selecting different periods, this year versus last year, budgets and so on (Figure 15-3 shows an example report).

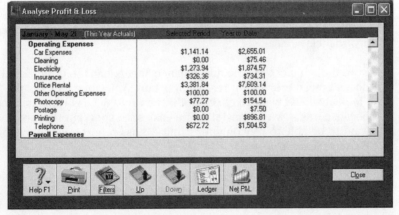

Figure 15-3: Go to your Analysis menu for a quick low-down on profitability.

For more detail or specific date ranges, I make my way to the main Reports menu and click the Accounts tab:

- ✔ The simple Profit & Loss [Accrual] report shows how much came in and how much went out for any date range. For a less detailed report, select Level 2 or Level 3 as the Report Level in the Advanced Filters.

- ✔ The Profit & Loss [Cash] report is the same as the Profit & Loss [Accrual], except the income only shows up on this report when you get paid and similarly, expenses only appear when you part with the cash. I like this report if I'm wondering why I've got no cash (a perennial event), but my regular Profit & Loss report shows a profit.

- ✔ The Profit & Loss Year to Date report shows how your business is faring for any date range and compares these figures with the year so far.

- ✔ The Profit & Loss Multi-Period Spreadsheet reports are great for sending into Excel. Click Customise to select a whole year as your reporting period and then click the Send To button followed by Excel. Your budget appears in Excel, with the figures for each month listed in a separate column, making an ideal starting point for budgets or cashflow reports.

- ✔ The Profit & Loss Last Year Analysis report compares how you're doing this year with how you did last year. I like to highlight a few months at a time to make this report more meaningful.

Giving your Balance Sheet a health check

Think of your Profit & Loss as a story of what goes on in your business over any period of time, and your Balance Sheet as a photograph. A Balance Sheet is really a picture of how much you own and how much you owe at any point in time, and the difference between how much you own and how much you owe is your stake in the business. (The Americans love to call this your net worth — personally, I prefer to calculate my net worth using other values as a yardstick!)

Even though most people find Balance Sheets hard to understand, that doesn't mean they're not really important. A Balance Sheet is the first report I look at when I want to check out if the Profit & Loss reports are accurate, because this is where mistakes are easiest to spot. In other words, if you want to be able to rely on your Profit & Loss reports, you have to sure your Balance Sheet is correct.

To check that your Balance Sheet makes sense (and that your company file is healthy and happy), work through the following points:

- ✔ Ask yourself whether every single line on your Balance Sheet makes sense. A simple idea, but it works.

✔ Check that every bank account shows the right balance. Savings and investment accounts are the most prone to neglect, so check the amount showing on the Balance Sheet against the latest bank statements.

✔ Consider the balances of your fixed assets. Do they make sense? Perhaps you have an old bomb that barely scrapes through rego, but Motor Vehicles shows up as a $50,000 asset in your Balance Sheet. In this case, something has gone astray.

✔ All accumulated depreciation accounts should be minus figures. They're not? Something is definitely crook.

✔ All liability accounts should be positive figures. They're not? Again, something is almost certainly wrong. (GST Paid on Purchases is an exception to this rule!)

✔ Your Historical Balancing account should always be zero.

Before you read on, check out the Balance Sheet in Figure 15-4 and see whether you can spot the five deliberate mistakes. Be sure you identify all five mistakes, even if it takes you ages. When you're happy with the results, check your answers against the list that follows. (Don't cheat by peeking at the answers!)

Analyse Balance Sheet

	This Year Actuals	
	Selected Period	% of Total
Assets		
Current Assets		
Business Bank Account	$13,500.00	22.4%
Petty Cash	$9,870.00	16.4%
Undeposited Funds	$1,200.00	2%
Electronic Clearing Account	-$356.00	-0.6%
Trade Debtors	$2,022.00	3.4%
Fixed Assets		
Furniture & Fittings	$22,000.00	36.5%
Furniture - Accum Depreciation	$12,056.00	20%
Total Assets	$60,292.00	100%
Liabilities		
Visa Card	-$2,342.00	-7.2%
Trade Creditors	$32,020.00	98.6%
GST Liabilities		
GST Collected	$5,310.00	16.4%
GST Paid	-$4,523.00	-13.9%
Total GST Liabilities	$787.00	2.4%
Superannuation Payable	$1,118.32	3.4%
PAYG Payable	$880.00	2.7%
Total Liabilities	$32,463.32	100%
Equity		
Retained Earnings	$0.00	0%
Current Earnings	$12,823.50	46.1%
Historical Balancing Account	$15,005.18	53.9%
Total Equity	$27,828.68	100%

Help F1   Print   Filters   Up   Down   Ledger   Asset   Liability   Equity   Close

Figure 15-4: Can you spot the five mistakes in this report?

Did you spot the five mistakes in the Balance Sheet in Figure 15-4? Here are the details:

- ✔ Petty cash is almost certainly wrong. A balance of $9,870 is much too high.

- ✔ Electronic Clearing Account is almost certainly wrong. Clearing accounts should normally have a zero balance.

- ✔ Furniture–Accum Depreciation is definitely wrong. Accumulated depreciation accounts are always minus amounts.

- ✔ Visa Card is almost certainly wrong. A minus balance for a credit card means that the credit card owes you money, not the other way around.

- ✔ Historical Balancing is definitely wrong. This account should always have a zero balance.

Setting up Profit & Loss budgets

Part of getting intimate with your financials is deciding what you *want* the figures to be (as opposed to just looking at what they are) and figuring out how you're going to get there. In order to do this, you need to get your hands dirty and draw up a few serious budgets.

Creating budgets is a piece of cake. Simply go to your Accounts List, highlight the account you want to create a budget for and click the Budgets button. You see a window similar to the one shown in Figure 15-5. Some comments:

- ✔ In recent versions of MYOB software, you can select your Financial Year at the top of the Prepare Budgets window. This is great, because you can keep going with budgets into the next year even if you haven't yet finalised last year's accounts.

- ✔ For an injection of realism, start the budget preparation process by clicking Copy Previous Year's Actual Data. If you increase an income account or decrease an expense account by more than 10 percent when compared to last year, you'd better have a really good reason!

- ✔ If an expense is the same every month (like rent or insurance), save time and click the Copy Amount to Following Months button.

- ✔ If you have a few people working in the business, ask for input into the budget. The more involved everyone is, the more realistic the budget.

- ✔ Remember that some expenses are irregular, such as quarterly electricity bills or one-off annual payments. Also, keep an eye out for months with five pay weeks, rather than four.

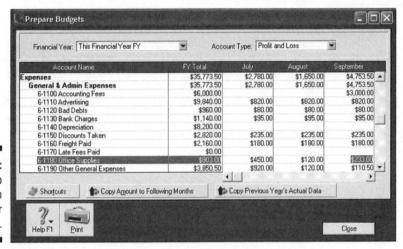

Figure 15-5:
Setting up
budgets in
your
accounts.

Setting up job budgets

Earlier in this chapter, I talked meaningfully (well, kind of) about setting up job reporting, so you could see where the real profits in your business lie. When you get the hang of how jobs work, you'll probably want to set up job budgets so you can make sure that everything stays on track.

To set up a job budget, go to your Jobs List, highlight the job in question and then click the Budget button. A list of all income, cost of goods sold and expense accounts appears on your screen. (By the way, you can't set up budgets for header jobs, only for detail jobs.) Work your way down the list of accounts, entering income and expense budgets one by one.

One drawback with job budget features is that you can only set up budgets for the entire duration of a job, meaning that you can't set up monthly or annual budgets. There's no easy way round this. You could consider sending your Job Budget into Excel and adapting it from there, or alternatively, you could contact Two Keys software, a company that distributes specialist job reporting software that hooks up with MYOB. (See www.twokeys.com.au for more details.)

After you've set up your job budgets, you're ready to produce some reports. You can either open your Analysis menu, select Jobs and punch in the job number, or you can select the Jobs Budget Analysis report in your Reports menu.

For either of these reports to make any sense, you have to specify the Percent Complete for the job. If you work from the Analysis menu, you enter this figure in the Percent Complete field at the top of the Analyse Jobs window; if you work from the Reports menu, you'll have to go to your Jobs List, edit the job in question and change the Percent Complete field there.

And here's where a trick-of-the-trade comes in. To generate a budget report that shows how much you've spent on the job to-date and compare this against what you budgeted for the job in total, enter 100% as the Percent Complete, regardless of how far along the job actually is.

Part IV
The Part of Tens

Glenn Lumsden

'I need help. All these pie charts
are making me hungry.'

In this part . . .

You either love lists or you hate them. I love lists because the very process of writing them makes me feel I've achieved something, even when I haven't moved an inch out of my deckchair.

This part of the book consists solely of lists. You'll find lists about stuff you absolutely have to do, as well as lists about stuff to avoid at all costs. There's a list of tips to transform you into an MYOB software wizard as well as a list of tips to keep your business in tip-top health. And last, but not least, there's a list about that very tricky but totally unavoidable event: Starting a new year.

Chapter 16

Ten Perilous Pitfalls

1 could rave on and on about how simple MYOB software is. About how easy it is to do your accounts, and how the amount of time you spend on bookkeeping is cut in half.

The problem is that if you relax too much, you can still come a cropper. Prevention is heaps better than cure, so in this chapter I tell you the things you should never, ever do.

Don't Chuck the Baby Out With the Bathwater

A few years ago, I remember dropping by a friend's house on 1 July for a cup of tea. Replying to my comment about what a busy time of year it was, my friend answered that she didn't get what all the fuss was about. She'd started a new financial year in her MYOB company file that morning, simply by choosing File⇨Start a New Financial Year and then carrying on as normal.

I felt rather anxious as I asked her if she'd backed up first.

'No,' she replied, 'I must back up soon, though. I've been meaning to do so for weeks.'

Her sunny demeanour rapidly faded as I explained that by starting a new financial year, she had just purged every single transaction from the previous year.

'Do you mean nothing's left?' she asked me.

'Nothing, nix, nada, zilch', I replied.

'What can I do?' she cried.

I shrugged my shoulders.

When you start a new financial year, it's a big deal. When you click that innocent Start a New Financial Year command (found on your File menu, by the way), you clean out every transaction from the previous year: sales, payments, receipts, purchases — everything (with the exception of any transactions that haven't been reconciled yet). It's like the biggest spring-clean you could ever imagine.

MYOB software knows that this is serious stuff and when you ask it to start a new financial year, it warns that you need to make a backup, as shown in Figure 16-1. Even so, I'm still amazed how many people think to themselves, 'Naah, I won't bother, I'll do that later,' and then proceed *without* making a backup.

Figure 16-1:
Always, always back up before starting a new financial year.

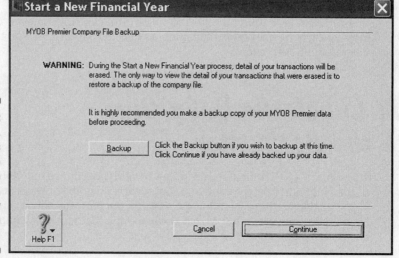

To not back up is like taking your files, your hard copy invoices and your receipts, and chucking them onto a big bonfire. Your accountant needs these records, the ATO will ask for them in the event of an audit, and there's every chance you'll need to refer to them at some stage.

So, please, please, please back up before starting a new financial year.

Danger — Don't Delete

Occasionally, when you try to change or delete a transaction, a message appears, similar to the one shown in Figure 16-2.

This kind of warning isn't there just for fun. It's serious business. When a transaction is already reconciled and you then delete it or change the amount, you throw your whole bank reconciliation out of balance. Worse still, you may not realise this has happened until you return to your reconciliation a few weeks later and by then there's every chance you will have forgotten what it was that you deleted.

I absolutely hate this problem. Sometimes, I have to ask clients to reconcile every single transaction in their file all over again, or trawl through page after page of printouts trying to work out what they've done. There should be no reason to delete a transaction once it's been reconciled in your account, so just don't.

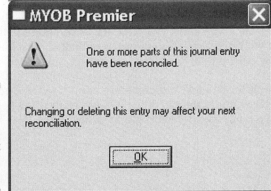

Figure 16-2:
Pay attention
to warnings
about
reconciled
transactions.

Never Give Away Your Password

In Chapter 14, 'Looking After Your Files', I talk about administrator passwords and sub-passwords. The idea is that the boss has the admin password and employees have sub-passwords. This may seem unnecessarily complicated, but there's method behind the madness.

I'd like to tell you a story about one of my slightly crustier clients. He went into his office one day to find his receptionist had resigned and was never coming back. Fine, he thought. Then he tried to open his MYOB company file. Every time he entered his password, it was rejected. It finally dawned on him that his receptionist's parting gift had been to change the administrator password.

My client sent his file off to MYOB software in Melbourne and they hacked into it to find out the password — for a fee, I might add. The file was returned and my client was given the embarrassing news that the password had been changed to become 'DEAD****' (I can't spell it out, because I'm not allowed to swear in this book).

Stay in charge of your business accounting. If you're the boss, you should have the administrator password. Employees should have sub-passwords. Revenge may be sweet, but not for those on the receiving end.

Don't Stick Your Head in the Sand

Do you have a sinking audit feeling in the pit of your stomach? Then now is the time to come clean. If you know you're about to be audited, own up and tell the ATO about your mistake. This counts as 'voluntary disclosure' and your penalty will be substantially reduced.

Better still, don't wait for an audit notice before admitting the error of your ways. If you voluntarily notify the tax office of any tax shortfall before an audit is declared, you may avoid penalties altogether.

Don't Fiddle with Linked Accounts

Linked accounts are a neat way to excuse you from having to think about debits and credits, which is a relief, because the logic of debits and credits can become pretty ugly, pretty quickly. Linked accounts tell MYOB software where to send the debits and credits of sales, purchases, payments, deposits and so on.

To see your linked accounts, go to the Setup menu, click Linked Accounts and then select either Accounts & Banking Accounts, Sales Accounts, Purchases Accounts or Payroll Accounts. However, look but don't touch! Because linked accounts are the nuts and bolts behind every single transaction you do, you must be absolutely sure about what you're doing before changing any of these settings. In fact, I suggest you either talk to your accountant or an MYOB Certified Consultant before you touch linked account settings.

Don't Do Anything Twice

Once is plenty. Life is short enough without doing deadly boring things more than you absolutely have to.

You may think that you're a picture of efficiency, but take a moment to ask yourself 'Does any data entry get done twice?' Here are some examples of what I'm on about:

- Employees filling out forms by hand, the information from which gets typed into a database at a later point.
- New customer details getting typed first into one database (such as the address book in Microsoft Outlook), and then into another (such as MYOB software).
- Daily takings reports getting printed out of your point-of-sale system and then totals re-entered into MYOB software.
- Customers placing orders online. These orders are then printed out and the details retyped into the MYOB company file.

If you can identify any work that's duplicated, you can almost certainly find a solution. In some situations, an off-the-shelf solution will fit the bill (like the Datapel utility that synchronises info between MYOB software and Microsoft Outlook). In other situations, especially if you're trying to synchronise data between a custom-written database and your MYOB company file, you'll need to get a third-party developer to whip up a custom solution (see Appendix C for a list of third-party developers).

If you ever find yourself typing something a second time, then stop, and think again. Data should be shared, not duplicated!

Don't Try to Do Everything at Once

When you first start using MYOB software, it's tempting to try to get everything perfect, right from the word go. But, just as you can't learn a new language overnight, MYOB software takes a little while to get accustomed to.

I often find it works best if businesses set up their company file a little at a time. Maybe start off by getting your sales, payments and customer receipts up to speed. When these basic transactions have been chugging along happily for a few weeks, move onto balancing your bank account. If you want, delay a few months or even the whole first year before plunging ahead with payroll.

As a newcomer to MYOB software, it's sometimes hard to differentiate between what's essential right away and what's icing on the cake. You may be better off getting an MYOB Certified Consultant to provide some training, or ask your accountant for some assistance.

Chapter 17

Ten Tricks to Speed Up Your Work

In This Chapter

▶ Learn how to type

▶ Create a shortcut on your desktop

▶ Memorise shortcut keys

▶ Do without your mouse

▶ Use cards as much as you can

▶ Get tricky with advanced searches

▶ Automate anything you can

▶ Link supplier cards to the right expense

*I*n this chapter I talk about a few tricks to make your bookwork as speedy and efficient as possible. None of these tricks is essential to using your MYOB software — your accounts will still balance and your accountant will still be quite happy even if you ignore every single one.

But if you like to live life to the full and spend as little time in front of a computer screen as possible, then this chapter is for you.

Use All Ten Fingers

I don't think that there's any other activity in the world that people spend so much time doing quite so badly. The average person on the street wouldn't consider using a Swiss army knife to chop down a tree, nor would they cut their lawns with nail scissors. However, many people persist in using a computer, hour after hour, without learning how to type.

It's basic. If you spend more than half an hour a day keying information into a computer, then you should learn to type. The average speed of a non-typist is about 15 words a minute — and that's for a pretty hot two-fingered typist — but by touch-typing, you can easily expect to key in 60 words a minute. That's four times faster!

So, if you're a non-typist and you usually spend just four hours a week in front of the computer and you learn to type, you'll save about three hours a week, every week, from now until you die. And, guess what? Learning how to type takes about an hour a day, every day, for six weeks. That's not so long.

Even if you can type properly, consider your employees. If they're spending time in front of the computer every day and they can't touch type, think about paying for them to have training or buy software so they can do it at work (Typequick is a product that's really popular — go to www.typequick.com.au to find out more). It's money well spent.

Take a Shortcut from Your Desktop

I hate pressing seventeen hundred buttons just to fire up MYOB software. Instead, I like to pop an icon on the desktop so that all I have to do is click and I'm away.

If you use a PC, go to Windows Explorer or My Computer and click once on the myob.exe file (myobp.exe in MYOB Premier, or bbasics.exe for MYOB BusinessBasics) that lives in your MYOB program folder. Then navigate to the File menu and click Create Shortcut, as shown in Figure 17-1.

Figure 17-1: Create a shortcut to your MYOB program on your desktop.

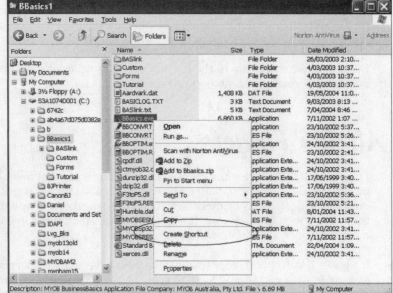

Next, look in your MYOB program folder and check that you have something called Shortcut to MYOB. Drag this file up to your Desktop folder (right in the top left) and drop it in there. Simple!

Macintosh people have to take a different approach. First, go to your MYOB program folder and highlight the MYOB Accounting, FirstEdge or AccountEdge icon. Then from the File menu, choose Make Alias. Finally, drag this alias onto your desktop. It's now ready for action.

If you're working on a network, make sure that your shortcut points to the MYOB program application that lives on your *local* machine, not to the one on the server.

Play Memory Games

This tip saves heaps of time and is incredibly impressive to anyone who may be looking over your shoulder . . .

Want to go to Spend Money? You don't have to quit out of wherever you are, navigate to the Banking command centre and then click Spend Money. No, you're much more intelligent than that. Instead, simply type Ctrl+H (Cmd+H on a Mac) and, in two shakes of a lamb's tail, you arrive at the Spend Money window.

For PC users, this means finding the Ctrl key (usually at the bottom left of your keyboard) and holding it down. Keep holding it down and then press the letter H. Let go and you're there.

You do the same if you're a Mac user, except use the Cmd key (that's the one with the squiggly ⌘ sign) instead of the Ctrl key.

Spend Money isn't the only place you can go to using shortcuts. Ctrl+J takes you to Sales, Ctrl+E to Purchases, Ctrl+D to Receive Money and so on — if you use a Mac, substitute Cmd for Ctrl in each case. I summarise these shortcut keys at the front of this book on the Cheat Sheet.

Enthused? Then try to memorise two or three shortcuts a week until you have them down pat.

Hurl Your Mouse Out the Window

Want to move faster? Then grab your mouse, kiss it a fond farewell and hurl it out of the window. Ignore the squeaking sounds and wish it a happy afterlife.

It may sound radical but, when using a PC, you can do just about every transaction without using your mouse. To see how this works, go to the Sales command centre and look at the Sales Register button. Can you see how the letter 'g' is underlined? This means that instead of clicking the Sales Register button with the mouse, you can press down the Alt button and then hit the letter 'g' at the same time.

When entering sales or payments, keep working without your mouse. Press the Tab key to go forwards, or the Shift key plus the Tab key to go backwards (the Tab key sits next to the letter 'Q' with the arrows pointing in either direction). It's quite possible to do most tasks without ever touching your mouse.

Create Cards Wherever Possible

Have you noticed that when you go to Spend Money or Receive Money, you can choose between writing the name of the company that you're paying in either the Card field or the Payee field?

Lots of people ignore the Card field and instead just complete the Payee field (as shown in Figure 17-2). This may seem speedy the first time you do it, but it's not in the long run — for two reasons.

The first reason is this: If you create a card for the person you're paying, the next time you record a payment for them, you only need to type the first few letters of their name into the Card field and MYOB software gets psychic, guesses the name and fills in the rest.

The second reason? After you've created a Card, any previous transactions for this person are much easier to find. That's because you can then use the Find Transactions menu the same way to list every transaction in that person's name.

The Card field makes it easier to complete transactions and to refer to them again later. Only ignore the Card field when completing a transaction if you think you'll never pay this person any money ever again.

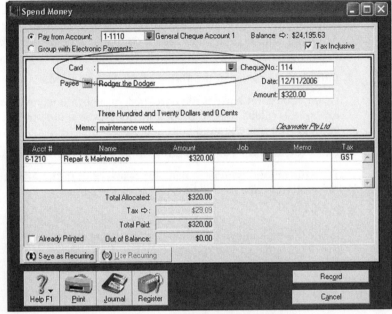

Figure 17-2:
Don't
overlook the
Card field, as
shown in this
example.

Move On to Advanced Searches

When looking for a transaction, instead of browsing through endless
transaction journals, take a shortcut and perform an advanced inquiry.

Imagine you're looking for a payment for $85.50. You can't remember the
exact date of the payment, nor which account you allocated it to. What you
need to do is search for every transaction in your company file for this
amount.

Here's how:

1. **Go to Find Transactions and click the Account tab.**

   The Find Transactions menu is on the bottom of every command centre.

2. **Click the Advanced button.**

   This button is in the top-right corner and has a magnifying glass next to
   it. I hope you're feeling clever already — the word Advanced alone
   makes me feel smart.

3. Ask to search by All Accounts.

You can choose to search through one specific account or through All Accounts. All Accounts may take a couple of seconds longer, but it's usually your best bet.

4. Enter a date range in the Dated From and To fields.

When you're not sure of the date, pick an enormously wide range, for example 1/7/2005 to 30/6/2050. Remember, the more specific your settings, the more limited your search will be.

5. Enter the amount you're looking for in the Amount From and To fields.

Type the amount you're looking for twice, both in the Amount From and Amount To fields. (See Figure 17-3 for an example.)

6. Click OK.

In the blink of an eye (well, almost), up pops every transaction that has the dollar amount you're searching for. It's so cool.

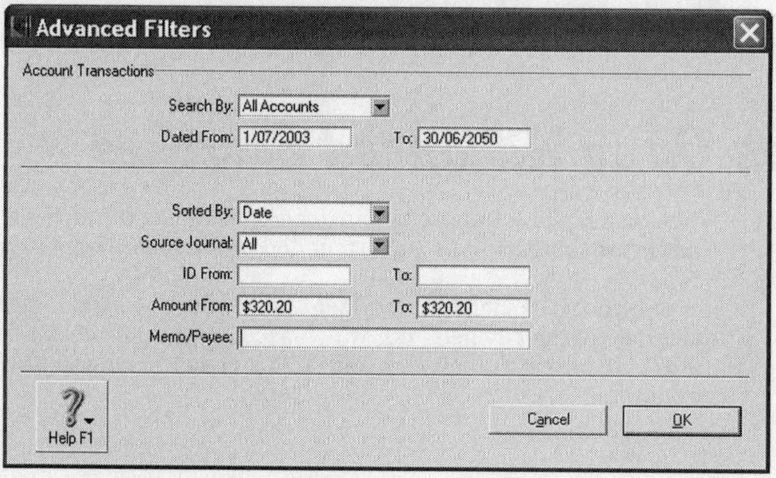

Figure 17-3:
Advanced
Filters are
terrific for
finding
transactions.

Advanced Filters	

Account Transactions

Search By: All Accounts

Dated From: 1/07/2003   To: 30/06/2050

Sorted By: Date

Source Journal: All

ID From: To:

Amount From: $320.20   To: $320.20

Memo/Payee:

Help F1   Cancel   OK

Memorise your Regular Transactions

Most businesses have a number of transactions that happen every week or every month. Regular lease payments, loan repayments, employee pays, rent payments and repeating sales are common examples of transactions that are made over and over.

If you have stuff like this in your business, then don't put yourself through the agony and toil of writing the details afresh each time. Instead, save these transactions as recurring. The recurring buttons sit at the bottom of most transactions: The Save Recurring button memorises regular transactions, and the Use Recurring button lets you can call up these regular transactions, ready to record them again.

For transactions that are the same every month, tell MYOB software to record each transaction automatically and notify you when it's done the deed. For transactions that vary, ask MYOB software to pop up a reminder to tell you that this transaction is due.

I explain the intricacies of recurring transactions in Chapter 3 and in Chapter 5.

Tell Suppliers Where to Go

Did you know you can set up your supplier cards so that every time you record a payment to a supplier, the correct expense account pops up automatically? This innocuous little trick can save you hours of time when it comes to recording payments, and as an extra bonus, makes for more reliable data entry as well.

Here's how it works:

1. **Go to your Cards List and double-click on a supplier card.**

   Pick any old card for the moment. I just want to show you how the whole idea works.

2. **Click the Buying Details tab.**

3. **In the Expense Account field, enter the expense account that payments for this supplier would normally go to.**

   For example, if you pick Telstra as your supplier card, the Expense Account is likely to be Telephone Expense, as shown in Figure 17-4. If you choose AMP as your supplier card, the Expense Account is probably Insurance Expense.

4. **Click OK to save your changes.**

5. **Go to Spend Money and experiment, entering a payment to this supplier.**

In the Spend Money window, enter the supplier's name as normal, then tab through the payment as you normally would. When you get to the Allocation Account, instead of entering an account number, simply press the Tab key and marvel as the allocation account pops up automatically. Yippee. Life doesn't get much easier than this.

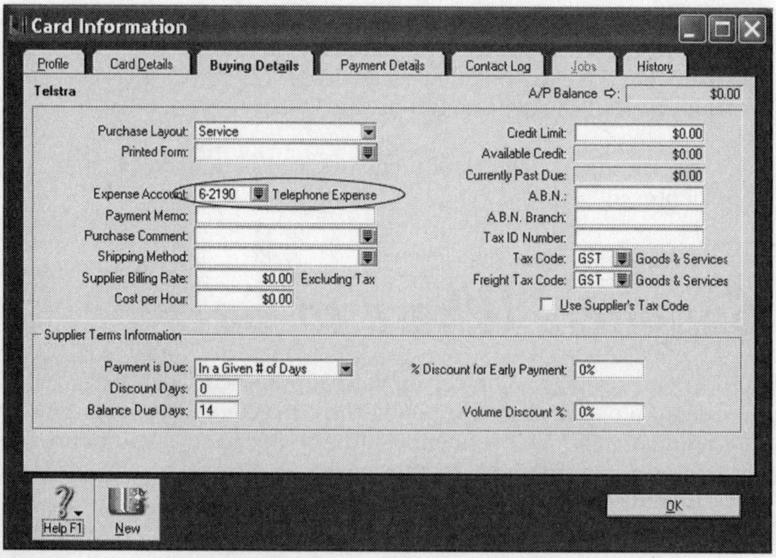

Figure 17-4:
Linking
expense
accounts for
each
supplier
makes for
speedy data-
entry.

Stop Printing Stuff

If you can avoid printing, then rest assured that not only will you save a few trees, but you'll save time as well. As long as you keep good backups of your MYOB company file (as explained in detail in Chapter 14), you don't need to hang on to paper records. Consider the following:

✔ **Customer invoices.** Why print a customer invoice? Email it instead. Certainly, don't bother with keeping copies of customer invoices on file. If a customer wants a duplicate copy of an invoice you can always open MYOB software and print it again.

✔ **Purchase orders.** Why on earth would you print a purchase order when you can fax or email them direct from your MYOB company file?

✔ **Profit & Loss reports.** So management wants a monthly Profit & Loss report? All you have to do is display the report and click the Send To button to create a PDF file that is automatically sent as an email.

✔ **Transaction reports.** I really hope no-one prints these any more. If your accountant asks for reports, backup your company file onto CD and pop it in the post (or, if your file is small enough, email a copy). Your accountant can print out reports if they're really needed!

✔ **Customer statements.** No need for all that printing and posting. Just email 'em.

✔ **Remittance advices and cheques for suppliers.** Move out of the Dark Ages and subscribe to M-Powered Payments. That way you can process payments online and email remittance advices direct to suppliers, without putting pen to paper or printing a single page.

I could go on and on, but I won't . . .

Chapter 18

Ten Tips for Small Business

As time goes by, I become more and more passionate about the art of running a small business. I think it takes a special kind of person to start up on their own, often risking most of their money and most of their spare time. The old picture of the small business boss exploiting underpaid workers while they relax under a palm tree sipping pina coladas couldn't be further from the truth.

I've been lucky over the last few years because there's no better way to find out how small businesses run than to go visit them, on-site, week after week, month after month. Theory is one thing, but seeing the pressures of small business and understanding what a balancing act it can be is quite another. These small businesses have taught me much more than I've ever been able to teach them.

Keep Chasing the Dollars

If you have trouble feeling excited about the idea of debt collection, then think of it this way: Imagine your monthly sales are $30,000 and your customers pay, on average, within 60 days (a few pay on time, others pay pretty late). If you can reduce this average from 60 days to 45 days, then you would generate an extra $15,000 of working capital for your business, interest-free!

So, if you want to be paid quicker, here are a few practical tips to make this a reality:

✔ **Chase money as soon as it's due.** Be sure to customise your invoice so that you tell customers when payment is due. If you want to get more heavy-handed, include a comment that says interest will have to be paid if these terms are not met. With this in place, don't wait until an account is overdue before you chase it. The longer you leave debts, the greater the risk of not getting paid.

✔ **Don't be shy about phoning customers with overdue accounts.** A polite phone call works infinitely better than statement reminders or standard debt collection letters.

✔ **Ask for a commitment.** When chasing money, ask your customer for a date that they promise to pay by. Thank them for their commitment and then note this date in the Recontact Date of their Contact Log, as shown in Figure 18-1. (To find a customer's Contact Log, go to their card and click the Log button.) That way, you receive a reminder on the Contact Alert tab of your To Do List when the date comes around and you can double-check that your customer has fulfilled their promise.

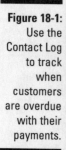

Figure 18-1:
Use the
Contact Log
to track
when
customers
are overdue
with their
payments.

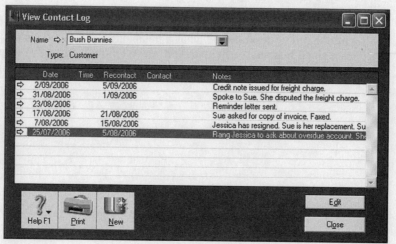

✔ **Send monthly statements.** Send statements promptly on the last day of each month to everyone with an outstanding account. A number of customers won't cough up unless they receive a statement.

✔ **Bring out the whip.** For customers who persist in paying late, consider implementing finance charges. MYOB software can calculate finance charges automatically on overdue accounts and they're often a pretty good deterrent.

✔ **Always carry out threats.** If you threaten to take legal action 'within 14 days', then send the lawyer's letter on the morning of the fifteenth day. If you threaten to cut off supply 'within 7 days', then cut deliveries off on the eighth day.

Plan for the Future

Business planning is like daily exercise: You know you should do it, but you keep putting it off. It's a shame, because not only do you become flabby and unhealthy, your business is also likely to flounder. I have seen studies that go as far as to say that businesses with a working business plan consistently achieve over 63 percent higher revenue growth and 58 percent higher profit growth than those without one. As well, these businesses have a much higher likelihood of not going belly-up in the long term.

If you've never created a business plan before, your best bet is to buy business planning software or download a few sample plans off the Internet. Both these methods are much quicker than slogging through a text book or wading through an eight-week TAFE course.

I reckon the best software around is an Australian product called CCH Masterplan. This software helps you create customised business and marketing plans to suit your industry, and walks you through the entire process of creating a business plan, with a series of simple questions. You can either devise your answers from scratch or adapt the example responses for your own needs.

Creating a business plan using Masterplan is much faster than the traditional method of using a word processor and spreadsheets — or, perish the thought, writing it out by hand. The software has lots of practical examples and, with a minimum of effort, you can string together a structured business plan with impressive financial forecasts and heaps of colourful graphs and charts.

You can check out CCH Masterplan at www.cch.com.au or by phoning 1300 300 586. The software costs about $299 (including GST).

If you don't want to spend any money on software straight away, sample business plans are available on the Internet. You can find a whole range of different sample business plans, marketing plans, Web strategy plans and advertising plans at www.bplans.com/sp.

Compare Your Business with Others

An acupuncturist once said to me, 'When you work for yourself, you work for a real bastard. No bonuses, no holiday pay, no sick leave . . . Who else could dish out such a raw deal?' At the time, those words rang all too true, as they no doubt do for many people reading this book.

Working for a real bastard is one thing, but worse still is when you're working for peanuts on top of that. If you just slogged through a 70-hour week to take home $600 in net profit, maybe it's time for a rethink.

One of the best ways to gauge the sanity of your business (and yourself) is to do a bit of *benchmarking*. This means comparing your business finances objectively with others in your industry, to see whether you come up to scratch or not.

If your business falls into a regular category (for example, you're an auto-electrician or a doctor, not an inventor or a film producer), then CCH Small Business provide what's probably the most accessible benchmark statistics. CCH researches thousands of businesses each year and, in doing so, builds up a remarkable picture of how different sectors perform, as well as what to expect. You can discover how the average business in your industry is faring, both in terms of finances and also in terms of other performance indicators — such as average consultation time, trading hours per week or number of staff.

For more information, visit www.cch.com.au and follow the link to the Small Business page or phone 1300 300 586.

Research First, Spend Later

Reconnaissance is time well-spent. Don't rush out and buy a hairdressing salon unless you understand the hairdressing business — and you don't mind doing the occasional blue rinse. Don't move to the bush and open a trendy inner-city style café just because you think the locals are dying to drink café lattés. (Hurling dollars and advertising at a dying swan does not a success story make.)

Researching your industry on a regular basis is invaluable and is especially important if you're starting up or buying an existing business and you lack hands-on experience. Your first stop in the research ritual should be local industry and trade associations, but expand this to browsing the Internet, talking to competitors and visiting your local chamber of commerce. In short, speak to anyone you think may be able to help you. Think of information as if it were gold — and don't assume anything!

It's also a good idea to research the demographics of your customers and, in the case of retail businesses, the demographics of your location. The Australian Bureau of Statistics (ABS) is your best bet for this. Go to the ABS Web site at www.abs.gov.au and search on Basic Community Profile. Type in the area that you want to know about to display a detailed community profile from the latest census, free of charge. Hopefully, this way you can avoid such disasters as opening up a hip-hop music store in an area that has the lowest percentage of 15-to-25-year-olds in Australia.

Borrow Wisely

The human species is composed of two distinct races: Those who lend and those who borrow. If you're like me and belong to the latter category, then it's important to learn how to borrow without the attitude of a pathetic, pleading underdog. Instead, you should approach it with the magnificent pride of someone who's doing the bank a favour (which indeed you are).

To compare the merits of different loans, hop onto the Internet and look for a Web site that publishes current interest rates for Australia's major lenders: Both www.artog.com.au and www.echoice.com.au are useful starting points.

After you figure out your likely interest rate, explore how different loan periods will affect your repayments. You can find loan calculators in Excel's add-ins, Microsoft Money's planning wizards or at www.yourmortgage.com.au. Work out what you can afford, but don't forget to give yourself some leeway for error (or rising interest rates, for that matter).

Armed with this information, shop around. Using a loan calculator, enter the interest rates and fees from different banks and compare the total amount of interest that you will pay for each one. They're often surprisingly different!

Double Your Money (or Your Debt)

The Rule of 72 is a little trick you can use to see if loan repayments, saving accounts or financial planning strategies make sense. It's a cool trick because you can use it in lots of different ways.

The idea of this rule is that if you divide the value 72 by an interest rate percentage, your result is approximately the number of years it will take to double your money. Here are a few examples of how it works:

- ✔ If you deposit funds into an investment that pays 12 percent interest, it takes roughly six years to double your money (that's because 72 divided by 12 equals 6).

- ✔ If your business is growing at 7 percent a year and you want to forecast how long it will take to double your sales volume, divide 72 by 7 and the result is about 10. In this case, you can expect to double the size of the business in approximately ten years from now.

- ✔ If you want to forecast how long it takes inflation to double the price of an item, divide 72 by the current inflation rate. For example, if inflation is 5 percent and you own an antique that you reckon should keep up with inflation, then divide 72 by 5 to see how long it will take for your antique to double in value. (About 14 years is your answer.)

Discover Your Break-Even Point

Okay, you may hate me for this, but I'm going to be merciless and torture you with mathematics. There's no avoiding it because I want to discuss calculating the break-even point for your business.

For the uninitiated, your *break-even point* is the amount of dollars you need to earn each week or each month in order to keep your head above water. Depending on what stage your business is at, this break-even point could be an aspiration, a goal, a bare minimum or, ideally, the point to which you never wish to sink.

If you have a service business, then working out your break-even point is easy. You just have to cover whatever your fixed costs are for the month. However, if you buy goods and then sell them for a profit — maybe you're a manufacturer, wholesaler or retailer — then you need to do some sums.

You also need to know two pieces of information:

- ✔ **Your fixed costs for every month:** These are the expenses you have to pay regardless of how much income you earn and usually includes items like wages, bank charges, leases and rent.

- ✔ **Your gross profit margin:** This is the average profit you make on each sale. If something costs you $40 and you sell it for $100, then your gross profit is $60. This means your gross profit margin is 60 percent.

When you establish these two amounts, you need to be really brave and do this formula:

Break even = Fixed costs/Gross Profit Margin

Here's an example of how it works. Imagine you sell homemade craft items at the markets. You know that materials — fabric, buttons and so on — usually cost 40 percent of the final price. This means your gross profit margin is about 60 percent. (For example, if you sell a teddy bear for $10, it costs about $4 to make it.) The rent for your market stall is $80 a day and you pay an assistant $120 per day. That means your fixed costs are $200 per day.

So, here it is . . . drum roll . . . the big formula:

Break even = Fixed Costs/Gross Profit Margin
= $200/60 percent = $333

This means you have to sell $333 worth of goods every day to break even. Any amount over that is icing on the cake.

Try calculating the break-even point for your business. Sure, it's not going to be as cut and dried as my example, because you may need to average your profit margin against the different goods you sell, and it may take longer to total up your fixed costs for each month. But, give it a go, because it's worth it.

Chapter 19

Ten Tricks to Starting a New Year

*B*eing a person of Scottish descent, I'm used to associating the words 'New Year' with raucous drinking parties, freezing cold winds and the warbling refrains of Auld Lang Syne.

In contrast, starting a new *financial* year with MYOB software is a time when you want to be as sober as a judge. It's a pretty involved process that no kind of liquor will make easier.

Run the Company Data Auditor

To make sure your file is squeaky-clean before starting a new year, your first port of call is the Company Data Auditor. To find this, go to your Accounts command centre and click . . . you guessed it . . . the Company Data Auditor button.

The Company Data Auditor is split into four sections. As long as you've reconciled all your bank accounts (refer to Chapter 7) and gone through the Tax Exception Review (explained in Chapter 12), the Transaction Review window is where you spend most of your time.

When you're preparing to finish up the financial year, go to the Transaction Review section of your Company Data Auditor and enter the first day of the financial year you're finalising as your Start Date and the last day as your End Date. Then click the Run Review button. Wait a few seconds and MYOB software pops up with a column of green ticks and red crosses (Figure 19-1).

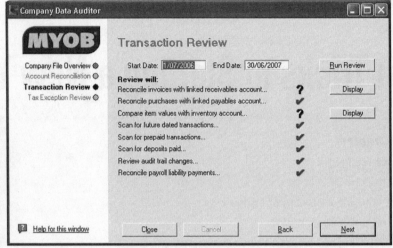

Figure 19-1:
Running the
Transaction
Review
in your
Company
Data Auditor.

With the following reviews, your aim is to get a green tick and not to give up until you do.

✔ **Reconcile invoices with linked receivables.** The idea here is that the total of your receivables report matches with the balance of Trade Debtors in your Balance Sheet. If it doesn't, then you need to find out why. See Support Note 9096 at www.myob.com.au/support to find out how to troubleshoot out of balance amounts.

✔ **Reconcile purchases with linked payables.** Similar to the receivables report, what you want is for the total of your payables report to match with the balance of Trade Creditors in your Balance Sheet. Support Note 9109 at www.myob.com.au/support explains what to do if this report doesn't balance.

✔ **Compare item values with inventory account.** If you don't get a green tick here, refer to 'Assessing the aftermath' in Chapter 8 for help.

✔ **Scan for future dated transactions.** The aim of the game here is to identify any transactions that are dated beyond your End Date. If the date is already beyond 30 June, you may get some transactions appearing on this report. If they're July transactions and you're in July, then that's okay. But problem transactions are ones that are dated *beyond* the current date. These transactions are almost always mistakes and need to be fixed up.

✔ **Scan for prepaid transactions.** This review highlights any transactions where the payment for a sale falls earlier than the date of the sale itself, or where the payment for a purchase falls earlier than the date of the purchase. Usually, prepaid transactions are gremlins that need your tender attention.

With the remaining reviews, your aim isn't necessarily to get a green tick. Sometimes it's okay to get a red cross, so long as you understand the reason why.

- ✔ **Scan for deposits paid.** If any customers have outstanding deposits, or you've currently got deposits to suppliers outstanding, then this report lists them. These deposits aren't necessarily mistakes — that's why you don't have to worry about the red crosses — but it's always worth reviewing anything that comes up on this report so you know for sure they're right.

- ✔ **Review audit trail changes.** The Audit Trail report shows if you've deleted transactions, changed transactions or altered your preferences (this report only comes up if you've selected to use Audit Trail Tracking in your Security preferences). Although a red cross against the audit review doesn't necessarily mean you have a problem — after all, it's usually fine to delete a transaction — it's worth looking at what comes up in this report and checking that everything looks cool.

- ✔ **Reconcile payroll liability payments.** What you're looking for here is that PAYG tax and superannuation balance correctly. This report only works if you record tax and superannuation payments using the Pay Liabilities feature in the Payroll command centre.

Become an Irritating Pedant

If ever there's a time for chilling logic, it's now. Follow this step-by-step guide and don't miss a beat:

1. **Complete every transaction up to 30 June, including payments, deposits, sales and purchases.**

   You don't have to finish recording transactions on the last day of June. In fact, it may be September, October or even later by the time you're finished recording everything for the previous year. MYOB software is very accommodating about this and allows you to start recording transactions in the new financial year before you've finished the last financial year.

2. **Reconcile all bank accounts, including credit cards, term deposits, savings accounts and loan accounts.**

   You can use the Reconciliation Review in the Company Data Auditor to check you've remembered to reconcile everything.

3. **Read through your Profit & Loss and Balance Sheet reports for the year just completed.**

   Ask yourself whether your financial statements make sense and seem right. Investigate any unusual figures. (For more about checking your financial statements, refer to Chapter 15.)

4. **Print any relevant end-of-year reports.**

   If you have adequate backup systems, you don't really need to print end-of-year reports. However, if there are any reports you'd like to print for future reference, do so now.

5. **Make a backup and then another one, just in case.**

   I talk about backups in Chapter 14. The only difference between end-of-year backups and regular backups is that you store end-of-year backups separately from your regular backups, never to be used again.

   After you've made one backup, make another. This end-of-year stuff is serious business.

6. **Supply your accountant with a backup or email the file.**

   Don't accommodate old-fashioned accountants who demand printed copies of your financial reports — why waste paper when you don't have to? Simply provide your accountant with a back up of your company file or, if your file is small enough, email the file direct.

7. **Lock periods so that you can't accidentally post transactions to last year.**

   See the section 'Lock Yourself Out' later in this chapter if you're not sure how to do this.

   When you lock the period you've just completed — usually June of the current financial year — you can't accidentally post stuff to the year you've just finished.

8. **Wait until your accountant provides you with completed financial reports.**

   This usually takes several weeks or months, and that's if you're lucky.

9. **Enter your accountant's adjustments for the end of the financial year.**

   This next step is pretty icky, so please pay attention. You need to enter your accountant's adjustments into your company file so that your final Balance Sheet for the year matches your accountant's final Balance Sheet. You may want to ask your accountant or an MYOB Certified Consultant for help to do this.

10. **Do a final backup and label it Final End of Year.**

11. **Go to File⇨Start a New Year⇨Start a New Financial Year and click OK.**

Figure 19-2 shows you how to take the plunge. This end-of-year process can take anywhere between a few minutes to a few hours, depending on the size of your file.

12. Go to File⇨Optimise Company File and click OK.

Optimising your file deletes the empty space left behind by the year-end process, reducing your file size and making everything run faster. (Refer to Chapter 14 for lots more about optimising and how it works.)

13. Pop the champagne bottle — you're done!

Wow! Thirteen steps — the longest set of instructions in this whole book . . .

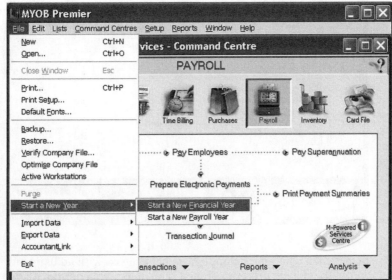

Figure 19-2: Starting a new financial year.

The only hitch with working in the way I outline in this section is if your accountant takes months to produce final accounts, leaving you working in a new year without closing off the old. The hassle about having two years open is that some reports aren't available until you close off the old year, such as last year comparisons.

An alternative way of working is to send your file to your accountant, backup carefully, and then start a new financial year without waiting for your accountant's adjustments. Much later, when your accountant produces final accounts, you can adjust the opening balances in your Balance Sheet so that your opening Balance Sheet on 1 July matches the accountant's closing Balance Sheet from 30 June. (Such journals are pretty technical stuff and you may want to ask either your accountant or an MYOB Certified Consultant to help you with this process.)

Lock Yourself Out

At Step 7 in the section 'Become an Irritating Pedant' earlier in this chapter, I talk about locking periods and protecting your company file so that no-one can accidentally create or edit transactions in the period that you've just competed.

To lock a period, go to Setup⇨Preferences and with a delicate flick of your little finger, press the Security tab. Select Lock Periods and then choose the month up to which you want to close off the accounts, as Figure 19-3 shows. Click OK and you're finished.

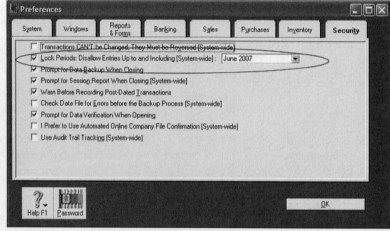

Figure 19-3:
Lock periods
after you
send the
accountant
your file.

Later, when your accountant comes back to you with adjustments, it's easy to return to your security preferences and unlock this period. All you have to do is remove the tick from Lock Periods and you're away.

Write Your Password On Your Backups

As a business you're obliged to maintain records going back for at least five years, if not seven (depending on where you live in Australia, and on the specific circumstances of the audit).

Hopefully, you already create a special backup at the end of each year and you store these backups separately in a safe place (if not, it's time to start, now!). However, if you change your password from time to time, can you guarantee that you'll be able to remember what your password was five, six or even seven years earlier? Probably not.

Save yourself from such dramas by writing your password on the front of your end-of-year backups. Or, if you intend to store backups in a place where others could see what's written on them, and you'd rather keep your password private, write a password 'clue' on the front of the backup instead.

Oh, and one more thing. Unless you have a fireproof safe, always keep two sets of archival backups and store one of those sets off-site, away from the office. This is the only way to protect your valuable data from fire and theft.

Switch Off Auto Confirmation

With most versions of MYOB software, every now and then you're prompted to 'confirm' your software serial number. If you're always connected to the Internet and you've set your preferences for automatic confirmation, chances are that you're hardly even aware of this process. Every few months a message pops up, you click OK and that's it.

However, if your accountant is working with a copy of your file and a confirmation message falls due when the accountant is connected to the Internet, your file will end up being confirmed twice. This can cause confusion and ultimately 'use up' the number of company files you can have activated (the limit is usually either five or ten company files, depending on the circumstances). However, there is an easy solution:

1. **Make a copy of your company file, ready to give to your accountant.**

2. **Open up this copy and select Preferences from the Setup menu.**

3. **Click the Security tab.**

4. **Unclick the option that reads 'I Prefer to Use Automated Online Company File Confirmation'.**

Another solution is to tell your accountant not to confirm your company file if they receive a message prompting them to do so. Instead, ask them to click the option Confirm Later.

Anticipate the Obvious

Make things easy for your accountant by anticipating the questions they have to ask every year, whether you like it or not:

- ✔ **Your motor vehicle percentage:** If you use a motor vehicle for part-business, part-personal use, you need to tell your accountant the percentage split. (You also need to do one of those mind-numbingly bureaucratic log books at least once every five years.)

- ✔ **Your home office percentage:** If you claim home office expenses such as rent, rates or mortgage interest, provide your accountant with a record of how you've calculated your home office percentages. Also, tell them how you've dealt with these expenses in your company file.

- ✔ **Medical expenses:** Your accountant always needs to know how much you spent on medical expenses. I create a special drawings account called Medical Expenses in my company file so that I can provide a summary of this info, at the drop of a hat.

- ✔ **The number of your dependants:** Always a tricky and contentious question. If only my dog were eligible for family tax benefit.

- ✔ **Interest or dividend income:** You need to tell your accountant about any interest or dividend income that you didn't bank in your business account (and therefore isn't showing in your company file).

Communicate More, Communicate Better

The biggest key to any relationship, whether it's with your accountant, your lover or your cat, is communication. With MYOB software, communicating with your accountant is easier than ever, so long as you know a few tricks of the trade:

- ✔ **If possible, send your company file via email.** Do you remember the hassle of gathering together your accounts and paperwork for your tax return? These days, it's simple. All you have to do is send an email to your accountant, with your MYOB company file as an attachment, or if your file is too big to send by email, burn it onto a CD and pop it in the mail.

- ✔ **Plan ahead for tax.** Don't wait until June has come and gone before worrying about your tax bill. Get your accountant to give your company file the once-over in April or May and ask them to help you minimise your tax, before it's too late.

- ✔ **Ask for advice instead of bookkeeping.** Have you ever heard of an accountant who lowered annual fees? No, me neither. So, if you've recently switched to MYOB software and you're doing 90 percent more of the work, harbour no illusions that your labours will save money. Instead, be realistic and get your pound of flesh by asking for business advice, in place of the bookkeeping services your accountant used to provide.

- ✔ **Ask for criticism.** Don't be too laissez-faire about your accounts, relying on your accountant to fix up all your mistakes every time your tax falls due. It's a waste to pay good money for your accountant to fix the same mistakes, year in, year out! A much healthier scenario is the one where you ask your accountant to explain what you're doing wrong and get them to teach you something new every time they work with your file.

- ✔ **Become more informed.** With MYOB software, you can produce your own Profit & Loss and Balance Sheet reports whenever you want, at the click of a button. Ask your accountant to look through these statements with you, explain what they mean and analyse what you could be doing better.

Part V
Appendixes

Glenn Lumsden

'Hello, tech support? MYOB is working fine,
but I was wondering how to set up a
firewall that lets the money come in
without the money going out.'

In this part . . .

My husband tells a story about the time his sister came down with appendicitis and received lots of attention and presents. So, in true malingering spirit, he concocted the same symptoms and, before he knew it, was whisked off to hospital. One general anesthetic and several very painful days later, he learnt to rue the error of his ways.

I still have my appendix and, not only that, I've written three more for this last part of *MYOB Software For Dummies*. There's an appendix about what to do when you need help (I don't recommend malingering), an appendix describing the MYOB software family and an appendix that lists the Web sites mentioned in this book, plus a few more besides.

Appendix A

A Helping Hand

S o you have a question and the answer isn't in this book? (Maybe you've forgotten to read the last few hundred pages?) Don't worry, here's a bunch of other places to look for help.

Finding Your Serial Number

Before you contact MYOB Technical Support, you're going to need your serial number. Look in any one of three places:

- ✔ **The CD envelope:** Look on the back of your MYOB software CD envelope.
- ✔ **Your registration card:** Your registration card comes in the box with your MYOB software.
- ✔ **Your Setup menu:** Make your way to the Setup menu and select Company Information. Your serial number appears in the top-left corner.

Paddling at the Water's Edge

You've just bought your MYOB software, the box is still sitting on the desk, manuals are littered everywhere and the computer is humming away. If you can't figure out where to start — you just want someone to make you a warm cup of milk, hold your hand and take you off to bed — this section is for you.

Sign up

When you first install MYOB software and open up your company file, a message appears asking you to register and activate your software (I talk about this in detail in Chapter 1). The goods news is that registration is free, the bad news is that you don't have any choice in the matter . . .

You can register your software using any one of the following methods:

- ✔ **Register online:** In Australia, the easiest way to register is to go to my.myob.com.au (yes, skip the 'www' bit). Follow the steps to register and my.MYOB automatically updates its database with your registration details. After online registration is complete, you return to your MYOB software to complete the activation process.

- ✔ **Register by phone:** Phone 1300 555 127 (Australia) or 0800 606962 (New Zealand). Don't be shy. If the person on the phone wants a recipe for French onion soup, make one up. If she asks you what type of printer you've got and you're not sure, make a wild guess. At the end of this little exchange (which usually only takes a couple of minutes), you're given your registration number.

- ✔ **Register by mail:** If you prefer to support the postal system, then complete the registration card that comes in the box with your MYOB software and mail or fax the card to the place printed on the card.

Get free installation support

The good part about registering and activating your MYOB software is that you're entitled to free installation support. In Australia, the phone number for Introductory Support is 1300 555 128. Ring between 9 a.m. and 5.30 p.m., Eastern Standard Time, Monday to Friday. In New Zealand, the phone number is 03 983 2636.

Take out insurance

Are you one of those slapdash types who leave the car key in the ignition? Maybe you don't lock your house when you go shopping? Or perhaps you're really radical and refuse to have your family pet micro-chipped (you know who's next after family pets, don't you)?

However carefree and optimistic your nature, I reckon that signing up for MYOB's software support is a good move — it's kind of like an insurance policy for your accounts.

The cost of technical support depends on which version of software you have and how long you subscribe. But, for what is usually a relatively modest sum, you receive unlimited phone or fax support (for the cost of a local call); free version upgrades; free subscriptions to M-Powered services (Australia only) and, if payroll tax scales change, free updates.

(Note that for MYOB BusinessBasics and FirstEdge, the support includes phone or fax support on a 1300 number only.)

To find out more about the various support services offered, go to www.myob.com.au/support or www.myob.co.nz and follow the links to Support.

Check out the support notes

There's not much point in struggling and cursing about something if someone has already struggled and cursed before you, and figured out a solution to boot.

So before the air turns blue, make your way to www.myob.com.au/support and follow the links to Support Notes. In the Search query box, type a couple of words about the nature of your problem, click Search and see what results come up. (I just typed in 'Not Enough Sleep' as my Search query, and the results showed me a document called *Performance Tips*. Bizarre.)

Call the experts

Everyone learns in different ways. Many people find out everything they need to know from illuminating publications such as this one. Others need more hands-on assistance, especially at the beginning when everything seems to be so overwhelming. If this applies to you, call on the help of an MYOB Certified Consultant (or, if you're on the other side of the Tasman, the correct terminology is an MYOB Approved Partner).

The fact that consultants are certified doesn't mean they're raving bonkers. Instead, it means they've done lots of training, passed an entrance exam and set up several referral sites. Consultants also have to sit renewal exams twice a year and commit to a minimum number of professional development hours. In short, they know their stuff.

The cost of having an MYOB Certified Consultant or Approved Partner come to your business and help set up your company file varies. They operate independently from MYOB Software and so each one has different charges and different approaches. You can ask a consultant for an estimate of how long training takes and what is covered during the consultation.

To find a consultant in your area in Australia, visit www.myob.com.au/support/ccmembers. In New Zealand, visit www.myob.co.nz and follow the links to Approved Partners.

Jumping In and Getting Wet

Even if you've more or less mastered MYOB software, you may still need help from time to time. You may want to fix up a gremlin that's been bothering you for ages, refine something you set up months before or maybe find out more about what the software can do. Here's where to look next.

Take a course

I come across lots of people who do a course before they set up MYOB software for their business. This is okay, but when they sit down to set up their own company file, they find they can't apply the stuff they learnt during the course to the real world. (After all, there are only so many water-filter businesses.)

What works best for most people is to install and start using MYOB software and then enroll in a course, preferably one that is run over a few weeks, requiring a couple of hours per week of your time. You can digest new information a bit at a time and apply it to your business as you go.

If you're working in a larger business that includes payroll and lots of complex transactions, then a course in MYOB software alone may not be enough: You may need to look for a course in bookkeeping to add extra background theory to what you're doing. Sure, this theory may seem old-fashioned at first, but it provides an unequalled level of understanding.

Hop on the blower

If you want information about other MYOB software products (maybe you're thinking about hand-held invoicing, point of sale or advanced payroll) and you want to speak to a real walking, talking person, you're best to phone MYOB on 1300 555 111 (in Australia) or 0800 60 69 62 (New Zealand).

Pay every time

If you really don't think you need to subscribe to MYOB Technical Support and you have a one-off problem you need to solve, you can try the Pay Per Call Support. The cost is a handsome $4.50 per minute, with a minimum call charge of $22 or, if you're in Kiwi-land, a set fee of $35 per call applies.

Call 1300 555 128 (in Australia) or 0900 55 789 (New Zealand) to take advantage of this service, remembering to have your serial number and credit card details ready when you call. And one more tip: When a call starts becoming expensive, you can always transfer the cost of the call towards a subscription to MYOB Technical Support or MYOB Cover.

Network with colleagues

If you belong to a certain industry — whether it's retailing, bed-and-breakfast accommodation, building or childcare — chances are lots of other businesses very similar to yours use MYOB software. Network with business associates, trade associations or your local chamber of commerce and seek out these businesses. Find out what they're doing with MYOB software — their tricks and tips, their headaches and difficulties.

Recently, I heard about a group of Sydney private schools that decided to ditch their old-fashioned DOS systems for MYOB software. They clubbed together and met every month to discuss their systems. They shared training sessions and paid a consultant to develop custom reports that they could all use. This co-operative approach works really well and everyone is happy.

Going for a Surf

Maybe I should have mentioned this bit first, it's so handy. Your first port of call in times of need is MYOB's Web site, which is a goldmine of information. Head to www.myob.com.au or www.myob.co.nz for lots of support documents, small business information, product news and consultant contact details. Bookmark it now!

The MYOB Software Family

The MYOB software family is one of those old-fashioned prolific dynasties spanning several generations, with lots of offspring and a wide network of in-laws and out-laws. Not only does the basic MYOB accounting software family range from MYOB BusinessBasics to MYOB Premier Enterprise, there's also an extended family that includes MYOB AssetManager Pro, MYOB RetailManager, MYOB PowerPay and MYOB ReportWriter. And guess what? In this appendix, I talk about each one.

The MYOB Accounting Software Family

I find the idea that computer software can produce offspring (thereby producing the MYOB family) rather grandiose, given that most software is not much more than a cardboard box with a bit of metal and paper inside. But to a certain extent calling the product group a family is an excellent analogy, with MYOB BusinessBasics the baby at the bottom and MYOB Premier Enterprise the benevolent but powerhouse grandma at the top. In this appendix, I describe each version in turn.

By the way, if you're in the Macintosh camp, MYOB FirstEdge and MYOB AccountEdge are the only software versions currently available.

MYOB BusinessBasics and FirstEdge

If you're a small service business with only a couple of employees — or maybe none, for that matter — then MYOB BusinessBasics (for Windows) or FirstEdge (for Macintosh) makes an excellent starting point. I have lots of clients who are very happy with these products, such as architects and hairdressers, builders and plumbers, landscape gardeners and restaurateurs, consultants and musicians.

One of the best aspects of both MYOB BusinessBasics and FirstEdge is that they're so easy to use. Sure, these products have fewer features than their big brothers and sisters, but this can work to your advantage: Because you have less to get your head around, your chances of making a mess of your work are massively reduced!

MYOB Accounting

The next rung up the ladder is MYOB Accounting, which has pretty much everything most businesses may need. Unlike MYOB BusinessBasics and FirstEdge, MYOB Accounting includes inventory, providing a practical solution for manufacturers, retailers and wholesalers, as well as service-type businesses.

MYOB Accounting also a few other extras designed to make your life that little bit more streamlined:

- ✔ Purchases management, so you can see how much you owe suppliers and report for GST on an accrual basis.
- ✔ More sophisticated reporting, including graphs and bar charts for key financial reports.
- ✔ Access to M-Powered Services, such as electronic supplier and employee payments.
- ✔ A link to Microsoft Word — ideal for customer letters and debt collection.
- ✔ A link to Microsoft Excel, opening the door to a whole range of custom reports and further analysis of business information.
- ✔ Salesperson tracking, including commission reports.
- ✔ Category tracking, so you can produce Profit & Loss and Balance Sheet reports for each cost centre in your business.

MYOB Accounting Plus

Further up the ladder, MYOB Accounting Plus has everything that MYOB Accounting has, but also includes Payroll and Time Billing.

I recommend Payroll for any business that has four employees or more, simply because you'll save so much time. No longer do you have to spend hours calculating tax, adding up super and working out holiday pay.

Instead, entire pay runs take a matter or minutes and payment summaries are printed at the click of a button.

The time-billing features come in handy if you bill for your time in small segments. Maybe you're a solicitor charging by the millisecond, a technician billing in ten-minute units, or an engineer accounting for time out in the field. The Time Billing command centre helps track your time down to the last moment, with the stopwatch timer clicking away and reciting 'time is money, time is money, time is money' as you go.

MYOB Premier and MYOB AccountEdge

The matriarchs of the family are MYOB Premier (for Windows) and MYOB AccountEdge (for Macintoshes). These grandmas have everything that you see in MYOB BusinessBasics, MYOB FirstEdge, MYOB Accounting and MYOB Accounting Plus, but with one big difference. These products are multi-user. (MYOB Premier comes with a three-user licence, but MYOB AccountEdge comes with a single-user licence only. You then purchase licences for additional users.)

The term *multi-user* may be one of the ugliest in the English language, but I like to explain it this way: More than one person can log onto MYOB Premier or MYOB AccountEdge at the same time so that several employees on a network can work simultaneously on the accounts. For example, someone can raise invoices, another can record expenses, a bookkeeper can reconcile the bank account and a manager can browse through financials — all at the same time.

MYOB Premier and MYOB AccountEdge also include multi-currency reporting — a life-saver for importers and exporters. The inventory features are also more sophisticated and allow for multiple pricing, pictures of stock items and a few more goodies besides.

MYOB Premier Enterprise

Last on the scene is the great-grandma, MYOB Premier Enterprise. Identical in almost all respects to MYOB Premier, the important distinction here is that Premier Expertise has been developed for use on networks running Windows Server 2003 in a Terminal Services environment (don't you love the way all this technical jargon just rolls off the tongue?). Included with MYOB Premier Enterprise is a five-user licence; five Terminal Server Client Access licences; MYOB BusinessAnalyst; and a year's support and upgrades. MYOB Premier Enterprise also caters for inventory in multiple locations.

Moving Up the Family Tree

So, you've outgrown your current version of MYOB software and want to move up a level? Then it's time to upgrade.

Many people don't realise that when upgrading with MYOB software, you don't have to go out and buy a whole new package. Instead, you can pay a smaller fee to purchase a *family upgrade*. For example, if you initially purchased MYOB BusinessBasics and now want to upgrade to MYOB Accounting Plus, you only have to pay for a family upgrade, which is a lot cheaper than going out and buying a whole new copy of MYOB Accounting Plus.

The other piece of good news is that you don't lose any of your work when you upgrade. You simply install the new software and ask it to do its stuff. It whizzes, groans, moans and grunts, but after only a few minutes the job is done. Every bit of information you had in your earlier version of MYOB software is carried across into the new format, without missing a beat.

The easiest way to upgrade your software is to phone MYOB Sales on 1300 555 151 and ask them to send you an upgrade form, or head to the Upgrades page at www.myob.com.au. Remember to dig out the serial number from your original software (refer to 'Finding Your Serial Number' in Appendix A).

Other MYOB Products

Once you've chosen your core MYOB accounting software, have a think about whether any other MYOB products may come in handy at your business.

MYOB AssetManager Pro

How is it that your accounts say you're making lots of money — and you're certainly shelling out heaps for tax! — but you don't have any cash? There can be a few reasons for this, but one cause of a cash drought may be that you've spent money building up your assets. (Assets include computers, cars, office equipments, tools, telephones and so on.) You pay big dollars for these things, but you're not allowed to claim these dollars all at once at tax time. Instead, you have to claim them bit by bit over several years, using the rather arcane process that accountants call *depreciation*.

Enough of my technical lecturing . . . MYOB AssetManager Pro is a special program designed to keep track of your fixed assets, as well as help you calculate depreciation. You can even keep records of any services carried out on your assets, and you can track assets by location, cost centre or any other way you choose.

MYOB AssetManager Pro looks similar to other MYOB products and employs similar account numbering and structures. At $899 (including GST), I reckon it's a bargain for any business that has lots of assets or major depreciation expenses every year. Go to www.myob.com.au and follow the links to Specialist products to find out more.

MYOB Retail Point-of-Sale Solutions

MYOB now offers a whole swag of specialist point-of-sale solutions for retailers, including MYOB RetailBasics, MYOB RetailReady, MYOB RetailManager and MYOB RetailHospitality.

The idea behind any point-of-sale software is to replace your old-fashioned cash register with a barcode system so that processing sales is quicker and easier, and so that you can get proper stock control and supplier management.

The thing I like best about MYOB's point-of-sale products is that they talk to other MYOB products, so that you import daily summaries of sales, stock movements, purchases and so on into your MYOB accounting software. This kind of close connection is like any good communication — it saves heaps of time and is much less hassle.

The current RRP of MYOB RetailManger (standard edition) is $1,990, but to read more about the different versions and pricing, visit www.myob.com.au/products.

MYOB PowerPay

The Payroll that comes with MYOB Accounting Plus and MYOB Premier is excellent for most businesses, but it does have its limits. As a rule of thumb, if you have more than 30 employees, you're likely to need more sophisticated software in order to cope with multiple awards, payroll tax calculations or termination pays.

The answer is MYOB PowerPay, a stand-alone payroll package that integrates seamlessly with MYOB Accounting, MYOB Accounting Plus and MYOB Premier. Included in PowerPay's list of can-dos is merged pay runs, payroll tax calculations across multiple Australian states, multi-level password protection, correct calculation of termination pays and much more.

The current RRP of MYOB PowerPay is $549.

MYOB ReportWriter

MYOB ReportWriter is the whizzbang, all singing-and-dancing approach to generating your own custom reports. You can draw on a whole range of information from your company file — including customer and sales details, purchasing information and financial indicators — and create impressive reports that present this information in a very graphical manner.

Sounds wonderful, but you need either programming experience or a whole lot of enthusiasm for a steep learning curve to make the most of MYOB ReportWriter. Happily, the current RRP of $1,195 includes a comprehensive training manual and 12 months' support.

Appendix C

Wonderful Web Sites

• •

I know what it's like when you want to find a specific Web site, yet you can't remember its address, or where you last saw a reference to it. That's why this appendix lists every single Web site mentioned in this edition of *MYOB Software For Dummies*, grouped so you can find the one you want, without batting an eyelid. I've even added a couple of extra sites.

Find Your Own Place

MYOB software offers my.myob.com.au as an online area exclusively for its customers. On your first visit, simply type in your serial number to receive your special password and gain access to the site. After that, you can download software patches, place orders for upgrades, check and update your registration details and access the latest MYOB software news and technical support information.

Here's a trick to getting started: Don't get fooled into typing 'www' in front of my.myob.com.au — it won't work!

One and One Make Three

It's a symbiotic kind of thing. These products work hand-in-hand with MYOB software, like familiar and sociable cousins. However, this list is only a small sample of what's available. For the latest (and greatest) in custom reporting, visit the Links page of my Website at www.veechicurtis.com.au.

✔ www.accountingpower.com.au: AccountingPower specialises in custom reports that hook up with MYOB software. The products include PerfectJobs (for reports with a job bent); PerfectReview (for in-depth analysis of your financial statements); and Perfect Reports (custom reports for sales, customers and inventory). If you're looking for a particular kind of report, then AccountingPower may just have what you need. Even if AccountingPower doesn't, chances are the people at the company can whip something up that does.

✔ www.addisons.com.au: The perfect spot to visit if you're looking for custom reports with an accountant's bent.

✔ www.datapel.com: Datapel distributes a nifty little utility called Cardfile Connect, which enables you to synchronise your Microsoft Outlook address book with the cards in your MYOB company file.

✔ www.dipity.com.au: For a sophisticated quoting system that hooks up with MYOB software — ideal for tradespeople and builders — check out Master Quote software distributed by Serendipity Consulting at this Web site.

✔ www.myob.creditcheck.com.au: This credit reference service taps into the databases of Credit Reference Limited, helping you to ascertain the credit worthiness of prospective customers. A fee applies (of course!) but if you're about to stick your neck out and offer a hefty amount of credit to someone, this service may save your bacon.

✔ www.formsexpress.com.au: Head here to order forms especially designed to work with MYOB software, such as pre-printed invoices, purchase orders, customer statements and pay slips.

✔ www.psr.com.au: If you're stretching the job features in MYOB software to the max, then JobsPlus may just help relieve the strain. Even better, JobsPlus integrates with all MYOB accounting software products.

✔ www.twokeys.com.au: Veterans of third-party products that link with MYOB software, Two Keys distributes a budget and cashflow forecasting product called MoneyManager, a specialised billing system called MoreWays and several add-ons for RetailManager.

Reach Out

Surf the Net and check out some of these great business resources:

✔ www.abs.gov.au: The Australian Bureau of Statistics site isn't the most scintillating place in the world, but it has some helpful demographic info if you're considering expanding your business to a new location.

✔ www.bplan.com/sp: Go here to download sample business plans from this site and to get an idea of what they're all about.

✔ www.business.gov.au: A compilation of all the government-related sites relevant to business in Australia, covering both state and federal levels.

✔ www.cchsmallbusiness.com.au: CCH produces a handy range of Business Start-Up Guides, benchmark statistics for different industry types (find out if you're making the profit you should be!) and a range of business planning software products, including Masterplan.

✔ www.cpaaustralia.com.au: This Certified Practising Accountants Web site has a surprising amount of useful stuff. Check it out.

Index

• N •

• O •

Notes

FOR DUMMIES®

Business

Small Business
1-74031-109-4
$39.95

Superannuation
1-74031-061-6
$39.95

Personal Finance
1-74031-004-7
$39.95

Business Plans
1-74031-124-8
$39.95

Buying & Selling Your Home
1-74031-166-3
$39.95

Investing
1-74031-041-1
$39.95

Australian Wills and Estates
1-74031-067-5
$39.95

GST and BAS
1-74031-033-0
$39.95

Reference

Superannuation - Choosing a Fund
1-74031-125-6
$29.95

Tracing Your Family History Online
1-74031-071-3
$39.95

Job Hunting
1-74031-030-6
$39.95

FOR DUMMIES®

Technology

1-74031-086-1
$39.95

1-74031-160-4
$39.95

1-7403-1159-0
$39.95

1-74031-123-X
$39.95

Cooking

Pets

1-74031-010-1
$39.95

1-74031-008-X
$39.95

1-74031-040-3
$39.95

1-74031-028-4
$39.95

Parenting

Health & Fitness

1-74031-103-5
$39.95

1-74031-042-X
$39.95

1-74031-143-4
$39.95

1-74031-140-X
$39.95

FOR DUMMIES®

Football

1-74031-122-1
$39.95

Diabetes

1-74031-094-2
$39.95

Asthma and Allergies

1-74031-054-3
$39.95

Fitness

1-74031-009-8
$39.95

Golf

1-74031-011-X
$39.95

Weight Training

1-74031-044-6
$39.95

Aussie Rules

1-74031-035-7
$39.95

Fishing

1-74031-006-3
$39.95

Gardening

Yoga

1-74031-059-4
$39.95

Pilates

1-74031-074-8
$39.95

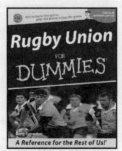

Rugby Union

1-74031-073-X
$39.95

Gardening

1-74031-007-1
$39.95